D0354374

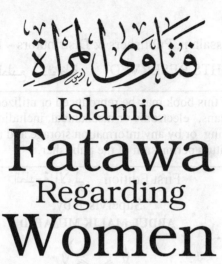

فتاوى المرأة

Islamic
Fatawa
Regarding
Women

[Shari'ah Rulings given by the Grand Mufti of Saudi Arabia
Sheikh Ibn Baz, Sheikh Ibn Uthaimin, Sheikh Ibn Jibreen and
others on matters pertaining to Women]

Compiled by

مُحـمَّد بن عَبد العزيز المسـند

Muhammad bin Abdul-Aziz Al-Musnad

Translated by

جمَـال الدّيـن زرابوزو

Jamaal Al-Din M. Zarabozo

Published by
DARUSSALAM
Publishers & Distributors
Saudi Arabia • UK • USA • Pakistan

First Edition   الطبعة الأولى

Supervised by:
ABDUL MALIK MUJAHID

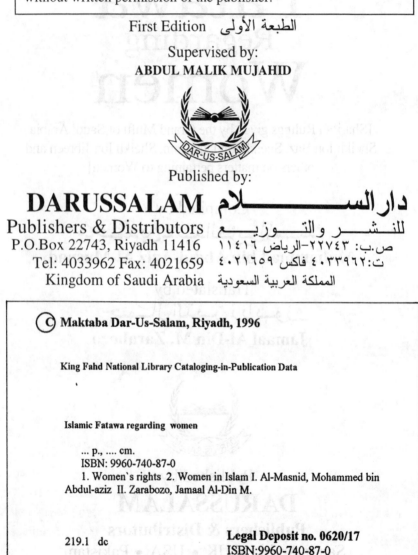

Published by:

DARUSSALAM   دار الســـــلام

Publishers & Distributors   للنـــشـــر والتـــوزيـــع
P.O.Box 22743, Riyadh 11416   ص.ب: ٢٢٧٤٣-الرياض ١١٤١٦
Tel: 4033962 Fax: 4021659   ت:٤٠٣٣٩٦٢ فاكس ٤٠٢١٦٥٩
Kingdom of Saudi Arabia   المملكة العربية السعودية

© Maktaba Dar-Us-Salam, Riyadh, 1996

King Fahd National Library Cataloging-in-Publication Data

Islamic Fatawa regarding women

   ... p., ... cm.
   ISBN: 9960-740-87-0
   1. Women's rights 2. Women in Islam I. Al-Masnid, Mohammed bin
Abdul-aziz II. Zarabozo, Jamaal Al-Din M.

219.1 dc   **Legal Deposit no. 0620/17**
                ISBN:9960-740-87-0

Translator's Introduction

All praises are due to Allah. We praise Him, and seek His Help, and ask for His forgiveness. We seek refuge in Allah from the evil in our souls and from our sinful deeds. Whoever Allah guides, no one can mislead. And whoever Allah misguides, no one can guide. I bear witness that there is no one worthy of worship except Allah. And I bear witness that Muhammad is His servant and messenger. O believers, have *taqwa* [fear] of Allah according to His right and die not save as Muslims. O mankind, have *taqwa* of your Lord, the One who created you from one soul and created from it its mate and from them spread many men and women. And fear Allah from whom you demand your mutual rights and [do not cut] familial relations. Surely, Allah is Ever an All-Watcher over you. O believers, have *taqwa* of Allah and always speak the truth. He will direct you to do righteous deeds and will forgive you your sins. And whosoever obeys Allah and His Messenger has indeed achieved a great achievement. To proceed:

In many parts of the Western or English speaking world, our Muslim sisters do not have as much access to scholars, lectures in the mosques, arenas in which they may ask questions, and so forth. Therefore there is a pressing need to get vital Islamic information out to them in means they can take advantage of. This book is a step, Allah willing, in that direction.

In this work, the collector has done a good job of compiling many of the most important and often asked questions from sisters. The responses are given by some of the top scholars in the Muslim world today, namely, Shaikh Abdul Aziz ibn Baz, Shaikh Muhammad ibn Uthaimin and Shaikh Abdullah ibn Jibrin. Some of the questions were responded to by the "Standing

Committee" made up of eminent scholars similar to those just mentioned.

My role in translating this work is just that: translating the work. Therefore, I have tried to keep my comments to a minimum— except for the comments on hadith that is referred to in the text paragraph. Usually, comments will only appear to make the meaning of the question or answer clearer to those who are from a different background from the questioners and scholars involved. Very rarely, there may be a comment of a different nature.

Due to the nature of *fatawa*, or giving answers to questions received, many times important information about the hadith quoted is not mentioned by the scholars. In those cases where the Shaikh did not give the needed information concerning a hadith, I have made the effort to trace the hadith and mention such information. In general, if a hadith was from *Sahih al-Bukhari* or *Sahih Muslim*, that is all I would mention about the hadith. Otherwise, I would mention only the most important hadith references in which that hadith is to be found. Since the scholars responding to the questions are excellent scholars and very knowledgeable of hadith, it is very rare that they quote any hadith which is not authentic. Still, just to give the reader more confidence in the work, I did quote hadith specialists concerning those Ahadith that were not taken from either *Sahih al-Bukhari* or *Sahih Muslim*.

It has been my attempt to limit the number of Arabic terms used in this translation. In this way, every English reader can, Allah willing, benefit completely from the work. However, on occasion, I was still forced to use some Arabic terms. Usually, when coming across such terms, they are defined in parenthesis or are clear from the context. Some of these Arabic terms are completely defined in the glossary at the end of the work.

I pray that Allah accepts this work from us and makes it beneficial for the Muslim community. I ask Allah to bless the Shaikhs who responded to these questions and to increase their knowledge and fear of Him. May Allah also bless Br. Muhammad al-Musnad for gathering these questions in one work and getting them published. May Allah also bless Br. Abdul Malik Mujahid of Darussalam for presenting this translation project to me as well as for his encouraging me to complete it. May Allah also especially bless three brothers (Br. Muhammad Tahlawi, Dr. Muhammad al-Osimi and Br. Fahd al-Yahya) who have assisted me a great deal over the years, although in very different ways.

I ask Allah to forgive my mistakes and shortcomings in this work and in general. O Allah, accept this work from me as a work done solely for your sake.

Br. Jamaal Zarabozo
May 30, 1996
Muharram 13, 1417

Publisher's Note

All praise be to Allah. By His grace and mercy, Darussalam is having the golden opportunity to publish the Book of Fatâwâ (Shari'ah Rulings) for women to present it to the English-speaking world for the first time ever since.

The Book of Fatâwâ has got a vital importance among the religious books. In day-to-day life, different people face different types of problems of varying nature and they need their proper solution in the light of the Qur'ân and Sunnah. In addition to the common problems faced by both men and women, women are to face a lot of special problems regarding their menses, post-partum bleeding, istihada, hijab, mixing with men; rights and duties with respect to their husband, husband's household, children; inheritance, marriage, divorce and so forth. Women apart, even educated men are not having proper knowledge of these issues.

It is only the scholars who can derive rulings from Shari'ah and give legal verdicts. Hence the people are commanded by Allah to have recourse to the pious scholars of religion.

Allah says,

فسئلوآ اهل الذكر ان كنتم لا تعلمون (16:43)

"So ask of those who know the Scripture if you know not." (al-Nahl 43)

Allah also describes the dignified station of the scholars in the following verse,

قل هل يستوى الذين يعلمون والذين لا يعلمون (39:9)

"Say: Are those who know equal to those who know not?" (al-Zumar 9)

In a Hadith, it is also stated by the Prophet صلى الله عليه وسلم that,

من يرد الله به خيرا يفقهه فى الدين (بخارى)

"If Allah wants to do good to a person, He makes him comprehend the religion (the understanding of the Qur'ân and Sunnah)."

In Saudi Arabia women have got the facility to put their questions regarding different kinds of problems faced by them in their day-to-day life, to the eminent scholars herein who are from amongst the best scholars of the world. These are such Fatâwâ (responses to their questions) compiled in this book for all the women to benefit from them.

Scholars' answers to the questions of the people, with respect to their problems and issues, are actually the gists of the vast studies over the Qur'ân and Ahadith. And a common man, thus, through the Book of Fatâwâ, gets the exact Shari'ah rulings with a very little effort. In this way, Fatâwâ are an authentic and easy accessible source of the knowledge.

In this regard, Muhammad bin Abdul Aziz al-Musnad is highly praiseworthy for his efforts to collect all the Fatâwâ in Arabic, wherefrom it could be rendered into English in view of its vast usefulness for the women.

I am much grateful to Br. Jamaal Zarabozo who has rendered it into a very simple and eloquent English, intelligible to all. His comments on Ahadith and also those clarifying the meaning of the question or answer are much appreciable and are an added value to the book. I express my sincere thanks to the companions of Br. Jamaal, who have assisted him in different ways. I am also thankful to all of my brothers, especially Md. Daud, who have exerted their best efforts in bringing out the book.

Abdul Malik Mujahid
General Manager

Biographies

Shaikh ibn Baz

Abu Abdullah Shaikh Abdul-Aziz bin Abdullah bin Abdur-Rahman Aal-Baz was born in the city of Riyadh in Dhul-Hijjah 1330H. He memorized the Qur'ân in his early age and then he acquired knowledge from many of the great scholars of the Kingdom. Some of his teachers were Shaikh Muhammad bin Abdul-Latif Aal-Shaikh, Shaikh Salih bin Abdul-Aziz Aal-Sahikh and the eminent Shaikh Muhammad bin Ibrahim Aal-Shaikh who, in his time, was the Mufti of Saudi Arabia. Shaikh ibn Baz accompanied the eminent Shaikh and learned from him for about ten years. Thus he gained his religious education from the family of Imam Muhammad bin Abdul-Wahab. Afterwards Shaikh ibn Baz was appointed as a Justice and he worked for fourteen years in the judiciary until he was deputed to the education faculty. He remained engaged in teaching for nine years at Riyadh Islamic Law College, Riyadh Religious Institute. Then he was appointed Vice-Chancellor of the Islamic University, Al-Madinah; but shortly afterwards, he was made the Chancellor with all the administrative powers.

Later he was appointed President of the General Presidency of Islamic Research, Ifta, Call and Propagation, Kingdom of Saudi Arabia. Presently he is the Grand Mufti of Saudi Arabia.

He is also the President of many Islamic Committees and Councils, the prominent among these are: Senior Scholars Committee of the Kingdom, Permanent Committee for Islamic and Educational Research, the Founding Committee of Muslim World League, World Supreme Council for Mosques, Islamic Jurisprudence Assembly Makkah; and the member of the Supreme Council of the Islamic University at Al-Madinah, and the Supreme Committee for Islamic Propagation.

He belongs to the Hanbali School of jurisprudence but his verdicts are based on the arguments from Qur'ân and Sunnah.

Shaikh ibn Uthaimin

Abu Abdullah Muhammad bin Salih bin Muhammad bin Uthaimin At-Tamimi An-Najdi was born in the city of Unaiza, Qaseem Region on 27th Ramadhan 1347H in a famous religious family. He got his education from many prominent scholars like Shaikh Abdur-Rahman Sa'di, Shaikh Muhammad Amin Shinqiti and Shaikh Abdul-Aziz bin Baz.

When he entered into teaching, a great number of students from inside and outside Saudi Arabia get benefited from him. He has his own unique style of interpretation and explanation of religious points. He is from among those scholars who served Islam without any type of religious prejudice and kept themselves away from the limitations of blind-following. He is distinguished in his great exertion of effort in religious matters and analogical deductions which clearly prove the religious understanding he possesses, and the correct usage of the principles of religion, he adopts.

In giving religious verdicts, like Shaikh ibn Baz, his Fatawa are based on evidence from Qur'ân and Sunnah. He has about fifty compilations to his credit. Presently he is teaching Religious Fundamentals at the Shariah Faculty of Imam Muhammad bin Sa'ud Islamic University, Qaseem Branch. He is also a member of the Senior Scholars Committee of the Kingdom, and is the Imam and Khatib of the big Mosque of Unaiza city.

Shaikh ibn Jibreen

Abdullah bin Abdur-Rahman Al-Jibreen is the member of the General Presidency of Islamic Research, Ifta, Call and Propagation, Kingdom of Saudi Arabia. He received his education from the great scholars of the Kingdom including the eminent Shaikh ibn Baz. He participates in various seminars and religious forums for the purpose of the propagation of the call to Islam. He also delivers special lectures for the same cause. He has compiled many books and pamphlets on various Islamic topics.

Contents

4 - Questions Related to Menstruation & Post Partum Bleeding

Contents   13

Contents   **14**

Contents 15

Contents

12 - Questions Related to Relations Between the Spouses

Contents

Contents

Contents   19

Contents

Contents 21

Contents 22

What Negates One's Islam

Shaikh-ul-Islam Muhammad bin Suleiman At-Tamimi stated, "Know that ten matters negate one's Islam. [They are:]

"First, associating partners in the worship of Allah. Allah says,

﴿ إِنَّ ٱللَّهَ لَا يَغْفِرُ أَن يُشْرَكَ بِهِۦ وَيَغْفِرُ مَا دُونَ ذَٰلِكَ لِمَن يَشَآءُ ﴾ [النساء: ١١٦]

"Verily, Allah forgives not (the sin of) setting up partners in worship with Him, but He forgives whom He pleases other sins than that" (al-Nisa 116).

Allah also says,

﴿ إِنَّهُۥ مَن يُشْرِكَ بِٱللَّهِ فَقَدْ حَرَّمَ ٱللَّهُ عَلَيْهِ ٱلْجَنَّةَ وَمَأْوَىٰهُ ٱلنَّارُ وَمَا لِلظَّٰلِمِينَ مِنْ أَنصَارٍ ﴾ [المائدة: ٧٢]

"Verily, whosoever sets up partners in worship with Allah, then Allah has forbidden Paradise for him, and the Fire will be his abode. And for the wrongdoers, there are no helpers" (al-Maidah 72).

Included in this category of deeds is sacrificing animals for the sake of jinn or graves.

"Second, whoever sets up an intermediary between himself and Allah, whom he prays to, seeks intercession from and puts his reliance in, has blasphemed according to the consensus of the scholars.

"Third, whoever does not consider the polytheists as disbelievers or whoever has doubt concerning their disbelief or whoever considers their way as correct has committed an act of disbelief himself.

"Fourth, if a person believes that some guidance other than the guidance of the Prophet (صلى الله عليه وسلم) is more complete than his or that another's judgment is better than the Prophet's, [then that person has committed an act of disbelief]. This would be like the one who prefers the rule and law of false gods [be they human or otherwise] over the Prophet's rule and law. This position is one of disbelief.

"Fifth, whoever dislikes anything the Prophet (صلى الله عليه وسلم) brought, even if he acts by it, has committed an act of disbelief.

"Sixth, whoever ridicules or jokes about any part of the religion of the Messenger (صلى الله عليه وسلم), or its rewards or its punishments, has committed an act of disbelief. The evidence for this is in the Words of Allah,

﴿ قُلْ أَبِٱللَّهِ وَءَايَٰتِهِۦ وَرَسُولِهِۦ كُنتُمْ تَسْتَهْزِءُونَ ۞ لَا تَعْتَذِرُواْ قَدْ كَفَرْتُم بَعْدَ إِيمَٰنِكُمْ ﴾ [التوبة: ٦٥-٦٦]

"Say: Was it Allah, or His signs or His Messenger that you were mocking? Make no excuse, you have disbelieved after you had believed." (*al-Tauba* 65-66).

"Seventh, the performing of magic [is an act of disbelief], this includes those magical incantations that make one love or hate another person. Whoever performs them or is pleased with them has committed an act of disbelief. Allah says in the Quran,

﴿ وَمَا يُعَلِّمَانِ مِنْ أَحَدٍ حَتَّىٰ يَقُولَا إِنَّمَا نَحْنُ فِتْنَةٌ فَلَا تَكْفُرْ ﴾ [البقرة: ١٠٢]

"But neither of these two (angels) taught anyone (such things) until they had said, 'We are only for trial, so disbelieve not [by learning such magic from us]'" (*al-Baqara* 102).

"Eighth, assisting and supporting the polytheists against the Muslims [is also a type of disbelief]. The proof for this is in Allah's statement,

﴿ وَمَن يَتَوَلَّهُم مِّنكُمْ فَإِنَّهُۥ مِنْهُمْ إِنَّ ٱللَّهَ لَا يَهْدِى ٱلْقَوْمَ ٱلظَّـٰلِمِينَ ﴾

[المائدة: ٥١]

"And if any among you takes them [the Jews and Christians] as helpers and protectors, then surely he is one of them. Verily, Allah guides not those people who are wrongdoing" (al-Maida 51).

"Ninth, if a person believes that some people are permitted to be free of the Law of Muhammad (peace be upon him), in the same way that Khidr was free of the law of Moses (peace be upon him), then that person is a disbeliever.

"Tenth, turning away from the religion of Allah, not learning it or applying it, [is also a form of disbelief]. The evidence for this is Allah's saying,

﴿ وَمَنْ أَظْلَمُ مِمَّن ذُكِّرَ بِـَٔايَـٰتِ رَبِّهِۦ ثُمَّ أَعْرَضَ عَنْهَآ إِنَّا مِنَ ٱلْمُجْرِمِينَ مُنتَقِمُونَ ﴾

[السجدة: ٢٢]

"And who does more wrong than he who is reminded of the signs of his Lord, then he turns aside therefrom? Verily, We shall exact retribution from the sinners" (al-Sajdah 22).

"There is no difference with respect to all of the above whether the act is done jokingly, seriously or out of fear. The only exception is one who is coerced. All of them are from the greatest of the dangerous acts and they are also among the most common in occurrence. A Muslim must be aware of them and fear for himself concerning such actions. We seek refuge in Allah from that which brings about His anger and the painfulness of His punishment."

Hypocrisy is of Two Types: With Respect to Belief and with Respect to Actions

Hypocrisy with respect to beliefs is of six types. The one who is guilty of any of them will be in the lowest pit of the Hell-fire. These are:

(1) Denying or disbelieving the Messenger (صلى الله عليه وسلم).

(2) Denying something that the Messenger (صلى الله عليه وسلم) presented or taught.

(3) Having hatred for the Messenger (صلى الله عليه وسلم).

(4) Having hatred for something the Messenger (صلى الله عليه وسلم) presented.

(5) Being pleased if the religion of the Messenger (صلى الله عليه وسلم) is diminished or weakened.

(6) Being displeased if the religion of the Messenger (صلى الله عليه وسلم) is strengthened or victorious

1. Questions Related to Aqidah (Faith).

The Ruling Concerning Visiting Graves and Using Them as a Means of Approach to Allah

Question 1: What is the ruling concerning visiting graves and seeking to get closer to Allah by means of mausoleums, and using sheep and wealth to get closer by them, such as visiting the mausoleum of al-Sayid al-Badawi, al-Husain and al-Sayidah Zainab.[1] Benefit us [by responding to our question], may Allah benefit you.

Response: The visiting of graves is of two types. The first type is legally sanctioned and desired. This is to visit the graves in order to supplicate for the deceased and to ask for mercy for them, and also to remember death and prepare for the Hereafter. This is based on the hadith of the Prophet (صلى الله عليه وسلم),

" زُورُوا القُبُورَ فَإِنَّها تُذَكِّرُكُمُ الآخِرَةَ "

"Visit the graves as they remind you of the Hereafter."[2]
The Prophet (صلى الله عليه وسلم) and his Companions used to visit the graves. However, this practice is for men only and not for women. As for women, it is not sanctioned for them to visit the graves. In fact, they must be prevented from doing so as it is confirmed from

---

[1] The question is referring to a common practice in many parts of the Muslim world. The three mausoleums mentioned in this question are located in Egypt. People visit them and offer wealth or animal sacrifices thinking that doing so in the honor of those deceased people will bring them closer to Allah and make Allah pleased with them.—JZ

[2] Part of a hadith recorded by Muslim, Ahmad, al-Nasai, Abu Dawud and ibn Majah with the last word being "death" instead of "the Hereafter." Ibn Majah also records something similar with the last word being "the Hereafter."—JZ

the Prophet (صلى الله عليه وسلم) that he cursed those women who visited graves.[1] This is because their visiting the graves is a great trial for them. It is also because [by their behavior] they become a trial for others due to their little patience and great griefing that overcomes them. Therefore, it is not legally sanctioned for them to visit the graves. It is also confirmed in the *Sahih* that Umm Atiyah said, "We were prohibited from following the funeral procession but this was not strictly enforced upon us." This shows that they were prevented from following the funeral procession to the grave site out of fear that it would be a trial for them or because of them and because of their little patience. The basic ruling when something is ordered against is that of prohibition. This is because Allah has stated,

$$ \text{﴿ وَمَا ءَاتَىٰكُمُ ٱلرَّسُولُ فَخُذُوهُ وَمَا نَهَىٰكُمْ عَنْهُ فَٱنتَهُوا۟ ﴾} $$

[الحشر: ٧]

"Whatsoever the Messenger gives you, take it; and whatsoever he forbids you, abstain from it" (*al-Hashr* 7).

---

[1] This is in a hadith recorded by al-Tirmidhi, al-Nasai, Abu Dawud, ibn Majah and Ahmad. However, all of them narrated this through Abu Saleh, who is a weak narrator. Hence, many scholars of hadith (such as ibn Hajr, al-Albani and others) consider that narration weak. The correct (*hasan*) narration of this hadith states that the Prophet (peace be upon him) cursed those women who frequently visited the graves. [Recorded by al-Tirmidhi, ibn Majah and Ahmad. According to al-Albani, this narration is *hasan*. See Muhammad Nasir al-Din al-Albani, *Sahih Sunan al-Tirmidhi* (Riyadh: Maktab al-Tarbiyah al-Arabi li-Daul al-Khaleej, 1988), vol. 1, p. 308.] This can give a very different interpretation of the hadith, as is given by Abdul Rahman al-Mubarakfoori, *Tuhfah al-Ahwadhi bi-Sharh Jami' al-Tirmidhi* (Beirut: Dar al-Fikr, n.d.), vol. 4, p. 160. Bakr Abu Zaid, however, interprets this hadith to mean the same as the previous hadith. [See Bakr Abu Zaid, *Juz` fi Ziyarat al-Nisa li-l-Quboor* (Riyadh: Dar al-Aasima, 1994), pp. 24-27.] If a woman is known not to behave herself within the limits of the *shariah* at a gravesite, then she should be prevented from visiting the graves according to the agreement of the scholars. Allah knows best.— JZ

As for saying prayers over the dead (as in the funeral prayer), this is sanctioned for both men and women. This has been authentically reported in the hadith from the Messenger of Allah (صلى الله عليه وسلم) and reports from the Companions.

As for following the funeral procession, the statement of Umm Atiyah, "but this was not strictly enforced upon us," is not an evidence that it is permissible for women to follow the funeral procession. This is because the prohibition has come from the Prophet (صلى الله عليه وسلم) and this forbids the act. Her statement, "but this was not strictly enforced upon us," may have been based on her own reasoning and what she suspected to be true, but her personal reasoning cannot be taken in opposition to the sunnah.

The second type of visiting is a kind of heresy. This is the visiting of the graves in order to make prayers to the deceased and ask for their help, or in order to make sacrifices or vows on their behalf. This is an evil and is a greater form of *shirk*.[1] We ask Allah for safety. Closely associated with that is visiting the graves in order to specifically make supplications, read the Quran or pray at the gravesites. These are all heresies. This type of visiting is not legally sanctioned and it is one of the roads that lead to *shirk*.

Therefore, there are actually three types of visitations:

The first type is legally sanctioned. This is where one visits the grave to pray for the deceased and to remember death.

The second type is where one visits the grave to read the Quran, pray there or make a sacrifice there. These are heresies and are actions that lead to *shirk*.

The third type is where one visits the grave in order to make a sacrifice in the name of the deceased in order to get closer to him, pray to the deceased instead of Allah in order to meet some need, or seek help, aid or victory from the deceased. These are all greater forms of *shirk*. We ask Allah for safety from them. One

---

[1] "Greater form of *shirk*" means that the act, given certain conditions, takes one out of the fold of Islam.— JZ

must be aware and cautious about such innovated visitations. It does not matter if the deceased called upon was a prophet, righteous person or otherwise. Included in this category is what some of the ignorant people do at the grave of the Prophet (صلى الله عليه وسلم), including supplicating to him and seeking his rescue. It also includes what people do at the grave of al-Husain, al-Badawi, Shaikh Abdul Qadir al-Jeelani or others. Allah is the One from whom we seek help.

Shaikh ibn Baz

The Ruling Concerning Posing Questions to the Fortunetellers and Soothsayers

Question 2: My father suffered from a psychological disease. This disease stayed with him for some time. There were visits to the hospital during that time. Some of our relatives advised us to visit a specific woman as they said that she knew a cure for that kind of disease. They also said that all you need to do is give her his name and she will tell you what is afflicting him and will give you a cure. Is it allowed for us to visit that woman? Help us, may Allah reward you with good.

Response: It is not allowed to either put questions to or to believe in that woman or any other like her. This is because she is from the fortunetellers and soothsayers, who claim to have knowledge of the unseen and who seek the help of jinn for their cures and their information about people. It has been authentically reported that the Messenger of Allah (صلى الله عليه وسلم) said,

"مَنْ أَتَى عَرَّافاً فَسَأَلَهُ عَن شَيءٍ لَمْ تُقْبَلْ لَه صَلاةُ أَرْبَعِينَ لَيْلَةً"

"If a person goes to a fortuneteller and asks him about something, his prayer will not be accepted for forty nights."

Muslim recorded this in his *Sahih*. It is also authentically narrated that he said,

"مَنْ أَتَى عَرَّافاً أَوْ كَاهِناً فَصَدَّقَهُ بِمَا يَقُولُ فَقَدْ كَفَرَ بِمَا أُنْزِلَ
عَلَى مُحَمَّدٍ صلى الله عليه وسلم"

"Whoever goes to a fortuneteller or soothsayer and believes in what he says, he has then disbelieved in what has been revealed to Muhammad صلى الله عليه وسلم"[1]

There are many Ahadith with that meaning. Therefore, it is a must to stop such people and those who visit them. They should not be questioned nor should they be believed. They should be taken to the people in authority in order to receive the punishment they deserve. Allowing them to be present and not taking them to the authorities harms society as a whole. Leaving them would also help them in deceiving the ignorant people, who will ask them questions and believe in them.[2]

The Prophet (صلى الله عليه وسلم) said,

"مَنْ رَأَى مِنْكُمْ مُنْكَراً فَلْيُغَيِّرْهُ بِيَدِهِ فَإِنْ لم يَسْتَطِعْ فَبِلِسَانِهِ فَإِنْ لـم
يَسْتَطِعْ فَبِقَلْبِهِ وَذلِكَ أَضْعَفُ الإِيمَانِ"

"If anyone of you sees an evil, he must change it with his hand. If he is not able to, then he should do so with his tongue. And if he is still not able to, then with his heart and that is the weakest faith."

This was recorded by Muslim in his *Sahih*. There is no doubt that taking them to the authorities, such as the mayor of the city, the

---

[1] Recorded by Ahmad. It seems that the correct version in *Sahih Muslim* is without the words, "and believes in what he says." Allah knows best.— JZ

[2] The ruling in this question also applies to all of the other forms of predicting the future that have become commonplace in the West, such as astrologers and psychic networks. Muslims must avoid them completely and must not believe in their statements.— JZ

people whose job is to enforce right and eradicate evil, and the courts, is part of the general concept of removing them by one's tongue. It is also part of helping one another in righteousness and piety. May Allah support all the Muslims in that which is best for them and protect them from every evil.

Shaikh ibn Baz

The Ruling Concerning One Who Opposes the Laws of Allah

Question 3: What is the ruling concerning one who says, "Some of the laws of the *Shariah* need to be reviewed, as they are in need of adjustment since they are not compatible with the developments of this day and age. For example, concerning inheritance, the law that says that a man gets twice the share of a woman needs to be reconsidered." What is the Islamic ruling concerning one who says something of that nature?

Response: The laws that Allah has laid down for His servants and has made clear in His Noble Book or upon the tongue of His Messenger (صلى الله عليه وسلم) — such as the laws of inheritance, the five daily prayers, *zakat*, fasting and so forth that Allah has made clear for His servants and concerning which the Muslim Nation (*ummah*) is in agreement— may not be opposed or changed by anyone as they have been laid down to be applied for this Nation for the time of the Prophet (صلى الله عليه وسلم) and after him until the Hour [of Judgment] is established. From those laws is the giving of preference [in inheritance] to male children over female children, and grandchildren, and full brothers and half-brothers from the father. Allah has made this clear in His Noble Book and there is a consensus of the Muslim scholars upon it. It is, therefore, obligatory to act upon it with faith and belief. If a person alleges that something different from what the *Shariah* has stated is better or more suitable, then he is a disbeliever. Similarly, anyone who says that it is permissible to go against the *shariah* is also a disbeliever. This is because he is opposing Allah and His messenger (صلى الله عليه وسلم), as well as the consensus of the *Ummah*. It is upon the ruler to ask him to repent if he is a Muslim. If he repents [that is accepted from him]. If he does not repent, then he must be killed as a disbelieving, apostate from Islam. This is because the Prophet (صلى الله عليه وسلم) said,

" مَنْ بَـدَّلَ دِينَـهُ فَـاقْتُلُـوُه "

"Whoever changes his religion is to be killed."[1]

We ask Allah for safety and for all Muslims safety from the misguidance of trials and from differing from the pure *shariah*.

Shaikh ibn Baz

The Ruling Concerning Celebrating Birthdays

Question 4: What is the ruling concerning celebrating birthdays?

Response: Celebrating birthdays has no source whatsoever in the pure *shariah*. In fact, it is an innovation, since the Messenger of Allah (صلى الله عليه وسلم) said,

" مَنْ أَحْدَثَ فِي أَمْرِنا هذَا مَالَيْسَ مِنهُ فَهُوَ رَدٌّ "

"Whoever introduces anything into this matter of ours that does not belong to it shall have that action rejected."

This was recorded by both al-Bukhari and Muslim. In a version recorded by Muslim and by al-Bukhari in definitive *muallaq* form[2],

" مَنْ عَمِلَ عَمَلاً لَيسَ عَلَيهِ أَمرُنا فَهُو رَدٌّ "

---

[1] Recorded by al-Bukhari, Ahmad, Abu Dawud, al-Nasai, al-Tirmidhi and ibn Majah.— JZ
[2] *Mualaq* is where al-Bukhari did not record the entire chain of the hadith. However, if it is in "definitive *mualaq* form," it shows that he considered it authentic back to the one he is quoting from.— JZ

"Whoever performs a deed which is not in accord with our affairs, that deed is rejected."

It is well-known that the Prophet (صلى الله عليه وسلم) did not celebrate his birthday at all during his lifetime nor did he ever order it to be celebrated. Nor did he teach such to his Companions. Therefore, the rightly-guided caliphs and all of his Companions did not celebrate it. They are the most knowledgeable of the people concerning his sunnah and they are the most beloved to the Prophet (صلى الله عليه وسلم). They were also the most keen upon following whatever the Prophet (صلى الله عليه وسلم) brought. Therefore, if one is supposed to celebrate the Prophet's birthday, this would have been made evident at their time. Similarly, not one of the scholars of the best generations[1] celebrated his birthday nor did they order it to be done.

Therefore, it is known from the above that such a celebration is not from the Law that Allah sent Muhammad (صلى الله عليه وسلم) with. We ask Allah and all Muslims to witness that if the Prophet (صلى الله عليه وسلم) had done so or ordered such to be done, or even if his Companions had done so, we would rush to do it and call others to do it. This is because, and all praises are due to Allah, we are the most keen in following his sunnah and respecting his commands and prohibitions. We ask Allah, for ourselves and for all of our brethren Muslims, steadfastness upon the truth, avoiding everything that differs from Allah's pure *shariah*. Verily, He is Generous and Noble.

Shaikh ibn Baz

How Does One Behave Toward a Relative who Does Not Pray?

Question 5: I have a brother-in-law who rarely prays. I live with my husband's family and [the female members of] his family sit with him even if the Imam is praying. What should I

---

[1] The first three generations of Islam, that is, the generation of the Prophet (peace be upon him) and the following two.— JZ

do? I am not one of his relatives (*mahram*). Is there any sin upon me since I do not have the ability to advise him?

Response: If he does not pray, then he is deserving to be boycotted. You should not greet him nor should you respond to his greeting, until he repents. This is because not praying is a greater form of *kufr* [that takes one out of the fold of Islam]. This is true even if the person does not deny that it is obligatory. This is according to the most correct opinion among the scholars. The Prophet (صلى الله عليه وسلم) said,

" العَهدُ الَّذِي بَينَنَا وبينَهُمُ الصَّلاةُ ، فمَنْ تَرَكَها فقد كَفَر "

> "The covenant that is between us and them [the disbelievers] is the prayer. Whoever abandons it has committed blasphemy."

This was recorded by Ahmad and the compilers of the *Sunan* with a sound chain. The Prophet (صلى الله عليه وسلم) also said,

" بَينَ الرَّجُـلِ وَبَينَ الكُفْـرِ والشِّـرْكِ تـركُ الصَّـلاةَ "

> "Between a man and disbelief and polytheism is the abandoning of the prayer."

This was recorded by Imam Muslim in his *Sahih*.

However, if a person denies the obligation of the prayers, then he is a disbeliever according to the consensus of the scholars.

Therefore, it is obligatory upon his family to advise him and to boycott him if he does not repent. It is also obligatory to take his matter to the ruler for him to be asked to repent. If he repents, [that is accepted from him]. If he does not repent, he is to be killed. This is because Allah has said in the Quran,

﴿ فَإِن تَابُوا۟ وَأَقَامُوا۟ ٱلصَّلَوٰةَ وَءَاتَوُا۟ ٱلزَّكَوٰةَ فَخَلُّوا۟ سَبِيلَهُمْ ﴾

[التوبة : ٥]

"But if they repent and offer prayer perfectly and give zakat, then leave their way free" (*al-Tauba* 5).

Also, the Prophet (صلى الله عليه وسلم) said,

" نُهِيــتُ عَــن قَتـلِ الـمُصَلّــين "

"I have been prohibited from killing those who pray."[1]

These evidences show that one who does not pray is not to have his "way left free" and there is no prohibition against killing him if he is taken to the authorities and he does not repent.

And Allah is the One who provides guidance.

Shaikh ibn Baz

Ruling About Hiring a Non-Muslim Maid [or Servant]

Question 6: I sent requests asking for a maid to help my wife with her housework. I discovered, through letters, that they did not find a Muslim in the country that I wanted a maid from. Is it allowed for me to hire a non-Muslim maid?

Response: It is not allowed to have a non-Muslim maid or a non-Muslim male servant, or a worker who is non-Muslim for anyone living in the Arabian Peninsula. This is because the Prophet (صلى الله عليه وسلم) ordered the Jews and Christians to be expelled from that land. He ordered that only Muslims should be left there. He decreed upon his death that all polytheists must be expelled from this Peninsula.

---

[1] Recorded by Abu Dawud. Some of the narrators in its chain are unknown. However, due to supporting evidence, al-Albani has called this hadith *sahih*. See Muhammad Nasir al-Din al-Albani, *Sahih Sunan Abu Dawud* (Riyadh: Maktaba al-Tarbiya al-Arabi li-Daul al-Khaleej, 1989), vol. 3, p. 931. He discusses it in some detail, although without mentioning that it is recorded by Abu Dawud, in Muhammad Nasir al-Din al-Albani, *Silsilat al-Ahadith al-Sahiha* (Riyadh: Maktaba al-Maarif, 1991), vol. 5, p. 493.— JZ

Furthermore, hiring disbelieving men and women is very dangerous for the Muslims, their faith, their behavior and the upbringing of their children. Therefore, such must be prevented in obedience to Allah, the Glorified, and His Messenger (صلى الله عليه وسلم), and to prevent a source of evil and immorality.

And Allah is the One who provides guidance.

Shaikh ibn Baz

The Ruling Concerning Washing with Blood

Question 7: My mother was ill and she visited a number of hospitals but without a cure. Finally, she went to a soothsayer who told her to wash herself with the blood of a goat. My mother actually did what he said, being ignorant of the religious ruling concerning such. Is there some expiation that we must perform and, if so, what is it? May Allah reward you with what is best.

Response: It is not allowed to go to soothsayers, astrologers, magicians or any of the other kind of charlatans. It is also not allowed to put questions to them or to believe them. Indeed, that is one of the greatest sins, since the Prophet (صلى الله عليه وسلم) said,

$$\text{"مَنْ أَتَى عَرَّافاً فَسَأَلَهُ عَن شَيءٍ لَمْ تُقْبَلْ لَه صَلاةُ أَربَعِينَ لَيلَةً "}$$

"If anyone goes to a fortuneteller and asks him about anything, then his prayer will not be accepted from him for forty nights."

Recorded by Muslim in his *Sahih*. The Prophet (صلى الله عليه وسلم) also said,

$$\text{"مَنْ أتى عَرَّافاً أو كَاهِناً فصَدَّقَه بِما يقُولُ فقَدْ كَفَرَ بِما أُنزِلَ عَلى مُحَمَّدٍ "}$$

"Whoever goes to a fortuneteller or soothsayer and believes in what he says has then disbelieved in what has been revealed to Muhammad."

This was recorded by the compilers of the *Sunan* with an authentic chain. Finally, the Prophet (صلى الله عليه وسلم) also said,

" لَيْسَ مِنَّا مَن سَحَرَ أَو سُحِرَ لَه أَو تَكَهَّنَ أَو تُكُهِّن لَه أَو تَطَيَّرَ أَو
تُطُيِّرَ لَه ومَنْ أَتَى كَاهِناً فَصَدَّقَه بِمَا يَقُولُ فَقَدْ كَفَرَ بِمَا أُنزِلَ
عَلَى مُحَمَّدٍ صلى الله عليه وسلم "

"He is not one of us: who performs magic, the one who
has magic performed for him, the one who reads
fortunes, the one who has his fortune read, whoever gives
omens or has omens done for him. And whoever goes to
a soothsayer and believes in what he said has disbelieved
in what is revealed to Muhammad صلى الله عليه وسلم."

Recorded by al-Bazaar with a good chain.

As for washing with blood, that is a clearly rejected act.
Blood is an impure, forbidden object. It is not allowed to use impure
items as medicine. This is based on what Abu Dawud recorded in his
Sunan from Abu al-Darda, that the Prophet (صلى الله عليه وسلم) said,

" إِنَّ اللهَ أَنزَلَ الدَّاءَ والدَّوَاءَ وجَعَلَ لِكُلِّ دَاءٍ دَوَاءً فَتَدَاوَوا
ولا تَدَاوَوا بِحَرَام "

"Allah has descended the illness and its remedy. And for every
illness, He has created its remedy. Therefore, use remedies for
each other but do not use anything forbidden as a remedy."

The Prophet (صلى الله عليه وسلم) also said,

" إِنَّ اللهَ لَمْ يَجْعَلْ شِفَاءَكُم فِيمَا حَرَّمَ علَيكُم "

"Allah did not place your cures in what He has
forbidden for you."

Recorded by al-Baihaqi. Ibn Hibban has declared it authentic,
from the hadith narrated by Umm Salama.

It is obligatory upon the aforementioned woman to repent to
Allah and not to repeat a similar action like the one she did. Whoever
sincerely repents, Allah returns back to him. Allah has said,

﴿ وَتُوبُوٓاْ إِلَى ٱللَّهِ جَمِيعًا أَيُّهَ ٱلْمُؤْمِنُونَ لَعَلَّكُمْ تُفْلِحُونَ ﴾

[النور : ٣١]

"And all of you repent to Allah, O believers, that you may be successful" (*al-Nur* 31).

Shaikh ibn Baz

Ruling Concerning Putting a Piece of Animal Skin or Leather Upon a Baby's Stomach

Question 8: Is it allowed to put a piece of animal skin, leather or such upon the stomach of a breastfeeding baby boy or girl or older child? We in the South of Saudi Arabia put such a piece of leather upon the stomach of the girl, small child or older. We hope that you will benefit us on this matter.

Answer: If that piece of animal skin is put on the child as a kind of amulet to protect the child from harm or to bring about some good, then that is forbidden, and could even be a form of *shirk*. If it is put for a sound reason, such as to keep the navel from bulging or to strengthen the back, then there is no harm in that.

The Standing Committee

The Ruling Concerning Putting a Knife On a Child in Order to Protect Him

Question 9: I have seen some people placing a knife on their small children and saying, "This is so the jinn do not come to him." Is this practice correct?

Response: This is an objectionable act and there is no sound source for it. It is not allowed to do such a thing. What is legally sanctioned is to seek refuge from them by Allah's complete words from every devil and poisonous pest, as has been confirmed from the Prophet (صلى الله عليه وسلم). He used to seek protection by those words for his grandsons al-Hasan and al-Husain ibn Ali. It is also sanctioned to make *dua* for them by asking Allah to protect them from every evil. As for putting a knife or something similar, of iron, wood or other substances, with the belief that such will protect them from the jinn, it is an evil practice that is not allowed.

Similar is the ruling with respect to hanging an amulet over them, which is what is called *al-tama'im*. This is not allowed because the Prophet (صلى الله عليه وسلم) said,

" مَنْ تَعلَّقَ تَمِيمَةً فَلاَ أَتَمَّ اللهُ لَـهُ "

"Whoever hangs an amulet, Allah will not complete [his affair] for him."[1]

In another narration, the Prophet (صلى الله عليه وسلم) said,

" مَنْ تَعَلَّقَ تَميمةً فَقـد أَشْــرَكَ "

"Whoever wears an amulet has committed *shirk*."[2]

May Allah bestow understanding of the religion upon all Muslims, and steadfastness in the religion. We seek refuge for ourselves and them[3] from everything that differs from His pure law.

Shaikh ibn Baz

It is Not Allowed to Seek Blessings Through the Dead

Question 10: In our land, a man died. The news of his death came during the day. We saw the elderly women of the land going to his house. He was laid out after being shrouded in the middle with the women around him. We asked them why they went to him and they said that they did so in order to get blessings from him [his body]. What is the ruling concerning what they did? Is that *sunnah*?

Response: That action is not allowed. In fact, it is an evil act. It is not allowed because one may not seek blessings through or from the dead or their graves. Nor is one allowed to supplicate to them

---

[1] Recorded by Ahmad, ibn Hibban and others. Salih al-Usaimi concludes that it is *hasan*. See Salih ibn Abdullah al-Usaimi, *al-Dur al-Nadheed fi Takhreej Kitab al-Tauheed* (Dar ibn Khuzaima, 1413 A.H.), p. 38.— JZ

[2] Recorded by Ahmad and al-Hakim. Al-Usaimi also concludes that this hadith is *hasan*. See al-Usaimi, p. 39.— JZ

[3] In English, the more proper manner is to invoke for others first and then for oneself. However, in Arabic, the opposite is considered the proper manner of speech.— JZ

instead of Allah. Nor can one ask them to fulfill a need or heal an ill person, and so forth. This is because acts of worship are the right of Allah alone. It is from Him that blessings are sought. He is described as being the Blessed, as Allah says in *surah al-Furqan*,

$$﴿ تَبَارَكَ ٱلَّذِى نَزَّلَ ٱلْفُرْقَانَ عَلَىٰ عَبْدِهِۦ لِيَكُونَ لِلْعَٰلَمِينَ نَذِيرًا ﴾$$

[الفرقان : ١]

"Blessed be He who sent down the Criterion to His slave that he may be a warner to the worlds" (*al-Furqan* 1).

Allah also says,

$$﴿ تَبَٰرَكَ ٱلَّذِى بِيَدِهِ ٱلْمُلْكُ ﴾$$　　[الملك : ١]

"Blessed be He in whose hand is the Dominion" (*al-Mulk* 1)
The meaning of that is that Allah is behooving of the greatest amount of veneration and blessing. As for the human, he is blessed if Allah guides him and makes his affairs good, and the others benefit from him. This is as Allah has stated about His servant and Messenger Jesus, son of Mary, (عليه السلام),

$$﴿ قَالَ إِنِّى عَبْدُ ٱللَّهِ ءَاتَىٰنِىَ ٱلْكِتَٰبَ وَجَعَلَنِى نَبِيًّا ۞ وَجَعَلَنِى مُبَارَكًا أَيْنَ مَا كُنتُ ﴾$$

[مريم : ٣٠-٣١]

"He [Jesus] said: Verily, I am a slave of Allah. He has given me the Scripture and made me a prophet. And He has made me blessed wherever I be" (*Maryam* 30-31).

Shaikh ibn Baz

Ruling Concerning Hanging and Possessing Pictures

Question 11: What is the ruling concerning hanging a picture on a wall? What is the ruling concerning owning pictures of people?

Response: It is not allowed to hang a picture or keep a picture of any being that possesses a soul. It is obligatory to destroy such pictures. This is because the Prophet (صلى الله عليه وسلم) told Ali,

$$ \text{" لاَ تدَعْ صُورَةً إلا طَمَسْتَهَـا "} $$

"Do not leave any image, but [instead] efface it."[1]

It is also confirmed in the hadith of Jabir that,

$$ \text{"ان النبى صلى الله عليه وسلم نَهَى عَنِ الصُّورَةِ فِي البَيْتِ "} $$

"The Prophet (صلى الله عليه وسلم) prohibited having pictures in houses."[2]

Therefore, all pictures meant for remembrance should be torn to pieces or burned. However, pictures that are needed out of necessity, such as for official identification purposes and so forth, may be kept.

Shaikh ibn Baz

Ruling Concerning the Papers that Contain the Name of Allah

Question 12: We find some of the verses of the Quran printed in the newspapers or writings, as well as, "In the name of Allah, the Compassionate, the Merciful",[3] at the beginning of some papers or letters. What do we do with such verses after we are finished reading the newspaper or letter? Should we tear it up or burn it or what should be done?

Response: It is a must, after one is done with the papers or pages that contain Allah's name, to safeguard the papers, by burning them or burying them in clean soil. This is to protect the Quranic verses and Allah's names from being degraded. It is not

---

[1] Recorded by Muslim.— JZ
[2] Recorded by al-Tirmidhi and Ahmad. Al-Albani says it is *sahih.*
[3] Of course, the question is talking about these words being written in Arabic.— JZ

allowed to throw them into the garbage heaps or into the streets or to use them as different kinds of sheets, such as tablecloths. Otherwise, one is degrading the names and verses and not safekeeping them.

Shaikh ibn Baz

Ruling Concerning Crying due to Illness

Question 13: I am ill and sometimes I cry because of what happens to me after my illness. Is this kind of crying considered an act of opposition to Allah and not being pleased with what He has decreed? I do not do this action willfully. Similarly, does that ruling also include when I talk to my relatives, telling them about my illness?

Response: There is no harm in crying if it is simply tears coming from the eyes, without wailing. This is based on the Prophet's statement, when his son Ibrahim had died,

" العَينُ تَدْمَعُ والقَلْبُ يَحْزَنُ ولا نَقُولُ إلا ما يُرضِي الـرَبَّ وإنّا لِفِراقِكَ يا إبراهيمُ لَحزُونُونَ "

"The eye tears, the heart grieves but we do not say anything except what is pleasing to the Lord. We are, by your departure Ibrahim, certainly grieved."[1]

Hadith with that meaning are many. There is also no harm in your talking to your relatives and friends about your disease as long as you praise Allah, thank Him and extol Him, and ask Him for health, following the permissible means. We advise you to have patience and hope for reward from Allah. I give you glad tidings, as Allah has stated,

﴿ إِنَّمَا يُوَفَّ ٱلصَّٰبِرُونَ أَجْرَهُم بِغَيْرِ حِسَابٍ ﴾   [الزمر : ١٠]

"Only those who are patient shall receive their rewards in full without reckoning" (al-Zumar 10).

---

[1] Recorded by al-Bukhari and Muslim.— JZ

The Prophet (صلى الله عليه وسلم) also said,

" لا يُصِيبُ المُسْلِمَ هَمٌّ ولا غَمٌّ ولا نَصَبٌ ولا وَصَبٌ (وهـو
المرض) وَلا أَذىً حَتَّى الشَّوْكةِ إلا كَفَّر اللهُ بها مِنْ خَطَايَاهُ "

"A Muslim is not afflicted with fatigue, sorrow, disease,
sadness, or hurt, even if it be the prick of a thorn, except that
due to it Allah expiates some of his sins."[1]

The Messenger of Allah (صلى الله عليه وسلم) also said,

" مَنْ يُــرِدِ اللهُ بــه خَــيراً يُصِــبْ مِنــه "

"If Allah wants good for a person, he afflicts him with trials."[2]

We ask Allah to grant you a cure and health, as well as goodness
of the heart and deeds. Verily, He is the Hearer, the Responder.

Shaikh ibn Baz

Women Visiting Graves

Question 14: What is the reason or cause for the
prohibition of women visiting graves?

Response: First, there is a strong prohibition of that action
in the statement of the Prophet (صلى الله عليه وسلم),

" لَعَــنَ اللهُ زائِــرَاتِ القُبُـــور "

"Allah curses those women who visit the graves."[3]

Also, the Prophet (صلى الله عليه وسلم) told Fatima, when she visited
some people to give them her condolences,

---

[1] Recorded by al-Bukhari. Muslim has something similar to it.— JZ

[2] Recorded by al-Bukhari. — JZ

[3] As was stated in a previous footnote, this is in a hadith recorded by al-
Tirmidhi, al-Nasai, Abu Dawud, ibn Majah and Ahmad. However, it is a
weak narration. The correct (*hasan*) narration of this hadith states that the
Prophet (peace be upon him) cursed those women who frequently visited
the graves.— JZ

"لَوْ بَلَغْتِ مَعَهُمُ الْكَدَاءَ (يعني أدنى المقابر) مَا رَأَيْتِ الْجَنَّــةَ..."

"If you would have reached with them the closest graves, you would not see Paradise..."[1]

Secondly, the cause for that was mentioned by the Prophet (صلى الله عليه وسلم) when he said to some women who followed a funeral procession,

" اِرْجِعْنَ مَأْزُورَاتٍ غَيْرَ مَأْجُورَاتٍ فَإِنَّكُنَّ تَفْتِنَّ الْحَيَّ وَتُؤْذِينَ الْمَيِّتَ "

"Go back bearing sin and not with reward. For verily you put the living to trial and you disturb the dead."[2]

Hence, the Prophet (صلى الله عليه وسلم) gave two reasons for such prohibition. [First,] they are a temptation or trial for the living because the woman is *aurah* [to be kept out of the public eye] and by her going out and being visited by men she is not related to she becomes a trial and may lead to a great sin. [Second,] she also harms the deceased because women have little patience and are weak of heart, without the ability to bear such trials. Therefore, one cannot be certain that they may not start weeping, wailing and

---

[1] The remainder of the hadith is, "Until your great grandfather sees it." This hadith, with slightly different wordings, is recorded by al-Nasai, Abu Dawud and Ahmad. After recording the hadith, al-Nasai points out that Rabia ibn Saif, one of the narrators, is weak. Al-Albani concludes that it is a weak hadith. Hence, it is not acceptable as proof in the realm of fiqh. See Muhammad Nasir al-Din al-Albani, *Dhaeef Sunan al-Nasai* (Beirut: al-Maktab al-Islami, 1990), p. 69.— JZ

[2] Ibn Majah and Abu Yala record this hadith without the words, "For verily..." The above narration is recorded by al-Khateeb al-Baghdadi, *Tarikh Baghdad* (Dar al-Fikr), vol. 6, p. 201. Both narrations, with and without the additional words, are weak and not authentic. See, for example, Abdul Rahman ibn al-Jauzi, *Al-Ilal al-Mutanahiyah fi al-Ahadith al-Wahiyah* (Beirut: Dar al-Kutub al-Ilmiyah, 1983), vol. 2, p. 902. Hence, once again, this hadith cannot be used as proof in a matter of fiqh.— JZ

raising their voice at the grave, that will then harm the deceased. That is why it is prohibited for them to visit the graves.

The Ruling Concerning Picture Making

Question 15: What is the ruling concerning picture making? What are the Ahadith concerning that topic? According to the strongest opinion among the scholars, is there a difference between pictures which have a shadow [three-dimensional pictures and statues] and those which do not [two-dimensional drawings]?

Response: Picture making is to make a representation of a living, willing, moving animal, such as a human, horse, animal and so forth. The ruling concerning that is that such representation or depiction is forbidden. The evidence for that is what is found in numerous Ahadith. In the *Sahih*ain, al-Bukhari and Muslim, it is recorded from ibn Masud that the Messenger of Allah (صلى الله عليه وسلم) said,

" إِنَّ أَشَــدَّ النَّـاسِ عَـذَاباً يــومَ القِيَامَـةِ المُصَـوِّرُونَ "

"The people with the severest punishment on the Day of Judgment are the picture makers."

Ibn Umar narrated that the Messenger of Allah (صلى الله عليه وسلم) said,

" إِنَّ الَّذِيــنَ يَصْنَعُــونَ هـذِهِ الصُّوَرَ يُعَذَّبُونَ يَـومَ القِيامَـةِ يُقَالُ لَهُـم أَحْيُـوا مَا خَلَقْتُــمْ "

"The people who make these pictures will be punished on the Day of Resurrection. It will be said to them, 'Give life to what you have created.'"

This was also recorded by al-Bukhari and Muslim. Muslim also recorded from ibn Abbas that the Prophet (صلى الله عليه وسلم) said,

" مِن صَوَّرَ صُورَةً فِي الدُّنيا كُلِّفَ أَن يَنْفُخَ فِيها الرُّوحَ وَلَيس بِنافِخٍ "

"Whoever makes a picture in this world will be held responsible to breathe a spirit into it and he is not one who can breathe such."

It is recorded by Muslim on the authority of Ibn Abbas that the Prophet (صلى الله عليه وسلم) said:

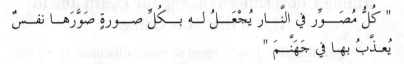

"All the picture makers would be put into Hell. For every picture he made, a soul would be created and punished".

It is also recorded on the authority of Abu Talha from the Prophet (صلى الله عليه وسلم) who said,

" لا تَدْخُلُ الْمَلائِكَةَ بَيتاً فِيه كَلْبٌ وَلا تَمَاثِيلُ "

"The angels do not enter a house wherein there is a dog or statues." (Muslim)

These hadith and others are general for every kind of representation, whether it has a shadow, like a figure, or if it does not have a shadow, which is like a drawing on a wall, paper, clothing and so forth. It is confirmed that the Prophet (صلى الله عليه وسلم) entered the Kaabah and it contained pictures and he asked for a pitcher of water and he began to efface them, saying,

" قَاتَلَ اللهُ قَوماً يُصَوِّرُون مَا لاَ يَخْلُقُـون "

"May Allah destroy those who make pictures of what they do not create."[1]

---

[1] This is recorded by al-Tayalisi and Dhiya al-Maqdisi. Al-Albani has concluded that it is "confirmed". See Muhammad Nasir al-Din al-Albani, *Silsilat al-Ahadith al-Sahiha* (Beirut: al-Maktab al-Islami, 1979), vol. 2, p. 731, hadith #996.— JZ

An exception to this ruling during this time is money containing the pictures of kings as well as passports and identification cards. Due to the need and necessity of these items, it is allowed to carry them according to need. And Allah knows best.

Shaikh ibn Jibreen

Ruling Concerning Wishing for Death due to Harm that Has Come

Question 16: I have faced so many difficulties in my life that it has made me hate this life. Every time I turned to Allah, I pleaded for Him to take my life away from me at the earliest. This is my wish until now as I do not see any solutions to my problems except death; it is the only thing that can save me from this punishment. Is this behavior forbidden for me?

Response: When a person wishes for death because of something that has afflicted him, he is doing something that the Prophet (صلى الله عليه وسلم) has prohibited. The Prophet (صلى الله عليه وسلم) said,

" لا يَتَمَنَّيَنَّ أَحَدُكمُ المَوتَ لِضُرٍّ نَزَلَ به فإن كان لاَ بُدَّ مُتَمَنِّياً فَلْيَقُلْ:
اللهم أَحْيِني ما عَلِمْتَ الحَيَاةَ خيراً لِي وتَوَفَّنِي ما عَلِمْتَ الوَفاةَ خيراً لِي "

"None of you should hope for death because of some harm that has come to him. If he has wish such, he should say, 'O Allah, give me life if You know that life is better for me. And give me death if You know that death is better for me.'"[1]

Therefore, it is not allowed for anyone to wish for death because of some harm, hardship or difficulty that has come to him. In fact, he should have patience and expect a reward from Allah for what he is passing through. He should also wait for relief to come, as the Prophet (صلى الله عليه وسلم) has said,

---

[1] The wording in the Arabic text is not quite exact, but this hadith is recorded by al-Bukhari and Muslim.— JZ

" وآعلَـم أَنَّ النَّصْـرَ مـعَ الصَّـبْرِ وأن الفَـرَج مَـنَ الكَـرْبِ وأَنَّ
مَعَ العُسْـرِ يُسْـراً "

"Know that victory comes with patience, relief with distress and ease with hardship."[1]

The one who is afflicted with any affliction should know that those afflictions expiate some of the sins that he has committed. No believer is afflicted with any kind of worry, grief or pain except that Allah expiates sins for him due to that, even the pricking of a thorn. When the person has patience and expects rewards from Allah, he reaches the stage of being among the patient. This stage is a very elevated stage. Allah has stated about its inhabitants,

﴿ . . . وَبَشِّرِ ٱلصَّٰبِرِينَ ○ ٱلَّذِينَ إِذَآ أَصَٰبَتْهُم مُّصِيبَةٌ قَالُوٓا۟ إِنَّا لِلَّهِ وَإِنَّآ إِلَيْهِ رَٰجِعُونَ ﴾ [البقرة: ١٥٥-١٥٦]

"And give glad tidings to the patient. Who, when afflicted with calamity, say, 'Truly, to Allah we belong and, truly, to Him we shall return'" (al-Baqara 155-156).

The woman in the question feels that there is no solution for her problems except death. I believe that this is a mistaken view. Death does not solve any problems. In fact, the situation of adversity may get even worse. How many humans die while being afflicted with pain and problems but they had been wronging themselves and did not give up their sins and repent to Allah. Then his death is just a quicker coming of his punishment. If he remained alive, perhaps Allah would have guided him to repentance, seeking forgiveness, patience, facing the problems, and expecting relief. This all would have been good for him.

---

[1] Ibn Uthaimin is probably referring to a lengthy hadith recorded by Ahmad. As a hadith by itself, these words, without the words, "Know that," are recorded by al-Khateeb al-Baghdadi. According to al-Albani, it is an authentic hadith. See al-Albani, *Sahih al-Jami al-Sagheer*, vol. 2, p. 1151.— JZ

Therefore, you, the questioner, must be patient and expect relief from Allah. Allah says in His book,

"So, verily, with the hardship there is relief. Verily, with the hardship, there is relief" (*al-Sharh* 5-6).

And the Prophet (صلى الله عليه وسلم) stated, in an authentic narration,

" وَآعلَــم أنَّ النَّصْـرَ مــع الصَّـبْرِ وأن الفَـرَج مَــع الكَــرْبِ وأنَّ مَعَ العُسْـرِ يُسْـراً "

"Know that victory comes with patience, relief with distress and ease with hardship."[1]

Shaikh ibn Uthaimin

Ruling Concerning Celebrating Specific Occasions, such as the Two *Eids*, the Night of *Isra* and the Middle of the Month of Shaban

Question 17: We have some practices that we have become accustomed to and have inherited concerning some special occasions for example, making cakes and biscuits on the day of Eid al-Fitr. We also prepare meat and fruit for the night of the 27th of Rajab and the night of the 15th of Shaban. Furthermore, there is a specific type of sweet that we must prepare during the day of *Ashura*. What is the ruling of the Islamic law concerning those things?

Response: As for displaying pleasure and happiness during the days of Eid al-Fitr and Eid al-Adha, there is no harm in that as long as it is within the limits of the *Shariah*. That would

---

[1] As just noted, Ibn Uthaimin is probably referring to a lengthy hadith recorded by Ahmad. As a hadith by itself, these words, without the words, "Know that," are recorded by al-Khateeb al-Baghdadi. According to al-Albani, it is an authentic hadith. See al-Albani, *Sahih al-Jami al-Sagheer*, vol. 2, p. 1151.— JZ

include people preparing food, drink and so forth. It has been confirmed that the Prophet (صلى الله عليه وسلم) said,

" أَيَّامُ التَّشْرِيقِ أَيَّامُ أَكْلٍ وشُرْبٍ وذِكْرٍ للهِ عزَّ وجلَّ "

"The Days of *Tashreeq* are days of eating and drinking and remembrance of Allah."[1]

The Days of *Tashreeq* are the three days following the Day of Eid al-Adhha in which the people slaughter their sacrifices, eat from that meat and enjoy the bounties Allah has bestowed on them. Similarly, during Eid al-Fitr there is no harm in showing one's pleasure and happiness as long as that does not go beyond the limits of the Shariah.

As for having merriment on the night of the 27th of Rajab, the night of the 15th of Shaban or during the Day of Ashura, such practices have no source for them whatsoever. Indeed, they are prohibited. No Muslim should attend such celebrations if he is invited to such gatherings. The Prophet (صلى الله عليه وسلم) said,

"إِيَّاكُم ومحدَثَاتِ الأُمُورِ فإِنَّ كُلَّ مُحدَثَةٍ بِدْعَةٌ وكُلَّ بِدعَةٍ ضَلاَلَةٌ"

"Stay away from innovated matters. Verily, every innovated matter is a heresy. And every heresy is a straying [from the Straight Path]."[2]

As for the night of the 17th of Rajab, some people claim that it is the night of the Miraj in which the Prophet (صلى الله عليه وسلم) ascended into heaven to Allah. However, historically speaking, that is not confirmed. Everything that is not confirmed is false. And everything that is built upon something false is also false. Even if, hypothetically speaking, that was the night of that event, it is not allowed for us to introduce any new practices with respect to

---

[1] Recorded by Muslim.— JZ
[2] Recorded by Abu Dawud and Ahmad. Muslim also has something very similar.— JZ

celebrations or acts of worship on that day, since such were not done by the Prophet (صلى الله عليه وسلم). In fact, such is not confirmed from the Companions who were the people who followed the sunnah and the Law of the Prophet (صلى الله عليه وسلم) most closely and enthusiastically. How is it permissible for us to invent something new that was not practiced during the time of the Messenger of Allah (صلى الله عليه وسلم) nor during the time of the Companions?

Even for the 15th of Shaban, there is nothing confirmed from the Messenger (صلى الله عليه وسلم) about venerating that day or praying during its night. Some of the Followers[1] used to spend its night in prayer and remembrance of Allah, and not in eating, celebrating or taking it as a holiday.

As for the Day of Ashura, the Prophet (صلى الله عليه وسلم) was asked about fasting on that day and he said,

$$\text{" يُكَفِّرُ السَّنَةَ الْمَاضِيَةَ "}$$

"It is an expiation for the previous year."[2]

Therefore, it is not allowed to display any form of celebration or grieving on that day as such a display of celebration or grieving goes against the sunnah. The only thing that is narrated from the Prophet (صلى الله عليه وسلم) is that one should fast that day, although he also ordered that a person should fast the day prior or the day after Ashura in order to be different from the Jews who simply fast on that day alone.

Shaikh ibn Uthaimin

The Impurity of the Disbelievers is a Spiritual Impurity

Question 18: We deal with some people who do not have a religion; they worship fire and also the cow. Allah has described them as impure and unclean. What is the essence of that impurity?

---

[1] This is reference to the generation that followed that of the Companions.— JZ
[2] Recorded by Muslim.— JZ

Should we keep our distance from them and not shake their hands. If they are impure, how do we deal with them. Are the things that they touch with their hands impure, given that they deal with merchandise and have contact with the public? We are hoping for you to help us.

Response: Allah says,

$$ ﴾ إِنَّمَا ٱلْمُشْرِكُونَ نَجَسٌ ﴿ \quad [التوبة: ٢٨] $$

"Verily, the polytheists are impure" (*al-Tauba* 28).

Allah also says about the hypocrites,

$$ ﴾ فَأَعْرِضُواْ عَنْهُمْ إِنَّهُمْ رِجْسٌ ﴿ \quad [التوبة: ٩٥] $$

"So turn away from them, for verily they are impure (*rijs*)" (*al-Tauba* 95).

Rijs means impure. However, their impurity is a spiritual impurity. It refers to their evil, harm and immorality. As for their physical bodies, as long as they are clean, one does not say that they are impure in a sensory or physical sense. Therefore, based on that, it is allowed to wear the clothing that they had worn if one knows that they are clean, unless it is the clothing that covered their private parts, since they do not protect themselves from urine and especially since they are not circumcised. Similar is the case if they come into direct contact with impurities, such as in cooking pork or preparing and dealing with wine. As for shaking hands with them and using what they manufacture, there is no harm in that. In fact, the Messenger of Allah (صلى الله عليه وسلم) and his Companions used to use what the disbelievers manufactured and made as long as they knew it was pure. Furthermore, the original or basic ruling concerning any matter is that of purity.

Shaikh ibn Jibreen

Ruling Concerning Mixing with the Disbelievers in order to Call Them to Islam

Question 19: Is it allowed to mix with the disbelievers, Christians, Hindus and others, and to eat and talk to them or even to be amicable with them as a means of calling them to Islam?

Response: It is allowed to mix with the disbelievers, sit with them and be polite with them as means of calling them to Allah, explaining to them the teachings of Islam, encouraging them to enter this religion and to make it clear to them the good result of accepting the religion and the evil result of punishment for those who turn away. For this purpose, being a companion to them and showing love for them is overlooked in order to reach that good final goal.

Shaikh ibn Jibreen

The Reward for Women in Paradise

Question 20: Whenever I read the Noble Quran, I find in many verses Allah giving glad tidings to His believing male servants of *al-hoor al-ain* who extol in beauty. Does the woman have any partner in Paradise other than her husband? Furthermore, most of the statements concerning bounties in Paradise are directed toward the believing men. Is the reward of the believing women in Paradise less than that of the believing men?

Response: There is no doubt that reward in the Hereafter encompasses both men and women. This is based on the following statements of Allah:

$$ \text{﴿ أَنِّي لَا أُضِيعُ عَمَلَ عَامِلٍ مِّنكُم مِّن ذَكَرٍ أَوْ أُنثَىٰ ﴾} $$

[آل عمران: ١٩٥]

"Never will I allow to be lost the work of any of you, male or female" (*al-Imran* 195).

﴿ مَنْ عَمِلَ صَٰلِحًا مِّن ذَكَرٍ أَوْ أُنثَىٰ وَهُوَ مُؤْمِنٌ فَلَنُحْيِيَنَّهُۥ حَيَوٰةً طَيِّبَةً ﴾ [النحل : ٩٧]

"Whosoever works righteousness, whether male or female, while he (or she) is a true believer, We will give a good life" (al-Nahl 97).

﴿ وَمَن يَعْمَلْ مِنَ ٱلصَّٰلِحَٰتِ مِن ذَكَرٍ أَوْ أُنثَىٰ وَهُوَ مُؤْمِنٌ فَأُوْلَٰٓئِكَ يَدْخُلُونَ ٱلْجَنَّةَ ﴾ [النساء : ١٢٤]

"And whoever does righteous good deeds, being a male or a female, and is a true believer, such will enter Paradise" (al-Nisa 124).

﴿ إِنَّ ٱلْمُسْلِمِينَ وَٱلْمُسْلِمَٰتِ - إلى قوله - أَعَدَّ ٱللَّهُ لَهُم مَّغْفِرَةً وَأَجْرًا عَظِيمًا ﴾ [الأحزاب : ٣٥]

"Verily, the Muslims, men and women, the believers, men and women... [up to the end of the verse where Allah says:] Allah has prepared for them forgiveness and a great reward" (al-Ahzab 35).

Allah mentions them entering into Paradise together,

﴿ هُمْ وَأَزْوَٰجُهُمْ فِي ظِلَٰلٍ ﴾ [يس : ٥٦]

"They and their wives will be in pleasant shade" (Ya Sin 56).

Also,

﴿ ٱدْخُلُوا ٱلْجَنَّةَ أَنتُمْ وَأَزْوَٰجُكُمْ تُحْبَرُونَ ﴾ [الزخرف : ٧٠]

"Enter Paradise, you and your wives, in happiness" (al-Zukhruf 70).

Allah also mentions that He will recreate the women in the verse,

﴿ إِنَّآ أَنشَأْنَٰهُنَّ إِنشَآءً ٠ فَجَعَلْنَٰهُنَّ أَبْكَارًا ﴾ [الواقعة : ٣٥-٣٦]

"Verily, We created them of special creation and made them virgins" (al-Waqia 35-36).

That is, Allah will recreate the elderly women and make them virgins. Similarly, Allah will recreate the elderly men and make them youths. It is also mentioned in the hadith that the women of this worldly life have a superiority over *al-hoor al-ain* due to the acts of worship and obedience that they performed [in this world]. Therefore, the believing women will enter Paradise just like the believing men. If a woman had a number of husbands and she enters Paradise with them, she will choose among them and will choose the one with the best character and behavior.

Shaikh ibn Jibreen

Purity and Ostentation

Question 21: Many times a person thinks about doing a good deed and then Satan comes to him and whispers to him, saying, "You are doing that ostentatiously, to be seen of men and for a good reputation." Therefore, he makes us go away from the good deed. How can one remain free of such occurrences?

Response: One can remain free of such occurrences by seeking refuge in Allah from the accursed Satan, as well as by continually performing good deeds. He should not pay attention to such whisperings that make him stop doing good deeds. If he turns away from such whisperings and seeks refuge in Allah from the accursed Satan, such whisperings will stop by the permission of Allah.

Shaikh ibn Uthaimin

Ruling Concerning Celebrating Mother's Day

Question 22: Every year we have a holiday on a particular day and it is called Mother's Day. It occurs on March 21. All the people gather and celebrate that day. Is this permissible or forbidden?

Response: Every holiday or celebration that differs from the *shariah* celebrations is a newly-invented innovation that was not known during the time of the Pious Predecessors. Furthermore, it may have begun as an imitation of the non-Muslims. Therefore, in addition to it being an innovation, it may also be an act of resembling the enemies of Allah.

The *shariah* holidays are well-known among the Muslims. These are the Eid al-Fitr, Eid al-Adhha and the weekly Eid [Fridays]. There is no holiday or festival in Islam other than those three. Every holiday that is invented besides them is to be rejected as an innovation and falsehood in the *shariah*. This is because the Prophet (صلى الله عليه وسلم) said,

" مَنْ أَحْدَثَ فِي أَمْرِنَا هَذَا مَا لَيْسَ مِنْهُ فَهُوَ رَدٌّ "

"Every deed introduced into our affair that does not belong to it is rejected."[1]

That is, it is rejected from that person and it will not be accepted by Allah. Another wording of the hadith states,

" مَنْ عَمِلَ عَمَلاً لَيْسَ عَلَيْهِ أَمْرُنَا فَهُوَ رَدٌّ "

"Whoever does a deed that is not what our affair is upon, will have it rejected."[2]

Since that is clear, the holiday that is mentioned by the questioner, known as Mother's Day, is not allowed. It is not allowed to have during such a day any kind of public display and celebration, happiness, giving of presents and so forth.

It is obligatory upon a Muslim to have pride and honor in his religion. He should also limit himself to what Allah and His Messenger (صلى الله عليه وسلم) have restricted this upright religion to. This is the religion that Allah is pleased to have His servants follow. There can be no addition or subtraction from this religion.

---

[1] Recorded by al-Bukhari and Muslim.— JZ

[2] Recorded by Muslim; also recorded by al-Bukhari in *mualaq* form.— JZ

Furthermore, a Muslim should not be a kind of weak person that follows every Tom, Dick and Harry. Instead, his personality should be that defined by the Law of Allah, such that he is followed and not a follower, such that he becomes an example and not a disciple. This should be the case because the law of Allah, praise be to Allah, is complete and perfect in all aspects. Allah says in the Quran,

$$﴿ ٱلۡيَوۡمَ أَكۡمَلۡتُ لَكُمۡ دِينَكُمۡ وَأَتۡمَمۡتُ عَلَيۡكُمۡ نِعۡمَتِي وَرَضِيتُ لَكُمُ الۡإِسۡلَٰمَ دِينࣰا ﴾$$

[المائدة: ٣]

"This day, I have perfected your religion for you, completed My favor upon you and have chosen for you Islam as your religion" (*al-Maidah* 3).

Furthermore, the mother has much more right than to have just one day in the year as a celebration for her. In fact, the woman has a right upon her children, that they will care for her, look after her, obey her in anything which is not sinful, during all times and at all places.

Shaikh ibn Uthaimin

The Wisdom Behind Creating Recording Angels

Question 23: Allah has created for us noble, recording angels that record everything we say and hear. What is the wisdom behind their creation while Allah has full knowledge, and nothing that we hide or reveal is hidden from Him?

Response: First, when it comes to matters of this nature, we may discover the wisdom behind it or we may not. There are many things concerning which we do not know their wisdom. As Allah has said,

$$﴿ وَيَسۡـَٔلُونَكَ عَنِ ٱلرُّوحِ قُلِ ٱلرُّوحُ مِنۡ أَمۡرِ رَبِّي وَمَآ أُوتِيتُم مِّنَ ٱلۡعِلۡمِ إِلَّا قَلِيلࣰا ﴾$$

[الإسراء: ٨٥]

"And they ask you about the *ruh* (Spirit). Say: As for the *Ruh*, its knowledge is with my Lord. And of knowledge, you (mankind) have been given only a little" (*al-Isra* 85).

As for that creation, it is as if the person would have asked me why did Allah create the camel in the form that it is in, or the horse, or the donkey, or human being, and questions such as that. Or if he would have asked me why Allah has made the *Dhuhr* prayer four *rakats*, *Asr* four and *Isha* four. As for questions of that matter, we cannot know their wisdom, as otherwise one might ask, why did Allah not make it eight or six *rakahs*. Therefore, we know that with respect to this creation and with respect to many aspects of the *shariah*, the wisdom behind them is simply hidden from us. However, if we do know some of the wisdom behind some of Allah's creation or parts of the *Shariah*, it is because Allah has given that to us and that is simply a greater excellence, knowledge and goodness. However, if we do not have that knowledge, we are not losing anything.

Now let me return to the question. What is the wisdom behind creating honorable, recording angels that know everything we do? The wisdom behind that is that it demonstrates that Allah has ordered all things and has laid everything down in perfection, to the extent that He has put above the actions of mankind noble recorders who are responsible for recording everything they do, even though Allah is knowledgeable of everything they do before they even do it. All of this is part of Allah's complete looking after of humans and His complete wisdom in this creation.

Allah knows best.

Shaikh ibn Uthaimin

2. Questions Related to Knowledge

Women and the Seeking of Knowledge

Question 24: The Messenger of Allah (صلى الله عليه وسلم) used to set a special day for teaching the matters of the religion to the women. He also used to permit them to be behind the men in the mosque in order to seek knowledge. Why do the scholars not follow the example of the Messenger of Allah (صلى الله عليه وسلم)? Although they do fulfill some of those needs, it is not sufficient and we need more. May Allah reward you.

Response: There is no doubt that such was the practice of the Messenger of Allah (صلى الله عليه وسلم), as well as the scholars. Indeed, I myself have done that here on a number of occasions as well as in Makkah, Taif and Jeddah.

I have no problem with setting apart a specific time for women in any locale if they want that from me. That is also the position of my scholar colleagues.

Furthermore, by the radio program *Noor ala al-Darb*,[1] Allah has opened the way to much good. A woman can send her question to the program and during the program it will be answered. This program is aired two nights a week on the stations *Nida al-Islam* and *al-Quran al-Kareem*.

Similarly, women may write to Dar al-Ifta. In this case, a committee of scholars may respond to their questions. It has been designed for that purpose. In any case, knowledge is equally obligatory for both men and women. There is nothing to prevent a woman from attending lectures, with the condition that she is properly dressed and is not exposing any of her beauty.

Shaikh ibn Baz

---

[1] This is a radio program in Saudi Arabia that the scholars participate in. It is basically a forum for questions to be put and answered.— JZ

Ruling Concerning Students Standing for their Teacher

Question 25: What is the ruling concerning female students [in a girls' school] standing for their female teacher as a sign of respect for her?

Response: The standing of the female students for their female teachers or the male students for their male teachers is an act that should not be done. At the very least, it is strongly disliked. This is based on Anas' statement, "No one was more beloved to them— the Companions— than the Messenger of Allah (peace be upon him). And they would not stand for him when he came to them, as they knew that he disliked such an act." The Prophet (peace be upon him) has also said,

$$\text{"}\ \text{مَنْ أَحَبَّ أَن يَتَمَثَّلَ لَه الرِّجَالُ قِيَاماً فَلْيَتَبَوَّأْ مَقْعَدَهُ مِنَ النَّارِ}\ \text{"}$$

"Whoever loves to have men stand for him shall take his abode in the Fire."[1]

On this matter, the ruling concerning men is the same as that concerning women. May Allah guide us all to what is pleasing to Him and keep us from everything that angers Him and is prohibited. May Allah bestow on all of us beneficial knowledge, as well as acting accordingly. He is the Generous, the Noble.

Shaikh ibn Baz

The Dangers of Having Female Teachers for Boys in Elementary Schools

I have come across what the newspaper *al-Madinah* printed in Issue #3898, dated 2-30-1397 A.H., written by one calling herself Nura bint Abdullah, under the title, "Face to Face." In sum, Nura is saying that she had a meeting with a number of women, including the female Dean of the College of Education in Jeddah, whose name is Faiza. Nura mentions Faiza's surprise that

---

[1] Recorded by Ahmad, Abu Dawud and al-Tirmidhi. Al-Albani states that it is *sahih*. Al-Albani, *Sahih al-Jami al-Sagheer*, vol. 2, p. 1033.—JZ

there are no female teachers teaching boys in the elementary level, even to the fifth grade. Nura supported Faiza's views in that article for a number of reasons. Personally, with thanks to Faiza, Nura and their colleagues for the concern about the teaching of our young boys and for their welfare, I find it an obligation upon myself to point out that their suggestion is filled with evil and harmful consequences. Having women teach boys at the elementary level means that they will have to mix with boys who are at puberty or adolescent stages, this is because some of the boys do not complete the elementary stage until they are already in adolescence, and some have already completed puberty. This is because, when a boy reaches ten years old, he is considered an adolescent. He naturally becomes inclined toward women. Someone like him can even get married and do what men do. And there is another matter, having women teach the boys will lead to mixing between the two sexes. That will then continue until the next level. This will open the door, without question, to mixing between the sexes at all levels. The evil results of such mixing in the schools are well-known. The devastating results that come from that type of teaching can be seen in other countries. Whoever has the smallest amount of knowledge of the *shariah* evidences and what is occurring to this *Ummah* during this age knows what definitely occurs to the boys and girls due to such practices. I believe that this suggestion has been inspired by Satan or some of his deputies upon the tongues of the above mentioned Faiza and Nura. It is, without doubt, something that is pleasing to our enemies and the enemies of Islam, and is from what those enemies are calling for, openly and privately.

Therefore, I see that the door to this kind of practice must be completely closed. Our boys must be left to be taught by men at all levels of instruction. Similarly, the girls must be left to be taught by female teachers at all levels of instruction. This will preserve our religion, our boys and our girls. It will be sufficient for us for our respected female teachers to fulfill their responsibilities to the best of their abilities with purity, sincerity and patience in teaching our girls. And the men must also fulfill their responsibilities with purity, sincerity and patience in teaching our boys at every level. It is also well-known that a man has more patience and is stronger in teaching boys and he can give him more teachings in every level of schooling. It is well-known that the boys, in the primary and higher levels of education, respect and esteem their male teacher. They will be more willing to submit and accept what he says. If the women were teaching them at those different levels, they would not have the characteristics, patience and strength with them that men have. It has been authentically narrated from the Prophet (صلى الله عليه وسلم) that he said,

" مُرُوا أَوْلادَكُم بِالصَّلاةِ لِسَبْعٍ، وَاضْرِبُوهُم عَلَيهَا لِعَشْرٍ، وَفَرِّقُوا بينَهُم فِي الْمَضَاجِعِ "

"Order your children to pray at the age of seven. And beat them [lightly] if they do not do so by the age of ten. And separate them in their bedding."[1]

This hadith points out what we have been saying about the dangers of mixing boys and girls at all levels of instruction. The evidence for that from the Quran, sunnah and the experience of the *ummah* today are many but I do not wish to mention them all here in order to be brief. The knowledge of our government, may Allah give them understanding, as well as the Minister of Education and the President of the Directory for Girls Education is sufficient for us to go into this matter here. I ask Allah to grant us all what is good for this *Ummah*. And to make us and our male and female youth good. And to give them happiness in both this life and the Hereafter. He is the Hearer, Responder. And peace and blessings be upon our Prophet Muhammad and his family and Companions.

Shaikh ibn Baz

---

[1] Recorded by Ahmad, Abu Dawud and al-Hakim. Al-Syuti has given it a notation signifying that it is authentic.

3. Questions Related to Physical Purification

The Ruling Concerning Stating One's Intention

Question 26: What is the ruling concerning stating one's intention for the prayer and ablution?

Response: The ruling is that such is an innovation. It has not been narrated from the Prophet (صلى الله عليه وسلم) or from his Companions. Therefore, one must avoid it. The place of the intention is the heart. It is never needed to state an intention.

Shaikh ibn Baz

A Baby Vomits on Clothing

Question 27: Is it allowed to pray in clothes that a breastfeeding baby has vomited on?

Response: One must wash the clothing by splashing water over it if the child is breastfeeding and does not eat hard food. It is similar to his urine, which is moistened with water and then one can pray in that clothing. The clothes are not to be prayed in until they are splashed with water.

Shaikh ibn Baz

If a Woman Washes Her Baby, Is Her Ablution Nullified?

Question 28: I have children and I wash and clean my child's impurities. Does this nullify my ablution or not?

Response: Washing the impurities off of the body that is being washed or otherwise does not invalidate the ablution unless one touches the private part. In that case, the ablution is nullified, as is the case if a person touches his/her own private part.[1]

The Standing Committee

Ruling About the Secretion that Comes from a Woman's Vagina

Question 29: I heard from a scholar that the liquid[2] that comes from a woman's vagina is pure and not impure. Since the time I heard that *fatwa*, I do not remove my underpants when I want to pray. After a lengthy period, I heard another scholar say that such liquid is impure. What is the correct opinion?

Response: Everything that secretes from the private parts, of liquid or otherwise, nullifies the ablution. The clothes and bodily parts that are touched by it are to be washed. If this happens on a continuous basis, the ruling is the same as that of *al-istihaadha*[3] and continuous seeping of urine [due to a lack of bladder control]. The impurity is to be washed off and the person makes ablution for every prayer, as the Prophet (صلى الله عليه وسلم) stated to the woman with continuous bleeding,

$$ " تَوَضَّئِي لِوَقْتِ كُلِّ صَـــلاةٍ " $$

---

[1] This is an issue in which there is a difference of opinion and the opinion expressed in this answer, although the safest opinion, may not be strongest opinion. In a few pages, a similar question is put to Shaikh ibn Jibreen and he comes to the opposite conclusion. Allah knows best.— JZ

[2] The term used in the question, *ratooba*, when used by earlier scholars, such as al-Shafi'i and al-Nawawi, is referring to the fluid that is produced upon sexual excitement. Many scholars consider that fluid pure, by analogy with semen. However, this particular question and others put to contemporary scholars is more in reference to the vaginal fluids that come out on a normal basis, especially in relation to ovulation.

[3] This is referring to the case of prolonged or continuous vaginal bleeding outside of the menses. It has specific rulings as described above in the response.— JZ

"Make ablution for the time of every prayer."[1]
However, this is not done in the case of passing gas. There is no washing in that case although one has to make ablution due to it. This ablution is to wash the face and hands, wipe the head, wash the feet, and rinse the mouth and nose while washing the face. Similarly, with respect to sleeping, touching one's private parts, eating camel's meat, one does not wash anything but one simply has to make ablution.[2]

Shaikh ibn Baz

Putting Henna in the Hair Does not Nullify the State of Purity

Question 30: A woman makes ablution and then puts henna in her hair and then stands to pray. Is her prayer valid or not? If her ablution is nullified, does she wipe over her henna or does she have to wash her hair and then make the minor ablution for the prayer?

---

[1] This translator was not able to find this hadith with this exact wording. The authentic narrations in al-Bukhari and Muslim simply state that she is to make ablution for every prayer.— JZ

[2] This question perhaps needs some more deliberation. It is very common for almost all healthy women to experience what is called leukorrhea. This is the secretion of vaginal mucous related to ovulation and other causes. It comes from the uterus and not through the urethra. Although this is something that must have afflicted women during the time of the Prophet (peace be upon him), there is no clear pronouncement about it as there is about, for example, menses and al-istihadha. The statement that everything that exits from the private parts is impure and nullifies ablution is not a hadith of the Prophet (peace be upon him) and, therefore, unchallengeable but it is simply the conclusion of many scholars based on the known examples. If this particular liquid nullifies ablution, then such women would have to make ablution for every prayer as this fluid exits from the body, like the case of istihadha. (Note that some women sometimes feel this fluid inside the body before it actually flows from the body. Until it flows out from the body, there is no question about its nullifying the ablution.) However, since there is no evidence for that in the hadith of the Prophet (peace be upon him), since this is a very common occurrence and since such a conclusion would involve hardship upon the women (especially at the time of the Prophet), it seems there is no evidence to declare such a secretion as nullifier of the ablution. Allah knows best.— JZ

Response: Putting henna in one's hair does not nullify the state of purity if she has completed her act of purity. If she makes ablution and upon her hair is henna or something similar that a woman needs, then it is allowed to wipe over it while making the minor ablution. As for the major act of ablution [*ghusl*], she must pour water over her hair three times and it is not sufficient for her just to wipe over the hair. This is based on what is confirmed in *Sahih Muslim* from Umm Salama who said, "O Messenger of Allah, I am a woman who has closely plaited hair on her head, should I undo it for making *ghusl* from sexual defilement or menstruation[1]?" The Prophet (صلى الله عليه وسلم) told her,

$$\text{" لا إنَّمَا يَكْفِيكِ أَنْ تَحْثِي عَلَيهِ ثَلَاثَ حَثَيَاتٍ، ثُمَّ تُفِيضِين}$$
$$\text{عَلَيكِ الْمَاء فَتَطْهُرِينَ "}$$

"No, it is sufficient for you to throw three handfuls of water on your head and then pour water over yourself, and you will be purified."

If you unplait your hair during your menses and then make *ghusl*, it will be best, due to other hadith narrated about that.

Shaikh ibn Baz

---

[1] The narration that mentions menstruation is only recorded by Muslim. Muslim, Abu Dawud, al-Tirmidhi and ibn Majah all record this hadith with Umm Salama only asking about sexual defilement. In fact, the way Muslim records the narration that also mentions menstruation gives a clue that that is not the correct narration. He specifically points out that of all the people who narrated that hadith, only Abdul Razzaq mentions menstruation. However, Abdul Razzaq was known to have lost some of his retentive ability by the end of his life. Hence, that addition, mentioning menstruation, must be considered "irregular" (*shadh*). This was the conclusion of ibn al-Qayyim in his discussion of the hadith of Abu Dawud. See the commentary of ibn al-Qayyim on the margin of Muhammad al-Adheemabadi, *Aun al-Mabood* (Cairo: Maktaba ibn Taimiya, 1987), vol. 1, pp. 429-430.—JZ

Ruling Concerning Doubt with Respect to Ablution

Question 31: What is the ruling concerning a person who doubts whether he nullified his ablution or not?

Answer: If a person has doubt whether he nullified his ablution or not, then his original state of being pure remains and his doubt does not have any effect. This is based on the Prophet's statement, when a man asked him about feelings he has in his stomach during the prayer,

" لا يَنْصَرِفْ حَتّى يَسْمَعَ صَوتاً أُو يَجِدَ رِيحاً "

"Do not leave [the prayer] until you hear a sound or you perceive a smell."[1]

The Prophet (صلى الله عليه وسلم) made it clear to him that the basic ruling is that of purity until one is certain that something has occurred to nullify it. As long as the person is simply in doubt, his state of purity is sound and confirmed. Therefore, he may continue to pray, circumambulate the Kaaba, read the Quran from a *mushaf* and so forth. That is the original ruling. This is, all praises are due to Allah, from the magnanimity and easiness of Islam.

Shaikh ibn Baz

How Does a Woman Wipe Her Head During Ablution

Question 32: What is the way in which a woman is to wipe her head during ablution? What is the ruling concerning wiping only part of the head if she is forced to do just that?

Response: The ruling concerning wiping their heads during ablution is exactly the same as that for men. She is to wipe all of her head until the last places where hair grows and as well as

---

[1] Recorded by al-Bukhari and Muslim.—JZ

the ears. She does not wipe over the portion of her hair that falls below that as it is confirmed in authentic hadith that the Prophet (صلى الله عليه وسلم) used to wipe his head from the forehead back to his nape, as well as his ears. The general principle is that the rules and regulations for men and women are the same unless there is evidence to show otherwise.

Shaikh ibn Baz

How Does a Woman Wash Herself After Sexual Defilement and Menses

Question 33: Is there any difference in the manner that a man and a woman wash themselves after sexual defilement? Does a woman have to undo her braids or is it sufficient for her just to pour three handfuls of water over her hair as mentioned in the hadith? What is the difference between the washing after sexual defilement and the washing after menses?

Response: There is no difference between men and women when it comes to *ghusl* after sexual defilement. Neither of them have to undo their hair for *ghusl*. It is sufficient to pour three handfuls of water over their hair and then to pour water over the rest of their bodies. This is based on the hadith of Umm Salama who said, "O Messenger of Allah,

" إنِّي امْرَأَةٌ أَشُدُّ ضَفْرَ رَأْسِي أَفَأَنْقُضُهُ للجَنَابةِ، قَالَ: لاَ ، إنَّمَا يكفيكِ أن تَحِثي على رَأْسِكِ ثلاَثَ حَثَيَاتٍ، ثم تُفِيضِي عَلَيهِ الماءَ فَتَطْهُري "

"I am a woman who has closely plaited hair on her head, should I undo it for making *ghusl* from sexual defilement?" The Prophet (صلى الله عليه وسلم) told her, "No, it is sufficient for you to throw three handfuls of water on your head and then pour water over yourself, and you will be purified." (Muslim)

However, if the man or woman has *sidr*, dye or something of that nature in his hair that would keep the water from reaching to the roots of the hair, he or she must remove that. If it is something light and does not keep the water from reaching the roots, it does not have to be removed.

As for the woman making *ghusl* after her menses, there is a difference of opinion over whether she must undo her hair or not. The correct opinion is that it is not obligatory upon her to do so. This is because it is mentioned in one of the narrations from Umm Salama, recorded by Muslim, that she said, to the Prophet (صلى الله عليه وسلم) "O Messenger of Allah,

" إِنِّي امْرَأَةٌ أَشُدُّ ضَفْرَ رَأْسِي أَفَأَنْقُضُهُ لِلْحَيْضِ وَالْجَنَابَةِ، قَالَ: لاَ ، إِنَّمَا يَكْفِيكِ أَن تَحْثِي عَلى رَأْسِكِ ثَلاَثَ حَثَيَاتٍ، ثُم تُفِيضِي عَلَيْهِ الْمَاءَ فَتَطْهُرِي "

"I am a woman who has closely plaited hair on her head, should I undo it for making *ghusl* from menstruation and sexual defilement?" The Prophet (صلى الله عليه وسلم) told her, "No, it is sufficient for you to throw three handfuls of water on your head and then pour water over yourself, and you will be purified."[1]

This narration is a clear text that it is not obligatory upon the woman to undo her plaits after either menses or sexual defilement.

However, it is best for her to undo her hair while making *ghusl* after menses as a precautionary measure, as a means of avoiding the thing in which there is a difference of opinion and as a way of reconciliation of the different evidences.

The Standing Committee

---

[1] The probable problem with this narration, mentioning both sexual defilement and menstruation, was discussed earlier.—JZ

The Ruling Concerning Praying in a Dress and Thin, Translucent Stockings

Question 34: What is the ruling concerning a woman dressing in a thin cloak that shows her clothing? Similarly, what is the ruling concerning wiping over thin, translucent stockings, called nylon stockings?

Response: It is not allowed for a woman to pray in a very thin garment or any other thin garment. The prayer in such clothing is not correct. Instead, it is obligatory upon her to pray in clothing which is covering and through which one cannot see what is behind it or the color of her skin. This is because the woman is *aurah* (meant to be covered). It is obligatory upon her to cover all of her body in the prayer, except for her face and hands. If she covers her hands also, that is better. As for her feet, she must either cover them with socks that cover and conceal them or with clothing [a dress, for example] that rests over them.

Shaikh ibn Baz

Ruling Concerning Wiping Over Thin, Translucent Socks

Question 35: What is the ruling concerning wiping over thin, translucent socks?

Response: From the conditions of wiping over socks is that the socks must be thick and concealing. If they are thin and translucent, it is not allowed to wipe over them. This is because, in that case, the foot is considered uncovered.

Shaikh ibn Baz

A Slight Tear in Socks is Overlooked

Question 36: What is the ruling if someone notices after the prayer, either a short or long time afterwards, that he had a medium size tear in one of his socks? Should he repeat his prayer or not?

Response: If the tear is small or the hole is small according to convention or custom, it is overlooked and the prayer is correct. However, it is safest for the believing men and women to be very careful about keeping their socks free from any kind of tear or hole. This is being more cautious with respect to their religion and it also avoids the difference of opinion [that exists concerning such torn socks]. This approach is indicated by the Prophet's statement,

" دَعْ مَا يَرِيبُك إِلَى مَا لَا يَرِيبُك "

"Leave what makes you doubt for that which does not make you doubt."[1]

The Prophet (صلى الله عليه وسلم) also said,

" فَمَنِ اتَّقَى الشُّبُهَاتِ فَقَدِ اسْتَبْـرَأَ لِدِينِـه وعِرْضِـه "

"Whoever avoids the doubtful matters clears himself in regard to his religion and his honor."[2]

Shaikh ibn Baz

Ruling Concerning Vaginal Discharge

Question 37: Is the discharge that comes from a woman's vagina pure or impure? May Allah reward you.

Response: What is well-known among the scholars is that anything that comes out of the private parts is impure, except for one thing, that is sperm which is pure. Otherwise, anything of mass or weight that comes from the private parts is impure and nullifies the ablution. Based on that principle, every liquid that flows from a woman's vagina is impure and requires ablution.

---

[1] Recorded by al-Tirmidhi and al-Nasai. It is an authentic hadith.—JZ
[2] Recorded by al-Bukhari and Muslim.— JZ

This is my conclusion after consulting with some scholars and doing some research. However, I have some problem with this conclusion because some women have such fluids at all times. If the flow is persistent, then the solution is to treat it in the same way that one treats the problem of uncontrollable urine flow. The person should make ablution for the prayer after the time of the prayer begins and then she prays. Then I researched this question with some doctors. They made it clear that if the liquid is from the urethra, then the ruling is as I have just stated. However, if it is from the uterus, then it is also as we have just stated, but, in that case, the liquid is considered pure and one does not have to wash it off of whatever it touches.

Shaikh ibn Uthaimin

Employing a Disbeliever For Cooking and Cleaning

Question 38: We have a non-Muslim maid. Is it permissible for me to leave her to wash the clothing while I pray? Can I eat what she has cooked? Is it permissible for me to point out the shortcoming and falsehood of her religion?

Response: It is permissible to employ a disbeliever and use them for cooking, washing and so forth. One may also eat the food they prepare and wear the clothing they have sewn or washed. This is because their outward body is clean and their impurity is a spiritual impurity. The Companions used to use non-Muslim male and female slaves and eat what they had prepared for them from the lands of the non-Muslims since they knew that their bodies were physically pure. However, it is mentioned in the hadith that one should wash their containers before cooking in them if those people used to drink alcohol or cook carrion and pork in them. Similarly, one should wash their clothing that is worn over the private parts. As for pointing out the shortcomings and falsity of their religion, that is permissible. Either their religion is paganism, distorted or abrogated, like Christianity. A distorted and changed religion is definitely blameworthy. However, you should call them to Islam and explain to them its teachings and superiority while showing them the difference between it and the other religions.

Shaikh ibn Jibreen

Dried Impurities Are No Problem

Question 39: Does dried urine not make clothing impure? That is, when a young child urinates on the ground and the urine remains there until it becomes dry, without it being washed away, and then a person sits on that dried urine, does his clothing get any of that impurity?

Response: There is no harm if a dried impurity comes into contact with a body or dry clothing. Similarly, there is no harm in entering a dry bathroom barefoot, while one's feet are dry. Impurities only move from one to another when they are wet.

Shaikh ibn Jibreen

Left-over Food in One's Teeth and Ablution

Question 40: A sister for the sake of Allah asks: Sometimes I find the remains of food in my teeth. Is it necessary for me to remove that leftover food before making ablution?

Response: It seems to me that it is not obligatory to remove such food remains before ablution. However, there is no doubt that it is better and cleaner to remove such from your teeth. Furthermore, this is better to keep illness away from your teeth and gums. A person should clean between his teeth after eating in order to remove any food remains. One should also use a

toothstick as food changes the smell of one's breath. The Prophet
(صلى الله عليه وسلم) also said about the toothstick,

" إِنَّـهُ مَطْهَـرَةٌ لِلفَـمِ ، مَرْضَـاةٌ لِلـرَّبِّ "

"It is purifying for the mouth and pleasing to the Lord."[1]

This indicates that whenever a mouth is in need of purification, it
is purified by using a toothstick. Allah knows best.

Shaikh ibn Uthaimin

Changing the Baby's Diapers
Does not Nullify Ablution

Question 41: If I were in a state of ablution and then I
changed my baby's diaper, does that nullify my ablution or not?

Response: If someone touches somebody else's private
parts with lust, then that invalidates his ablution. However, there
is a difference of opinion when such is touched without lust. The
strongest opinion is that touching the private parts of a baby in
order to clean the baby does not nullify ablution because such is
not a cause of sexual desire. Furthermore, it is something that
almost all people have to go through and if it were to nullify
ablution it would cause great hardship. And if it did nullify
ablution, this would have been well-known among the
Companions and those who came afterwards.

Shaikh ibn Jibreen

---

[1] Al-Bukhari has recorded this in definitive *mualaq* form from Aisha. It is
recorded by al-Nasai, Ahmad and al-Darimi with complete chains.
According to al-Albani, it is authentic. Al-Albani, *Sahih al-Jami*, vol. 1,
p. 688.— JZ

Is Cooking Oil Considered Something that Keeps Water from Reaching the Skin During Ablution?

Question 42: I heard one of the scholars saying that cooking oil is considered something that prevents water from reaching the skin during ablution. Sometimes when I cook, drops of oil spill onto my hair and extremities. Do I then, when I am going to make ablution, first have to wash myself with soap to remove that oil so the water can reach the skin? Similarly, I sometimes put oil on my hair as a kind of remedy for me, what should I do then?

Response: Before responding to that question, I would like to make it clear that Allah has said in His Book,

﴿ يَـٰٓأَيُّهَا ٱلَّذِينَ ءَامَنُوٓاْ إِذَا قُمْتُمْ إِلَى ٱلصَّلَوٰةِ فَٱغْسِلُواْ وُجُوهَكُمْ وَأَيْدِيَكُمْ إِلَى ٱلْمَرَافِقِ وَٱمْسَحُواْ بِرُءُوسِكُمْ وَأَرْجُلَكُمْ إِلَى ٱلْكَعْبَيْنِ ﴾

[المائدة: ٦]

"O believers! When you intend to offer prayer, wash your faces and your arms up to the elbows, rub your heads and (wash) your feet to the ankles" (*al-Maida* 6).

The order to wash those extremities and to wipe what is to be wiped requires the removal of anything that would prevent the water from reaching them. This is because if there is some obstacle preventing water from reaching them, they would not be washed. Based on that, we say that if a person uses oil [or cream] on the extremities that must be washed during ablution and that oil stays and becomes solid, then it must be removed before the extremities are washed. If it stays in that matter, it has weight and mass to it and it prevents the water from reaching the skin and, therefore, the act of purification is not valid.

However, if the oil has no mass or weight to it and its effects remain on the parts that must be washed, then it does not cause a problem. But, in that case, the person must make certain to pass his hands over all of the parts of the body that are to be washed. This is because oil usually keeps the water apart from it and, therefore, perhaps the water may not reach all of the extremity that must be washed.

So we say to the questioner that if the oil that is on your extremity is dry and has mass to it such that it keeps the water from reaching the skin, then you must remove it before purifying yourself. However, if it has no mass, then there is no harm in purifying yourself without washing with soap. But pass your hand over the entire part of your extremity when purifying yourself in order to make sure that the water does not miss it.

Shaikh ibn Uthaimin

Washing One's Face and Hands with Soap While Making Ablution

Question 43: What is the ruling concerning washing one's face and hands with soap while making ablution?

Response: The washing of the hands and face with soap while making ablution is not sanctioned. Indeed, it is from the actions that are considered overzealousness and being extreme. It is confirmed that the Prophet (صلى الله عليه وسلم) said,

" هَــلكَ المُتَنَطِّعُـــون هَــلكَ المُتَنَطِّعُـــون "

"Destroyed are the overzealous; destroyed are the overzealous." He said that three times.[1]

---

[1] Recorded by Muslim. It is sometimes translated as those who are hair-splitting.— JZ

Yes, if someone has some filth on his hands that cannot be removed except by using soap or other similar pure substance, then there is no harm in him using soap on that occasion. However, if he makes this his regular practice, then it is considered a case of overzealousness and extremism. In that case, it should not be used.

Shaikh ibn Uthaimin

Kissing Does not Nullify Ablution

Question 44: My husband always kisses me when he is leaving the house, even if he is leaving to the prayer in the mosque. Sometimes, I feel that he is kissing me in a lustful manner. What is the ruling concerning his ablution in that case?

Response: Aisha narrated that the Prophet (صلى الله عليه وسلم) kissed one of his wives and then went to pray without making ablution.[1] This hadith clarifies the question of touching or kissing a woman: does that nullify ablution or not? The scholars have different opinions on this point.[2] Some scholars say that it nullifies ablution in all cases- if one touches a woman it nullifies his ablution in all cases. Some say that if he touches a woman in a lustful way it nullifies ablution; otherwise, it does not. Some

---

[1] This hadith was recorded by Ahmad, al-Tirmidhi, Abu Dawud, al-Nasai and ibn Majah. Historically, there has been a great deal of difference of opinion over the authenticity of this hadith. Al-Albani, Shuaib al-Arnaut and al-Zailai concluded that it is authentic. See Muhammad Nasir al-Din al-Albani, *Sahih Sunan al-Tirmidhi* (Riyadh: Maktab al-Tarbiya al-Arabi li-Daul al-Khaleej, 1988), vol. 1, p. 26; Al-Husain al-Baghawi, *Sharh al-Sunnah*, Zuhair al-Shawish and Shuaib al-Arnaut, eds. (Beirut: al-Maktab al-Islami, 1983), vol. 1, p. 346, fns. 1 and 2.— JZ

[2] One important reason for that difference of opinion is that many scholars do not accept the above hadith as being authentic.— JZ

others say that it does not invalidate ablution in any case. This last opinion is the strongest opinion. That is, if a man kisses, touches or embraces his wife and he does not ejaculate or release any fluid, then his ablution is not ruined nor is hers. This is because the principle is that his ablution continues to be valid until there is some evidence that it has been nullified. There is no evidence, either in the Quran or the Sunnah, to show that touching a woman invalidates ablution. Based on that, if a person touches a woman, even without anything between their skins and even if in a lustful manner or a kiss or hug, all of that does not nullify the ablution. Allah knows best.

Shaikh ibn Uthaimin

Yes, She Must Make *Ghusl*

Question 45: Does my wife have to make the *ghusl* due to sexual defilement after insertion [of the male organ] during sexual intercourse but without ejaculation inside the vagina? Does she have to make that *ghusl* when she has inserted an IUD inside her vagina or is it sufficient for her just to wash her body and extremities?

Response: Yes, she must make *ghusl* due to penetration [of the male organ into the female], even if it is simply a little penetration. This is due to the hadith,

" إذا جَلَسَ بين شُعَبِهَا الأرْبَعِ ثُمَّ جَهَدَهَا فقـدْ وَجَـبَ الغَسْلُ وإن لم يُـنْزِلْ "

"When anyone sits between the four parts of her [his wife's] body and then makes an effort, *ghusl* becomes obligatory, even if he did not ejaculate."[1]

---

[1] Recorded by Muslim. Also recorded by al-Bukhari but without the words, "Even if he does not ejaculate."— JZ

Another hadith states,

" إِذَا آلتَقَى الخِتَـانَـان فَقَـدْ وَجَـبَ الغُسْـل "

"If the circumcised parts enter[1], ghusl is obligatory."[2]

She also must make *ghusl* even if she had an IUD in her vagina because of the penetration [of the male organ] and usually some ejaculation. However, she need only make ablution (*wudhu*) if there was simply touching without penetration.

Shaikh ibn Jibreen

---

[1] That is, if circumcised part of male organ is covered by female organ, *ghusl* is obligatory.
[2] Recorded by ibn Majah. Others have hadith with the same meaning. This hadith is graded authentic by al-Albani. Al-Albani, *Sahih al-Jami al-Sagheer*, vol. 1, p. 130.—JZ

4. Question Related to Menstruation and Post-Partum Bleeding

A Woman Does not Become Impure Due to Menstruation or Post-Partum Bleeding

Question 46: My wife gave birth and one of my friends prevented me from entering my house, arguing that it is not allowed for a person to eat what a woman has prepared while she is experiencing post-partum bleeding. She is considered physically and practically impure. I hope you will help me on this issue. According to what I know, the women with post-natal bleeding is not allowed to pray, fast or read the Quran?

Response: A woman does not become impure by menstruation or post-partum bleeding. One may eat with her and one may also come into physical contact with her, avoiding the vagina. However, it is disliked to come into contact with the area between the navel and the knees only. This is based on what Muslim recorded from Anas: Among the Jews, when a woman had her menses, they would not eat with her. The Messenger of Allah (صلى الله عليه وسلم) said,

" اصْنَعُـوا كلَّ شــيءٍ إلا النِّـكَاحَ "

"Do everything with them [as you please, as normal,] except sexual intercourse."

Al-Bukhari and Muslim also record from Aisha who said that the Prophet (صلى الله عليه وسلم) would tell her to put on a waist cloth and then he would have physical contact with her while she was menstruating. There is no effect from the prohibition of prayer, fasting and reciting the

Quran[1] during her menses and post-partum bleeding upon eating with her or eating the food that she has prepared.

The Standing Committee

Using Pills that Prevent Menstruation

Question 47: There are pills that will prevent the menses or delay their occurrence. Is it allowed to use such pills during the time of pilgrimage only out of fear of one's menses coming?

Response: It is allowed for a woman to use pills that will prevent her menses during the time of pilgrimage out of fear that her menses may come. But this should be after she has consulted with a specialist who makes certain that her health will be fine. Similarly, she may do the same during Ramadhan if she desires to fast with the people.[2]

The Standing Committee

Discontinuation of Bleeding During the Menses

Question 48: Sometimes it happens to me, during my menses, that I have blood for four days and then the blood stops for three days. Then on the seventh day the blood returns, but not as intense as previously. Then it turns to a brown color until the twelfth day. I hope you will guide me to what is correct in this matter.

Response: The days that you mentioned, the four and the six day periods, are days of menstruation. You should not pray or fast during those days. It is not allowed for your husband to have

---

[1] It is not prohibited for a menstruating woman or a woman with post-natal bleeding to recite from her memory without actually touching the Quran.— JZ

[2] There seems to be no need for women to go to such lengths. This probably could be considered a kind of overzealousness. There is no real certainty as to the health risks of such pills, like birth control pills. Furthermore, the menses are a natural matter that Allah has ordained for women and there is no need to flee from them. Hence, it must be considered best for women to abstain from such pills since there is no call for them and they cannot be certain of their side effects. Allah knows best.— JZ

sexual intercourse with you during those days. You should make *ghusl* after the four days and then pray and your husband may have intercourse with you during that period between the four and the six days. Also, there is no prohibition upon your fasting. If that occurs during Ramadhan, it is obligatory upon you to fast. And when you become pure after those six days, you must make *ghusl*, pray and fast like any other time of purity. This is because the monthly menses can increase or decrease. Its days are sometimes together and sometimes separated.[1] May Allah guide us all to what pleases Him. May He provide us, you and all the Muslims with understanding and steadfastness in the religion.

Shaikh ibn Baz

Drops of Blood After Making *Ghusl*

Question 49: I notice that sometimes after making *ghusl* due to my monthly menses, after having had my period for a normal amount of time, five days, I have a very small amount of drops coming out. This occurs right after I make *ghusl*. After that, nothing else comes out. I do not know what to do. Should I follow my normal five-day period and simply ignore what occurs after that and continue to pray and fast? Or should I consider that day also part of my period and not pray or fast during it? Note that such does not always occur to me but only occurs every two or three, or so, monthly cycles. I hope you will benefit me on this matter.

Response: If what comes out after your washing is either yellow or brown, it is not to be taken into consideration [as menses] and it takes the same ruling as urine.[2]

---

[1] In response to this question, the Shaikh has basically given the Hanbali view of the question. There are some other views, that state that the entire period is that of menstruation, which may carry more weight to them. Allah knows best.— JZ

[2] Meaning, it must be washed off the clothing and the person must make ablution from such discharge.— JZ

However, if it is clearly blood, it will then be considered part of the menses and you must repeat the *ghusl* due to what is confirmed from Umm Atiya, one of the Companions of the Messenger of Allah (صلى الله عليه وسلم), who said, "We would not consider yellowish or brownish discharge as anything[1] after we had been purified [from menses]."[2]

Shaikh ibn Baz

If a Woman Ends Her Menses Before Sunset, She Must Perform the *Dhuhr* and *Asr* Prayers

Question 50: When a menstruating woman becomes pure before sunrise is it obligatory upon her to perform the *Maghrib* and *Isha* prayers? Similarly, if she becomes pure before sunset, is it obligatory upon her to perform the *Dhuhr* and *Asr* prayers?

Response: If a menstruating or post-partum bleeding woman becomes pure before sunset, it is obligatory upon her to perform both the *Dhuhr* and *Asr* prayers according to the strongest opinion among the scholars. Similar is the case if she becomes pure before dawn. In that case, she must perform the *Maghrib* and *Isha* prayers. This has been narrated from Abdul Rahman ibn Auf and Abdullah ibn Abbas. This is the opinion of the majority of the scholars. Similarly, if a menstruating or post-partum bleeding woman becomes pure before sunrise, it is obligatory upon her to perform the *Fajr* prayer. And from Allah is guidance.

Shaikh ibn Baz

The Menstruating Woman Keeping Herself Clean From Urine

Question 51: When I am menstruating, I do not clean myself from urine with water because I fear that the water may harm me. What is the ruling concerning that?

---

[1] That is, "We would not consider it as menses."
[2] Recorded by al-Bukhari.— JZ

Response: It suffices, in place of water, to clean yourself with clean tissue paper or any other pure solid object that will remove the impure substance, such as a rock, piece of wood or similar substances. This wiping should be done three times or more, until the impure substance is removed. This ruling is not just for you or anyone in a case like yours. However, it is for all Muslim men and women. This is based on what has been confirmed from Aisha that the Prophet (صلى الله عليه وسلم) said,

" إِذَا ذَهَبَ أَحَدُكُم إِلَى الغَائِطِ فَلِيَسْتَطِبْ بِثَلاَثَةِ أَحجَارٍ فَإِنَّها تُجزِىُء عنه "

"When one of you goes to relieve himself, he should clean himself with three stones and that will be sufficient for him."

This was recorded by Ahmad, al-Nasai and Abu Dawud, as well as al-Daraqutni who said its chain is *sahih hasan*. It is also confirmed from Salman al-Farsi that it was said to him, "Your Prophet teaches you everything, even how to go to the bathroom." Salman said, "Certainly! He prohibited us from facing the *qibla* while defecating or urinating, from cleaning our genitals with our right hand, from cleaning ourselves with less than three stones and from cleaning ourselves with dung or bone." This was recorded by Muslim, Abu Dawud and al-Tirmidhi.

Shaikh ibn Baz

Getting Her Menses While She is in the Mosque

Question 52: A woman had blood starting to flow while she was in the Mosque of the Prophet (صلى الله عليه وسلم). She stayed in the mosque for a little while until her husband had finished the prayer and she could leave with him. Did she commit a sin?

Response: If she was not able to depart from the mosque by herself, then there is no harm in what she did. However, if she was able to leave by herself, it is obligatory upon her to exit as quickly as possible. This is because the menstruating woman, post-partum bleeding woman and sexually defiled person are not allowed to sit in the mosques. This is based on Allah's statement,

﴿ وَلَا جُنُبًا إِلَّا عَابِرِى سَبِيلٍ ﴾ [النساء : ٤٣]

"Nor while sexually defiled except when traveling on a road" (al-Nisa 43).[1]

It is also narrated from the Prophet (صلى الله عليه وسلم) that he said,

" إِنِّي لَا أُحِلُّ المَسْجِدَ لِحَائِضٍ ولا جُنُبٍ "

"I do not permit the menstruating woman or the sexually defiled person to enter the mosque."[2]

Shaikh ibn Baz

A Menstruating Woman May Read the Books of Quranic Commentary

Question 53: I read some of the books of *tafseer* (Quranic exegesis) while I am not in a state of purity, such as during my monthly period. Is there any harm in that? Am I being sinful in doing so? Please give me a ruling, may Allah reward you.

---

[1] Note that the verse is in reference only to those who are sexually defiled. Obviously, the differences between a menstruating women and a sexually defiled person are very great. Hence, one cannot make an analogy between the two. Furthermore, there is also a difference of opinion concerning whether this verse implies anyone who becomes sexually defiled or only the travelers who become sexually defiled.— JZ

[2] Recorded by Abu Dawud and, with a different wording, by ibn Majah. The authenticity of this hadith is greatly debated among the scholars of hadith. The way Shaikh ibn Baz has presented the hadith shows that either he has some doubt about the hadith or he himself considers the hadith to be weak. If this hadith is weak and the above verse is not in reference to menstruating women, there is no strong evidence that states that a menstruating woman may not enter the mosque. Unfortunately, this is not the proper place for a detailed presentation of the different views on that question.— JZ

Response: There is no harm if a menstruating or post-natal bleeding woman reads books of *tafseer* nor in her reciting the Quran without actually touching the *mushaf* [the physical copy of the Quran] according to the strongest opinion among the scholars.[1] As for the sexually defiled person, he may not recite the Quran in any manner until he makes *ghusl*. However, he may read the books of *tafseer*, hadith and so forth without reciting what they contain of verses of the Quran. This is based on the hadith that states that nothing would keep the Prophet (صلى الله عليه وسلم) from reciting the Quran except being in a state of sexual defilement. In another wording of the hadith, the Prophet (صلى الله عليه وسلم) states, as recorded by Ahmad with a good chain,

$$ \text{" فَأَمَّا الجُنُبُ فَـلاَ وَلا آيَـةً "} $$

"As for the sexually defiled, he may not [recite], not even one verse."[2]

Shaikh ibn Baz

---

[1] The question of the menstruating woman touching a physical copy of the Quran is another controversial issue which cannot be discussed in detail here. The interested reader may consult the translator's, "The Condition of *Tahara* for Reciting/Touching the Quran," *Al-Basheer* (Volume 7, Number 6, March-April 1994), pp. 8-22.— JZ

[2] Shaikh ibn Baz (may Allah prolong and bless his life) has stated that Ahmad recorded this hadith with a good chain. However, the hadith is transmitted through Abdullah ibn Salima who became senile toward the end of his life. Many scholars accept this hadith while a number of scholars, perhaps one could call them stricter scholars, reject this hadith. Furthermore, ibn Khuzaima, who accepts this hadith, states that the hadith does not prohibit a sexually defiled person from reciting the Quran. For more details, see the translator's, "The Condition of *Tahara*..." Ibid., pp. 9-14.—JZ

It is Permissible for a Menstruating Woman to Recite the Quran and Books of Supplications

Question 54: Is it allowed for a menstruating woman to read a book of supplications on the Day of Arafah, given the fact that the book contains Quranic verses?

Response: There is no harm in a menstruating or post-partum bleeding woman reading the books of supplications that are written for the rites of the pilgrimage. In fact, there is nothing wrong with her reciting the Quran according to the correct opinion. There is no authentic, clear text prohibiting a menstruating or post-partum bleeding woman from reciting the Quran. The thing that is narrated is concerned with the sexually defiled person only, as such should not recite the Quran while he is sexually defiled. This is based on the hadith of Ali. As for the menstruating or post-partum bleeding woman, there is the hadith of ibn Umar which states,

" لاَتَقْرَأَ الحَائِــضُ ولا الجُنُــبُ شيئـاً مَنْ القُــرآن "

"Neither the menstruating woman nor the sexually defiled person is to recite anything from the Quran."

However, this is weak. This is because it is from the narrations of Ismail ibn Iyyash on the authority of people from the Hijaz and he is weak when he narrates from them. However, she may recite from her memory without touching the Quran. As for the sexually defiled person, he/she may not even recite the Quran from memory or touch the *mushaf* until he/she makes *ghusl*. The difference between the two is that the amount of time one is sexually defiled is very short as he may make *ghusl* as soon as he has done the act with his spouse. The amount of time is not long and he is in control of its length as he may make *ghusl* whenever he wishes. Even if he cannot find water, he can make *tayammum* and pray or recite the Quran. However, the menstruating or post-partum

bleeding woman does not have control over their lengths, such
control is in the hand of Allah. Menstruation and post-partum
bleeding take days. Therefore, it is allowed for them to recite the
Quran so that they do not forget what they have memorized and so
they will not lose the merits of reciting it. It is also so they may
learn the laws of the *Shariah* from the Book of Allah. Therefore,
it is even more permissible for her to read the books of
supplications that have verses and hadith intermixed with them.
This is the correct view and is the correct opinion of the scholars-
may Allah have mercy on them- on that point.

Shaikh ibn Baz

The Prayer of the *Mustahaadha*[1]

Question 55: A woman who has reached the age of fifty-
two years has strong bleeding for three days and then light
bleeding for the rest of the month. Should that [heavy] bleeding be
considered menses, given that that blood only comes to her on an
irregular bases, such as once every two or three months? Should
she perform the obligatory prayers when the blood is flowing?
Similarly, does she pray the voluntary prayers, such as the *sunnan*
prayers and *salat al-witr*?

Response: A woman like her should consider that blood
that she has blood due to illness. This conclusion is based on her
age and because it occurs irregularly. It is known from experience
and from what is related from Aisha that when a woman reaches
fifty years of age her menses and chance of pregnancy come to an
end or the blood comes in a strange, irregular fashion. This irregular
fashion is proof that it is not blood of the menses. Therefore, she

---

[1] The *mustahaadha* is the woman with *istihaadha*. *Istihaadha* is either a
prolonged flow of blood (called menorrhagia in English) or bleeding
outside of the menses (called metrorrhagia in English). Many hospitals
and medical clinics in the United States have pamphlets stating what
women should do in such cases. In some cases, especially when the
bleeding is prolonged, it may be a symptom of some other disorder.— JZ

should pray and fast and consider that continuous flowing blood as *istihaadha* that does not prevent her from praying and fasting or prevent her husband from having sexual intercourse with her, according to the strongest opinion among the scholars. However, she must make ablution for every prayer and protect herself from the blood with a panty liner, pad or something of that nature. The Prophet (صلى الله عليه وسلم) said to a woman with *istihaadha*,

$$ " تَـوَضَّـئِــي لِــكُلِّ صَــلاةٍ " $$

"Make ablution for every prayer."

Recorded by al-Bukhari in his *Sahih*.

Shaikh ibn Baz

If a Woman with Post-Partum Bleeding Stops Bleeding Before the Fortieth Day, She Must Make *Ghusl*, Pray and Fast

Question 56: If a woman becomes pure from post-natal bleeding before her fortieth day, should she fast and pray or not? If her menses come after that, does she break her fast? If she becomes pure again, does she then fast and pray or not?

Response: If the woman with post-natal bleeding becomes pure before the 40th day [that is, the blood stops before then], it is obligatory upon her to make *ghusl*, pray and fast the month of Ramadhan and she becomes legal for her husband [to have intercourse with her]. If the blood returns to her before the 40th day, she must stop praying and fasting and her husband can no longer have intercourse with her according to the strongest of the two opinions among the scholars. She becomes again like the one with post-partum bleeding until the bleeding stops or until she completes forty days. If she then becomes pure before the 40th day or on the 40th day, she must make *ghusl*, pray, fast and may have intercourse with her husband. If the blood continues after the 40th day, this is considered blood due to illness and she does not abandon the prayers or fasting on account of it. Indeed, she must pray and fast and she is permissible for her husband, like the *mustahaadha*. She must clean herself and keep herself clean from the blood by using some cotton or something similar [like a panty liner or pad]. She should make ablution for the time of every prayer because the Prophet (صلى الله عليه وسلم) ordered the *mustaahadha* to do such. But if her monthly period should come, she abandons the prayer and fast and she becomes illegal for her husband until she becomes clean of her menses.

Shaikh ibn Baz

Ruling Concerning a Miscarriage

Question 57: Some women have miscarriages. Sometimes the fetus comes out fully formed while at another times it does not. I would like you to make clear the ruling for prayer in both of those situations.

Response: If a woman has a miscarriage and the fetus has clearly human figures to it, such as a head, hand, leg and so forth, then her bleeding is post-natal bleeding. She follows the rulings of post-natal bleeding. She does not pray or fast and her husband cannot have sexual intercourse with her until the bleeding stops or she completes forty days. If the bleeding stops before the 40th day, she must make *ghusl*, pray, fast during Ramadhan and her husband may have sexual intercourse with her.

There is no minimum length of time for post-partum bleeding. The bleeding could stop after ten days, more or less, and then she must make *ghusl* and all the laws of a ritually pure person apply to her. If she sees any blood after the fortieth day, it is considered bleeding from illness. She would then fast and pray with that bleeding and it is permissible for her husband to have intercourse with her. She must make ablution for the time of every prayer, like the *mustahaadha*, as the Prophet (صلى الله عليه وسلم) told Fatima bint Abu Hubaish,

" وَتَوَضَّئِـي لِوَقْتِ كُلِّ صَـــلاةٍ "

"Make ablution for the time of every prayer."[1]

If the blood that flows from her after the forty-day period coincides with the time of her menses, then it takes on the ruling of menses. It is forbidden for her to pray or fast until she becomes pure. And it is forbidden for her husband to have intercourse with her.

However, if what comes out of the woman does not resemble a human being, such as when it is simply a smooth lump of flesh or clot of blood, then she takes the ruling of *istihaadha* and not that of post-partum bleeding. She should pray, fast during Ramadhan and may have intercourse with her husband. She should make ablution for the time of every prayer while keeping herself clean from the blood by a panty liner or something similar, like the *mustahaadha*, until the bleeding stops. She may also combine the *Dhuhr* and *Asr* prayers together and the *Maghrib* and *Isha* prayers together. She may also make a *ghusl* for the combined prayers and a separate *ghusl* for the *Fajr* prayer based on the confirmed hadith of Hamnah bint Jahsh. This is because she is to be treated like a *mustahaadha* according to the people of knowledge.

Shaikh ibn Baz

Ruling Concerning a Discharge of Blood Five Days Before Giving Birth

Question 58: A woman had bleeding during pregnancy, five days before giving birth, during the month of Ramadhan. Should that blood be considered menstruation or *istihaadha* and what are the obligations upon her?

Response: If the matter is as mentioned, with her seeing blood five days before giving birth, and she did not have any signs

---

[1] As mentioned earlier, this translator was not able to find this hadith with this exact wording. The authentic narrations in al-Bukhari and Muslim simply state that she is to make ablution for every prayer.— JZ

that labor would be soon, such as contractions, in that case, the blood is neither menstruation nor post-partum bleeding. It is simply irregular blood. Therefore, she should not abandon the acts of worship but she must fast and pray. If along with the blood she has signs that her labor is near, such as contractions, then it is considered post-partum bleeding and she abandons, due to it, praying and fasting. Then if she becomes pure after giving birth, she must make up the days of fasting but not the prayers.

The Standing Committee

The Meaning of the Word *Quru'*

Question 59: Allah says in the Quran,

﴾ يَتَرَبَّصْنَ بِأَنفُسِهِنَّ ثَلَٰثَةَ قُرُوٓءٍ ﴿   [البقرة: ٢٢٨]

"And [divorced women] shall wait for three *quru'*" (al-Baqara 228).

What is the meaning here of the word *quru'*?

Response: Lexically, *quru'* can mean the time of purity and it can also mean the menses itself. However, the correct meaning in the verse is the menses as this is its most often usage by the Lawgiver and is the opinion of the majority of the Companions.

Shaikh ibn Jibreen

Breaking the Fast Due to Menses and Not Making the Days Up Due to Shyness

Question 60: When I was young, thirteen years old, I fasted the month of Ramadhan and broke my fast on four days due to menses. However, due to shyness, I did not inform anyone about that. Now, it has been eight years since that event, what should I do?

Response: You have made a mistake by not making up those days for all of this time. Menses is something that is prescribed, by Allah upon the females and there is no shyness when it comes to the religion. You must quickly make up those four days and then, along with making up those days, you must also make an expiation by feeding a poor person for every day. You must give about two *sa's* of the normal staple food of the country to a poor person or poor persons.[1]

Shaikh ibn Jibreen

If the Menses Continue for More Than Their Normal Length

Question 61: If a woman normally has menses for eight or seven days but once or twice she has them for a longer period, what is the ruling concerning that?

Response: If that woman normally has her menses for six or seven days and then they become longer, becoming eight, nine, ten or eleven days, then she remains not praying until she becomes pure. This is because the Prophet (صلى الله عليه وسلم) did not set any specific limit for menstruation. Allah says in the Quran,

﴿ وَيَسْـَٔلُونَكَ عَنِ ٱلْمَحِيضِ قُلْ هُوَ أَذًى ﴾   [البقرة: ٢٢٢]

"They ask you concerning menstruation. Say: It is a harmful thing..." (*al-Baqara* 222).

As long as that blood is flowing, the woman remains in her state of menses until she becomes pure [the blood stops] and she makes *ghusl* and prays. If, in the following month, the blood comes for a shorter period of time, she makes *ghusl* when the blood stops even if it was not as long as the previous period. The important point is that as long as the woman is having menses, she remains in that state as long as she has bleeding and she does not pray, regardless of whether that amount of time is the same, longer or shorter than her previous menses. When the blood stops, she prays.

Shaikh ibn Uthaimin

---

[1] The Shaikh says two *sa's* because the person has to give a half a *sa'* for each day and the total number of days was four.—JZ

If a Woman Has a Miscarriage in the Third Month of Her Pregnancy

Question 62: A year ago, I had a miscarriage in my third month of pregnancy. I stopped praying until the blood stopped. It was said to me that I should have prayed. What should I do now since I do not know the exact number of days I did not pray?

Response: What is well-known and accepted among the scholars is that if a woman has a miscarriage in the third month, she does not pray. This is because when the woman has such a miscarriage, the fetus has clear signs of being a human. Therefore, the blood that then flows is considered post-partum bleeding and the woman does not pray. The scholars say that fetus take on the shape of a human after eighty-one days, which is less than three months. If you are certain that you had a miscarriage after three months, the blood that came was post-partum bleeding. However, if it were before eighty days, then the blood that came is irregular or abnormal blood and she should not leave the prayer due to it. So the one who asked the question must see if the miscarriage was before eighty days, in which case she must make up the prayers she missed. If she does not know how many days she missed, she must estimate the matter and make up what she believes she has missed.

Shaikh ibn Uthaimin

Sexual Intercourse Before Completing Forty Days

Question 63: Is it allowed for a man to have sexual intercourse with his wife after she gave birth before the forty-day period is up? If he has intercourse with her after thirty or thirty-five days and she is clean [having no bleeding] but she has not completed the forty days, is there any sin upon him?

Response: It is not allowed to have intercourse with one's wife during the time of post-partum bleeding. This is when the bleeding occurs after delivery. If the bleeding stops before forty days, it is disliked to have intercourse with her. However, it is allowed and there is no sin, Allah willing, upon the person given the condition that the woman is completely free from blood, and she is required to pray, fast and so forth.

Shaikh ibn Jibreen

Supplication of Menstruating Women

Question 64: Does Allah accept the supplications and asking forgiveness of the menstruating woman?

Response: Yes, it is allowed- in fact recommended- for the menstruating woman to often supplicate, ask for Allah's forgiveness, make remembrance of Allah and humble herself to Allah, especially during the noble times. When the conditions for a supplication to be answered are met, the supplication is answered for a menstruating woman or for others.

Shaikh ibn Jibreen

Prayer of a Menstruating Woman

Question 65: While I was praying, my menses began. What should I do? Do I make up the prayers of the time of my menses?

Response: If the menses come after the beginning of a time for prayer, for example, if you receive your menses a half an hour after high noon, then you must make up that prayer after your bleeding has ended since when its time began you were in a state of purity. This is based on Allah's statement,

﴿ إِنَّ ٱلصَّلَوٰةَ كَانَتْ عَلَى ٱلْمُؤْمِنِينَ كِتَٰبًا مَّوْقُوتًا ﴾

[النساء: ١٠٣]

"Verily, the prayer is enjoined upon the believers at fixed hours" (al-Nisa 103).

Do not make up the prayers you missed while menstruating. This is based on the lengthy hadith in which the Prophet (صلى الله عليه وسلم) said,

" أَلَيْسَتْ إِذَا حَاضَتْ لَمْ تُصَلِّ وَلَمْ تَصُمْ "

"Is it not the case that when you menstruate, you do not pray or fast?"[1]

There is a consensus of the scholars that the prayers missed during menstruation are not to be made up. However, if she becomes pure [the bleeding stops] and she has enough time to pray one *rakah* or more of a prayer, then she must pray the prayer of that time in which she became pure. This is based on the hadith of the Messenger of Allah (صلى الله عليه وسلم),

" مَنْ أَدْرَكَ رَكْعَةً مِنَ الْعَصْرِ قَبْلَ أَن تَغْرُبَ الشَّمْسُ فَقَدْ أَدْرَكَ الْعَصْرَ "

"Whoever catches one *rakah* of the Asr Prayer before sunset has caught the Asr Prayer."[2]

If the woman becomes pure during the time of Asr or before sunrise and there is enough time before sunset or sunrise to pray one *rakah*, then she prays Asr in the former case and Fajr in the latter case.

Shaikh ibn Uthaimin

Brownish or Yellowish Discharge After Purity is to be Ignored

Question 66: My period usually lasts for six days and sometimes for seven days. I make *ghusl* after I am certain that I am pure. I remain in such a state for a complete day. Then I notice

---

[1] Recorded by al-Bukhari. This is the hadith that is mentioned in the Arabic text but it seems that there is something wrong here. This hadith in no way proves what the Shaikh is trying to prove. Indeed, one could conclude from the printed text that the woman does not make up her missed days of fasting either. That is clearly wrong and not the opinion of Shaikh ibn Uthaimin. Hence, he must have been quoting or referring to a different hadith.—JZ

[2] Recorded by al-Bukhari and Muslim.—JZ

a brown drop and I do not know what is the ruling concerning that. I am confused whether I should pray or not and whether I should fast or not. I am also confused concerning other deeds. What should I do in such a state? May Allah reward you.

Response: As long as you know the time for your period and its length, and you went through that time and then prayed and fasted, if you then see yellow or brown spotting after being in purity, such spotting does not keep you from prayer and acts of worship. The state of purity has a clear sign that women know, known as the white clear discharge. If a woman sees that, that is the sign that her menses have come to an end and her state of purity is beginning. Hence, she must then make *ghusl* afterwards and perform the ritual acts of worship, such as prayer, fasting, reading the Quran and so forth.

Shaikh ibn Uthaimin

A Menstruating Woman May Use Henna

Question 67: I heard that it is not allowed to apply henna to one's hair and hands while menstruating.

Response: It is allowed for the menstruating woman to apply henna to her hands and hair while menstruating. There is no sin or harm in that. Those who say it is prohibited or disliked have no evidence to support them. When the woman's menses end, she must make *ghusl* and should remove what she can of the henna. However, there is no harm in leaving what is difficult to remove.

Shaikh ibn Jibreen

Menstruating Women and Writing the Quran

Question 68: Is it allowed for a menstruating woman to recite the Quran, to use it in an example or to use it as evidence for something? And is it permissible for her to write verses of the Quran or hadith?

Response: There is no harm in menstruating women reading books which contain verses of the Quran or verses which are commented upon. There is no harm in her writing them as part of an article or something similar. Similarly, it is permissible for her to quote them as a type of evidence for a ruling or to recite them like a kind of supplication. This is not called "recitation" of the Quran. Similarly, she may carry books of *tafseer* and similar books if she needs to do so.

Shaikh ibn Jibreen

Don't Be Hasty

Question 69: My monthly period fluctuates between seven to eight days. Sometimes on the seventh day I do not see any blood or any sign of purity. What is the ruling in that case concerning prayer, fasting and sexual intercourse?

Response: Do not be hasty until you see the white clear discharge that is well-known among women as the sign of purity. The stopping of bleeding is not purity. Purity is when the sign that the menses has ended is seen and the period is finished.

Shaikh ibn Jibreen

The Blood that Comes Just Prior to the Menses is Irregular Blood and One Does not Stop Praying Due to It

Question 70: Three or four days before my period arrives I get some brown spotting. I do not know the ruling concerning that. Is it pure or impure? I am in a very confused and difficult state, should I pray or not?

Response: If the woman knows her menses by calculation, color or timing, she stops praying when her period comes and then makes *ghusl* and prays afterwards. The blood that comes just before the period is considered irregular or abnormal blood and one does not stop praying or fasting due to it. However, she must wash the blood away and keep herself clean of it for every prayer and make ablution for every prayer. She then prays even if the blood continues to flow. She is treated like *mustahaadha*. If she did abandon the prayer due to that bleeding, then it would be safest for her to make up those prayers and there is no hardship upon her, Allah willing.

Shaikh ibn Jibreen

5. Questions Related to Prayer

The Ruling Concerning One Who Does Not Pray

Question 71: What is the ruling concerning a person who died and he did not pray, although his parents were Muslims? How should he be dealt with concerning the washing of his body, shrouding, prayer, burial, supplications and asking for mercy upon him?

Response: Any sane adult person who dies and does not pray, given that he knows the Islamic ruling about prayer, is a disbeliever. He is not to be washed nor should he be prayed over. He is not to be buried in the Muslim cemetery. His Muslim relatives do not inherit from him. In fact, his wealth is to be given to the state treasury according to the strongest opinion among the scholars. This is based on the authentic hadith in which the Prophet (صلى الله عليه وسلم) said,

" بينَ الرَّجُلِ وبينَ الكُفْرِ والشِّرْكِ تركُ الصَّلاة "

"Between a person and *kufr* (disbelief) and *shirk* (associating partners with Allah) is the abandonment of the prayer."

This was recorded by Imam Muslim in his *Sahih*. The Prophet (صلى الله عليه وسلم) also said,

" العَهدُ الَّذي بينَنَا وبينهُمُ الصَّلاةُ فمن تَرَكَها فقد كَفَرَ "

"The covenant dividing us and them is the prayer. Whoever abandons it has committed *kufr* (apostasy)."

This was recorded by Ahmad and the Compilers of the *Sunan* with an authentic chain from the Hadith of Buraidah. Abdullah ibn Shaqeeq al-Aqeely, one of the Noble Followers, stated, "The

Companions of the Prophet (صلى الله عليـه وسلم) did not consider the abandonment of any act as *kufr* except the [abandonment of] prayer." There are many Ahadith and reports with that meaning. This is concerning the one who does not pray out of laziness. The one who refuses to accept it as being obligatory is an apostatizing disbeliever according to all of the scholars of Islam. We ask Allah to make the affairs of the Muslims good and lead them to follow the Straight Path. He is the All-Hearing, the Responder.

Shaikh ibn Baz

It is Not Sanctioned for the Women to Make the *Adhan* or *Iqama*

Question 72: There is a mosque in the College wherein the female students pray Dhuhr. One of them makes the *iqama* for the prayer. Is this legally sanctioned for women?

Response: It is not legally sanctioned for women to give the *adhan* or the *iqama*. That is something sanctioned for men only.

Shaikh ibn Baz

Ruling Concerning a Muslim Woman Praying without *Hijab*

Question 73: If a woman who does not wear *hijab* is forced to pray or if her *hijab* is not in accord with the *shariah*, for example, some of her hair or her shin is exposed for some reason, what is the ruling?

Response: First, it is necessary that one realize that *hijab* is obligatory upon women. It is not allowed for her to abandon it or be lackadaisical towards it. If the time for prayer comes and the woman is not properly attired or properly covered, then her situation may be broken down into the following cases:

If she is not wearing *hijab* or is not properly covered due
to circumstances forcing her to be in that state,[1] then she prays in
the situation that she is in. Her prayer will then be valid and there
will be no sin upon her. This is based on Allah's statement,

﴿ لَا يُكَلِّفُ ٱللَّهُ نَفْسًا إِلَّا وُسْعَهَآ ﴾ [البقرة: ٢٨٦]

"Allah burdens not a person beyond his scope" (*al-Baqara* 286).
Allah also says,

﴿ فَٱتَّقُوا۟ ٱللَّهَ مَا ٱسْتَطَعْتُمْ ﴾ [التغابن: ١٦]

"So keep your duty to Allah (and fear Him) as much as you
can" (*al-Taghabun* 16).

However, if the woman is not wearing *hijab* or is not
properly covered out of a voluntary choice, such as following the
customs or mode of the people, and the lack of *hijab* here means
not covering her face and hands, then her prayer is correct. But
she is committing a sin if she is doing that in the presence of men
that she is not related to.

Furthermore, if she is uncovering her shin, forearms, hair
on her head and so forth, then it is not permissible for her to pray
in that state. If she prays in that state, her prayer is not valid. And
she is committing a sin on two counts. First, she is sinful because
she is not covering herself in general. Second, she is sinful for
performing the prayer in that state.

Shaikh ibn Baz

---

[1] Here the Shaikh is referring to situations where women are not allowed
to wear *hijab* in public, at work or in school. Unfortunately, this situation
exists today in some Muslim countries.—JZ

Suffering From Uncontrollable Urine Flow: Should One Stop Praying Then?

Question 74: A pregnant woman in her ninth month had uncontrollable urine flows all the time and, therefore, she stopped praying during that final month. Should she have stopped praying? What should she do now?

Response: That woman and others like her should not stop praying. In fact, it is obligatory upon her to pray while in that state. She should make ablution for the time of every prayer, like the *mustahaadha*. She should keep herself clean, to the best of her ability, from the discharge by using cotton or something of that nature [such as a panty liner]. She should perform the prayers in their times. It is also legal for her to perform voluntary prayers during their times. She may also combine the two prayers of Dhuhr and Asr as well as combine Maghrib and Isha, like the *mustahaadha*. This is based on Allah's statement,

[التغابن: ١٦]　　　　　　　　　﴿ فَٱتَّقُوا۟ ٱللَّهَ مَا ٱسْتَطَعْتُمْ ﴾

"So keep your duty to Allah (and fear Him) as much as you can" (*al-Taghabun* 16).

She must make up the prayers that she missed while, at the same time, repenting to Allah by remorse and resolving never to do that act again. Allah has said,

﴿ وَتُوبُوٓا۟ إِلَى ٱللَّهِ جَمِيعًا أَيُّهَ ٱلْمُؤْمِنُونَ لَعَلَّكُمْ تُفْلِحُونَ ﴾

[النور: ٣١]

"And repent, all of you, to Allah, O believers, that you may be successful" (*al-Nur* 31).

Shaikh ibn Baz

Ruling Concerning Women Covering Their Hands and Feet During the Prayer

Question 75: What is the ruling concerning covering hands and feet in the prayer? Is it obligatory upon a woman or is it allowed for her to uncover them, in particular, if there are no non-related men around her or if she is in a group of women?

Response: As for the face, it is *sunnah* for her to uncover it during the prayer if there are no non-related men around her. As for the feet, it is obligatory upon her to cover them according to the majority of the scholars. Some scholars allow the feet to be uncovered but the majority say it is prohibited to uncover them and she must cover them. Abu Dawud recorded that Umm Salama was asked about a woman praying in a headcovering and long gown and she said, "There is no harm in that as long as the gown covers the top of her feet." So covering the feet is better and safest under all circumstances. As for the hands, their situation is simpler. If she uncovers them, there is no harm. If she covers them, there is no harm. Some scholars say it is better to cover them. And from Allah comes guidance to the correct path.

Shaikh ibn Baz

Ruling Concerning Praying While Wearing Gloves

Question 76: What is the ruling concerning praying while wearing gloves?

Response: There is no harm in a woman praying while wearing gloves since she has been ordered to cover herself in the prayer, except for her face when there are no non-related men around. Wearing gloves covers the hands. If, however, she covers the hands with her outer garments, that is sufficient. If non-related men are around then she must cover her face as well as the rest of the body. As for men, it is not sanctioned for them to cover their hands in the prayer, not with gloves or anything else. In fact, the *sunnah* is for them to directly touch with the skin of their hands and face the place of their prayer, in imitation of the Messenger of Allah (صلى الله عليه وسلم) and his Companions.

Shaikh ibn Baz

The Times in Which the Hands are Raised in Prayer

Question 77: To what level does one raise his hands in the prayer, opposite the shoulders or to the ears? Is this done repeatedly in the prayer or just in the first *rakah*?

Response: It is preferred to raise the hands opposite the shoulder or the ears when making the first *takbeer*, when bowing and when coming up from bowing. It is also done when standing from the first sitting during the Dhuhr, Asr, Maghrib and Isha prayers. These are all confirmed in the hadith of the Prophet (صلى الله عليه وسلم).

Shaikh ibn Baz

The Placing of the Hands During the Prayer

Question 78: Before and after bowing, where does one place his hands during the prayer?

Response: It is *sunnah* to put one's hands on the chest while standing in the prayer, both before the bowing and afterwards. It is confirmed in authentic hadith from Wail ibn Hujr who said, "I saw the Prophet (peace be upon him), when he was standing in the prayer, putting his right hand over the back of his left hand, wrist and forearm." This was recorded by Abu Dawud and al-Nasai with an authentic chain. Similarly, Imam Ahmad recorded with a good chain that the Prophet (peace be upon him) used to put his right hand over his left hand upon his chest while standing in the prayer. This is also what al-Bukhari recorded in the *Sahih* from Sahl ibn Saad, through Abu Haazim, who said, "The people were ordered to put their right hands over the left forearms in the prayer." Abu Haazim said, "I knew that the order was from the Prophet (صلى الله عليه وسلم)." This indicates that while standing in prayer, the person puts his right hand on his left. This is general for every standing, before the bowing and afterwards.

Shaikh ibn Baz

What is Placed Down First While Prostrating: The Knees or the Hands

Question 79: What is more proper, putting the hands down first on the ground or putting the knees down first while prostrating?

Response: The more proper way is to place the knees down, then the hands and then the face, based on the hadith of Wail and others with similar meaning.

Shaikh ibn Baz

Devilish Prompting and Confusion While in the Prayer

Question 80: I get confused a lot concerning how many *rakat*s I perform, even though I pray in a loud voice in order to remember what I have recited. However, I still get doubts. When I finish the prayer, I feel that I have missed a *rakah*, prostration or sitting, even though I try very hard not have doubts during my prayer. But still this is without benefit. I hope you will guide me to what will benefit me in such a case. Do I have to repeat the prayer when I have such confusion? Is there some supplication that I can make at the beginning of the prayer that will remove such confusion?

Response: You must fight against such devilish prompting and be cautious about them. You must increase your seeking of refuge in Allah from the accursed Satan. Allah has said,

﴿ قُلْ أَعُوذُ بِرَبِّ ٱلنَّاسِ ٥ مَلِكِ ٱلنَّاسِ ٥ إِلَٰهِ ٱلنَّاسِ ٥ مِن شَرِّ ٱلْوَسْوَاسِ ٱلْخَنَّاسِ ﴾ [النَّاس: ١-٤]

"Say: I seek refuge with [Allah] the Lord of Mankind, the King of Mankind, the God of Mankind, from the evil of the whisperer who withdraws from his whispering..." to the end of the *surah* (*surah al-Nass*).

Allah also says,

﴿ وَإِمَّا يَنزَغَنَّكَ مِنَ ٱلشَّيْطَٰنِ نَزْغٌ فَٱسْتَعِذْ بِٱللَّهِ إِنَّهُۥ سَمِيعٌ

عَلِيمٌ ﴾ [الأعراف : ٢٠٠]

"And if an evil whisper comes to you from Satan, then
seek refuge with Allah. Verily, He is All-Hearer, All-
Knower"(al-Araf 200).

If you have finished your prayer or ablution and then such
doubts come to your mind, then turn away from them and don't give
them any attention. Consider your prayer and ablution as proper and
sound.   If doubts come to you while you are praying, such as whether
you have prayed three or four *rakats*, then consider them as three and
finish your prayer, making two prostrations of forgetfulness before the
salutations at the end of the prayer. This is what the Prophet (صلى الله عليه
وسلم) ordered one who had similar doubts to do. We seek refuge in
Allah for ourselves and you from Satan.

Shaikh ibn Baz

Doorbell Rings While I am Praying

Question 81: If I am praying and somebody rings the
doorbell, and nobody is in the house except me, what shall I do?

Response: If the prayer is a voluntary prayer, the matter is
much easier as there is nothing from preventing you from stopping
your prayer and seeing who is at the door. However, if it is an
obligatory prayer, then you should not rush your prayer unless it is
something very important that you fear will be missed. If possible,
you may alert the person at the door that you are busy in prayer, by
saying *subhanallah* for men or clapping for women, that would be
sufficient. The Prophet (صلى الله عليه وسلم) said,

" مَنْ نَابَهُ شِيءٌ فِي صَلَاتِهِ فَلْيُسَبِّحِ الرِّجَالُ وَلْتُصَفِّقِ النِّسَاءُ "

"If anything happens to someone during the prayer, the men should say *subhanallah* and the women should clap."[1]

If you can make it clear to the one at the door that you are in prayer, by the man saying *subhanallah* and the woman clapping, then you should do that. However, if that will not help because the door is far away and the person will not hear you, then there is no harm in you breaking off the prayer, in particular if it is a voluntary prayer. If it is an obligatory prayer, you should only do that if it is expected that that is something very important. In that case, you may break off the prayer and then repeat it from its beginning afterwards. And all praises belong to Allah.

Shaikh ibn Baz

A Woman in Her House Does Not Pray Following the Imam

Question 82: My mother lives next to a congregational mosque. Between her and the mosque is a small street. She hears the *adhan* and the prayer and she continues to follow the Imam in her prayer in her house. Is that allowable for her? If it is not allowed, what should she do about the prayers that she performed in that manner over the years. I hope you can benefit us in this matter, may Allah reward you.

Response: If the situation is as you mentioned in the question, she cannot follow the Imam of the mosque in her prayer unless she sees the Imam or some of the rows of the followers. If she does not see any of them, then the strongest opinion among the statements of the scholars is that she does not follow the Imam in the prayer. As for what has passed of her prayers, she does not have to repeat them, Allah willing, because there is no clear evidence that they are invalid prayers. This question is an area of

---

[1] With the exact wording in the text, this was recorded by Abu Dawud. Al-Bukhari has something extremely close to it.—JZ

ijtehad [juristic reasoning] by the scholars. The safest and strongest opinion is as we have mentioned.

Shaikh ibn Baz

There is No Harm in Reading from a Copy of the Qur'an During the *Tahajjud* Prayer

Question 83: Is it allowed to read from a Quran during the late-night [tahajjud] prayer since I have memorized very little and I desire to finish the Quran during the late-night prayers?

Response: There is no harm in that. Dhakwan, the freed slave of Aisha, used to lead them in prayer during Ramadhan reading from a copy of the Quran. Al-Bukhari recorded that in his *Sahih* with a definitively-stated discontinuous chain. This is the opinion of a large number of scholars. Those who don't allow it have no evidence to support them. Not everyone has the Quran memorized and, therefore, there is a need to read it from a copy of the Quran in the prayer and otherwise. This is especially true for the late night prayers and during the night prayers of Ramadhan for those who have not memorized the Quran in their hearts.

Shaikh ibn Baz

Ruling Concerning Raising One's Hands During the Supplications of the *Witr* Prayer

Question 84: What is the ruling concerning raising one's hands during the *Witr* Prayer?

Response: It is legally sanctioned to raise one's hands during the supplications of the *Witr* Prayer. This is because it is similar to the supplications during times of affliction. It is confirmed that the Prophet (صلى الله عليه وسلم) used to raise his hands while supplicating during times of affliction. This was recorded by al-Baihaqi, may Allah have mercy on him, with an authentic chain.

Shaikh ibn Baz

Performed *Witr* During the First Part of the Night and then Got Up During the Latter Part...

Question 85: If I performed the *Witr* prayer during the first part of the night and then I woke up during the latter part of the night, how shall I pray?

Response: If you made *Witr* during the first part of the night and then Allah made it easy for you to get up in the later part of the night, then pray whatever Allah has made easy for you in sets of two without performing another *Witr*. This is because the Prophet (صلى الله عليه وسلم) said,

" لا وِترانِ في لَيلَة "

"There are not to be two *Witr*s in one night."[1]

Furthermore, Aisha reported that the Prophet (صلى الله عليه وسلم) used to pray two *rakat*s after *Witr*, while he was sitting. The wisdom behind that, Allah knows best, is to show the people that it is permissible to pray after the *Witr* prayer.

Shaikh ibn Baz

The Last Time for the *Witr* Prayer

Question 86: What is the latest time in which one may catch the *Witr* Prayer?

Response: It is the last portion of the night before dawn, since the Prophet (صلى الله عليه وسلم) said,

" صلاةُ اللَّيلِ مَثنى مَثنى.. فإذا خَشِيَ أحدُكُمُ الصُّبحَ صلّى ركعةً
واحدةً تُوتِرُ له ما قَد صَلّى "

---

[1] This hadith was recorded by Ahmad, Abu Dawud, al-Nasai and al-Tirmidhi. According to al-Albani, it is authentic. Al-Albani, *Sahih al-Jami*, vol. 2, p. 1256.

"The late-night prayer is two and then two. If one of you fears the coming of the morning, he should pray one *rakah*. That will make all that he prayed an odd number."

This hadith is agreed upon by al-Bukhari and Muslim.

Shaikh ibn Baz

Ruling of Woman Uncovering Her Hands and Feet During the Prayer

Question 87: What is the ruling concerning the uncovering of the hands and feet of the woman in the prayer, given that she is not in the presence of men but alone in her home?

Response: The well-known opinion among the Hanbalis is that a free adult woman should cover all of herself, except her face, for the prayer. Based on that, it is not allowed for her to uncover her hands and feet. Many of the scholars say that it is allowed for the woman to uncover her face and hands. What is safest is for the women to avoid all of that. However, assuming that she did uncover that and she comes to ask about it, a person should not be so bold as to ask her to repeat her prayers.

Shaikh ibn Uthaimin

Specifying the Last Third of the Night by Its Time

Question 88: I want to know about the last third of the night. What time of the watch is it?

Response: That cannot be specified by a specific time. But everyone may know it by dividing the night from sunset until dawn into three equal parts. After the first two parts, that is two-thirds of the night, pass, the third part is the last third of the night. It is confirmed in the *Sahihain* of al-Bukhari and Muslim from the Hadith of Abu Huraira [that the Prophet (صلى الله عليه وسلم) said],

" إِنَّ اللهَ عَزَّ وجَلَّ يَنْزِلُ كُلَّ لَيْلَةٍ إِلَى السَّمَاءِ الدُّنْيَا حِينَ يَبْقَى ثُلُثُ اللَّيْلِ الآخِرُ فيَقُولُ مَن يَدعُونِي فأَستَجِيبَ لَهُ، مَن يسأَلُنِي فأَعطِيَه مِن يَسْتَغْفِرُنِي فأَغْفِرَ لَهُ "

"Allah, the Glorified, descends every night to the lowest heaven when there remains a third of the night remaining. He then says, 'Who is calling on Me so I may respond to him? Who is asking of Me so I may give him? Who is seeking My forgiveness so I may forgive him?'"

The believer must take advantage of this time, even if just a small amount of that time, in order that he may attain that great bounty. He might catch one of the presents of his Lord as Allah responds to what he calls on Him for.

Shaikh ibn Uthaimin

Permissibility of a Woman Praying in the Marketplace

Question 89: Is it allowed to perform the prayer in the marketplace?

Response: A man must perform the obligatory prayers in the mosque in congregation. As for a woman, her house is best for her. If she needs to pray in a marketplace and there is a concealed place, there is no prohibition for that, Allah willing.

Shaikh ibn Uthaimin

Ruling of Prostration of Recitation

Question 90: If I recite a verse of prostration from the Quran, is it obligatory upon me to prostrate or not?

Response: Prostration of recitation is a stressed sunnah that one should not leave. If a person passes by a verse of prostration, he should prostrate regardless of whether he read that from a copy of the Quran, from his memory, during the prayer or outside of the prayer.

As for it being obligatory, it is not obligatory and there is no sin upon a person for not performing it. This is because it is confirmed that the Leader of the Believers, Umar ibn al-Khattab (رضي الله عنه), read a verse of prostration from *surah al-Nahl* while upon the *minbar* ("pulpit"). He got down and made prostration. Then he recited it on a following Friday and he did not prostrate. Then he said, "Allah did not oblige us to prostrate unless we wish to do so." This was in the presence of the Companions (رضي الله عنهم).[1]

It is also confirmed that Zaid ibn Thabit read a verse of prostration to the Prophet (صلى الله عليه وسلم) from *surah al-Najm* and he did not prostrate. If it were obligatory to do so, the Prophet (صلى الله عليه وسلم) would have ordered him to do it. Therefore, it is a stressed sunnah. It is best not to abandon it, even if it is during a time in which one is not allowed to pray, such as after *Fajr* or after *Asr*, for example. This is because that prostration has a specific reason for it and every prayer [or prostration] that has a specific reason for it may be performed even during such times of prohibition, such as prostration of recitation or prayers of greeting the mosque and so forth.

Shaikh ibn Uthaimin

If A Woman Cannot Pray Standing, Can She Sit?

Question 91: There is a lady who is injured with a bad back. She has a cast on. She cannot pray standing, as is normally done. So she has prayed sitting for a month. She bows simply by motioning. Is her prayer valid or not?

Response: Yes, her prayer is proper because she has not the ability to stand. To stand is obligatory in the mandatory prayers if one has the ability to do so. If she cannot stand due to an injured back, she prays sitting. If she can stand while leaning

---

[1] It seems that this sentence should be completed by saying, "And none of them objected to that, meaning they were in agreement with it."—JZ

on a stick or wall, then she can pray standing. Therefore, the prayers of that woman during the past month are sound because she does not have the ability to stand. This is based on the hadith in which the Prophet (صلى الله عليه وسلم) said to Imran ibn Husain,

" صَلِّ قَائِماً فَإِن لَم تَسْتَطِعْ فَقَاعِداً فَإِن لَم تستَطِعْ فَعَلَى جَنْبٍ "

"Pray standing. If you cannot do so, then [pray] sitting. If you cannot [do that either], then [pray] while on your side."[1]

Shaikh ibn Uthaimin

Delaying the Prayer Due to Sleep

Question 92: I am a young lady. Many times I miss the Maghrib prayer due to sleep and then make it up in the morning or at some late time. What is the ruling concerning that?

Response: The ruling is that it is not allowed for anyone to be lackadaisical when it comes to prayer until the time is missed. If a person is sleeping, he may entrust someone to wake him up so he may pray. Indeed, he must do so. One may not delay the Maghrib or Isha prayers until the morning. It is obligatory to pray the prayer in its time. Therefore, this young lady should encourage her family to wake her up. If, hypothetically speaking, one faces a difficult situation or need, such as he is extremely tired and sleepy and has just prayed Maghrib and fears that if he does not pray the Isha prayer he will be overcome with sleep and will not pray it until the morning, then, in that case, there is no harm in combining the Isha Prayer with the Maghrib Prayer in order to not miss the Isha Prayer in its time. This is not to be done unless such a situation arises, such as if a person had been up for many days straight or is just recovering from an illness.

Shaikh ibn Uthaimin

---

[1] Recorded by al-Bukhari.—JZ

Doubt During the Prayer

Question 93: Sometimes in the prayer I forget if I had recited *Surah al-Fatiha* or not. Therefore, I recite it a second time. Is this action proper? Should I then perform the prostration of forgetfulness?

Response: Many people get numerous devilish whisperings during the prayer. This causes them to doubt if they had recited [*al-Fatiha*] or made the *tashahud* [and so forth]. The cure for that is to make sure that one really gets attuned to the prayer and the heart is fully conscious during it, fearing mistakes or devilish prompting. If that happens a lot and one usually recites *al-Fatiha*, then it is disliked to recite it again. However, if one does repeat *al-Fatiha* just to make certain and be on the safe side, then he does not have to make the prostration of forgetfulness.

Shaikh ibn Jibreen

Delaying the *Isha* Prayer

Question 94: What is the ruling concerning delaying the *Isha* Prayer to a late time?

Response: The best act with respect to the *Isha* Prayer is to delay it until its last time. Whatever amount it is delayed is better. This is true except in the case of men. If a man is going to delay the *Isha* Prayer and by so doing is going to miss performing it in congregation, then it is not allowed for him to delay it and miss the congregation. As for women in their homes, the more they delay the *Isha* Prayer, the better for them. However, they cannot delay it beyond half of the night.

Shaikh ibn Uthaimin

Repentance Wipes Out What Occurred Before It

Question 95: I am a young lady of 25 years old. However, from the time I was young until the time I was 21 years old, I did not fast or pray simply out of laziness. My father and mother advised me but to no avail. What should I now do given that Allah has now guided me and I do fast and pray and I feel remorse for what I did in the past?

Response: Repentance obliviates or wipes away whatever preceded it. You must have remorse, resolve not to do such again and have sincerity in your acts of worship. You should also increase your voluntary prayers during the night and day as well as perform voluntary fasts, remembrance of Allah, reciting of the Quran and supplications. Allah accepts the repentance of His servants and overlooks their sins.

Shaikh ibn Jibreen

Ruling of Women Praying Behind the Men in the "Prayer for Rain"

Question 96: Is it proper for women to pray behind the men in the prayer for rain (*salat al-istisqa*)?

Response: Yes. It is allowed for women to attend the prayer for rain but they must be behind the men. The farther they are from the men the better. This is because the Prophet (صلى الله عليه وسلم) said,

" خَيْرُ صُفُوفِ النِّسَاءِ آخِرُهَا وشَرُّهَا أَوَّلُها "

"The best rows for women are the last rows and the worst are the front rows."[1]

It is also confirmed that the Prophet (صلى الله عليه وسلم) ordered the women to go to attend the good deeds and the supplications of the Muslims at the *Eid* prayer. If the women go out to the location of the Prayer for Rain to attend the supplication of the Muslims and to catch some of the good deeds therein, there is no harm in that but they must not go out exposing their beauty.

There is another matter that must be pointed out. This is that sometimes when the women go to pray in the mosque with the

---

[1] Recorded by Muslim.—JZ

congregation, some of them pray behind the rows by themselves alone. This goes against the *sunnah*, as the Prophet (صلى الله عليه وسلم) said,

" خَيْرُ صُفُوفِ النِّسَاءِ آخِرُهَا "

"The best rows for women are..."
This shows that the women pray in rows. Furthermore, the Prophet (صلى الله عليه وسلم) said,

" لاَ صَلاَةَ لِمُنْفَرِدٍ خَلْفَ الصَّفِّ "

"There is no prayer for the one by himself behind the rows."[1]

Shaikh ibn Uthaimin

The Ruling Concerning Delaying the Prayer

Question 97: What is the ruling concerning a person who prays the Fajr Prayer two hours, for example, before Dhuhr, given that he was sleeping the entire time before that?

Response: It is not allowed to delay a prayer beyond its proper time except for an excuse. Sleep is not necessarily an excuse for everyone. One could possibly sleep early and therefore

---

[1] This hadith was recorded by ibn Khuzaima. Ibn Hibban has almost exactly the same thing (less one letter). In *Fath al-Bari* (vol. 2, p. 450), ibn Hajr mentions that this hadith is recorded by ibn Hibban and that there is some doubt about this hadith, which, he says, he will discuss in a later section. However, in that later section (vol. 2, p. 520), he simply mentions that it is recorded by ibn Khuzaima without mentioning that there is any problem with the hadith. Hence, it is not possible to determine why ibn Hajr questioned this hadith. In any case, both al-Albani (in his footnotes to al-Adhami's edition of *Sahih ibn Khuzaima*) and al-Arnaut (in his footnotes to *Sahih ibn Hibban*) state that the chain of the hadith is authentic. See Ahmad ibn Hajr, *Fath al-Bari bi-Sharh Sahih al-Bukhari* (Makkah: al-Maktaba al-Tijariyya, 1993), vol. 2, pp. 450 and 520; Al-Ameer Ala al-Din al-Farisi, *Al-Ihsan fi Taqrib Sahih ibn Hibban*, Shuaib al-Arnaut, ed. (Beirut: Muassassat al-Risalah, 1988), vol. 5, p. 580; Abu Bakr ibn Khuzaima, *Sahih ibn Khuzaima*, Muhammad Mustafa al-Adhami, ed. (Beirut: al-Maktab al-Islami, 1975), vol. 3, p. 30.

wake up for the time of prayer. Similarly, one could assign one of his parents, brethren, neighbors or so forth to wake him up. In addition, one must be concerned with the prayer and have one's heart attuned to it so that when its time approaches one perceives it, even if one is sleeping. So the heart of the person who always does not pray Fajr except in the late morning is a heart which has the least bit of concern about the prayer. In any case, the person is ordered to perform the prayer in the best manner that he is capable of. If he was asleep, he must perform it as soon as he gets up. The same kind of ruling applies to the one who forgot the prayer as well as the negligent.

Shaikh ibn Jibreen

The Most and Least Number of the Statements in the Bowing and Prostration

Question 98: What is the most and the least that one can say, "*Subhanallah*" in the bowing and prostrations?

Response: The statement in the bowing is, "*Subhana Rabbiy al-'Adheem* (Glory be to my Lord, the Great)" and in the prostration it is, "*Subhana Rabbiy al-'Ala* (Glory be to my Lord, the Most High)." The least amount which is still considered complete is to say it three times. The most for the Imam is to say it eleven times. It is also recommended to praise Allah afterwards in the bowing and to make supplications in the prostration.

Shaikh ibn Jibreen

Devilish Whispers During the Prayer

Question 99: I am a woman who performs what Allah has obligated on me concerning the ritual acts of worship. However, while in prayer, I often forget what I have prayed. I also think about what has occurred to me during that day. I do not think of those things except when I begin the prayer and I cannot seem to free myself from these thoughts unless I recite aloud. What do you advise me to do?

Response: This matter that you complain about is something that many of those who pray also complain about. This is where Satan has the door of whispering open to him during the prayer. Perhaps the person finishes without knowing what he has said in his prayer. However, the Prophet (صلى الله عليه وسلم) has guided us to the cure for that. The person should blow out on his left side three times and say, "I seek refuge in Allah from the accursed Satan." If the person does that, his problem will come to an end, Allah willing. When the person enters the prayer, he must firmly believe that he is standing in front of Allah. He is in private conversation with Allah. He should get closer to Allah by his stating *Allahu akbar*, his glorification of Allah, and his reciting of Allah's word. Also, he should get closer to Allah by means of the places of supplication in the prayer If a person has this feeling and consciousness in him, he will approach his Lord with humility and submission to Him. He will love what Allah has of good and fear from His punishment if he fails in what Allah has obliged him to do.

Shaikh ibn Uthaimin

The One Who Sleeps Through the Time of Prayer

Question 100: When should the *Isha* Prayer be made up when someone slept through it and did not remember it until after the *Fajr* Prayer? Should he pray it at its next appointed time or when he remembers it?

Response: It is recorded in an authentic Hadith that the Prophet (صلى الله عليه وسلم) said,

"مَنْ نَامَ عَنْ صَلاَةٍ أَو نَسِيَها فَلْيُصَلِّها إِذَا ذَكَرَهَا لاَ كَفَّارَةَ لَهَا إِلا ذَلِكَ"

"Whoever sleeps through a prayer or forgets it should pray it when he remembers it and there is no expiation for it but that."

And then the Prophet (صلى الله عليه وسلم) recited the Quranic verse,

﴿ وَأَقِمِ ٱلصَّلَوٰةَ لِذِكۡرِىٓ ﴾ [طه : ١٤]

"Establish the prayer for My remembrance" (*Taha* 14).

(This was recorded by al-Bukhari, number 597, and by Muslim, p. 477, as well as by others, from Anas, may Allah be pleased with him.)

Based on this Hadith, there is no difference between the *Isha* Prayer or other prayers. When the person wakes up, even though its time is finished, he must pray it at that time and cannot delay it until the similar prayer time comes again. He prays it whenever it comes to his mind, even if it is during one of the times in which it is prohibited to pray or even if it is during the time of another prayer. However, if he fears that the time for the present prayer will be missed, he prays the present prayer first and then prays the prayer that he had missed afterwards. And Allah knows best.

Shaikh ibn Jibreen

If a Barrier or Wall is Placed Between the Men and Women, Which Row of the Prayer is then the Best for the Women?

Question 101: If there is some sort of covering or wall between the men and women in the mosque, does the Hadith of the Prophet (صلى الله عليه وسلم) still apply, "The best rows for the men are the first rows and the worst rows are the last rows. And the best rows for the women are the last rows and the worst rows are the front rows," or does this Hadith no longer apply and the best rows for the women become the front rows? Benefit us, may Allah benefit you!

Response: It is apparent that the reason the best rows for the women are the last rows is because they are further away from the men. The further a woman is from the men, the better and more chaste that is for her person and honor. It also keeps her further away from being enticed to do evil. However, if the place of prayer for the women is far from the men and is separated by a wall or barrier, and they rely upon a microphone to follow the Imam, then, in that case, the strongest view is that the best rows for the women are the front rows since they are in front and closer to the *qibla* and so forth.

Shaikh ibn Jibreen

The *Iqama* for Women

Question 102: When the women gather to perform the prayer, do they make the *iqama* for the prayer?

Response: If they make the *iqama*, there is no harm in that. If they do not do so, there is no harm in that either. This is because the *adhan* and *iqama* are only obligatory upon the men.

Shaikh ibn Uthaimin

The "Prayer of Need" and "Prayer for Memorizing the Quran" are Unfounded and Do Not Form Part of the *Shariah*

Question 103: I have heard about the "Prayer of Need" (*Salat al-Haajah*) and the "Prayer for Memorizing the Quran". Are these actual prayers or not?

Response: Both of them are not correct. There is no such thing as "Prayer of Need" or "Prayer for Memorizing the Quran." This is because these kinds of acts of worship can only be confirmed through legal evidences. Neither of these have any evidences for them that can be considered proofs and acceptable in Islamic Law. Therefore, they are not sanctioned by Islamic law.

Shaikh ibn Uthaimin

Interrupting One's Prayer

Question 104: If I forgot and prayed in clothes that contained some impurity and then, during the prayer, I remembered it, is it allowed for me to discontinue my prayer and pray again? What are the cases in which one can discontinue his prayer?

Response: If someone prayed and had some impurity on his person or body, and he was knowledgeable of that, then his prayer is invalid. If he was not aware of that until after he finished his prayer, then his prayer suffices and it is not necessary for him to repeat it. If he discovers it while praying and he can easily remove the impurity, then he should do so and continue to complete his prayer. It is confirmed that the Prophet (صلى الله عليه وسلم) removed his shoes once in the prayer when the Angel Gabriel informed him that it contained some harmful matter. This did not invalidate the beginning of his prayer. Therefore, if the impurity is on one's headdress, he simply removes the headdress quickly and continues his prayer.[1] However, if the removal requires a great deal of movements, such as when removing one's shirt, pants and so forth, then after removing it, one will have to rebegin his prayer. The same is the case if one breaks off the prayer because he remembered that he had invalidated his ablution or if he does so in the prayer or if he invalidates the prayer by laughing and so forth.

Shaikh ibn Jibreen

Labor Pains and Prayer

Question 105: Is it allowed for me to pray while I feel labor pains?

Response: The woman prays whenever she is free of menstruation and post-partum bleeding. However, if you see blood a day or two before giving birth, that blood is considered post-partum bleeding. Therefore, you do not pray. On the other

---

[1] Obviously, the reference to removing the headdress is respect to men only since that is not part of the *aurah* that they must keep covered.—JZ

hand, if you do not see any blood, then you continue praying even if you are having labor pains, in the same way that an ill person prays while feeling the pangs of his illness. He still has to pray as long as he is conscious.

Shaikh ibn Jibreen

The *Witr* Prayer and the Late-Night (*Tahajjud*) Prayer

Question 106: I am a woman who when I go to bed I am very tired. Is it all right for me to pray the *Witr* Prayer before I sleep because I get up at the time of the *Fajr* Prayer? Will that be considered late-night prayer for me?

Response: If it is your custom not to get up until the time of the *adhan* for Fajr, then it is best for you to pray the prayers you want to pray before you go to bed. This is based on the Prophet's advise to Abu Huraira that he should perform the *Witr* Prayer before he slept. You pray whatever Allah has recorded [destined] for you to pray and then perform the *Witr* Prayer before you sleep and sleep after having performed *Witr.* If you have the ability to get up before the *adhan* of *Fajr* and you wish to pray, then there is no harm if you pray two *rakat*s, then two *rakat*s, without repeating the *Witr* Prayer.

Shaikh ibn Uthaimin

Complete What You Had Forgotten of the Prayer if it was Relatively Recent

Question 107: I prayed the *Dhuhr* Prayer. Afterwards, I recalled that I had only prayed three *rakat*s. Shall I pray the fourth and then make the prostrations of forgetfulness or shall I completely repeat my prayer?

Response: If the worshipper forgot a *rakah* or more of a prayer and then remembered it when he is in the place of the prayer or in the mosque, after a short period, like five minutes or so, then he completes the prayer. He performs what he missed, then he makes the greetings, then he prostrates the prostrations of forgetfulness and then he makes the salutations again. If he does not recall that except after a lengthy period of time, such as half an hour or after he has left the mosque and it became a long time, then he completely re-performs the prayer and he discounts the first one because the acts of the prayer were not done in consecutive, one-after-the-other fashion.

Shaikh ibn Jibreen

Women Going Out to the *Eid* Prayer

Question 108: Is it allowed for a woman to go out to the *Eid* Prayer?

Response: Yes, it is sanctioned for them to go out to the two *Eid* Prayers and this is stressed for women. It is recorded in the two *Sahihs* from Umm Atiya who said, "We were ordered to go out on the Day of Eid, even including the young virgin in her house and the menstruating woman. They would make the *takbeer* with the others and supplicate with them and hope for the blessings of that day." Another narration states that the Messenger of Allah (صلى الله عليه وسلم) used to tell the virgins, young women secluded in their houses and menstruating women to go to the *Eid* Prayer. But the menstruating women would remain away from the place of prayer and would join in the good deeds and supplications of the Muslims. Umm Atiya stated that a woman asked the Prophet (صلى الله عليه وسلم), "But one of us may not have a *jilbab*[1]!" The Prophet (صلى الله عليه وسلم) told her,

$$\text{" لِتُلْبِسْهَا أُخْتُهَا مِنْ جِلْبَابِهَا "}$$

---

[1] The *jilbab* is the outer garment or cloak that covers the woman from the top of her head to her feet. This is what the Muslim woman is commanded to wear in *surah al-Ahzab*. The hadith above is further evidence that they would not leave their houses unless they were so attired.—JZ

"Her sister may clothe her from her *jilbab*."

The woman, though, must go out without perfume and without displaying her beauty. Furthermore, she must remain away from mixing with the men.

Shaikh ibn Jibreen

The Prostration of Recitation is Permissible Under Any Conditions

Question 109: Is it true that a disbeliever cannot afflict a Muslim with the Evil Eye? What is the evidence for that? When I am reading a verse of prostration from the Quran, can I prostrate in whatever condition I am in even without covering my head or body?

Response: It is not true. In fact, a disbeliever like any other may afflict with the Evil Eye for the Evil Eye is factual.

There is no harm in making the prostration in whatever condition you are in, even if your head is uncovered and so forth. This is because the strongest opinion is that such a prostration does not have the same rulings as the prayer.

Shaikh ibn Jibreen

It is Not Necessary for Him to Make Up the Prayers He Missed

Question 110: Previously, I used not to perform the prayers. Allah blessed me with guidance. I became very keen on performing them. My question is about the prayers in all of those previous years that I missed. Is it obligatory upon me to make them up or not?

Response: When a person abandons the prayer for a number of years and then repents and performs them regularly, it is not necessary for him to make up the prayers that he missed. If that were a condition, it would make many people flee from repentance itself. However, the repenting person is to perform the prayers regularly in the future and to increase his voluntary prayers, acts of obedience, good deeds, getting closer to Allah and his fear of Allah.

Shaikh ibn Jibreen

The Ruling Concerning Uncovering the Head while Praying or Reading the Quran

Question 111: What is the ruling concerning a Muslim woman who reads the Quran, prays and fasts but she does not cover her head?

Response: It is not a condition for the reciting of the Quran that one have her head covered. As for the prayer, the prayer is not valid unless the "private area" is covered, which for the prayer of the adult, free woman implies everything but her face. She is not required to cover her face during the prayer unless there are non-related men around her. She must then cover her face from them, as it is not allowed for a woman to uncover her face except to her husband and her male relatives [within the prohibited degrees of marriage] i.e., mahram.

Shaikh ibn Uthaimin

Labor Pains Are Expiation of Sins

Question 112: My wife used to pray regularly until her first child. After that she became quite lazy, claiming that a woman's sins are all forgiven due to the pain she faces during labor. What do you say to her?

Response: This is not true. If the woman, like other humans, faces some hardship and she is patient and hopes for reward for that, she will be rewarded due to that pain and affliction. In fact, the Prophet (صلى الله عليه وسلم) gave examples of much lesser types of pain which expiate sins, such as being pricked by a thorn. Know that if a person has patience and expects reward from Allah for anything that has afflicted him, he will be rewarded according to what he has of patience and expectations. The essence of affliction is the removal of his sins. The one who is afflicted has his sins removed under any circumstance. Furthermore, if this is accompanied with patience, the person will also be rewarded for his patience with his affliction. When a woman gives birth, there is no doubt that she suffers a lot of pain and hardship. That pain removes some of her sins from her. If she is also patient and expecting reward from Allah, then, in addition to having sins removed, she will also be rewarded and have good deeds recorded for her.

Shaikh ibn Uthaimin

"The Imam of the People is the One Best in Quran" Does Not Apply Between Women and Men

Question 113: Is it allowed for me to lead my husband in prayer since I am more knowledgeable and educated than him, since I study in the College of *Shariah* and he is semi-illiterate?

Response: It is not allowed for a woman to lead men in prayer, regardless if he is her husband, son or brother. This is because such is not a possibility due to the Prophet's statement,

" لَنْ يُفْلِحَ قَوماً وَلَّوا أَمْرَهُمُ آمْرَأَةً "

"A people whose affairs are in the hands of a woman will not prosper."[1]

Even if she is more knowledgeable of the Quran, she does not lead him in prayer. The Prophet's statement,

---

[1] Recorded by al-Bukhari.—JZ

" يَؤُمُّ القَومَ أَقرَؤُهُم لِكِتَابِ اللهِ "

"The Imam of a people is the most knowledgeable of the Book of Allah"[1]

does not include women among its addressees in the presence of men. Allah has said,

﴿ يَٰٓأَيُّهَا ٱلَّذِينَ ءَامَنُواْ لَا يَسۡخَرۡ قَوۡمٞ مِّن قَوۡمٍ عَسَىٰٓ أَن يَكُونُواْ خَيۡرٗا مِّنۡهُمۡ وَلَا نِسَآءٞ مِّن نِّسَآءٍ عَسَىٰٓ أَن يَكُنَّ خَيۡرٗا مِّنۡهُنَّۖ ﴾   [الحجرات: ١١]

"O you who believe! Let not a group [of men] scoff at another group, it may be that the latter are better than the former; nor let some women scoff at other women, it may be that the latter are better than the former" (al-Hujurat 11).

Allah has divided society into two parts, men and women. Based on that, women are not included in the generality of the Prophet's statement,

" يَؤُمُّ القَومَ أَقرَؤُهُم لِكِتَابِ اللهِ "

"The Imam of a people is the most knowledgeable of the Book of Allah"[2]

Shaikh ibn Uthaimin

Wearing Forbidden Clothing Could Invalidate One's Prayer

Question 114: A woman uses a particular clothing for prayer and it is clothing for men. Is her prayer permissible? Is this considered part of imitating men?

Response: If the clothing is something particular for men, then it is forbidden for her to wear it regardless of whether she is praying or is outside of the prayer. This is because it is confirmed

---

[1] Recorded by Muslim.— JZ
[2] Recorded by Muslim.— JZ

from the Prophet (صلى الله عليه وسلم) that he cursed those women who imitate and appear like men as well as those men who imitate and appear like women. It is not allowed for a woman to wear clothing that are particular for men and it is not allowed for men to wear clothing that are particular for women.

However, we must understand the concept of "particularity". Particularity is not with respect to color but it is with respect to color and description. It is, then, permissible for women to wear white clothing as long as it is not the same as the white clothing of men. If it is clear, though, that woman wearing men's clothing is forbidden, then her prayer in such clothing is not valid according to those scholars who say that the covering in the prayer must be a covering which is permissible.

This is a question in which there is a difference of opinion among the scholars. Some scholars say that it is a condition that the covering or clothing be clothing that is in itself permissible. Some do not lay down such a condition. The proof for those who lay down such a condition is that the covering of the *aurah* [what must be covered] in the prayer is one of the conditions for the prayer and the covering must be something that Allah has permitted. If it is something that Allah has not permitted, then it is not considered a legal covering since it goes against what is commanded. The proof of those who say that the prayer is still valid while the person is committing a sin is that the woman has actually covered herself and the sinful aspect is something that is external and is not particularly related to the prayer. In any case, the person who prays in forbidden clothing is in a dangerous situation since her prayer may be rejected and not accepted from her.

Shaikh ibn Uthaimin

6.Questions Related to Funerals

There is No Harm in the Husband Washing His Wife's Body

Question 115: I have often heard from the general public that when a wife dies, it is no longer permissible for her husband to look at her or to place her in the grave. Is this correct? Please respond, may Allah bless you.

Response: The *Shariah* evidences indicate that there is no harm in the husband washing his wife or for him to look at her. There is also no harm in her washing him or looking at him. In fact, Asma bint Umais washed her husband's body, Abu Bakr al-Sideeq. And Fatima willed that she be washed by her husband Ali.

Shaikh ibn Baz

The Funeral Prayer is Not Just For Men

Question 116: It is noted that women do not attend the Funeral Prayer. The question to the noted shaikh is whether or not such an act is forbidden by the *Shariah*?

Response: The Funeral Prayer is sanctioned for both men and women since the Prophet (صلى الله عليه وسلم) said,

"مَنْ صَلَّى عَلَىَ الْجَنَازَةِ فَلَهِ قِيراطٌ وَمَنْ تَبِعَهَا حَتَّى تُدْفَنَ فَلَهُ قِيرَاطَانِ. قِيلَ يَارَسُولَ اللهِ وَمَا الْقِيرَاطَانِ. قَالَ: مِثْلُ جَبَلَيْنِ عَظِيمَيْنِ يَعْنِي مِنَ الأَجْرِ"

"Whoever performs the funeral prayer shall receive a *qirat* [from Allah as reward]. And whoever follows the funeral procession until the burial shall receive two *qirats*." It was said, "O Messenger of Allah (صلى الله عليه وسلم), what are two *qirats*?" He said, "They are like two great mountains of rewards."

This was recorded by al-Bukhari and Muslim.

However, women are not to follow the funeral procession to the grave, as they have been prohibited from doing so. It is recorded in the *Sahihain* of al-Bukhari and Muslim that Umm Atiya said, "We were forbidden from following the funeral procession but such was not stressed upon us." However, as for the funeral prayer, such has not been forbidden for women, regardless of whether it is held in the mosque, a house or the prayer grounds. The women used to perform the funeral prayer in the Prophet's mosque, with the Prophet (صلى الله عليه وسلم) and after his death.

As for visiting the grave, this is something specific for men only, like following the funeral procession to the grave. This is because the Messenger (صلى الله عليه وسلم) cursed the women who visit graves.[1] The wisdom behind that— and Allah knows best— is that it is feared that if they are allowed to follow the funeral procession to the grave, it may become a trial for themselves and for others. This is because the Prophet (صلى الله عليه وسلم) said,

" مَا تَرَكْتُ بَعْدِيْ فِتْنَةً أَضَرَّ عَلَى الرِّجَالِ مِنَ النِّسَآءِ "

"I have not left anything after me that is a more harmful trial for men than women."

Recorded by al-Bukhari and Muslim.

Shaikh ibn Baz

Ruling Concerning Post-Burial Gathering

Question 117: What is the ruling concerning what is known as *al-ma`tim*, in which people gather for three days after the burial in order to recite the Quran?

Response: The gathering in the house of the deceased to eat, drink and recite the Quran is an innovation. Similarly, their getting together to pray for the person and make supplications for

---

[1] The referred to hadith was discussed in detail in an earlier footnote.—JZ

him are also innovations. There is no source for it. All that should be done is that people come to pay condolences, pray for the person, ask for mercy for them, console their grieving and encourage them to be patient. To gather for what they call *al-ma`tim*, to make particular supplications, particular prayers or reading of the Quran has no basis whatsoever. If that were a good act, our pious predecessors would have done it. The Messenger of Allah (صلى الله عليه وسلم) did not do it. When Jafar ibn Abu Talib, Abdullah ibn Rawaaha and Zaid ibn Haaritha were killed at the Battle of Mu`tah and the Prophet (صلى الله عليه وسلم) received that news through revelation, the Prophet (صلى الله عليه وسلم) announced that to the Companions and told them their news. He supplicated for them and asked Allah to be pleased with them. He did not make a gathering. He did not prepare a meal or have a *ma`tim*. All of that he did not do even though the three who died were from the most virtuous of the Companions. When Abu Bakr died, also, no one made a *ma`tim*, even though he was the best of the Companions. When Umar was killed, no one made a *ma`tim*. The people did not gather to pray or read the Quran for him. Uthman and Ali were killed and the people did not gather after a specific time to pray for them, ask mercy for them or prepare food for them. It is, however, recommended for the relatives or neighbors of the deceased to prepare food for the deceased's family and to send that food to them. This is similar to what the Prophet (صلى الله عليه وسلم) did when the news of Jafar's death came to him. He said to his family,

" اصْنَعُوا لِآلِ جَعْفَرَ طَعَاماً فَقَدْ جَاءَهُمْ مَا يُشْغِلُهُمْ "

"Prepare food for the family of Jafar as something has occurred to them that is preoccupying them."[1]

The family of the deceased are preoccupied with their loss. To prepare food for them and send it to them is what is legally sanctioned. However, to add to their affliction and to put more

---

[1] Recorded by al-Tirmidhi, Abu Dawud and ibn Majah. According to al-Albani, it is *hasan*. Al-Albani, *Sahih al-Jami*, vol. 1, p. 234.—JZ

responsibilities on their shoulders by making them prepare food for the people goes completely against the sunnah. In fact, it is an innovation. Jarir ibn Abdullah al-Bajali said, "We used to consider gathering with the family of the deceased and preparing food after the burial as a kind of lamentation." And lamentation is forbidden. This is to raise one's voice, while the deceased is punished in the grave due to the wailing over him. One must avoid such practices. However, there is no harm in crying with tears.

Shaikh ibn Baz

There is No Particular Day for the Paying of Condolences

Question 118: Is specifying three days for the paying of condolences considered an innovation? Is there paying of condolences for young children, elderly women and ill people from whom one does not expect intercession after their death?

Response: Giving condolences is *sunnah* as it strengthens the one afflicted and contains supplications for what is better for them. There is no difference in this matter between the deceased being young or old. Furthermore, there is no specific expression that one should use. Instead, the Muslim consoles his brother with whatever expression seems suitable at that time, such as saying, "May Allah make your grief easier and forgive your deceased." This is if the deceased were a Muslim. If the deceased were a disbeliever, then supplications should not be made for him. One only consoles for his Muslim relatives with the words above.

There is no specific time for it, nor any specific days. It is legally sanctioned from the time of death, before Funeral Prayer or afterwards, as well as before the burial or afterwards. It is best to do it soon after the death when the affliction is still strong. However, it is permissible after three days of the death since there is no evidence to restrict it [to the first three days only].

Shaikh ibn Baz

Wailing Over the Dead

Question 119: Is it allowed to cry for someone after they die? If the crying includes wailing, slapping the cheeks and tearing the clothes, is the deceased affected by it?

Response: Neither lamenting nor wailing is allowed. Tearing clothing, slapping one's cheeks and similar deeds are also not allowed. It is confirmed in the *Sahihs* of al-Bukhari and Muslim from ibn Masud that the Prophet (صلى الله عليه وسلم) said,

" لَيْسَ مِنَّا مَنْ لَطَمَ الْخُدُودَ وشَقَّ الْجُيُوبَ ودَعَا بِدَعْوَى الْجَاهِلِيَّةِ "

"Not from us is the one who slaps the cheeks, tears the front opening of the shirt or makes the calls of the Days of Ignorance."

It is also confirmed that the Prophet (صلى الله عليه وسلم) cursed the wailer and its audience.[1]

It is also authentically reported that the Prophet (صلى الله عليه وسلم) said,

" إن الْمَيِّتَ يُعَذَّبُ في قَبْرِهِ بِمَا يُنَاحَ عَلَيهِ "

"The deceased is punished in his grave due to the wailing over him"

In another narration, it states,

" إن الْمَيِّتَ يُعَذَّبُ بِبُكَاءِ أَهْلِهِ عَلَيهِ "

"The deceased is punished due to the crying of the family over him."[2]

The Standing Committee

---

[1] Recorded by Abu Dawud and Ahmad. According to al-Albani, the chain of this narration is weak. Muhammad Nasir al-Din al-Albani, *Dhaeef Sunan Abu Dawud* (Beirut: al-Maktab al-Islami, 1991), p. 317.—JZ

[2] Recorded by al-Bukhari and Muslim.— JZ

Ruling Concerning Slapping One's Cheeks and Tearing One's Clothing During Times of Affliction

Question 120: What is the Islamic ruling concerning women slapping their cheeks when somebody dies?

Response: Slapping the cheek, tearing the front part of the clothing and wailing at the time of affliction are all forbidden and not permissible. The Prophet (صلى الله عليه وسلم) said,

$$\text{"لَيْسَ مِنَّا مَنْ ضَرَبَ الخُدُودَ وشَقَّ الجُيُوبَ وَدَعَا بِدَعْوَى الجَاهِلِيَّةِ"}$$

"Not from us is one who slaps the cheeks, tears the front opening of the shirt or makes the calls of the Days of Ignorance."

This was recorded by al-Bukhari and Muslim. The Prophet (صلى الله عليه وسلم) also said,

$$\text{" أَنَا بَرِيءٌ مِنَ الصَّالِقَةِ والحَالِقَةِ والشَّاقَّةِ "}$$

"I have nothing to do with the wailer, the one who shaves her head and the one who tears her clothing [at the time of an affliction]."

This was also recorded by al-Bukhari and Muslim. The wailer is the one who raises her voice at the time of an affliction. The *haliqah* is the one who shaves her hair off of her head at the time of an affliction. And *al-shaaqah* is the one who tears the front opening of her garment. The Prophet (صلى الله عليه وسلم) also said,

$$\text{"أَرْبَعٌ فِي أُمَّتِي مِنْ أَمْرِ الجَاهِلِيَّةِ لَا يَتْرُكُونَهُنَّ، الفَخْرُ بالأَحْسَابِ،}$$
$$\text{والطَّعْنُ فِي الأَنْسَابِ، والاسْتِسْقَاءُ بالنُّجُومِ، وَالنِّيَاحَةُ عَلَى المَيِّتِ"}$$

"Four matters among my Nation are from the Days of Ignorance the people will not abandon: boasting about high rank, reviling other peoples' lineage, seeking rain by invoking the stars and wailing." Then he said, "If the wailer does not repent before her death, she will be resurrected on the Day of Resurrection wearing a garment of pitch and a chemise of mange."

This was recorded by Muslim in his *Sahih*.

It is obligatory to have patience and hope for reward at times of affliction. One must avoid those above mentioned evil acts and repent to Allah for what was done in the past. Allah has said,

$$﴿ وَبَشِّرِ ٱلصَّٰبِرِينَ ۝ ٱلَّذِينَ إِذَآ أَصَٰبَتۡهُم مُّصِيبَةٌ قَالُوٓاْ إِنَّا لِلَّهِ وَإِنَّآ إِلَيۡهِ رَٰجِعُونَ ﴾ [البقرة: ١٥٥-١٥٦]$$

"But give glad tidings to the patient who, when afflicted with calamity, say, 'Truly! To Allah we belong and, truly, to Him we shall return'" (*al-Baqara* 155-156).

Allah has promised them a great deal of good:

$$﴿ أُوْلَٰٓئِكَ عَلَيۡهِمۡ صَلَوَٰتٌ مِّن رَّبِّهِمۡ وَرَحۡمَةٌ وَأُوْلَٰٓئِكَ هُمُ ٱلۡمُهۡتَدُونَ ﴾ [البقرة: ١٥٧]$$

"They are those on whom are blessings from their Lord, and (who) receive His mercy, and it is they who are the guided" (*al-Baqara* 157).

Shaikh ibn Baz

7. Questions Related to Zakat

Zakat on Jewelry is an Obligation

Question 121: Is Zakat obligatory upon the gold that a woman purchases for the purpose of beautification and wearing and not for the purpose of trade or merchandise?

Response: There is a difference of opinion among the scholars concerning the obligation of Zakat on jewelry if that jewelry reaches the *nisab* [1] and is not for business purposes. The correct opinion is that there is Zakat on it, if it reaches the level of *nisab*, even if it is just for the purposes of being worn and beautification.

The *nisab* for gold is twenty *mithqaals*. In grams, this is ninety-two grams. If the amount of gold is less than that, there is no *Zakat* on it— unless it be a type of merchandise in which case there is always zakat on it if its value of gold and silver reaches the level of *nisab*. The *nisab* for silver is one hundred and forty *mithqaals*. If the amount of silver is less than that, there is no *Zakat* on it — unless it be merchandise in which case there is always *Zakat* on it if they reach the amount of *nisab* for gold and silver.

The evidence that it is obligatory to pay Zakat on gold and silver jewelry which is just for the purpose of wearing is the generality of the statement of the Prophet (صلى الله عليه وسلم)

" مَا مِنْ صَاحِبِ ذَهَبٍ وَلاَ فِضَّةٍ لاَ يُؤَدِّي زَكَاتَهـا إِلاَّ إِذَا كَـانَ يَـومُ
الْقِيَامَةِ صُفِّحَتْ لَهُ صَفَائِحُ مِنْ نار فَيُكْوَى بِهَا جَنْبُهُ وجَبِينُهُ وظَهْرُهُ "

"Anyone who owns gold or silver and does not pay Zakat on them will, on the Day of Resurrection, have them be made

---

[1] The *nisab* is the minimum amount that one must possess before he is liable to pay zakat on his wealth. Different forms of wealth have different levels of *nisab*.—JZ

into plates of fire and they will then burn his sides, forehead and back."[1]

There is also the Hadith of Abdullah ibn Amr ibn al-As which states that a woman came to the Prophet (صلى الله عليه وسلم) and upon the wrist of her daughter were two bracelets of gold. He said, "Have you paid the Zakat on them?" She said, "No." He said,

$$\text{" أَيَسُرُّكِ أَنْ يُسَوِّرَكِ اللهُ بِهِمَا يَومَ الْقِيَامَةِ سِوَارَينِ مِنْ نَار "}$$

"Would you be pleased to have Allah make out of them two bracelets of fire on the Day of Judgment?"

She removed them and said, "They are [charity] for Allah and His Messenger." This was recorded by Abu Dawud and al-Nasai with a *hasan* chain.

There is also the Hadith of Umm Salamah in which she was wearing gold jewelry. She said, "O Messenger of Allah (صلى الله عليه وسلم), is this a hoarded treasure?" He said,

$$\text{" مَا بَلَغَ أَنْ يُزَكَّى فَزُكِّيَ فَلَيْسَ بِكَنْزٍ "}$$

"Whatever reaches the amount that one must pay Zakat on and the Zakat is actually paid on it, then it is not a hoarded treasure."

This was recorded by Abu Dawud and al-Daraqutni. Al-Hakim declared it authentic. The Prophet (صلى الله عليه وسلم) did not tell her that there is no zakat on jewelry!

As for what is narrated, that the Prophet (صلى الله عليه وسلم) said,

$$\text{" لَيْسَ فِي الْحَلِيِّ زَكَاةٌ "}$$

"There is no Zakat on jewelry,"

it is a weak Hadith and it cannot be used to oppose what is firmly established or an authentic hadith.

Shaikh ibn Baz

---

[1] Recorded by Muslim.

Zakat on Jewelry with Stone Inlays

Question 122: How does one pay Zakat on jewelry that is not simply gold but is gold with precious stone inlays? Does one also include the weight of those stones since it would be very difficult to remove the gold and weight it by itself?

Response: Gold is the thing upon which Zakat must be paid, even if it is simply for wearing. As for the precious stones, such as pearls, diamonds and so forth, there is no Zakat on them. If a necklace, for example, has both gold and these other stones, the woman, her husband or guardian then must ponder the matter and try to estimate the amount of gold or give it to an expert to estimate it. It is sufficient to be fairly certain about the matter [and one need not be exact]. If the amount of the *nisab* is reached, Zakat must be paid. The *nisab* is twenty *mithqaals..* which is ninety-two grams. The Zakat is to be paid every year [once a year]. The amount is 2.5%. For example, on one thousand, a person pays twenty-five. This is the correct opinion among the views of the scholars. If the jewelry is for business purposes, then one pays Zakat on all of it, including pearls and diamonds, according to their [market] value, which is the same with all types of merchandise goods. This is the opinion of the majority of the scholars.

Shaikh ibn Baz

I Sold the Gold Before I Paid Zakat on It, What Should I Now Do?

Question 123: I sold gold [jewelry] that I used to wear for some time but I did not pay zakat on it. I would like from you to make it clear to me what I should do about its zakat, given that I sold it for four thousand *riyals*.

Response: If you did not know that you had to pay Zakat on it until after you had sold it, then there is nothing that you must do. However, if you knew that you had to pay Zakat on it, then you should pay 2.5% per year. You should pay that for each previous year according to the value of gold in the marketplace. You must pay 2.5% in cash. However, if you did not know about that until the last year, then you should pay Zakat just for the last year.

Shaikh ibn Baz

Can My Husband Pay My Zakat for Me? Can One Give Zakat to One's Nephew?

Question 124: Is it allowed for my husband to pay the Zakat on my wealth on my behalf, given that he is the one who gave me the wealth? Is it allowable to give the Zakat to my nephew, whose wife passed away and he is a young man who is thinking about getting married?

Response: Zakat is obligatory upon your wealth, if you have the *nisab* or more of gold, silver or other forms of zakatable wealth. If your husband, with your permission, pays it for you, there is no harm. The same is true if your father, brother or others, with your permission, pay it on your behalf. It is allowed for you to pay the Zakat to your nephew to help him get married if he is not able to support himself.

Shaikh ibn Baz

There is No Harm in Her Paying Her Zakat on Jewelry to Her Poor or Debtor Husband

Question 125: Can a wife pay the Zakat on her jewelry to her husband given that he receives a salary of about 4,000 *riyal*s but is in debt 30,000 *riyal*s?

Response: There is no harm in a woman paying the Zakat of her jewelry or other Zakat to her husband if he is poor or is in debt and he is not able to pay off the debt, according to the strongest of the two opinions among the scholars. This opinion is based on the generality of the evidences, including Allah's statement,

﴿ ۞ إِنَّمَا ٱلصَّدَقَٰتُ لِلۡفُقَرَآءِ وَٱلۡمَسَٰكِينِ . . ﴾   [التوبة: ٦٠]

"Zakat are only for the poor and the indigent..." (*al-Tauba* 60).

Shaikh ibn Baz

Giving Zakat to One's Mother

Question 126: Is it allowed for a person to give his zakat to his own mother?

Response: A Muslim may not give his Zakat to his parents or to his children. But, in fact, it is obligatory upon him to spend on their behalf from his own wealth if they are in need of it and he has the ability to spend on their behalf.

Shaikh ibn Baz

There is No Zakat on the Household Utensils

Question 127: I have a large number of household utensils [silverware and diningware] for use on a daily basis as well as for regularly guests and some others for special occasions. I use these many utensils instead of borrowing them from others or renting them, as sometimes one gets dirty or old utensils that one cannot use in any social setting. I keep my utensils in a cabinet in my home. If my neighbors or relatives ask to borrow them, I give it to them, trying to help them.

During a sisters' meeting, I heard one of the sisters say that a person is going to be held accountable for everything that he leaves behind, including household utensils. She said that we will be punished by them if we leave them behind and they will be heated and will brand us on the Day of Resurrection. Please assist me, may Allah assist you. Should I give them away in charity and then borrow from the people for special occasions or should I keep them and pay Zakat on them or is there no zakat on them or what should I do?

Response: There is no harm in what you have mentioned. There is no Zakat on such household utensils, since they are not for sale but are for need and for lending out. The one who told you that possessing such utensils is not allowed is an ignorant, mistaken person. He[1] has said something about Allah and about Allah's religion without knowledge. He must repent from that sin and be careful and avoiding making *fatwas* without knowledge. Allah has stated in stern words that such is forbidden. Allah has stated,

﴿ قُلْ إِنَّمَا حَرَّمَ رَبِّيَ ٱلْفَوَٰحِشَ مَا ظَهَرَ مِنْهَا وَمَا بَطَنَ وَٱلْإِثْمَ وَٱلْبَغْىَ
بِغَيْرِ ٱلْحَقِّ وَأَن تُشْرِكُوا۟ بِٱللَّهِ مَا لَمْ يُنَزِّلْ بِهِۦ سُلْطَٰنًا وَأَن تَقُولُوا۟ عَلَى ٱللَّهِ مَا
لَا تَعْلَمُونَ ﴾   [الأعراف: ٣٣]

"Say: The things that my Lord has forbidden are great evil sins, whether committed openly or secretly, sins [of all kinds], unrighteous oppression, joining partners with Allah for which He has given no authority, and saying things about Allah of which you have no knowledge" (*al-Araf* 33).

In a separate verse, Allah has stated that making statements about Allah without knowledge is something that Satan orders and requests. This is in Allah's words,

﴿ يَٰٓأَيُّهَا ٱلنَّاسُ كُلُوا۟ مِمَّا فِى ٱلْأَرْضِ حَلَٰلًا طَيِّبًا وَلَا تَتَّبِعُوا۟
خُطُوَٰتِ ٱلشَّيْطَٰنِ إِنَّهُۥ لَكُمْ عَدُوٌّ مُّبِينٌ ٠ إِنَّمَا يَأْمُرُكُم بِٱلسُّوٓءِ
وَٱلْفَحْشَآءِ وَأَن تَقُولُوا۟ عَلَى ٱللَّهِ مَا لَا تَعْلَمُونَ ﴾   [البقرة: ١٦٨-١٦٩]

"O mankind! Eat of that which is lawful and good on the Earth, and follow not the footsteps of Satan. Verily, he is to you an open enemy. [Satan] commands only what is evil and sinful, and that you should say about Allah what you know not" (*al-Baqara* 168-169).

Shaikh ibn Baz

---

[1] The answer states "he" but the question was clearly in reference to a "she".—JZ

Giving the Zakat to the *Mujahideen*

Question 128: A trustworthy man says that he is able to take the Zakat and give it to a trustworthy person to give it to the *mujahideen.* May I give him the Zakat of my wealth or is there a better place to give my Zakat? It is difficult for me as a woman to search for those people who are in need and deserving.

Response: It is correct to give the Zakat to the *mujahideen* as the scholars have stated, since they are fighting the disbelieving enemy. If a person knows someone that he has reason to trust, it is permissible for him to give him the Zakat to send it to the *mujahideen* or one may send it with a trustworthy person to them. In doing so, one has fulfilled his responsibility of paying Zakat and his reward will be from Allah.

Shaikh ibn Jibreen

Zakat of Jewelry

Question 129: A woman has jewelry that has reached the level of *nisab.* How does she pay Zakat on it, in Saudi *riyals*[1]? And what is its amount?

Response: Every year, she should ask those who sell gold or others about the value of used gold and so forth. If she knows its value in Saudi *riyals* at the present time, she may pay its value. There is no need to know the original capital amount since its payment is based on its value at the present time.

Shaikh ibn Jibreen

---

[1] Obviously, the non-Saudi can read whatever currency she may use into this question. Hence, for an American, it would be American dollars.—JZ

8. Questions Related to Fasting

Question 130: I never made up the days that I missed from the month of Ramadhan due to my monthly period and I am not able to determine how many days they were. What shall I now do?

Response: Dear sister in Islam, you must investigate the matter and fast what you believe you missed of the days of fasting. And Ask Allah for help and assistance.

﴿ لَا يُكَلِّفُ ٱللَّهُ نَفْسًا إِلَّا وُسْعَهَا ﴾   [البقرة: ٢٨٦]

"Allah burdens not a person beyond his scope" (*al-Baqara* 286).

Do your best and investigate the matter and be cautious with respect to yourself until you have fasted what you believe must be the amount that you missed. You must also repent to Allah.

Shaikh ibn Baz

You Must Make Up the Missed Days and Feed A Poor Person

Question 131: About ten years ago I passed through the well-known stages of puberty. However, in the first year of my adulthood, I did not fast the month of Ramadhan although I had no physical excuse. It was my ignorance at that time, not realizing that it was obligatory. Do I now have to make those days up? In addition to making up those days, do I now have to make some expiation?

Response: It is a must upon you to make up that month in which you did not fast while, at the same, repenting and seeking Allah's forgiveness. You must also feed a poor person for every day the amount of half a *sa'* of the staple food of dates, rice or other such foods if you have the ability to do so. If you are poor and do not have the ability to do so, then there is nothing upon you besides the making up of the fast.

Shaikh ibn Baz

Ruling Concerning Delaying the Making Up of the Days of Ramadhan

Question 132: What is the ruling concerning delaying the making up of the days of Ramadhan until after the following Ramadhan?

Response: Whoever broke his fast during Ramadhan due to traveling, illness and so forth, must make up those days before the next Ramadhan. Between the two Ramadhans our Lord has given us ample time. If one delays it until beyond the next Ramadhan, one must make up the missed days as well as feed a poor person for every day. This was the ruling of a group of the Companions of the Prophet (صلى الله عليه وسلم). One should give half a *sa'* of the staple food of a land. This is approximately one and half kilograms of dates, rice or something of that nature. If the person makes up the fasts before the next Ramadhan, there is no obligation to feed others.

Shaikh ibn Baz

9.Questions Regarding Hajj and Umrah

Menses Came Before She Made the Umrah

Question 133: [This question is] about a woman who was going to perform the Hajj and Umrah as *Tamattu* and she entered the state of *ihram*[1]. However, before she reached the Inviolable House, her menses came. What should she do? Should she perform the Hajj before she makes the Umrah?

Response: She should remain in her state of *ihram* for her Umrah. If she becomes pure before the ninth [of Dhul-Hijjah] and she has the ability to complete the Umrah, she should do so. Then she enters the inviolable state for the Hajj and goes to Arafah to finish the rest of the rites of Hajj. If she does not become pure before the Day of Arafah (the Ninth), she then combines the Hajj with the Umrah, by saying, "O Allah, I have entered the inviolable state for Hajj with my Umrah." She then is performing it as *Qiraan*. She stays with the people and completes all of the acts. Her entering the inviolable state and her circumambulation on the Day of Eid or afterwards suffices for her visiting circumambulation and the running between the two hills for both the Hajj and Umrah. She must also offer the sacrifice of *Qiraan*, as also the one who does *Tamattu* must do.

Shaikh ibn Jibreen

No Harm Has Been Done

Question 134: My wife was entering the inviolable state for Umrah and before she came out of the bathroom and put on her clothing, she cut some of her hair. What is now obligatory upon her?

---

[1] The "state of *ihram*" is the inviolable state of Hajj or Umrah in which one must be dressed in a certain fashion and one is no longer allowed to do certain acts until he or she finishes the rites of the Hajj or Umrah.—JZ

Response: There is no harm in what she has done. She does not have to offer a sacrifice. The prohibition to cut one's hair is for after one has actually begun the state of *ihram*. She had not yet entered that state and had not yet put on her clothing. Hence, there is no harm in what she did. However, if she did it after she entered the state of *ihram* out of ignorance or forgetfulness, then she also would not have had to offer a sacrifice since she would be excused due to her ignorance.

Shaikh ibn Jibreen

I Want to Make Hajj but My Husband Prevents Me

Question 135: I am an elderly, wealthy woman. I presented the idea of making Hajj to my husband more than once but he refused without having any reason. I have an old brother who intends to make Hajj. Should I make Hajj with him even if my husband does not permit me or should I abandon the Hajj and stay in my land out of obedience to my husband? Give me a ruling, may Allah reward you.

Response: Since Hajj is an obligation that must be met at its first opportunity and since that woman has the responsibility, ability and male relative to go with her, it is obligatory upon her to go immediately to Hajj and it is forbidden for her husband to prevent her without any reason.

It is permissible for her, in the state just described, to make Hajj with her brother even if her husband does not agree to it because it is an individual obligation, like the prayer and fasting, and the right of Allah takes precedence. That husband has no right to prevent his wife from fulfilling her obligation of Hajj. And Allah is the Guide to the Straight Path.

Shaikh ibn Jibreen

The Face Veil is From the Matters Not Allowed while in the State of *Ihram*

Question 136: I wore a face veil while performing Umrah, not knowing that it was not allowed. What is the expiation for that?

Response: Since the face veil is one of the matters that is not allowed during the state of *ihram*, it is obligatory upon the woman who wore it to pay a "ransom", that is, to offer a sacrifice, feed sixty poor people or fast three days. However, this is conditional upon knowledge and cognizance. If one wore it and she was ignorant of its ruling or she had forgotten that she was in *ihram* or that it was forbidden, then there is no "ransom" upon her for the "ransom" is only upon the one who does something deliberately.

Shaikh ibn Jibreen

Using Pills that Stop the Menses in Order to Perform Hajj

Question 137: Is it allowed for women to use such pills that prevent or delay her menses during the time of Hajj?

Response: It is allowed for a woman to use pills that prevent the menses during the time of Hajj out of fear that her menses will come. That must be done only after she consults a specialist doctor who has her safety and interest in mind. The same is true with respect to Ramadhan if she wishes to fast with the people.

The Standing Committee

The One Who Does not Have a "Male Relative" is Not Obliged to Perform Hajj

Question 138: A woman well-known for her piety, in her middle ages or close to being elderly, wants to make the Hajj of Islam. However, she does not have a *mahram*[1]. From the same

---

[1] *Mahram* refers to the husband or a male relative whose relationship to the woman, due to blood, breastfeeding or marriage relations, is such that they are never allowed to be married.—JZ

country there is a man who is well-known for his piety who wants to make Hajj and he is traveling with women whom he is related to. Is it proper for that woman to make Hajj with this man and the women he is traveling with, being among the women with the man watching over them? Does she have to perform the Hajj or is this requirement dropped from her since she does not have a *mahram*, even though she is financially capable? Give us a response, may Allah reward you.

Response: The woman who does not have a *mahram* is not obligated to perform the Hajj. This is because a *mahram*, with respect to her, is part of the necessary aspects of having the means to perform the Hajj. Having the means is one of the conditions for the obligatory nature of Hajj.

Allah Says:

﴿ وَلِلَّهِ عَلَى ٱلنَّاسِ حِجُّ ٱلْبَيْتِ مَنِ ٱسْتَطَاعَ إِلَيْهِ سَبِيلًا ﴾

[آل عمران: ٩٧]

"And Hajj to the House is a duty that mankind owes to Allah, those who can afford the expenses." (al-Imran 97)

It is not allowed for her to travel for Hajj or otherwise without her husband or a *mahram*. This is based on what al-Bukhari recorded that the Prophet (صلى الله عليه وسلم) said,

" لَا يَحِلُّ لِامْرَأَةٍ تُسَافِرُ مَسِيرَةَ يَوْمٍ وَلَيْلَةٍ إِلَّا مَعَ ذِي مَحْرَمٍ "

"It is not allowed for a woman to travel a day and night's distance except with a *mahram*."

Al-Bukhari and Muslim also recorded from ibn Abbas that he heard the Prophet (صلى الله عليه وسلم) say,

"لَا يَخْلُو رَجُلٌ بِامْرَأَةٍ إِلَّا وَمَعَهَا ذُو مَحْرَمٍ، وَلَا تُسَافِرُ الْمَرْأَةُ إِلَّا وَمَعَهَا ذُو مَحْرَمٍ " فَقَامَ رَجُلٌ فَقَالَ: يَارَسُولَ اللهِ إِنَّ امْرَأَتِى خَرَجَتْ حَاجَّةً، وَإِنِّى اكْتُتِبْتُ فِى غَزْوَةِ كَذَا وَكَذَا قَالَ: "فَانْطَلِقْ فَحُجَّ مَعَ امْرَأَتِكَ"

"A man cannot be alone with a woman unless in the presence of a *mahram* of hers. And a woman does not travel except along with a *mahram*." A man said, "O Messenger of Allah (صلى الله عليه وسلم), my wife has left to make the Hajj and I have enlisted for such and such expedition." He said, "Go and make Hajj with your wife."

This is the opinion of al-Hasan, al-Nakhai, Ahmad, Ishaq, ibn al-Mundhir and the scholars of juristic reasoning (*ashab al-ra'i*). It is the correct opinion because it is in agreement with the generality of the Hadith of the Prophet that prohibits women from travelling without a husband or *mahram*. Malik, al-Shafi'i and al-Auza'i have a differing opinion. They all state conditions for which they have no evidence. Ibn al-Mundhir stated, "They all abandon the clear, obvious meaning of the Hadith and lay down conditions for which they have no evidence."

The Standing Committee

Ruling Concerning the Hajj of a Woman without a *Mahram*

Question 139: A poor woman made Hajj with a group of people she was not related to because she asked her relatives to make Hajj with her but they refused. She went with a man who was travelling with two women and she made the third. Was her Hajj valid or not?

Response: Her Hajj is valid. However, she is considered sinful for travelling without a *mahram* due to the evidences related to that. She must, therefore, repent to Allah for that deed.

Shaikh ibn Baz

Ruling Concerning a Woman Entering the State of *Ihram* While Wearing Socks and Gloves

Question 140: What is the ruling concerning a woman who entered the state of *ihram* while wearing socks and gloves? Is it allowed for her to remove what she was wearing while entering the state?

Response: It is best for her to enter the *ihram* while wearing socks. This is better and covers her better. However, if she is wearing a wide and long dress, that would be sufficient. If she entered the state of *ihram* while wearing socks and then later removed them, this is permissible, as it is like a man who entered the state of *ihram* while wearing sandals and he removes them at any time he wishes without doing any harm. However, she cannot enter the state of *ihram* with gloves. This is because it is prohibited for the one in the state of *ihram* to wear gloves. Similarly, she does not wear a face veil or *burqa'* [also a kind of face veil] while in that state. This is because the Messenger of Allah (صلى الله عليه وسلم) prohibited that. At the same time, though, she should lower her headcovering or outer cloak over her face when she is in the presence of non-*mahram* men. This is to be done when she is circumambulating the Kaaba or going between the hills of Safa and Marwa. This is based on the Hadith of Aisha who said, "The riders would pass us while we were with the Messenger of Allah (صلى الله عليه وسلم). When they got close to us, we would draw our outer cloak from our heads over our faces. When they passed by, we would uncover our faces." (Recorded by Abu Dawud and ibn Majah.[1])

---

[1] In *Dhaeef Sunan Abu Dawud* (pp. 182-183), it states that according to al-Albani, this narration is weak. There definitely is some weakness in its chain. However, in his work *Jilbab al-Marah al-Muslimah*, al-Albani states (p. 108) that it is *hasan* due to corroborating evidence. [See Muhammad Nasir al-Din al-Albani, *Jilbab al-Marah al-Muslima fi al-Kitab wa al-Sunnah* (Beirut: Dar ibn Hazm, 1994), pp. 108f.] Perhaps even more important is a narration from Asma, with a *sahih* chain, that states virtually the same. This is "perhaps more important" because some could argue that Aisha, being one of the Prophet's wives, must cover her face at all times in front of men. However, Asma was not one of the Prophet's wives and she used to also do the same. Hence, this is not a practice that was specific for the Prophet's wives.—JZ

It is also allowed for men to wear leather socks even if they are not cut off according to the strongest opinion. The majority of the scholars say that they should be cut off [below the ankles]. The correct opinion is that they need not be cut off because the Prophet (صلى الله عليه وسلم) addressed the people at Arafah and said,

" مَنْ لَم يَجِدْ إِزَاراً فَلْيَلْبَس السَّرَاوِيلَ، وَمَـنْ لَـمْ يَجِـدْ نَعْلَـين فَلَيْلَبَس الخُفَّينِ "

"Whoever does not have a waistcloth should wear pants. And whoever does not have sandals [or shoes] should wear leather socks."

(This was recorded by al-Bukhari and Muslim.) He did not order them to cut them off [at the ankles]. This is evidence that the order to cut them off had been abrogated.

Shaikh ibn Baz

Women Enter the *Ihram* in any Clothing They Wish

Question 141: Is it allowed for a woman to enter the state of *ihram* in any clothing she wishes?

Response: Yes, she may enter the *ihram* in whatever clothing she wishes. She does not have any specific type of clothing that she must wear for *ihram* as many of the general public think. But it is best for her to enter the *ihram* in clothing which is not beautiful and will not attract the one who sees it. This is because she is going to be mixing with men, so her clothing must not be such that it tempts the looker. It should not be beautiful but should be customary and not a temptation.

Shaikh ibn Baz

Ruling Concerning Changing the Clothing of *Ihram*

Question 142: Can a person change the clothing of *ihram* in order to wash them?

Response: There is no harm in washing the clothes during the *ihram*. There is no harm in exchanging them for others and putting on new or washed clothing.

Shaikh ibn Baz

Ruling Concerning the Hajj of a Menstruating Woman

Question 143: What is the ruling concerning a woman who had her menses during the days of her Hajj? Is the Hajj she performed valid?

Response: If a woman gets her menses during the days of Hajj, she performs all of the deeds of the Hajj except for the circumambulation of the Kaaba and the going between the hills of Safa and Marwa. She does not do those acts until she becomes pure. When she becomes pure, she makes *ghusl*, and performs the circumambulation and the circuits. If the menses come and the only rite she has not performed is the farewell circumambulation, then she goes home without performing it as it is no longer required of her [due to her state] and her Hajj is correct. The basis for this is what is recorded by al-Tirmidhi and Abu Dawud from Abdullah ibn Abbas that the Messenger of Allah (صلى الله عليه وسلم) said,

" النُّفَسَاءُ وَالْحَائِضُ إِذَا أَتَتَا عَلَى الْمِيْقَاتِ تَغْتَسِلاَنِ وَتُحْرِمَـانِ وَتَقْضِيَانِ الْمَنَاسِكَ كُلَّهَا غَيْرَ الطَّوَافِ بِالْبَيْتِ "

"The woman with post-partum bleeding and the menstruating women, when they come to the *miqat* [the place to enter the state of *ihram*] are to make *ghusl*, enter the state of *ihram* and perform all of the rites of the Hajj save for the circumambulation of the House [Kaaba]."[1]

In the *Sahih*, it is recorded from Aisha that she had her menses before completing the rites of the Umrah and the Prophet (صلى الله عليه وسلم) told her to enter the state of *ihram* for Hajj and to not circumambulate the House [Kaaba] until she was pure. He told her to do all of the rites of the Hajj and to combine it with the Umrah.

Al-Bukhari recorded from Aisha that Safiya, the wife of the Prophet (صلى الله عليه وسلم), received her menses and mentioned that to the Messenger of Allah (صلى الله عليه وسلم). He said, "Is she going to hold us up?" They said, "She has already made the *Ifadha* circumambulation." He said, "In that case, she is not [going to hold us up]." In another narration, Aisha said, "Safiya had her menses after she finished the *Ifadha* circumambulation. I mentioned her menses to the Messenger of Allah (صلى الله عليه وسلم) and he said, 'Is she going to hold us up?' I said, 'O Messenger of Allah, she has already performed the *Ifadha* circumambulation of the mosque.' So the Prophet (صلى الله عليه وسلم) said, 'Then let us go.'" And peace and blessings of Allah be upon the Prophet Muhammad and his family and Companions.

The Standing Committee

Ruling Concerning One Who Entered the *Ihram* While She Was Menstruating

Question 144: A woman asks: She was excused, that is menstruating, and her family wanted to go to make Umrah and if she lagged behind, there would be no one to stay with her. Therefore, she went with them to the Umrah and performed all of the rites of the Umrah, including the circumambulation and the circuits, as if she was not menstruating. She did this out of ignorance and out of shyness, not wanting to tell her guardian.

---

[1] According to al-Albani, this hadith is *sahih*. Al-Albani, *Sahih al-Jami*, vol. 1, p. 605.—JZ

You should know that she is illiterate and does not know how to read or write. What must she do?

Response: If she made the *ihram* for Umrah, then she must repeat the circumambulation after making *ghusl* and repeat the act of cutting some of the hair. As for her making the rounds between Safa and Marwa, they are proper according to the strongest opinion among the scholars. If she repeats them after the circumambulation, that would be better and safer. She must repent to Allah for her circumambulations and prayer of two *rakat*s while she was menstruating.

If she is married, her husband cannot have sexual intercourse with her until she completes her Umrah. If he has already had sexual intercourse with her, then her Umrah has been nullified and she must sacrifice a year old woolen sheep or a two year old goat in Makkah to be distributed to the poor. She must also complete her *umrah* as was mentioned previously. She must perform a new *umrah* from the same *miqaat*[1] that she entered the *ihram* from previously, in replacement of her spoiled *umrah*.

But if she simply performed the *Umrah* with them out of courtesy and bashfulness and she did not [actually and intentionally] enter the state of *ihram* from the *miqaat*, then the only thing upon her is to repent to Allah. This is because Hajj and *Umrah* are not valid without entering the state of *ihram*. And the *Ihram* is the intention for Hajj or *Umrah* or both.

We ask Allah for guidance and safety for all of us from the whisperings of Satan.

Shaikh ibn Baz

Waiting Until She Becomes Pure

Question 145: There is no doubt that the circumambulation known as *Ifadha* is one of the pillars and essential acts of the Hajj. If the menstruating women did not perform it due to lack of time and the time was not such that

---

[1] This is the place where the pilgrim enters the inviolable state of Hajj.

she could wait for her menses to end, what is the ruling concerning that?

Response: It is obligatory upon her and her guardian to wait until she becomes pure and then to perform the *Ifadha* circumambulation. This is based on the Prophet's (صلى الله عليه وسلم) statement when he was told that Safiyah had received her menses, "Is she going to hold us up?" When he was told that she had performed the *Ifadha* circumambulation, he said, "Then let's go."[1]

If she is not able to wait but she has the ability to return to Makkah to perform the circumambulation, then she may travel and return after she becomes pure to perform the circumambulation. If she does not have the ability to return or she fears that she would not be able to return, like those who live in far away places from Makkah, like the people of the West, Indonesia and so forth, then, according to the correct opinion, she may protect [her blood from dripping on to the floor] and perform the circumambulation with the intention of Hajj. This is considered permissible by a number of scholars, including Shaikh al-Islam ibn Taimiya and his student ibn al-Qayyim as well as other scholars.

Shaikh ibn Baz

She Did Not Cut Her Hair Out of Ignorance

Question 146: A woman performed the Hajj and fulfilled all of its rites except that she did not cut her hair, either out of ignorance or forgetfulness. She has reached her native land and has done all of the deeds that are not allowed for one in the state of *ihram*. What is obligatory upon her now?

Response: If the matter is as you have stated, that she performed all the rites except for cutting her hair, out of forgetfulness or ignorance, then she must cut her hair in her land whenever she recalls that and there is nothing else upon her due to her ignorance or forgetfulness, as long as she does such with the

---

[1] This was recorded by al-Bukhari.—JZ

intention to complete the Hajj. We ask Allah to guide us and accept our deeds. However, if her husband had intercourse with her before she cut her hair, then she must offer a sacrifice. This is either a sheep, one-seventh of a camel or one-seventh of a cow that is proper for the sacrifice. This is to be slaughtered in Makkah and distributed among the poor of Makkah. But if the intercourse was after she left the land of Makkah, in her own land or elsewhere, then she may offer a sacrifice anywhere she wishes. This sacrifice is to be distributed among the poor. And peace and blessings be upon our Prophet Muhammad, his family and Companions.

The Standing Committee

Does a Woman Uncover Her Face and Hands During the Hajj

Question 147: The woman is to be completely covered in prayer save for her face and hands. If she is in Hajj or traveling with non-*mahram* males and she prays in congregation with them, should she uncover her face and hands in the prayer or should she cover them out of fear of being seen by non-*mahram* men? Similarly, in the *Haram*[1], does she lower her outer cloak over her face and cover her hands also or does she leave them exposed?

Response: The free woman is to be covered completely and it is forbidden for her to expose her face and hands in the presence of non-*mahram* men. This is the case regardless if she is in prayer or in the state of *ihram* or other common situations, according to the strongest of the two opinions among the scholars. This is also based on what has been narrated from Aisha who said, "The riders would pass by us while we were with the Messenger of

---

[1] The *haram* is the place of the Kaaba and its surrounding areas.—JZ

Allah (صلى الله عليه وسلم) in the inviolable state of pilgrimage. When they got close to us, we would lower our outer cloak from our heads over our faces. When they passed by, we would uncover them." Recorded by Ahmad, Abu Dawud and ibn Majah.[1] If this [act of covering the face] is requested from the women during the state of *ihram* when she is to [otherwise] uncover her face, then obviously it is more so requested from them during other times. In addition, there is the general nature of the verse that states [and also supports the view that the woman must cover her face],

$$ ﴿ وَإِذَا سَأَلْتُمُوهُنَّ مَتَٰعًا فَسْـَٔلُوهُنَّ مِن وَرَآءِ حِجَابٍ ذَٰلِكُمْ $$
$$ أَطْهَرُ لِقُلُوبِكُمْ وَقُلُوبِهِنَّ ﴾ \quad [الأحزاب : ٥٣] $$

"And when you ask them, ask them from behind a screen, that is purer for your hearts and for their hearts"(*al-Ahzab* 53).

The Standing Committee

Make Hajj on Behalf of Your Father

Question 148: My father (may Allah have mercy on him) died about ten years ago. He used to perform all of the obligatory acts. However, he did not perform the Hajj due to straitened circumstances. Then, by the will of Allah, I came to Saudi Arabia to teach. I performed the Hajj of Islam on my own behalf. Now, I would like to perform the Hajj on behalf of my father who passed away. Is it allowed for me to perform the Hajj on his behalf? And do I also earn reward?

Response: It is legally sanctioned for you to perform the Hajj on behalf of your father and you will get a great reward. May Allah accept it from you and make things easy for you.

Shaikh ibn Baz

---

[1] This seems to be a *hasan* report. It was discussed in detail earlier.—JZ

The Ruling of the "Farewell *Tawaf¹*" for the One Performing *Umrah* and Purchasing Something After that *Tawaf*

Question 149: Is the "Farewell Circumambulation of the Kaaba" obligatory for the one making *Umrah*? Is it allowed to purchase something in Makkah after making the "Farewell Circumambulation," regardless of whether that was for the Hajj or *Umrah*?

Response: The "Farewell Circumambulation" is not obligatory for the *Umrah*. However, it is best to do it. If, though, someone leaves and did not perform it, then there is no harm. However, for the Hajj, it is obligatory, because the Prophet (صلى الله عليه وسلم) said,

$$ " \ \text{لاَ يَنْفِرَنَّ أَحَدٌ مِنْكُمْ حَتَّى يَكُونَ آخِرُ عَهْدِهِ بِالْبَيْتِ} \ " $$

"None of you should leave until he performs the last circumambulation around the house."[2]

These words were directed to the pilgrims.

The person may purchase whatever he needs to purchase afterwards. He may even purchase items for business purposes. But the time interval must be short. If he spends a lengthy time [in Makkah after performing Farewell circumambulation], he must then repeat his circumambulation. If, according to custom, his stay afterwards was not lengthy, he does not repeat the circumambulation in any case.

Shaikh ibn Baz

---

[1] The *tawaf* is the circumambulation of the Kaaba. There are different types of *tawaf*. The most important is known as the *Ifadha* circumambulation. (See the glossary for its definition.)

[2] Recorded by Muslim.—JZ

10.Questions Related to the Sacrifice

Combing One's Hair by the One who Intends to Slaughter

Question 150: If a woman intends to offer a sacrificial animal, is it a must that she not comb her hair, even though it would be difficult upon her not to comb her hair for those ten days?

Response: In an authentic Hadith, narrated from Umm Salama, the Prophet (صلى الله عليه وسلم) said,

"إِذَا دَخَلَتِ الْعَشْرُ وَأَرَادَ أَحَدُكُمْ أَنْ يُضَحِّيَ فَلَا يَمَسَّ مِنْ شَعْرِهِ وَبَشَرِهِ شَيْئاً"

"If the ten days begin [the first ten days of Dhul-Hijjah] and one of you wants to slaughter, he should not touch [remove] his hair [on his head] or skin at all."[1]

In another narration it states,

"فَلْيُمْسِكْ عَنْ شَعَرِهِ وَأَظْفَارِهِ"

"He should refrain from [removing] his hair and nails."[2]

The scholars state that the meaning of this Hadith is that it is prohibited to remove any hair by means of shaving it, shortening it, cutting it, burning it off and so forth. Therefore, combing and arranging one's hair is not part of that prohibition. In the same way, it is permissible to wash and part the hair. Even if some of it should fall out, as long as that was not intentional, there is no harm. Therefore, it is allowed for a woman to comb her hair if needed. And there is no difference between the one who is offering an obligatory sacrifice or voluntary one. And Allah knows best.

Shaikh ibn Jibreen

---

[1] Recorded by Muslim.—JZ
[2]This narration is also recorded by Muslim.— JZ

Washing and Combing the Hair During the First Ten Days of Dhul-Hijjah

Question 151: Is it allowed for a person to comb his hair during the first ten days of Dhul-Hijjah?

Response: There is no harm in washing one's hair or parting the hair during the first ten days of Dhul-Hijjah. This is true even if some hair thereby fall out. The reward of the sacrifice will not be lessened, Allah willing. Furthermore, if a person intentionally removes some hair or trims his nails, he should still perform the sacrifice and the reward for the sacrifice itself will still be complete, Allah willing.

Shaikh ibn Jibreen

It is Allowed for the Woman to do Her Own Slaughtering if Needed

Question 152: If the time for slaughtering comes and there is no man in the house, is it allowed for the women to perform the slaughtering herself?

Response: Yes. It is allowed for a woman to perform the sacrificial slaughtering or any other [slaughtering of animals] if there is need to do so, as long as the other conditions for the sacrifice are met. It is recommended that upon sacrifice, the person mentions on whose behalf the sacrifice is being performed, whether the person be living or dead. However, if this is not done, the intention in the heart without stating it is sufficient. If the person mentions the wrong name by mistake, there is also no harm as Allah is most knowledgeable of the intentions.

Shaikh ibn Jibreen

11.Questions Related to Marriage

Ruling Concerning Using Birth Control Pills

Question 153: What is the ruling concerning the use of birth control pills by a married couple?

Response: It is not allowed for a wife to use birth control pills out of dislike for having many children or out of fear of having to support the children. It is permissible to use them to prevent pregnancy due to some illness that may harm the woman if she becomes pregnant or if she cannot give birth in the natural fashion but is in need of a medical operation to give birth. This and other cases are permissible due to necessity. In those types of cases, she may use birth control pills unless she learns from specialized doctors that those pills may be harmful to her in some other fashion.

The Standing Committee

Ruling Concerning Birth Control

Question 154: What is the ruling concerning birth control?

Response: This is a contemporary issue and many people ask about it. In the previous session of the Conference of the Leading Scholars [of Saudi Arabia], there was a study of this issue. They issued a verdict according to their opinion on this issue. In sum, they concluded that it is not allowed to take birth control pills. Allah has sanctioned the means that lead to procreation and a larger Muslim nation. The Prophet (صلى الله عليه وسلم) said,

" تَزَوَّجُوا الوَلُودَ الوَدُودَ فَإِنِّي مُكَاثِرٌ بِكُمُ الأُمَمَ يَوْمَ القِيَامَةِ "

"Marry the child-bearing, loving woman for I shall outnumber the peoples by you on the Day of Resurrection."[1]

Another narration states at the end, "[outnumber] the prophets on the Day of Resurrection." The Muslim Nation is in need of being increased in numbers so that it may worship Allah, strive in His way, and defend the Muslims, by the will of Allah, from the plots of their enemies. It is a must to avoid such things [as birth control] and not to use them except in the cases of dire necessity. If there is a necessity, there is no harm. [This would be,] for example, if the woman has some illness in her uterus or so forth that would harm her if she were to become pregnant. Then she may use such pills to the extent of her need. This is also the case if she already has many children and it would become a hardship on her to have another one soon, then she may use the birth control pills for a specific amount of time, such as one year or two years, which is the amount of time designated for breast feeding, until she reaches the stage where she would be able to raise the child properly. But if the women is taking them just so she will be free of responsibility or to be able to work or to live a comfortable life and other similar reasons why women take such pills these days, [it should be understood that] for these reasons it is not allowed to take birth control pills.

Shaikh ibn Baz

---

[1] This hadith is recorded by ibn Hibban, Ahmad, al-Tabarani and others. Without the words, "the Day of Resurrection," it is also narrated by Abu Dawud and al-Nasai. According to al-Albani, it is an authentic hadith due to its supporting chains. Muhammad Nasir al-Din al-Albani, *Irwa al-Ghaleel fi Takhreej Ahadeeth Manaar al-Sabeel* (Beirut: al-Maktab al-Islami, 1979), vol. 6, p. 195.—JZ

The Appropriate Age for Marriage

Question 155: What is the appropriate age for men and women to marry? Some of the young ladies of today do not accept to be married to men older than them and also some of the men do not get married from anyone older than them either. We hope for a response, may Allah reward you.

Response: I advise the young ladies not to refuse a man because of his older age. Even if he be ten, twenty or thirty years older, this is not a valid excuse. The Prophet (صلى الله عليه وسلم) married Aisha when he was fifty-three years old and she was nine years old. Older age is not harmful. There is no problem if the woman is older than the man and there is no problem if the man is older than the woman. The Prophet (صلى الله عليه وسلم) married Khadijah when she was forty years old and he was twenty-five years old, before he received his first revelation. That is, she was fifteen years older than him (may Allah be pleased with her). And Aisha was married when she was a young lady of six or seven years and the Prophet (صلى الله عليه وسلم) consummated the marriage when she was nine years old and he was fifty-three years old. Many of those who talk on the radio or television and speak against having disparaging ages between husband and wife are wrong. It is not permissible for them to say such things. Instead, what must be done, is the woman must look at the prospective husband and, if he be pious and appropriate, she must agree to him, even if he is older than her. Similarly, the man must try to marry a woman who is pious and virtuous, even if she is older than him, especially if she is still less than midlife. In any case, age should not be taken as an excuse. It should also not be considered a shortcoming, as long as the man is pious or the woman is pious. May Allah make the affairs good for everyone.

Shaikh ibn Baz

Marriage Comes First

Question 156: A common custom among the people nowadays is for a woman or her father to refuse a man's proposal so that she may finish high school, college or some specific amount of studying. What is the ruling concerning that? What is your advice for those who fall into that trap? Sometimes, the woman reaches the age of thirty or more and she has yet to get married!

Response: My advice to all young men and young women is to get married quickly if the means to it are made possible for you. This is because the Prophet (صلى الله عليه وسلم) has said,

" يَا مَعْشَرَ الشَّبَابِ مَنِ اسْتَطَاعَ مِنْكُمُ الْبَاءَةَ فَلْيَتَزَوَّجْ فَإِنَّهُ أَغَضُّ لِلْبَصَرِ وَأَحْصَنُ لِلْفَرْجِ. وَمَنْ لَمْ يَسْتَطِعْ فَعَلَيْهِ بِالصَّوْمِ فَإِنَّهُ لَهُ وِجَاءٌ "

"O youthful people, if any of you have the means to, he should get married, as it lowers the eyesight and protects the private parts. Those who have not the ability to do so should fast, as it will be a shield for him."

This was recorded by al-Bukhari and Muslim. The Prophet (صلى الله عليه وسلم) also said,

" إِذَا خَطَبَ إِلَيْكُمْ مَنْ تَرْضَوْنَ دِينَهُ وخُلُقَهُ فَزَوِّجُوهُ إِنْ لَا تَفْعَلُوهُ تَكُنْ فِتْنَةٌ فِي الْأَرْضِ وفَسَادٌ عَرِيضٌ "

"If one whose religion and character pleases you proposes to you, you should marry him. If you do not do so, there will be tribulations in the land and great evil."

This was recorded by al-Tirmidhi with a *hasan* chain. The Prophet (صلى الله عليه وسلم) also said,

" تَزَوَّجُوا الْوَلُودَ الْوَدُودَ فَإِنِّي مُكَاثِرٌ بِكُمُ الْأُمَمَ يَوْمَ الْقِيَامَةِ "

"Marry the child-bearing, loving woman for I shall outnumber the peoples by you on the Day of Resurrection."

This was recorded by Ahmad and graded *sahih* by ibn Hibban. Therefore, there are many benefits to marriage which the Prophet (صلى الله عليه وسلم) alluded to, including lowering the gaze, protecting the private parts, increasing the numbers of the Muslim Nation and being saved from great evil and misfortune.

May Allah grant to all what is best for their religion and worldly lives. He is All-Hearing, Close.

Shaikh ibn Baz

The Young Lady is Not to be Forced to Marry a Man She Does Not Want to Marry

Question 157: Is it allowed for a father to force his daughter to marry a specific man that she does not want to marry?

Response: Neither the father nor anyone other than the father may force a woman who is under his guardianship to marry a man that she does not want to marry. In fact, her permission must be sought. The Messenger of Allah (صلى الله عليه وسلم) said,

" لاَ تُنْكَحُ الأَيِّمُ حَتَّى تُسْتَأْمَرَ، وَلاَ تُنْكَحُ الْبِكْرُ حَتَّى تُسْتَأْذَنَ " قَـالُوا يَا رَسُولَ اللهِ كَيفَ إِذْنُها؟ قَالَ: "أَنْ تَسْكُتَ"، وَفِي لَفْظٍ آخَرَ قَالَ: "إِذْنُها صُمَاتُها"، وفي اللَّفْظِ الثَّالِثِ: "والبِكْرُ يَسْتَأْذِنُها أَبُوها وإِذْنُها سُكُوتُهَا" .

"The non-virgin [without a husband] must not be married until she is consulted. A virgin must not be married until her permission is sought." They said, "O Messenger of Allah (صلى الله عليه وسلم), how is her permission given?" He said, "By her being silent." Another narration states, "Her silence is her permission."

Yet a third narration states, "A virgin's father seeks her permission and her permission is her remaining silent."[1]

The father must seek her permission if she is nine years of age or above. Similarly, her other guardians may not marry her off except by her permission. This is obligatory upon all of them. If one is married without permission, then the marriage is not valid. This is because one of the conditions of the marriage is that both partners accept the marriage. If she is married without her permission, by threat or coercion, then the marriage is not valid. The only exception is in the case of the father and his daughter who is less than nine years of age. There is no harm if he gets her married while she is less than nine years old, according to the correct opinion. This is based on the Messenger of Allah (صلى الله عليه وسلم) marrying Aisha without her consent when she was less than nine years old, as is stated in authentic Hadith. However, if she is nine years old or more, she cannot be married, even by her father, except with her consent. The husband should not approach the woman if he knows that she does not want him, even if the father approves of it. He must fear Allah and not approach any wife that did not want him even if her father claims that he did not coerce her. He must avoid what Allah has forbidden for him. This is because the Messenger of Allah (صلى الله عليه وسلم) ordered that her permission must be sought. We also advise the woman to fear Allah and to accept the man if her father finds that he is suitable to marry her, as long as the prospective groom is good in his religion and character. This is true even if the one who is doing the marrying is not the girl's father [but her legal guardian]. We make this advice because there is lots of good and lot of benefits in marriage. Also, there are lots of hazards in living as a maiden. I advise all young ladies to accept those men who come to them if

---

[1] These narrations are recorded by al-Bukhari, Muslim and others.—JZ

they are qualified. They should not use schooling, teaching or
other causes as an excuse to avoid marriage.

Shaikh ibn Baz

A Religious Young Man Proposed to Me but My Mother Refused

Question 158: I am seeking a solution to my problem. I am
twenty-four years old. A young man proposed to me. He has finished
college. He is from a religious family. After my father agreed to
him, he asked me to come to see him. I saw him and was pleased
with him and he was pleased with me. [We saw each other] because
our pure religion has stated that I should see him and he should see
me. However, when my mother came to realize that he was from a
religious family, she became harsh against him and my father. She
swore that such a marriage would never take place in anyway. My
father desperately tried to persuade her, but to no avail. Do I have
the right to seek the Law to intervene in this matter?

Response: If the matter is as you have mentioned in your
question, then your mother has no right to make any objection. Indeed,
such a stance is forbidden. You are not obliged to obey your mother in
that matter. This is because the Prophet (صلى الله عليه وسلم) said,

" إِنَّمَا الطَّاعَةُ فِي الْمَعْرُوفِ "

"Obedience is in what is good and right."[1]
Rejecting a suitable proposal is not from what is good and right.
In fact, it has been narrated that the Prophet (صلى الله عليه وسلم) said,

" إِذَا خَطَبَ إِلَيْكُمْ مَن تَرْضَوْنَ دِينَهُ وخُلُقَه فَزَوِّجُوهُ إِلاَّ تَفْعَلُوا
تَكُنْ فِتْنَةٌ فِي الأَرْضِ وفَسَادٌ عَرِيضٌ "

---

[1] Recorded by al-Bukhari and Muslim.—JZ

"If one whose religion and character pleases you proposes to you, you should marry him. If you do not do so, there will be tribulations in the land and great evil."[1]

If you have need to take your matter to a court of law, you would not be wrong in doing so.

Shaikh ibn Baz

If Someone is Known Not to Perform the Prayers in Congregation, One Should Not Marry Him

Question 159: A young man came to me asking for my sister's hand in marriage. I inquired about him and discovered that he does not perform the prayer in congregation. Therefore, we differed about whether or not we should allow this marriage to take place. My brother said, "Marry him for perhaps Allah will guide him." However, my father refused. I want to know the Islamic ruling concerning this matter.

Response: If someone is known not to pray in congregation, then he should not be wedded to. This is because not praying in congregation is an open, public display of disobedience to Allah. This is one of the characteristics of the people of hypocrisy and it is one of the steps that leads to abandoning the prayer in totality. And abandoning the prayer completely is a greater form of *kufr* [that takes one out of the fold of Islam]. Allah has stated,

﴿ إِنَّ ٱلْمُنَٰفِقِينَ يُخَٰدِعُونَ ٱللَّهَ وَهُوَ خَٰدِعُهُمْ وَإِذَا قَامُوٓا۟ إِلَى

ٱلصَّلَوٰةِ قَامُوا۟ كُسَالَىٰ﴾ [النساء: ١٤٢]

---

[1] Recorded by al-Tirmidhi and ibn Majah, with the last word being *'areedh* instead of *kabeer*, as written in this text. (The two words are very close in meaning.) Shaikh ibn Baz presents the hadith in his answer in a form that implies that he does not consider the hadith authentic. However, in an answer to another question, he stated that it was recorded by al-Tirmidhi with a *hasan* chain. Similarly, al-Albani has concluded that it is *hasan*. Al-Albani, *Sahih al-Jami*, vol. 1, p. 112.—JZ

"Verily, the hypocrites seek to deceive Allah, but it is He who deceives them. And when they stand to pray, they stand with laziness" (*al-Nisa* 142).

The Prophet (صلى الله عليه وسلم) said,

" أَثْقَلُ الصَّلاَةِ عَلَى الْمُنَافِقِينَ صَلاَةُ الْعِشَاءِ وصَلاَةُ الفَجْرِ، وَلَوْ
يَعْلَمُونَ مَا فِيهِمَا لأَتَوْهُمَا وَلَوْ حَبْواً "

"The hardest prayers upon the hypocrites are the *Isha* Prayers and the *Fajr* Prayers. If they knew what they had [of reward and blessings], they would come to them even if they had to crawl."

This was recorded by al-Bukhari and Muslim.

In this regard, ibn Masud said, "During our time, none would lag behind the prayer in congregation except for the hypocrite who was well-known for his hypocrisy." This was recorded by Muslim in his *Sahih*.

It is also confirmed that the Prophet (صلى الله عليه وسلم) said,

" الْعَهْدُ الَّذِي بَيْنَنَا وَبَيْنَهُمُ الصَّلاَةُ فَمَنْ تَرَكَهَا فَقَدْ كَفَرَ "

"The covenant between us and them is the prayer. Whoever abandons it has committed *kufr* (infidelity)."

This was recorded by Ahmad and the compilers of the *Sunan* collections with a *sahih* chain. The Messenger of Allah (صلى الله عليه وسلم) also said,

"بَيْنَ الرَّجُلِ وَبَيْنَ الكُفْرِ وَالشِّرْكِ تَرْكُ الصَّـلاَةِ "

"Between a man and disbelief and polytheism is the abandoning of the prayer."

This was recorded by Imam Muslim in his *Sahih*. There is no doubt that abandoning the prayer in congregation is one of the means that leads to abandoning the prayer in its totality, as we mentioned earlier. We ask Allah for guidance for all of us.

Shaikh ibn Baz

Ruling Concerning a Christian Man Marrying a Muslim Woman

Question 160: What is the Islamic ruling concerning a Christian man marrying a Muslim woman? If they have children, what is the ruling concerning those children in Islamic law?

Response: The marriage of a Christian man to a Muslim woman is an invalid marriage. Allah says in the Quran,

[البقرة: ٢٢١]   ﴿ وَلَا تُنكِحُوا ٱلْمُشْرِكِينَ حَتَّىٰ يُؤْمِنُوا ﴾

"And give not [Muslim women] in marriage to idolaters until they believe" (*al-Baqara* 221).

Therefore, it is not allowed for a disbeliever to marry a Muslim woman. Allah also says,

[الممتحنة: ١٠]   ﴿ لَا هُنَّ حِلٌّ لَّهُمْ وَلَا هُمْ يَحِلُّونَ لَهُنَّ ﴾

"They [Muslim women] are not lawful for them [the disbelievers] nor are they [the disbelievers] lawful for them" (*al-Mumtahana* 10).

If he does marry her, the marriage is invalid. The children are the children of fornication. They are to be given to their mother and ascribed to her alone — unless that was done out of ignorance concerning such law. For ignorant people, the matter is different. In their case, the marriage is still invalid. However, the children will be ascribed to the father since the act was done out of ignorance. That is, if he was ignorant of the law and she was also, the marriage is still invalid but the children will be ascribed to their parents due to their ignorance and there was some doubtful aspect to their intercourse.[1] But if he knew the Islamic ruling and she knew the Islamic ruling and they were being lax and disrespectful of the law of Allah, then the children are children of fornication. They will be ascribed to their mother and will not be ascribed to their father at all. The couple should be reprimanded and the penal punishment should be enforced upon him for having intercourse with a Muslim woman when he did not have the legal right to do so. This is what must be done if the Islamic state has the ability to do it. If he becomes Muslim after that and Allah guides him, then he can marry her with a new contract.

Shaikh ibn Baz

The Condition that Has the Most Right to be Fulfilled

Question 161: A prospective wife laid down a stipulation that her husband will not prevent her from teaching and he agreed to that so they got married. Does he then still have to maintain her and her children although she is an employee? Is it permissible for him to take some of her salary without her approval? If the woman is religious and does not wish to hear singing and music but the husband and his family constantly listen to music and say that the one who does not permit music is being misled by the devil, is it allowed for the wife to stay or remain in her family's house due to such a state?

Response: If the woman stipulates to her fiance that he will not prevent her from teaching or from studying and he accepts that stipulation, such a stipulation is sound and he cannot prevent her from that after he has conjugated the marriage. This is because the Prophet (صلى الله عليه وسلم) has said,

---

[1] That is, they did not knowingly and intentionally violate the law. Therefore, there is room to consider their marital relations as "acceptable" in the sense that the children will be ascribed to both of the parents.—JZ

" إِنَّ أَحَقَّ الشُّرُوطِ أَنْ يُوفَى بِهِ مَا اسْتَحْلَلْتُمْ بِهِ الفُرُوجَ "

"The conditions that have the most right to be fulfilled are those that make sexual intercourse lawful [i.e., those of the marriage contract]."

This was recorded by al-Bukhari and Muslim. If he then prevents her from teaching, she has the option to stay with him or to seek a separation from the *Shariah* judge. However, the husband and his family listening to singing and music does not invalidate the marriage contract. She must advise them and inform them that such is prohibited. She also should not be with them when they partake in that evil. The Prophet (صلى الله عليه وسلم) has said,

" الــدِّيــنُ النَّصِيْحَــةُ .. "

"The religion is sincere advice..."

Recorded by Muslim in his *Sahih*. The Prophet (صلى الله عليه وسلم) also said,

" مَنْ رأى مِنْكُمْ مُنْكَراً فَلْيُغَيِّرْهُ بِيَدِهِ، فَإِنْ لَمْ يَسْتَطِعْ فَبِلِسَانِهِ، فَــإِنْ
لَمْ يَسْتَطِعْ فَبِقَلْبِهِ وَذلِكَ أَضْعَفُ الإِيمَانَ "

"Whoever of you who sees an evil must change it with his hand. If he cannot do so, then with his tongue. And whoever cannot do that, then with his heart and that is the weakest of faith."

Recorded by Muslim in his *Sahih*. Verses of the Quran and Hadith on this topic are numerous. The husband must also maintain her and his children from her. He may not take anything from her salary unless it be by her permission and approval. And she may not leave his house to go to her family's house or elsewhere except with his permission.

Shaikh ibn Baz

Ruling Concerning Having Wedding Parties in Hotels

Question 162: What is your opinion about the parties that are held in hotels?

Response: The parties that are held in hotels have many things wrong about them and may be criticized for many reasons. First, they are usually done extravagantly and beyond what is needed. Second, this leads to the extra financial burden of having wedding parties in hotels and the presence of people for whom there is no need. Third, it may lead to mixing between the men and women of the hotel and others. This mixing is a disgraceful evil. This is why the leading scholars issued a decree and gave it to the King advising him not to allow parties and wedding parties to be held in hotels. Instead, they said, the wedding parties should be held in the houses and hotels should not be hired, as such wedding parties lead to lots of evil. Similar is the case with the halls that are rented for a great deal of money. This advice was all concluded out of concern for the people, economic considerations, avoiding of extravagance and luxury. Also, this will allow those who are of the middle class to be able to afford to get married and will not be a great burden upon them. If they see their cousin or relative getting married in an expensive hotel party, he must compete with him or do something similar. This will drive him to borrow money. Otherwise, he may have to delay his marriage out of fear of such heavy expenses.

My advice to all Muslim brethren is that they should not hold their wedding parties in such hotels nor in the expensive halls that are rented for that purpose. They should hold them in inexpensive halls or not hold them in the halls at all. To hold them in the houses is preferred anyway. Or one could hold them in his relatives' house if that is possible.

Shaikh ibn Baz

Ruling Concerning Women Attending Wedding and Birthday Parties Which Have Objectionable Aspects

Question 163: What is the ruling concerning women attending wedding parties and birthday parties although they are innovations and every innovation is misguidance? Also, one finds in such parties singers to entertain the people. Is it forbidden if a woman simply goes their to witness the wedding and out of respect for the family of the bride and not to listen to the singing?

Response: If the wedding party has no objectionable aspects, such as mixing between men and women, shameless singing, or if the person attending has the ability to put an end to those aspects, it is then allowed for her to attend such a gathering to participate with the others in their happiness. In fact, it is a must to attend if the person has the ability to remove the objectionable aspects. If the party, though, has objectionable aspects and the person does not have the ability to stop them, then she is not allowed to attend such a party. This is based on the generality of Allah's statement,

﴿ وَذَرِ ٱلَّذِينَ ٱتَّخَذُواْ دِينَهُمْ لَعِبًا وَلَهْوًا وَغَرَّتْهُمُ ٱلْحَيَوٰةُ ٱلدُّنْيَا وَذَكِّرْ بِهِ أَن تُبْسَلَ نَفْسٌ بِمَا كَسَبَتْ لَيْسَ لَهَا مِن دُونِ ٱللَّهِ ﴾   [الأنعام : ٧٠]

"And leave alone those who take their religion as play and amusement, and are deceived by the life of this world. But remind [them] with it [the Quran], lest a person be given up to destruction for that which he has earned, when he will not find for himself any protector or intercessor besides Allah" (al-Anam 70).

Allah also says,

﴿ وَمِنَ ٱلنَّاسِ مَن يَشْتَرِى لَهْوَ ٱلْحَدِيثِ لِيُضِلَّ عَن سَبِيلِ ٱللَّهِ بِغَيْرِ عِلْمٍ وَيَتَّخِذَهَا هُزُوًا أُوْلَٰٓئِكَ لَهُمْ عَذَابٌ مُّهِينٌ ﴾   [لقمان : ٦]

"And of mankind is he who purchases idle talks [singing, music] to mislead (men) from the Path of Allah without knowledge, and takes it by way of mockery. For such there will be a humiliating torment" (*Luqman* 6).

The Hadith that have been narrated condemning singing and musical instruments are numerous.

As for birthday parties, neither a Muslim man or a Muslim woman should attend them because they are innovations. The only exception would be to attend them to put a stop to them and explain the rule of Allah concerning such parties.

The Standing Committee

The Dower is the Right of the Woman

Question 164: Can a man use his daughter's or sister's dower in order to get married?

Response: The dower of his daughter or sister is one of her rights and is a portion of her wealth. If she gives it as a gift to him or part of it, voluntarily and out of free choice and she is someone legally capable of such an offer, then it is permissible for him to take it. If she does not give it as a gift, it is not allowed for him to take it or take any portion of it as it is something that specifically belongs to her. However, the father may take a portion of it, but only if such is not harmful to her and only if he does not take specifically from some of his children. This is based on the Prophet's statement,

"إِنَّ أَطْيَبَ مَا أَكَلْتُمْ مِنْ كَسْبِكُمْ وَإِنَّ أَوْلَادَكُم مِنْ كَسْبِكُمْ"

"The best of what you consume is that which you have earned. And your children are part of what you have earned."[1]

The Standing Committee

---

[1] Recorded by al-Tirmidhi and al-Nasai. Al-Albani has graded it *sahih*. Al-Albani, *Sahih al-Jami*, vol. 1, p. 326.—JZ

Concerning Polygyny

Question 165: Some people say that marrying more than one wife is not allowed unless a person has orphans under his care and he fears that he will not do justice between them. Then he may marry their mother or one of her daughters. For evidence, they quote the verse,

﴿ وَإِنۡ خِفۡتُمۡ أَلَّا تُقۡسِطُواْ فِي ٱلۡيَتَٰمَىٰ فَٱنكِحُواْ مَا طَابَ لَكُم مِّنَ ٱلنِّسَآءِ

مَثۡنَىٰ وَثُلَٰثَ وَرُبَٰعَ ﴾   [النساء: ٣]

"And if you fear that you shall not be able to deal justly with the orphan-girls, then marry women of your choice, two, three or four..." (al-Nisa 3).

Response: This statement is false. The meaning of the verse is that if a person has under his care an orphan and he fears that he will not give her the proper amount of dower, then he should marry other women, for there are many women and Allah will not make things difficult for him. The verse points to the legality of marrying two, three or four wives. This is allowed because it leads to more chastity, lowering of eyesight and guarding of the private parts. Furthermore, that is a cause for more children and the chastity of more women, as well as them being treated properly and cared for. There is no doubt that the woman who has one-half of a husband or one-third or one-fourth is better off than the one who has no husband at all. However, one must meet the condition of justice among the wives and the ability to take care of and tend to the wives. If a person fears that he will not do justice, then he may only marry one wife in addition to having slaves. The practice of the Prophet (صلى الله عليه وسلم) indicates and stresses that. When he died, he had nine wives. And Allah says about him,

﴿ لَّقَدۡ كَانَ لَكُمۡ فِي رَسُولِ ٱللَّهِ أُسۡوَةٌ حَسَنَةٌ ﴾   [الأحزاب: ٢١]

"Indeed in the Messenger of Allah you have a good example to follow" (al-Ahzab 21).

The Prophet (صلى الله عليه وسلم) made it clear to his Nation that it was
allowed for him to have more than four wives. Therefore,
following his example on this point would mean taking four wives
or less. Beyond four wives is something that is specific for the
Prophet (صلى الله عليه وسلم) only.

Shaikh ibn Baz

There is No Contradiction in the Verses
Regarding Polygyny

Question 166: Concerning polygyny, it is stated in the Quran,

[النساء : ٣]   ﴿ فَإِنْ خِفْتُمْ أَلَّا تَعْدِلُوا فَوَاحِدَةً ﴾

"If you fear that you will not be able to deal justly [with
more then one wife], than [marry] only one" (*al-Nisa* 3).

However, in another place, it states,

﴿ لَقَدْ كَانَ لَكُمْ فِي رَسُولِ اللَّهِ أُسْوَةٌ حَسَنَةٌ ﴾

[الأحزاب : ١٢٩]

"You will never be able to do perfect justice between your
wives even if it is your ardent desire" (*al-Nisa* 129).

In the first verse, the condition of being just among the wives is
stated while in the second it makes it clear that the condition of
justice could never be met. Does this mean that the first verse is
abrogated and that it is not allowed to marry more than one woman
since the condition of justice cannot be fulfilled? Benefit us, may
Allah reward you.

Response: There is no contradiction between the two
verses. There is also no abrogation by one verse of the other. The
justice that is mentioned in the first verse is the justice within
one's ability, which is related to being fair in division of time and
maintenance. As for being just with respect to love and sexual

relations, this is not within one's ability. This is what is being referred to in the verse,

$$ ﴿ وَلَن تَسْتَطِيعُوٓا۟ أَن تَعْدِلُوا۟ بَيْنَ ٱلنِّسَآءِ وَلَوْ حَرَصْتُمْ ﴾ $$

[النساء: ١٢٩]

"You will never be able to do perfect justice between your wives even if it is your ardent desire" (*al-Nisa* 129).

In a Hadith about the Prophet (صلى الله عليه وسلم), Aisha stated,

"كَانَ رَسُولُ اللهِ، صلى الله عليه وسلم، يَقْسِمُ بين نِسَائِهِ فَيَعْدِلُ.

ويقُولُ: "اللهُمَّ هذَا قَسْمِي فِيمَا أَمْلِكُ فَلاَ تَلُمْنِي فِيمَا تَمَلِكُ وَلاَ أَمْلِكُ"

"The Messenger of Allah (صلى الله عليه وسلم) used to divide his time between his wives and he was fair. He used to say, 'O Allah, that is my division with respect to what I have control over. Do not blame me for what You control and over which I have no control.'"[1]

This was recorded by Abu Dawud, al-Tirmidhi, al-Nasai, ibn Majah. It was graded *sahih* by ibn Hibban and al-Haakim.

Shaikh ibn Baz

Ruling Concerning a Woman Looking at Men

Question 167: What is the ruling concerning a woman looking at men on television or casual looks in the streets?

Response: A woman looking at a man must be one of two cases, regardless of whether it be on television or otherwise. First

---

[1] This hadith seems to be one of those hadith where the specialists have noted a mistake in its transmission. Hence, they have concluded that it is a weak hadith. See, for example, al-Albani, *Irwa*, vol. 7, pp. 81-83; Shuaib al-Arnaut's footnotes to *Sahih ibn Hibban*, vol. 10, p. 5. The first part of the hadith, though, that the Prophet (peace be upon him) was just among his wives has supporting evidence and is considered confirmed.— JZ

is a look with lust. This is forbidden as it contains evil and temptation. Second is a simple look free of any kind of lust and desire. There is no harm in that kind of look according to the correct opinion of the scholars. It is permissible because it is confirmed in the *Sahih*s of al-Bukhari and Muslim that Aisha watched the Abbysinians doing their war dance. The Prophet (صلى الله عليه وسلم) was concealing her from them and he approved of what she was doing. Furthermore, women walk in the streets and they look at men although they are wearing *hijab*. A woman may look at a man even though he does not see her. However, this is conditional that the look not be accompanied with lust, desire or temptation. If it is a look of lust or temptation, then it is forbidden regardless of whether it be on television or otherwise.

Shaikh ibn Uthaimin

Ruling Concerning Women Looking at Non-*Mahram* Men

Question 168: What is the ruling concerning a woman looking at non-*mahram* men?

Response: We advise women not to look at non-*mahram* men. It is best for the woman if she is not seen by the men and she does not see them. There is no difference on this point between a battlefield or a sports field. A woman is weak and can easily be swayed. Many times, a woman looks at a movie or picture of a young man and her emotions and desires are excited. This exposes her to temptation. Being away from the causes of temptation is always the safest approach.

Shaikh ibn Jibreen

Correspondence between Young Men and Women is Not Allowed

Question 169: What is the ruling concerning letters or correspondence between young men and women, given that these correspondences do not contain any lewdness, passion or amorous flavor?[1]

Response: It is not allowed for a man to have correspondence with any woman whom he is not related to. This is because this is a source of temptation. The one involved may think that there is no temptation involved but the Devil may continue to work on him until he becomes enticed by her and her by him. The Prophet (صلى الله عليه وسلم) ordered that the one who heard about the anti-Christ's arrival should remain far away from him. He said that a man will come to him as a believer but the anti-Christ will keep working on him until he tempts him. Similarly, correspondence between young men and women is a great temptation and something very much to be avoided. One must refrain from it even if he claims that there is no lewdness or passion involved. As for correspondence between men and men or between women and women, there is no harm in that as long as such correspondence does not contain anything forbidden.

Shaikh ibn Jibreen

A Horrendous Crime

Question 170: A woman hired a lawyer to help her get her share of inheritance from her father. The lawyer charged her an amount larger than what she possessed. So he asked her to marry him due to the services he rendered for her. However, that woman was

---

[1] Obviously, the answer to this question also applies to the kind of correspondence that goes on over the Internet, especially the chat rooms. This is a new area that many young Muslims have gotten involved in and many times the results are very unfortunate.—JZ

already married. Her husband was not present, as he was out of the country. So that woman hired that same lawyer to have her marriage annulled. This was done without the husband being contacted in any manner, although the wife had his address and he used to send money to her to support her and their daughter of eleven years and son of eight years. What is the ruling concerning that marriage? Who has the right to take custody of that boy and that girl?

Response: There is no question that what was done was illegal, a heinous crime and a malicious attempt to get around the law. The woman was still under the marriage ties with her husband; he was still supporting her and their children. The lawyer only attempted to dissolve the marriage so that he could marry her even though he had every ability to contact the first husband and see what was his excuse for not being with her. Therefore, if this marriage was nullified by a *Shariah* judge after the causes and mandate for it were proven, then the marriage from the first husband is dissolved by the act of the judge. Otherwise, what was done was forbidden. Therefore, she would still be considered the wife of the first husband and the second marriage would be considered forbidden. As for the children, they stay with their mother. If the second husband refuses them, their custody goes to her closest relative or relatives of their father. If the husband returns soon, he can seek whatever he sees fit in this matter.

Shaikh ibn Jibreen

One Should Not Burden His Wife with Toilsome and Difficult Work

Question 171: I read in a newspaper a *fatwa* [religious ruling] from one of the scholars who said that it is not obligatory for the wife to serve a husband and such does not actually fall under the marriage contract which only implies his right to "enjoy" his wife sexually. As for her serving him, this is a type of good behavior from her only. He also said that it is obligatory upon the man to provide a servant for his wife if he does not serve her or she does not serve herself for any reason. Is this correct? If it is not correct, then I thank Allah that this newspaper is not widespread as, otherwise, some husbands would become like bachelors when their wives would read that *fatwa*.

Response: That *fatwa* is not correct and is not to be acted upon. The wives of the Companions used to serve their husbands. Asma bint Abu Bakr narrated how she served her husband al-Zubair ibn al-Awwam. Similarly, Fatima used to serve Ali. Such was the case with others also. The custom of the Muslims continues to be that the wife serves the husband in a customary fashion with respect to preparing food, washing clothing, washing utensils, cleaning the house and even watering and milking animals and helping in the farm. All of this is with respect to the customs of the people that have continued since the time of the Prophet (صلى الله عليه وسلم) until our times without it being refuted. However, one should not burden one's wife with work that is toilsome and hard upon her. This is determined by her abilities and custom.

Shaikh ibn Jibreen

There is No Wedding Procession with the Bride and the Groom Together

Question 172: Is it allowed to have a wedding procession with the groom being with the bride among the women during the wedding parting?

Response: That act is not allowed. It is an indication that modesty has been lost. It is also an imitation of the people of obscenity and lewdness. In fact, the matter is very clear. The groom is too shy to be brought in front of the people! Then how is he going to be brought in front of those in attendance?

Shaikh ibn Jibreen

A Muslim Woman may not Be Wed to a Disbeliever

Question 173: Is it allowed for a Muslim woman to marry a Muslim man who embraced Islam simply because of her? That is, he asked her to marry him and told her that he would leave his religion and enter Islam. Please help me for I know that I am the only reason that he entered into Islam.

Response: It is not allowed for a Muslim woman to marry a non-Muslim man. This is because Allah has said,

[الممتحنة: ١٠] ﴿لَا هُنَّ حِلٌّ لَّهُمْ وَلَا هُمْ يَحِلُّونَ لَهُنَّ﴾

"They [Muslim women] are not lawful for them [the disbelievers] nor are they [the disbelievers] lawful for them" (al-Mumtahana 10).

Allah has also said,

﴿وَلَا تُنكِحُوا ٱلْمُشْرِكِينَ حَتَّىٰ يُؤْمِنُوا۟ وَلَعَبْدٌ مُّؤْمِنٌ خَيْرٌ مِّن مُّشْرِكٍ وَلَوْ أَعْجَبَكُمْ﴾ [البقرة: ٢٢١]

"And give not [Muslim women] in marriage to polytheists until they believe and verily, a believing slave is better than a polytheist, even though he pleases you." (al-Baqara 221).

If he enters into Islam and truly practices Islam, then it is allowable. However, he must be "tested" first to make sure that he performs his prayers, fasts and other acts of worship. Also, he must be learning the Quran, learning the laws of Islam, abandoning *shirk*, avoiding alcohol and all other forbidden acts. He should also change his religion on his passport and identification papers. One should wait for some time after he embraces Islam to make sure that he is truly a Muslim and has not simply embraced Islam as a trick to be able to marry the woman. Otherwise, afterwards, he may apostate as soon as he gets married. If he does that, he must then be killed for the Prophet (صلى الله عليه وسلم) has said,

" مَـنْ بَـدَّلَ دِينَـهُ فَاقْتُلُـوهُ "

"The one who changes his religion is to be killed."[1]

Shaikh ibn Jibreen

A Muslim Woman Marrying a Christian Man

Question 174: What is the ruling concerning the marriage of a Muslim woman with a Christian man? What is the ruling concerning the children of such a marriage? What is the ruling concerning the one who gave the permission for such a marriage to take place? What is the ruling concerning the wife if she knew that such a marriage was invalid? Should she have the legal punishment inflicted upon her or not? If the husband embraces Islam, what is the ruling concerning the first marriage agreement and how do they make a new marriage contract?

Response: It is not permissible for a Muslim woman to marry a Christian man or other male disbeliever. Allah has stated,

﴿ وَلَا تُنكِحُوا ٱلْمُشْرِكِينَ حَتَّىٰ يُؤْمِنُوا۟ ﴾   [البقرة: ٢٢١]

"And give not [Muslim women] in marriage to polytheists until they believe" (al-Baqara 221).

Allah has also said,

﴿ لَا هُنَّ حِلٌّ لَّهُمْ وَلَا هُمْ يَحِلُّونَ لَهُنَّ ﴾   [الممتحنة: ١٠]

"They [Muslim women] are not lawful for them [the disbelievers] nor are they [the disbelievers] lawful for them" (al-Mumtahana 10).

The marriage must be annulled as soon as possible if such a wedding has taken place. If the woman knew about the ruling

---

[1] Recorded by al-Bukhari.—JZ

beforehand, she is liable to a legal punishment[1]. Similarly, the guardian, the witnesses and the one overseeing the wedding are to be punished if they were aware of what they were doing. If she gives birth, the children follow the mother in Islam. If the man becomes Muslim after the contract, a new contract must be made. However, that must be made after it is made certain that his conversion is a true one. Otherwise, it may just be maneuvering around the law. If he apostates afterwards, his neck must be struck off, based on the hadith,

$$ \text{" مَـنْ بَـدَّلَ دِينَـهُ فَاقْتُلُـوهُ "} $$

"The one who changes his religion is to be killed."[2]

Shaikh ibn Jibreen

Marriage from Distant or Non-Relatives is Preferred

Question 175: One of my relatives has come to me for the purpose of marriage but I heard that to marry from non-relatives or distant relatives is preferred for the sake of the future of the children and other reasons. What is your opinion on that matter?

Response: That principle has been stated by a number of scholars. It points to the fact that genetics and heredity has an effect. There is no doubt that genetics has an effect on the physical and psychological make-up of the person. This is shown in the Hadith where a man came to the Messenger of Allah (صلى الله عليه وسلم) and said, "My wife has given birth to a black child." (He was opposing that child because all of his ascendants were of light skin.) The Messenger of Allah (صلى الله عليه وسلم) told him, "Do you own camels?" He said, "Yes." The Prophet (peace be upon him)

---

[1] The reply states *tazeer* which is a discretionary punishment from a judge as opposed to *hadd* which is a quantified punishment from the Law.—JZ
[2] Recorded by al-Bukhari.—JZ

said, "What color are they?" He said, "Red." The Prophet (صلى الله عليه وسلم) asked him, "Is there a dusky one among them?" He said, "Yes." The Prophet (صلى الله عليه وسلم) then said, "How has that come about?" The man replied, "It is perhaps due to the strain to which it has reverted." So the Prophet (صلى الله عليه وسلم) told him, "Perhaps that son of yours is due to the strain to which it has reverted."[1] This is evidence that genetics has an effect and there is no doubt about that. However, the Prophet (صلى الله عليه وسلم) also said,

$$ " تُنْكَحُ الْمَرْأَةُ لِأَرْبَعٍ : لِمَالِهَا وَحَسَبِهَا وَجَمَالِهَا وَدِينِهَا. فَاظْفَرْ بِذَاتِ الدِّينِ تَرِبَتْ يَـدَاكَ" $$

"A woman is married for [any of] four reasons: for her wealth, for her lineage, for her beauty or for her religion. So try to marry one who is religious, may your hands be smeared with dust."[2]

Therefore, the most important matter in proposing to a woman is her piety. The more religious she is and the more beautiful she is then the better she is, regardless if she be a close relative or distant [or non-] relative. The religious woman will protect the man's wealth, children, and house. Beauty fulfills his needs and lowers his gaze and he will not look to others. And Allah knows best.

Shaikh ibn Uthaimin

For The Father to Force His Daughter into Marriage is Forbidden

Question 176: I have a half-sister from my father. My father married her to a man without her approval and without taking her opinion. She is twenty-one years old. The witnesses

---

[1] Recorded by al-Bukhari and Muslim.—JZ
[2] Recorded by al-Bukhari and Muslim. The expression, "may your hands be smeared with dust," is an Arabic expression encouraging the person to perform the action.—JZ

made a false witness, stating that she had agreed to the marriage. Her mother signed instead of her on the marriage contract. This is how the marriage was finalized. Until now, she still refuses this marriage. What is the ruling concerning that marriage contract and those who gave false testimony?

Response: If that sister were virgin and her father compelled her to marry that man, then, according to some scholars, that marriage is valid. They are of the opinion that a father may compel his daughter to marry someone she does not want if he is suitable. However, the stronger opinion on this question is that it is not allowed for a father or anyone else to compel a young lady to get married to one she does not want, even if he is suitable. The proof for this is the Prophet's statement,

" لاَ تُنْكَــحُ الِبــكْرُ حَــتَّى تُسْــتَأْذَنَ "

"A virgin must not be married until her permission is sought."[1]

This statement is general and there is no exception to it for any of the possible guardians. In *Sahih Muslim*, it is recorded as,

" البِــكْرُ يَسْتَأْذِنُهَــا أَبُوهــا "

"A virgin's father seeks her permission."

This version makes specific mention of the virgin girl and the father. This is a clear text on this disputed issue and what it states must be followed. Therefore, it is forbidden for a man to compel his daughter to marry a man that she does not want to marry. And the act that is forbidden cannot be valid or implemented. This is because it being considered valid or implemented flies in the face of it being prohibited. If the Lawgiver forbids something, it means that the people cannot do it. If we then say it is valid, this means

---

[1] These narrations are recorded by al-Bukhari, Muslim and others.—JZ

that we are accepting it, acting upon it and giving it the same status as a contract that is approved by the *Shariah*. Based on this stronger opinion, the marriage by your father of your sister to one she does not want is an invalid marriage. The contract is null and void. The case must then be taken to a court of law.[1]

As for those who gave false witness, they have committed one of the great sins. It is confirmed that the Prophet (صلى الله عليه وسلم) said,

$$\text{"أَلا أُخْبِرُكُمْ بِأَكْبَرِ الْكَبَائِرِ فَذَكَرَهَا ...وَكَانَ مُتَّكِئاً فَجَلَسَ ثُمَّ}$$
$$\text{قَالَ: أَلاَ وَقَوْلُ الزُّورِ أَلاَ وَقَوْلُ الزُّورِ أَلاَ وَشَهَادَةُ الزُّورِ"}$$

"Let me inform you of the greatest of the great sins." He then mentioned them. At the time, he was reclining. Then he sat up straight and said, "And certainly false witness [is one of them]. And certainly false witness. And certainly false witness." He continued to repeat that until they said, "Would that he would be quiet."[2]

Those who gave false witness must repent to Allah, state the truth and make it clear to the *Shariah* judge that they gave false witness and they are now taking back what they stated. Similarly, the mother, who falsely signed on behalf of her daughter, is sinful. She must repent to Allah and not repeat such an act ever again.

Shaikh ibn Uthaimin

Marriage with the Intention of Divorcing After a Period of Time

Question 177: A person is going abroad to study and he wants to protect his chastity there by getting married for a specific period of time. Afterwards, he will divorce his wife although he

---

[1] Here, obviously, the Shaikh is referring to a court of law in which the *Shariah* rulings will be implemented.— JZ
[2] Recorded by al-Bukhari and Muslim.—JZ

does not inform her that he is planning on divorcing after a specific time period. What is the ruling concerning such behavior?

Response: Marriage with the intention of divorce must fall into one of two cases. First, it is explicitly stipulated in the marriage contract that the marriage is for a month, year, until he finishes his studies and so forth. This is known as *muta*. This is forbidden. The second case is where the person has that as his intention [in his heart] but it is not put as a stipulation in the contract. The widespread opinion among the Hanbalis is that that is forbidden and the contract is void. They say that what is intended is equivalent to what is actually stipulated, since the Prophet (صلى الله عليه وسلم) said,

$$\text{" إنَّمَا الأعْمَالُ بِالنِّيَّاتِ وإنَّمَا لِكُلِّ امْرِيءٍ مَانَوَى "}$$

"Actions are based on intentions and for everyone is what he intended."[1]

They also say that if a man marries and plans on divorcing a thrice-divorced woman simply in order to make her permissible for her previous husband, that marriage is not valid even if what was intended is not stipulated in the marriage contract. Again, this is because what is intended is like what is stipulated. So if the intention of making the wife "legal" for her previous husband makes the contract null and void, the intention to perform [something similar to] *muta* also makes the contract null and void. This is the opinion of the Hanbalis.

The second opinion among the scholars is that it is permissible for the man to marry that woman with the intention that he will divorce her after he leaves her land, such as those who go to the West to study or for other purposes. They say that it is sound because it is not stipulated in the contract and this distinguishes it from *muta*. Furthermore, in the case of *muta*, as

---

[1] Recorded by al-Bukhari and Muslim.—JZ

soon as the period finishes, the two are separated whether they still want that or not. In this case, though, it could be the case that he desires his wife and decides to remain with her. This is one of the opinions held by Shaikh al-Islam ibn Taimiya.

In my opinion, such a marriage is not *muta* since it does not meet the definition of *muta*. However, it is still forbidden since it is a type of deception of the wife and her family. The Prophet (صلى الله عليه وسلم) has forbidden deception and mendacity. If the woman knew that the man only intends to be married with her for that specific time, she would not agree to the marriage nor would her family. In the same way, he would not be pleased to marry his daughter to a man who intends to divorce her when he has fulfilled his needs from her. How can he be pleased with doing to others what he would not be pleased to have done to himself? This goes against the foundations of faith. The Prophet (صلى الله عليه وسلم) has stated,

$$\text{"لاَ يُؤْمِنُ أَحَدُكُمْ حَتَّى يُحِبَّ لِأَخِيهِ مَا يُحِبُّ لِنَفْسِهِ"}$$

"None of you truly believes until he loves for his brother what he loves for himself."[1]

I have also heard that this opinion has led some people to do something that none of the scholars would be in agreement with. That is, some people travel to such lands with the sole purpose of performing such a marriage and then they return to their countries. This is also a greatly forbidden act. Therefore, one must close the door that leads to such a possible practice. Furthermore, the act contains deception and cheating. And it opens a very dangerous door since people, in general, are ignorant and most of the people's desires will not keep them from violating what Allah has prohibited.

Shaikh ibn Uthaimin

---

[1] Recorded by al-Bukhari and Muslim.—JZ

The Marriage with the Greatest Blessings is that with the Lesser Financial Burden

Question 178: What is your opinion of the large dowers and expensive parties and honeymoons that cost a great deal of money? Does the *Shariah* approve of such things?

Response: Having very expensive dowers and extravagant wedding parties is something that goes against the *shariah*. The marriage that has the greatest blessings is the one with lesser financial burden. Any time the burdens are lessened, the blessings are increased. This is a matter that is many times caused by women. Women are the ones that often insist upon their husbands to set a very high dower [for their daughters]. If a lesser dower is offered, they will say that their daughter is deserving of such and such. Furthermore, expensive and luxurious wedding parties are prohibited by the *Shariah*. They fall under the command of the verse,

﴿ وَلَا تُسْرِفُوٓاْ إِنَّهُۥ لَا يُحِبُّ ٱلْمُسْرِفِينَ ﴾   [الأنعام : ١٤١]

"But be not extravagant. Verily, He loves not those who are extravagant" (*al-Anam* 141).

Again, many times it is the women who force their husbands to do such things. They say that in so and so's party they had this and that. However, such gatherings must be according to the *Shariah*. The person should not spend what is beyond his means. He must also never be extravagant for Allah has prohibited extravagance.

﴿ . . . إِنَّهُۥ لَا يُحِبُّ ٱلْمُسْرِفِينَ ﴾   [الأنعام : ١٤١]

"Verily, He loves not those who are extravagant" (*al-Anam* 141).

Honeymoons are worse and even more evil. This is because they are an imitation of non-Muslims. They also are a waste of lots of wealth. It also leads people to being lax with respect to their religious duties when such honeymoons take place in non-Muslim areas. The people come back with customs and behavior that are harmful for them and for the Muslim community. This is something that is to be feared for the *Ummah*. However, there is no harm, Allah willing, if a man travels with his wife to make *Umrah* or to visit Madinah.

Shaikh ibn Uthaimin

Choosing a Husband

Question 179: What are the most important considerations a young lady should make when choosing a husband? If she refuses someone simply for economic or worldly reasons, will that expose her to the punishment of Allah?

Response: The most important attributes that a woman must look for in selecting a husband are character and piety. Wealth and lineage are secondary considerations. The most important aspect is that the proposed groom be a person of piety and proper behavior. The person of proper behavior and piety will not do his wife wrong.   Either he will keep her in a way that is proper or he will leave her to go free in the best way. Furthermore, the person of religion and behavior may be a blessing for her and her children. She may learn manners and religion from him. If he does not have those characteristics, she should stay away from him, especially if he is one of those who is lax with respect to performing the prayers or if he is known to drink alcohol, may Allah save us. As for those who never pray, they are disbelievers. Believing women are not permissible for them nor are they permissible for the believing women. The important point is that the woman should stress character and piety.   If he is also of a noble lineage, that is to be preferred. This is due to the Messenger of Allah's (صلى الله عليه وسلم) statement,

" إِذَا أَتَاكُمْ مَنْ تَرْضَوْنَ دِينَهُ وَخُلُقَهُ فَأَنْكِحُوهُ "

"If a person whose religion and character you approve of comes to you, then marry him."[1]

However, if he is also suitable [in other ways, such as economic standing and so forth], that is better.

Shaikh ibn Uthaimin

Relations Before Marriage

Question 180: What is the view of the religion concerning [pre-marital] relations?

Response: If the questioner means by "before marriage," before consummation of the marriage but after the contract[2], then there is no harm in such relations since she is his wife by virtue of the contract, even though they have not decorously consummated the marriage. However, if it is before the marriage, such as during the period of engagement or otherwise, such contact is forbidden and impermissible. It is not allowed for a man to enjoy a non-related woman's company, either by speech, look or private company. It is confirmed that the Prophet (صلى الله عليه وسلم) said,

" لاَ يَخْلُوَنَّ رَجُلٌ بِآمْرَأَةٍ إلا مَعَ ذِي مَحْرَمٍ، ولاَ تُسَافِرِ امْرَأَةٌ

إلاَّ مَعَ ذِي مَحْرَمٍ "

---

[1] Recorded by al-Tirmidhi and ibn Majah. As discussed earlier, it is a *hasan* hadith.—JZ

[2] Here the Shaikh is referring to a practice which is quite common in the Muslim world. Sometimes, the marriage contract is performed but the two will not live together as husband and wife for some time. However, as soon as the marriage contract is done, the two are husband and wife and are legally free to behave as such toward one another (although "custom" may say otherwise). This is not to be confused with the period of engagement. During engagement, the two have agreed that they will get married but they yet to actually perform the marriage contract and become truly husband and wife.—JZ

"A man cannot be alone with a woman except in the presence of [one of her] *mahram*. And a woman cannot travel except with a *mahram*."[1]

In sum, if that contact or association is after the marriage contract, there is no harm in it. If it is before the marriage ceremony, even if it is after proposal and acceptance, it is not allowed. Such behavior is forbidden for him since the woman is a non-relative and non-wife until they conclude the marriage contract.

Shaikh ibn Uthaimin

One Can Only Practice Coitus Interruptus with the Permission of the Wife

Question 181: When is it allowed for a woman to use birth control pills? Is there a clear text or opinion of the jurists on birth control? Is it allowed for a Muslim to practice coitus interruptus for no reason?

Response: Muslims must increase their numbers to the best of their ability. This is the command that the Prophet (صلى الله عليه وسلم) gave to the Muslims when he said,

$$\text{"تَزَوَّجُوا الْوَدُودَ الْوَلُودَ فَإِنِّي مُكَاثِرٌ بِكُمِ الأُمَمَ "}$$

"Marry the child-bearing, loving woman for I shall outnumber the peoples by you."[2]

Having more children means the Muslim nation will be larger. This is an honor for the Muslim Nation. Allah stated while talking about His blessings on the Tribes of Israel,

---

[1] Recorded by Muslim. Al-Bukhari has something similar.—JZ

[2] This hadith is recorded by Abu Dawud, al-Nasai, ibn Hibban, Ahmad, al-Tabarani and others. According to al-Albani, it is an authentic hadith due to its supporting chains, as was discussed earlier. Al-Albani, *Irwa*, vol. 6, p. 195.—JZ

﴾ وَجَعَلْنَـٰكُمْ أَكْثَرَ نَفِـيرًا ﴿ [الإسراء:٦]

"We made you more numerous in man-power" (*al-Isra* 6).

And Shuaib said to his people,

﴾ وَاذْكُرُوٓاْ إِذْ كُنتُمْ قَلِيلًا فَكَثَّرَكُمْ ﴿ [الأعراف:٨٦]

"And remember when you were but few and He multiplied you" (*al-Araf* 86).

No one can deny that the larger the Nation, the greater its honor and strength. This is the opposite of those who falsely and wrongfully claim that large population is a cause for poverty and hunger. If the Nation becomes larger, relies upon Allah and believes in the promise Allah has made in the verse,

﴾ وَمَا مِن دَآبَّةٍ فِى ٱلْأَرْضِ إِلَّا عَلَى ٱللَّهِ رِزْقُهَا ﴿ [هود:٦]

"And no moving (living) creature is there on earth but its provision is due from Allah" (*Hud* 6)

Allah will make their affairs easy for them and enrich them from His bounty. Based on that comes the answer to the question. A woman should not use birth control unless two conditions are met:

The first condition is that she is in need of such a practice. For example, she may be ill and cannot sustain bearing a child every year, her body might be weak or other causes that may make it difficult for her to be pregnant every year.

The second condition is that the husband gives his permission for the practice. This is because it is the right of the husband to have children. Furthermore, they must consult with a doctor concerning those pills. They have to see if taking them or not taking them could be hazardous to her health.

If these two conditions are met, there is no harm in her using those pills. But such procedures as pills or other forms must not be of a permanent nature. That is, one cannot use a form of birth control that is of a permanent nature as that will cut off the possibility of procreation.

As for the second part of the question, the answer is that, in reality, birth control is something that is not possible. This is because pregnancy and non-pregnancy are both in the hand of Allah. If humans try to limit their children to a specific number, it is possible that all of them may die in one year due to some cause and they will be left with no children at all. Birth control is something that is not considered acceptable by the *Shariah*. However, temporary limitation of pregnancy due to necessity, as was mentioned above, is permissible. As for coitus interruptus that is done for no sanctioning cause, according to the correct opinion among the scholars, it is permissible. This is based on the hadith of Jabir who said, "We used to perform coitus interruptus during the time that the Quran was being revealed," that is, during the lifetime of the Prophet Muhammad (صلى الله عليه وسلم).

If that act were forbidden, Allah would have forbidden them from it. However, the scholars say that coitus interruptus must not be done with a free [non-slave] wife except with her permission. This is because she also has the right to have children. It also reduces her sexual pleasure. The pleasure of the woman is not complete until after the male ejaculation. Therefore, for these two causes just mentioned, it is not allowed to perform coitus interruptus with one's free wife except with her consent.

Shaikh ibn Uthaimin

Ruling Concerning Remaining with a Husband who Does Not Pray

Question 182: My husband is heedless with respect to his religion. He does not fast Ramadhan or pray. In fact, he keeps me from doing any type of good. Now, he has started to have doubts about me to the point that he has left his job so he can stay home and watch me. What shall I do?

Response: It is not allowed to remain with such a husband. By his not praying, he has become a disbeliever. And it is not allowed for a Muslim woman to remain with a disbeliever. Allah has said,

﴿ فَإِنْ عَلِمْتُمُوهُنَّ مُؤْمِنَٰتٍ فَلَا تَرْجِعُوهُنَّ إِلَى ٱلْكُفَّارِ لَا هُنَّ حِلٌّ لَّهُمْ وَلَا هُمْ

يَحِلُّونَ لَهُنَّ ﴾   [الممتحنة: ١٠]

"If you know them [the women] to be true believers, send
them not back to the disbelievers. They are not lawful
[wives] for the disbelievers nor are the disbelievers lawful
[husbands] for them" (al-Mumtahana 10).

The marriage between you and him is annulled. There is no
marriage between the two of you unless Allah guides him, he
repents and returns to Islam. Then you will remain his wife. As
for the husband, his behavior is very wrong. In my opinion, it is a
kind of illness. It is the illness of doubt, suspicion and whisperings
that some people are exposed to with respect to their worship and
dealings with others. The only thing that can remove that sickness
is the remembrance of Allah, turning to Him and putting one's
complete trust in His decree. The important point, with respect to
you and him, is that you must separate from that husband and not
remain with him. This is because he is a disbeliever while you are
a believer. As for the husband, we advise him to return to his
religion and to seek refuge in Allah from the accursed Satan. He
should also be very keen on beneficial words of remembrance that
will repel these whisperings from his heart. We ask Allah to
benefit him. Allah knows best.

Shaikh ibn Uthaimin

The Son is for the Second Husband and the Missing Husband has the Right of Option

Question 183: A husband was missing for a long time, to
the point that his wife had thought he had died. His wife,
therefore, married another man and had a child from him. After
some years, the first husband returned. Does the wife now stay
with the second husband or is that marriage dissolved? Does the

first husband have the right to ask for his wife back? If he does, do they have to perform a new contract?

Response: This is the issue of the marriage of the wife of a missing husband. [This is the case where] the husband is missing and searched for over a long period of time, it is concluded that he is dead, the woman marries somebody else and then the husband reappears. He then will have the choice of keeping the new marriage in tact or in having his wife returned to him. If the new marriage is left in tact, the matter is clear. The contract is valid. If he does not choose that and he wants his wife back, the wife is returned to him. However, he cannot have intercourse with her until she finishes her waiting period from the second husband. There is no need to make a new contract for the first husband because there was nothing that invalidated the previous contract. As for her child from the second husband, it is a legal child and will be ascribed to its father because the child was the res:.t of a proper marriage.

Shaikh ibn Uthaimin

No Limit to What May Be Seen

Question 184: Is it allowed for a woman to look at all of the parts of her husband's body or for him to look at all of her with the intention of enjoying what is permissible?

Response: It is allowed for a woman to look at any part of her husband's body and it is allowed for a man to look at all of his wife's body without any exception. This is based on the Quranic verse,

﴿ وَٱلَّذِينَ هُمْ لِفُرُوجِهِمْ حَـٰفِظُونَ ٥ إِلَّا عَلَىٰٓ أَزْوَٰجِهِمْ أَوْ مَا مَلَكَتْ أَيْمَـٰنُهُمْ فَإِنَّهُمْ غَيْرُ مَلُومِينَ ٥ فَمَنِ ٱبْتَغَىٰ وَرَآءَ ذَٰلِكَ فَأُوْلَـٰٓئِكَ هُمُ ٱلْعَادُونَ ﴾
[المؤمنين: ٥-٧]

"And those who guard their private parts except from their wives or slaves, for then, they are free from blame. But whoever seeks beyond that, then those are the transgressors" (*al-Muminoon* 5-7).

Shaikh ibn Uthaimin

Ruling Concerning a Young Lady who Refuses Marriage in Order to Finish Her Studies

Question 185: A common practice today is for a young lady or her father to refuse one who proposes in order for the woman to finish her high school, college or study of certain years. What is the ruling concerning that? What is your advice to those who do such, given that many times the woman reaches the age of thirty or more without getting married?

Response: This practice goes against what the Prophet (صلى الله عليه وسلم) commanded. The Prophet (صلى الله عليه وسلم) said,

"إِذَا أَتَاكُمْ مَنْ تَرْضَوْنَ دِينَهُ وَخُلُقَهُ فَأَنْكِحُوهُ"

"If one whose religion and character pleases you comes to you [for proposal], then marry him."[1]

The Messenger of Allah (صلى الله عليه وسلم) also said,

" يَا مَعْشَرَ الشَّبَابِ مَنِ اسْتَطَاعَ مِنْكُمُ الْبَاءَةَ فَلْيَتَزَوَّجْ فَإِنَّهُ أَغَضُّ لِلْبَصَرِ وَأَحْصَنُ لِلْفَرْجِ."

"O youth, whoever of you has the means to get married should get married for it lowers the gaze and protects the chastity."[2]

By preventing marriage, one loses out on the benefits of marriage. I advise my brother Muslims who are the guardians of women and my sister Muslims not to keep from marriage due to finishing school or teaching. In fact, the woman may put a condition upon her husband that she may remain studying until she finishes her studies or she remain teaching for a year or two, given that she does not become busy with her children. There is no harm in such an act. However, a matter which needs further consideration is where the woman is continuing her studies in an area that is not

---

[1] Recorded by al-Tirmidhi and ibn Majah. Discussed earlier.—JZ
[2] Recorded by al-Bukhari and Muslim.—JZ

truly needed. In my view, when a woman finishes the elementary stages and has the ability to read and write, thereby being able to benefit from her knowledge through reading the Book of Allah, its *tafseer*, the hadith of the Prophet (صلى الله عليه وسلم) and their explanation, that is all she really needs. Unless, of course, she is continuing her studies in an area that the people need, such as medicine and similar fields This is also conditional that the study not involve aspects which are forbidden, such as mixing with men and so forth.

Shaikh ibn Uthaimin

Is the Marriage Contracting Valid if the Woman is Menstruating?

Question 186: I am a young woman who finalized my marriage contract with a young man some time ago. It happened that it occurred on a day in which I was having my menses. I did not agree to the contract until I asked the official about this matter and he said that such a marriage is valid and legal. However, I am not satisfied with that contract. I want you to help me by telling me if that contract was correct or not? Is it a must that I repeat the contract at a time when I am not on my menses?

Response: Performing a marriage contract with a woman while she is menstruating is permissible and valid. There is no harm in it. The basic ruling concerning contracts is that of permissibility and legality unless there is evidence to show that it is not allowed. There is no evidence to show that one may not finalize a marriage contract while the woman is menstruating. Therefore, the aforementioned contract is sound. There is no harm in it. One must also understand and know the difference between the marriage contract and divorce. Divorce is not permissible while the woman is menstruating. In fact, it is forbidden. The Messenger of Allah (صلى الله عليه وسلم) became angry when it reached him that Abdullah ibn Umar ibn al-Khattab had divorced his wife

while she was menstruating. The Prophet (صلى الله عليه وسلم) ordered
that he go back to her and not touch her until she became pure, had
her menses again and then became pure again. Then he could
afterwards remain with her or divorce her.[1] Furthermore, Allah
has stated,

﴿ يَٰٓأَيُّهَا ٱلنَّبِىُّ إِذَا طَلَّقْتُمُ ٱلنِّسَآءَ فَطَلِّقُوهُنَّ لِعِدَّتِهِنَّ وَأَحْصُوا۟ ٱلْعِدَّةَ
وَٱتَّقُوا۟ ٱللَّهَ رَبَّكُمْ لَا تُخْرِجُوهُنَّ مِنۢ بُيُوتِهِنَّ وَلَا يَخْرُجْنَ
إِلَّآ أَن يَأْتِينَ بِفَٰحِشَةٍ مُّبَيِّنَةٍ وَتِلْكَ حُدُودُ ٱللَّهِ وَمَن يَتَعَدَّ حُدُودَ
ٱللَّهِ فَقَدْ ظَلَمَ نَفْسَهُ ﴾ [الطلاق : ١]

"O Prophet! When you divorce women, divorce them at
their prescribed periods (*iddah*) and count (accurately) their
periods. And fear Allah your Lord. And turn them not out
of their [husband's] homes, nor shall they [themselves]
leave, except in cases where they are guilty of open illegal
sexual intercourse. Those are the set limits of Allah.
Whosoever transgresses the set limits of Allah, then indeed
he has wronged himself" (*al-Talaq* 1).

So it is not allowed for a man to divorce his wife while she is
menstruating. He also cannot divorce her during a time of purity
in which they had had sexual intercourse, unless it is clear that she
is pregnant. If it is clear that she is pregnant, he may divorce her
whenever he wishes and that divorce will take effect.

It is very strange that among the masses there is a common
misconception that a divorce stated while the woman is pregnant does
not take effect. This is not correct. The divorce of a pregnant woman
does take effect. In fact, the rules are more liberal concerning it. For
example, it is permissible for a man to divorce his pregnant wife even if
he had just recently had sexual intercourse with her. This is not so for a
woman who is not known to be pregnant. If he has intercourse with her,
he must wait until her next menses and their finishing or it becomes clear

---

[1] Recorded by al-Bukhari and Muslim.—JZ

that she is pregnant before he pronounces divorce. In *Surah al-Talaq*,
Allah states,

﴿ وَأُوْلَٰتُ ٱلۡأَحۡمَالِ أَجَلُهُنَّ أَن يَضَعۡنَ حَمۡلَهُنَّ ﴾ [الطلاق : ٤]

"For those who are pregnant, their waiting period is until
they deliver" (*al-Talaq* 4).

This is a clear indication that such a divorce does take effect.
Furthermore, in some of the hadith of ibn Umar, it is narrated that
the Prophet (صلى الله عليه وسلم) said,

" مُــرْه فَلۡيُراجِعۡهَــا ثُمَّ لِيُطَلِّقۡهَــا طَاهِــراً أَوْ حَامِــلاً "

"Order him to return to his wife and then divorce her when
she is pure [of her menses] or she is pregnant."[1]

If it is clear that the marriage contract done while the
woman is menstruating is a sound marriage contract, I still feel
that the man should not enter upon the woman [be with her alone]
until her menses come to an end. This is because if he does join
her before she becomes pure, it is feared that he may engage in an
act which is forbidden while she is menstruating, especially if he is
not able to control himself. Especially if he is a young man, he
should wait until she becomes pure, at a time when he is able to
enjoy her company by sexual intercourse. Allah knows best.

Shaikh ibn Uthaimin

Ruling Concerning Anal Intercourse

Question 187: A man asked his wife to have anal
intercourse with him. Is this acceptable behavior from the point of
view of the religion?

Response: That is an evil act. Abu Dawud, al-Nasai and
others record with a good chain that the Prophet (صلى الله عليه وسلم) said,

---

[1] This version was recorded by Muslim.—JZ

" مَلْعُونٌ مَنْ أَتَى امْرَأَتَهُ فِي دُبُرِهَا "

"Accursed is the one who has anal intercourse with his wife."

Shaikh ibn Uthaimin

Prohibition of Shaking Hands with a Non-Related Woman

Question 188: Why does Islam forbid a man from shaking the hand of a woman whom he is not related to? Does shaking hands without lust invalidate one's ablution?

Response: Islam has forbidden that because it is a temptation.[1] One of the greatest forms of temptation is for a man to touch a woman he is not related to. Everything that leads to temptation is prohibited by the Law. This is why one is required to lower one's gaze as a means of blocking that evil. As for a man touching his wife, it does not invalidate the ablution. This is so even if it is done with lust— unless he releases some prostatic fluid or sperm. In that case, he must make *ghusl* if it were sperm; he must make ablution and wash his male organ and testicles if it were prostatic fluid.

Shaikh ibn Uthaimin

Advice to "Old Maids"

Question 189: I would like your advice concerning a matter that affects me and my fellow sisters. This matter is that it has been written [by Allah] for us that we should live without a husband. We have passed through the age of marriage and we are getting close to menopause. This is the case even though, and all

---

[1] This word "temptation" found throughout this translation is actually an admittedly poor translation of the Arabic word *fitnah*. *Fitnah* has many connotations, including trial, tribulation and so forth. What it conveys here is the environment or actions that may lead to or induce one to commit a sin.—JZ

praises are due to Allah and Allah is witness to what I state, we are
women of character and we have all earned college degrees.
However, this is what is destined for us and all praises are due to
Allah. It is simply financial reasons that have kept people from
proposing to us. The customs surrounding a marriage, especially
in our land, are built upon cooperation between the spouses
concerning what will take place in the future. I ask for your advice
for me and my sisters.

Response: The advice that I direct to such women who
have delayed marriage is what was suggested in the question itself:
they should turn to Allah with supplications and submission so that
Allah may grant them one whose religion and character is pleasing
to them. If a person sincerely and resolutely turns to Allah,
seeking His help, following the manners of supplications and
being free of anything that prevents supplications from being
answered, then Allah has said,

﴿ وَإِذَا سَأَلَكَ عِبَادِى عَنِّى فَإِنِّى قَرِيبٌ أُجِيبُ دَعْوَةَ ٱلدَّاعِ إِذَا

دَعَانِ﴾   [البقرة: ١٨٦]

"And when My servants ask you [Muhammad] concerning
me, then (answer them), I am indeed near (to them by My
knowledge). I respond to the invocations of the supplicant
when he calls on Me" (*al-Baqara* 186).

Another verse states,

[غافر: ٦٠]   ﴿ وَقَالَ رَبُّكُمُ ٱدْعُونِى أَسْتَجِبْ لَكُمْ﴾

"And your Lord said, 'Invoke Me, I will respond to your
(invocation)'" (*Ghafir* 60).

Allah has stated that the response to the invocation comes after the
person responds to Allah and believes in Him. I do not see
anything stronger than turning to Allah, supplicating to Him,
humbling oneself to Him and waiting for the solution. It has been
confirmed that the Prophet (صلى الله عليه وسلم) said,

$$\text{"واعلَمْ أَنَّ النَّصْرَ مَعَ الصَّبْرِ، وَأَنَّ الفَرَجَ مَعَ الْكَرْبِ ، وَأَنَّ}$$
$$\text{مَعَ الْعُسْرِ يُسْراً"}$$

"Know that victory comes with patience, relief with distress and ease with hardship."[1]

I ask Allah for these women and others like them that Allah makes their affairs easy and grants them pious husbands who marry them for betterment in their religion and worldly lives. And Allah knows best.

Shaikh ibn Uthaimin

The Family Driver and Women

Question 190: What is the ruling concerning the family driver[2] mixing with the women and young girls of the family and him taking them to the market or schools?

Response: It is confirmed in the Hadith that the Prophet (صلى الله عليه وسلم) said,

$$\text{" لاَ يَخْلُوَنَّ رَجُلٌ بِامْرَأَةٍ إلا كَانَ الشَّيْطَانُ ثَالِثُهُمَا "}$$

"A man is never alone with a woman except that Satan is the third."[3]

Privacy is a general concept that applies to the house, car, market and so forth. When the two are in private, they are not safe from talking about private matters or what stirs the desires. Even

---

[1] Recorded by Ahmad and others. Al-Albani has graded it *sahih*. Al-Albani, *Sahih al-Jami*, vol. 2, p. 1151.—JZ
[2] In many Muslim countries, it has become the custom to have family chauffeurs. The question is in reference to these chauffeurs being the only other one in the car with the females of the family.—JZ
[3] Recorded by Ahmad and al-Tirmidhi. Al-Albani says it is *sahih*. Al-Albani, *Sahih al-Jami*, vol. 1, p. 234.—JZ

though many men and women have a fear of Allah and piety, and they hate sin and evil, Satan enters between them and makes sins look like light matters and opens the door to getting around the law. Therefore, remaining away from such deeds will be safer and more protecting.

Shaikh ibn Jibreen

Ruling Concerning Correspondence between Members of the Opposite Sex

Question 191: If a man has correspondence with a non-*mahram* woman and they fall in love with each other, is that act considered forbidden?

Response: Such an act is not allowed. It stirs up desires between the two. It stirs impulses in the two to meet and contact each other. Many times, the correspondence turns into soft speech that is a temptation and plants the love for fornication in the heart. I advise anyone who wants what is best for himself to remain away from such correspondence and speech in order to preserve one's religion and honor.

Shaikh ibn Jibreen

The Brother-in-Law is Not *Mahram*

Question 192: Is it allowed for my sister to wear *hijab* in front of her cousin even though he is going to be related to us [through marriage]. That is, his daughter is going to marry my brother, although the marriage has yet to take place.

Response: Your sister must wear *hijab* in front of her cousin because he is not a *mahram* for her, even if he is related through marriage and even if his daughter marries her brother. This is because the wife of the brother is still not a *mahram* as is also the case with the father of the brother's wife and so forth.

Shaikh ibn Jibreen

Speaking to Women on the Phone

Question 193: What is the ruling concerning a young man who is not married speaking to a young lady who is also not married over the telephone?

Response: It is not allowed to speak with a non-related woman with any speech that stirs desires, such as in a flirtatious, coquettish or soft manner. This is not allowed whether it is over the telephone or otherwise. Allah has said,

﴿ فَلَا تَخْضَعْنَ بِالْقَوْلِ فَيَطْمَعَ ٱلَّذِى فِى قَلْبِهِۦ مَرَضٌ ﴾

[الأحزاب: ٣٢]

"Be not soft in speech, lest those in whose heart is a disease should be moved with desire" (al-Ahzab 32).

There is no harm in casual speech due to some need if it is free from any sort of evil. However, such speech must be restricted to only what is necessary.

Shaikh ibn Jibreen

12. Questions Related to Relation Between the Spouses

My Husband Is Not Concerned with Me at All

Question 194: My husband, may Allah forgive him, although he has noble character and fear of Allah, is not concerned with me at all in the home. He is always frowning and depressing. One might claim that I am the cause but, and Allah knows this, I am, and all praises are due to Allah, fulfilling his rights and I try my best to make everything very pleasant and nice for him. I also keep anything harmful from him and I am patient with how he treats me.

Every time I ask him about something or speak to him, he gets upset and agitated. He claims that it is ridiculous and useless speech, although he is very friendly with his companions and friends. As for me, I only see harshness and contempt. This hurts me very much and I really suffer from it. Many times I have thought about simply leaving the home.

I am a woman, and all praises are due to Allah, who has an average education and I fulfill the obligations Allah has put upon me.

Dear Shaikh, if I leave the house, bring up my children alone and take on my worldly needs by myself, would I be sinful? Or should I stay with him in this situation and just stop talking and participating with him?

Response: There is no doubt that it is obligatory upon the spouses to treat each other in a kind and respectable manner. They should treat each other with love, good disposition and beautiful manners. Allah has stated,

﴿ وَعَاشِرُوهُنَّ بِٱلْمَعْرُوفِ﴾   [النساء: ١٩]

"Live with them honorably" (*al-Nisa* 19).

Allah also says,

﴿ وَلَهُنَّ مِثْلُ ٱلَّذِى عَلَيْهِنَّ بِٱلْمَعْرُوفِ وَلِلرِّجَالِ عَلَيْهِنَّ دَرَجَةٌ ﴾

[البقرة: ٢٢٨]

"And they (women) have rights similar to [those] over them according to what is reasonable, but men have a degree [of responsibility] over them" (*al-Baqara* 228).

The Prophet (صلى الله عليه وسلم) also said,

" الـــــبِرُّ حُسْـــــنُ الخُلُـــــقِ "

"Piety is good behavior."[1]

In another hadith, the Prophet (صلى الله عليه وسلم) said,

"لَا تَحْقِرَنَّ مِنَ الْمَعْـــرُوفِ شَيْئاً ولَو أَنْ تَلقَى أخَاكَ بَوَجْهٍ طَلْقٍ"

"Do not discount any deed of goodness, even greeting your brother with a smiling face."

Muslim recorded both of them in his *Sahih*. The Prophet also said,

"أَكْمَـلُ الْمُؤْمِنِـينَ إِيمَاناً أَحْسَنُهم خُلُقـاً وخِيارُكُم خِيَارُكُم لِنِسَآئِهِم وأَنَا خَيرُكُم لأَهْلِي"

"The believer with the most complete faith is the one with the best character. The best of you are those who are best to their wives and I am best to my family."[2]

---

[1] Recorded by Muslim.—JZ

[2] This translator was not able to find this complete text in any of the hadith books available to him. It seems, Allah knows best, that the Shaikh has combined two hadith in this reply. (It could simply be a typographical error.) One hadith states, "The believer with the most complete faith is the one with the best character. And the best of you is the one who is best to his wives." This is an authentic hadith recorded by al-Tirmidhi, Ahmad and others. The second hadith states, "The best of you is the best to his

There are many other Ahadith that are exhortations to behaving properly, dealing nicely with each other and having good relations with other Muslims in general. Therefore, what obviously must be the case concerning the relation between spouses and close relatives?

You have done well by being patient and bearing the coldness and bad behavior from your husband. I advise you to increase your patience and not leave the home. Allah willing, that will bring about lots of good and a praiseworthy solution. Allah has stated,

[الأنفال : ٤٦] ﴿ وَٱصۡبِرُوٓاْ إِنَّ ٱللَّهَ مَعَ ٱلصَّٰبِرِينَ ﴾

"Be patient. Surely, Allah is with those who are patient" (*al-Anfal* 46).

Allah also says,

﴿ إِنَّهُۥ مَن يَتَّقِ وَيَصۡبِرۡ فَإِنَّ ٱللَّهَ لَا يُضِيعُ أَجۡرَ ٱلۡمُحۡسِنِينَ ﴾ [يوسف : ٩٠]

"Verily, he who fears Allah and is patient, then surely, Allah makes not the reward of the doers of good to be lost" (*Yusuf* 90).

Again, Allah says,

[الزمر : ١٠] ﴿ إِنَّمَا يُوَفَّى ٱلصَّٰبِرُونَ أَجۡرَهُم بِغَيۡرِ حِسَابٍ ﴾

"Only those who are patient shall receive their rewards in full without reckoning" (*al-Zumar* 10).

Finally, Allah says in yet another verse,

[هود : ٤٩] ﴿ فَٱصۡبِرۡ إِنَّ ٱلۡعَٰقِبَةَ لِلۡمُتَّقِينَ ﴾

"So be patient, surely, the good end is for those who fear Allah" (*Hud* 49).

---

wife and I am the best to my wife." This was recorded by al-Tirmidhi and ibn Majah. It is also an authentic hadith. See Muhammad Nasir al-Din al-Albani, *Silsilat al-Ahadith al-Sahiha* (Beirut: al-Maktab al-Islami, 1979), vol. 1, hadith #284 and 285.—JZ

There is nothing to prevent you from joking with him and speaking with him in words that will soften his heart, acts that will cause him to smile at you and recognize your rights. Avoid seeking worldly needs from him as long as he is fulfilling your most important rights. Then when his heart becomes at ease, then you can get what you need and you both will praise Allah for the end result, Allah willing. May Allah grant you increase in every good. May He also correct the situation of your husband and guide him to what is right and proper behavior and fulfilling what is right. Allah is the Best one to ask and He is the guide to the straight way.

Shaikh ibn Baz

My Husband Does not Treat Me in a Good and Proper Fashion

Question 195: I have been married for about 25 years. I have numerous sons and daughters. I always face difficulties from my husband. He humiliates me in front of my children, close relatives and others. He never gives me any credit. The only time I feel rest is when I leave the house, although he does pray and he fears Allah. Please guide me to the best path I should follow.

Response: It is obligatory upon you to have patience and to advise him to act in the best way. Remind him of Allah and the Hereafter. Perhaps he will respond and return to what is correct. Perhaps he will give up his evil behavior. If he does not, the sin is upon him and you will get a great reward for your patience and bearing his harm. It is sanctioned for you to supplicate for him in your prayer and at other times, that Allah may guide him to what is correct, bless him with proper behavior and protect you from his evil and the evil of others. You also should take account of yourself and be steadfast in your faith. You should also repent to Allah for whatever you have done in the past of evils and mistakes with respect to the right of Allah, the right of your husband or others' rights. Perhaps he has been given this control over you because of some sin that you have committed. Allah has stated,

$$﴿ وَمَآ أَصَٰبَكُم مِّن مُّصِيبَةٍ فَبِمَا كَسَبَتْ أَيْدِيكُمْ وَيَعْفُوا عَن كَثِيرٍ ﴾ [الشورى: ٣٠]$$

"And whatever of misfortune befalls you, it is because of what your hands have earned. And He pardons much" (al-Shura 30).

There is nothing to keep you from asking his father, mother, older brothers, any relative he respects or neighbors to advise him and encourage him to treat you properly, in response to Allah's statements,

$$﴿ وَعَاشِرُوهُنَّ بِالْمَعْرُوفِ ﴾ [النساء: ١٩]$$

"Live with them honorably" (al-Nisa 19).

Allah also says,

$$﴿ وَلَهُنَّ مِثْلُ الَّذِى عَلَيْهِنَّ بِالْمَعْرُوفِ وَلِلرِّجَالِ عَلَيْهِنَّ دَرَجَةٌ ﴾ . . [البقرة: ٢٢٨]$$

"And they (women) have rights similar to those over them according to what is reasonable. But men have a degree [of responsibility] over them" (al-Baqara 228).

May Allah improve your affairs, guide your husband and return him to what is correct. May Allah also gather the two of you together in goodness and guidance. He is the Generous, the Noble.

Shaikh ibn Baz

My Husband Curses and Abuses Me

Question 196: What is the legal ruling concerning seeking a divorce when proper relations become an impossibility? This is due to the following reasons: First, my husband is ignorant and he does not recognize any rights for me. He curses me and my father and calls us Jews, Christians and Shia. However, I was patient with his evil manners because of my child. But when I became ill

with arthritis, I no longer had the ability to bear his behavior. I
began to hate him a great deal, to the point that I cannot stand even
talking to him. I asked him for a divorce but he refused. Now I have
been living with him for six years with my children and he treats me
like a divorced woman or a woman who is not related to him. But he
still refuses divorce. I beg for your answer to my question.

Response: If the situation is as you have just described,
there is nothing wrong in seeking divorce. There is no harm also
in you ransoming yourself by paying him some wealth in order for
him to divorce you. This is due to his improper behavior and
wronging you by evil speech. If you think it feasible, for the sake
of your children and your need for his maintenance as well as the
children's, to be patient and advise him to behave properly and ask
Allah to guide him, there is great reward and a good end. We ask
Allah to guide him and make him firm in his religion. This answer
is assuming that he prays and does not curse the religion. If he
does not pray or if he curses the religion, he is a disbeliever. Then
it is not permissible for you to stay with him or allow him control
over you. This is because cursing and ridiculing the religion is
disbelief and straying. It is apostasy from Islam according to the
consensus of the scholars. This is based on Allah's statement,

$$ \text{﴿ قُلْ أَبِٱللَّهِ وَءَايَـٰتِهِۦ وَرَسُولِهِۦ كُنتُمْ تَسْتَهْزِءُونَ ۝ لَا تَعْتَذِرُواْ} $$
$$ \text{قَدْ كَفَرْتُم بَعْدَ إِيمَـٰنِكُمْ ﴾ [التوبة: ٦٥-٦٦]} $$

"Say: Was it Allah, and His signs and His Messenger that
you were mocking? Make no excuse! You have disbelieved
after you had believed" (*al-Tauba* 65-66).

Also, abandoning the prayer is a greater form of disbelief, even if a
person does not deny its obligation, according to the stronger
opinion among the scholars. This is based on what has been
confirmed from the Prophet (صلى الله عليه وسلم) in *Sahih Muslim* from
Jabir ibn Abdullah that the Prophet (صلى الله عليه وسلم) said,

" بَيْنَ الرَّجُـلِ وَبَيْنَ الْكُفْـرِ وَالشِّـرْكِ تَـرْكُ الصَّـلاَةَ "

"Between a man and disbelief and polytheism is the abandoning of the prayer."

Also, Imam Ahmad and the compilers of the *Sunan* recorded with a *sahih* chain from Buraida ibn al-Hasib that the Prophet (صلى الله عليه وسلم) said,

" العَهدُ الَّذِي بَيْنَنَا وبينَهُمُ الصَّلاةُ ، فَمَنْ تَرَكَها فقَدْ كَفَرَ "

"The covenant between us and them is the prayer. Whoever abandons it has committed disbelief."

There are also other evidences from the Quran and sunnah besides what we have mentioned.

Shaikh ibn Baz

A Woman Takes Money from Her Husband without His Knowledge

Question 197: My husband does not give me my expenses, neither for me nor my children. Sometimes, we take money from him without his knowledge. Is there any sin upon us?

Response: It is allowed for a woman to take wealth from her husband without his knowledge to meet her and her children's needs if he is not giving them what they are customarily entitled to. She must take the money without extravagance or waste if he does not give her what suffices her. This is based on what is recorded in *Sahih al-Bukhari* and *Sahih Muslim* from Aisha who stated that Hind bint Utbah came to the Prophet (صلى الله عليه وسلم) and said, "O Messenger of Allah (صلى الله عليه وسلم), Abu Sufyan does not give me what is sufficient for me or for my children." The Prophet (صلى الله عليه وسلم) said,

" خُذِي مِنْ مَّالِهِ بِالْمَعْرُوفِ مَايَكْفِيكِ ويَكْفِي بَنِيكِ "

"Take from his wealth according to what is right and good which will suffice you and your child."

Shaikh ibn Baz

Obedience is in What is Right and Good

Question 198: I married a man. After the marriage, he requested that I should not cover my face in front of his brothers, otherwise he would divorce me. What should I do while I fear divorce?

Response: It is not allowed for a man to be flexible with respect to his wife and allow her to uncover her face in front of men. It is not proper for him to be weak and give into his family to the point that his wife uncovers her face in front of his brothers, uncles, brother-in-laws, cousins and others who are not *mahram* for her. This is not allowed. She does not obey him in that matter as obedience is only in what is good and right. In fact, she must wear *hijab* and cover her face even if he divorces her. If he does divorce her, soon Allah will provide her with someone better than him, Allah willing. Allah says in the Quran,

$$ \text{﴿ وَإِن يَتَفَرَّقَا يُغْنِ ٱللَّهُ كُلًّا مِّن سَعَتِهِۦ ﴾ [النساء: ١٣٠]} $$

"But if they separate [by divorce], Allah will provide abundance for everyone of them from His Bounty" (*al-Nisa* 130).

It is also narrated that the Prophet (صلى الله عليه وسلم) said,

$$ \text{" مَنْ تَرَكَ شَيْئاً لِلَّهِ عَوَّضَهُ اللَّهُ خَيْراً مِّنْهُ "} $$

"If someone abandons something for the sake of Allah, Allah will replace it with something better than it."[1]
Allah says:

---

[1] The Shaikh has presented this hadith in such a way that it looks like he considers it weak. However, with a different wording but the same meaning, the hadith is narrated by Ahmad with a chain of trustworthy narrators. See Muhammad al-Sakhawi, *al-Maqasid al-Hasana* (Beirut: Dar al-Kitab al-Arabi, 1985), p. 576.—JZ

$$\text{﴿ وَمَن يَتَّقِ ٱللَّهَ يَجْعَل لَّهُۥ مِنْ أَمْرِهِۦ يُسْرًا ﴾}$$ [الطلاق : ٤]

"And whosoever fears Allah and keeps his duty to Him, He will make his matter easy for him." (al-Talâq 4)

It is not allowed for the husband to threaten her with divorce if she wears *hijab* and follows those guidelines that lead to chastity and modesty. We ask Allah for safety and health.

Shaikh ibn Baz

If a Woman Advised Her Husband

Question 199: If a woman advised her husband who is lazy with respect to performing the prayers in the mosque and she shows her anger towards him, is she being sinful because of his greater right over her?

Response: There is no sin upon a woman if she advises her husband when he performs something that Allah has forbidden, such as being lazy with respect to performing the prayer with the congregation, drinking alcohol or having entertainment during the night. In fact, she will be rewarded. The advice should be in a good and kind way. In this way, it will more likely be accepted and benefited from.

Shaikh ibn Baz

My Husband is Addicted to Smoking

Question 200: My husband is addicted to smoking and is afflicted with asthma. We have faced many problems between us from trying to get him to quit. Five months ago, my husband prayed two *rakat*s to Allah and swore that he would not smoke again. Just one week after his oath, he smoked again and the problems began between us again. I sought divorce from him. However, he promised that he would not smoke again forever. However, I have no trust in him whatsoever. What is your sound opinion? What should he do as an expiation for his oath? What do you advise me to do? May Allah reward you.

Response: Smoking is an evil, forbidden act. It is very harmful. In *Surah al-Maidah* of the Noble Book, Allah has said,

﴿ يَسْتَلُونَكَ مَاذَآ أُحِلَّ لَهُمْ قُلْ أُحِلَّ لَكُمُ ٱلطَّيِّبَتُ ﴾ [المائدة : ٤]

"They ask you what is lawful for them. Say, 'Lawful unto you are the good, wholesome foods" (*al-Maida* 4).

In *Surah al-Araf*, Allah has stated in describing the Prophet Muhammad (صلى الله عليه وسلم),

﴿ وَيُحِلُّ لَهُمُ ٱلطَّيِّبَتِ وَيُحَرِّمُ عَلَيْهِمُ ٱلْخَبَئِثَ ﴾
[الأعراف : ١٥٧]

"[He] who permits for them good things and prohibits for them as unlawful all evil things" (*al-Araf* 157).

There is no doubt that smoking is one of the evil, unwholesome things. It is obligatory upon your husband to stop smoking and remain away from it in obedience to Allah and His Messenger (صلى الله عليه وسلم). He must also avoid any cause of Allah's displeasure and he must safeguard the well-being of his religion and health as well as deal with you in a proper manner.

He must make an expiation for the vow he broke. In addition to repenting to Allah due to his returning to smoking, he must feed ten poor people or clothe them or free a believing slave. It is sufficient for him to give them dinners or lunch or to give each a half of *sa'* of the staple food of the land. Half of a *sa* is approximately one and a half kilograms.

I advise you not to seek divorce if he prays, behaves well and gives up smoking. However, if he continues to perform this sinful act, there is nothing to prevent you from seeking divorce. We ask Allah for guidance and aid for a sincere repentance.

Shaikh ibn Baz

Psychological Conditions may Allow a Wife to Prevent Her Husband

Question 201: Is a woman sinful if she prevents her husband when he desires her for sexual intercourse due to her psychological state or due to an illness that is hurting her?

Response: It is obligatory upon the wife to respond to her husband if he calls her to his bed. However, if she is psychologically ill and is not able to actively respond to his call or if she has a physical illness, then in such cases it is not allowed for the husband to call upon her. This is because the Prophet (صلى الله عليه وسلم) said,

$$" \ \text{لاَ ضَـــرَرَ وَلاَ ضِـــرَارَ} \ "$$

"There is to be no harm done or reciprocation of harm."[1]

He should either refrain or enjoy her company in such a way that does not harm her.

Shaikh ibn Uthaimin

---

[1] Recorded by Ahmad, Malik and ibn Majah. Al-Albani has graded it *sahih*. Al-Albani, *Sahih al-Jami*, vol. 2, p. 1249.

13.Questions Related to Breast Feeding

Breast Feeding After Menopause is Treated the Same as Breast Feeding in Earlier Years

Question 202: What is the ruling concerning a woman who has reached the age of menopause and she breastfeeds a child five sucklings or more during the first two years of that child's life. Does this breastfeeding make them illegal for each other [and all the other ramifications], giving him a foster father even though the breastfeeding woman may be without a husband?

Response: Breastfeeding makes forbidden what blood relations make forbidden. Therefore, the breastfeeding mentioned in the question, five sucklings in the first two years, makes the woman a [breastfeeding] mother to that child due to that breastfeeding. This is based on the generality of the Quranic verse,

[النساء: ٢٣]   ﴿ وَأُمَّهَٰتُكُمُ ٱلَّٰتِيٓ أَرْضَعْنَكُمْ﴾

"[Forbidden to you for marriage are] your foster mother who gave you suck" (*al-Nisa* 23).

Even if the milk was produced after she reached the age of menopause, the ruling is the same. If that woman was married, the child would be her [foster] child and the son of the one whom the milk is ascribed to. If she was not married, perhaps she was not married and produced milk, then she is the [foster] mother of that child and he has no foster father.

Do not consider it strange that one may have a milking mother and not a foster father. Also, do not consider it strange that one may have a foster father but no foster mother. An example of the first case is where a woman gave two sucklings to a child, the milk that was the result of her first husband. Then she separated from that husband and married another after her waiting period expired. She becomes pregnant and has a child from the second husband. She then suckles her foster child again for the remainder of the suckling amount [with the milk that is the result of a child with the second husband]. She now has become that child's foster mother due to the five sucklings but he has no foster father because he did not suckle at least five sucklings that were the result of one man with the woman. As for the second case, this is where the child has a foster father but no foster mother. An example is where a man has two wives. One of them suckles the child twice and the other suckles the child three times. In that case, he will be a foster child of the husband since he was breastfed over five times from milk that was the result of intercourse with him. But he will not have a foster mother because neither the first nor the second woman suckled him the minimum amount of times required.

Shaikh ibn Uthaimin

They are Your Maternal Uncles and Aunts from Breastfeeding

Question 203: My mother was breastfed by a woman who had co-wives. Are the children of those co-wives considered my brothers or not?

Response: That breastfeeding woman is considered your [foster] grandmother by virtue of her breastfeeding your mother. Her husband is the [foster] father of your mother and your maternal grandfather. Therefore, her co-wives are treated the same as the wives of your maternal grandfather. The co-wives' children are your maternal uncles and aunts and the siblings of your mother. Since their father is your grandfather, they are the children of your grandfather and are your paternal aunts and uncles from breastfeeding.

Shaikh ibn Jibreen

14. Questions Related to Divorce

Asking for Divorce Due to Need

Question 204: My husband wants to marry a second wife and informed me of that. I refused. My reasoning was that he is not in need of that since I have given him children and fulfill his rights. So I said to him, "In that case, divorce me." Am I in the right?

Response: You do not have the right to prevent him from marrying again no matter what your actions are toward him. He may desire more children or he may feel that having only one wife does not keep him completely chaste. In any case, the wife does not have the right to keep him from marrying another. However, if she fears that she will treat the other wife unfairly or she believes that she will not be able to live with a co-wife, then she may seek divorce due to that need. It is not allowed to seek a divorce without the presence of a necessity.

Shaikh ibn Jibreen

Impotence Permits One to Seek a Divorce

Question 205: A woman was married for many years and did not have any children. After an examination, it was determined that the problem was from her husband and it would be impossible for the two of them to have children. Does she have the right to seek a divorce?

Response: That woman has a right to ask for divorce from her husband if it is shown that the infertility problem is from him alone. If he divorces her, that is final. If he does not divorce her, a judge may dissolve her marriage. This is because the woman has the right to have children and many women do not even get married except to have children. If the man she is married to is impotent or sterile, she has the right to ask for divorce and have her marriage dissolved. This is the stronger opinion among the scholars.

Shaikh ibn Uthaimin

I Do Not Love Him and I Want Him to Divorce Me

Question 206: My older brother married me off without my approval. Even though, I stayed with my husband for six years. I am still with him now and we do not have any children. However, I do not love him and I would like for him to divorce me. But I heard a hadith whose meaning is, "If a woman seeks a divorce due to no harm, she will not enter Paradise." What is the solution?

Response: Since you permitted the actions of your brother and went with your husband without preventing it and then stayed with him for that lengthy period of time, the marriage contract is valid. It is valid due to the implicit permission given. However, since you have found that you find no happiness or tranquillity with him, in fact, you have felt unhappiness and dislike and fear that you may not fulfill his rights and you have not had any child with him, due to those reasons, it is allowed for you to seek a separation.

Shaikh ibn Jibreen

Ruling Concerning Divorcing a Menstruating Woman and Its Legal Effect

Question 207: A mother of two children was divorced by her husband but at the time of the divorce she was not in a state of purity. However, she did not tell her husband that until the time that they went to the judge. She hid that information from him but not from her mother. The mother told her not to tell the judge for, if she did, the judge would not pronounce the divorce. Afterwards, she stayed with her family and then she wanted to be reunited with her husband out of fear that her children would grow up lost and uncared for [since their father would not be present]. What is the ruling concerning that divorce that took place while she was menstruating?

Response: Divorce that takes place while the woman is menstruating is disputed among the scholars. Indeed, the discussion over it is quite lengthy. The question is whether it was a divorce that took place or a divorce with no meaning to it whatsoever. The majority of the scholars say that it is a divorce that takes place and has legal effect. That is, it is considered a divorce but, at the same time, the person is ordered to take her back and to not touch her until she becomes pure from the menses and then gets her menses a second time. Then when she becomes pure after that second period, he may either keep her or he may divorce her. This is the approach of the majority of the scholars, including the four Imams, Imams Ahmad, al-Shafi'i, Malik and Abu Hanifah. However, the strongest opinion, we feel, is the conclusion of Shaikh al-Islam ibn Taimiya. This is that the divorce said during the menses does not take place and has no legal effect. This is because it goes against what Allah and His Messenger (صلى الله عليه وسلم) have ordered. The Prophet (صلى الله عليه وسلم) has stated,

$$\text{" مَنْ عَمِلَ عَمَلاً لَيْسَ عَلَيْهِ أَمْرُنَا فَهُوَ رَدٌّ "}$$

"Whoever does a deed that is not in accord with our affair shall have it rejected."[1]

The evidence for the particular case of the menstruating woman is the hadith of Abdullah ibn Umar. He had divorced his wife when

---

[1] Recorded by al-Bukhari and Muslim.—JZ

she was menstruating. The Prophet (صلى الله عليه وسلم) was informed of that and he became angry. He said,

$$\text{"مُرْهُ فَلْيُرَاجِعْهَا ثم يَتْرُكْهَا حَتَى تَطْهُرَ ثُمَّ تَحِيضَ ثُمَّ تَطْهُرَ ثُمَّ إِنْ شَآءَ أَمْسَكَ بَعْدُ وَإِنْ شَآءَ طَلَّقَ"}$$

"Order him to return to her and then leave her until she becomes pure and then has her menses again and then becomes pure again. At that time, he may keep her or he may divorce her."[1]

The Prophet (صلى الله عليه وسلم) said,

$$\text{"فَتِلْكَ العِدَّةُ الَّتِي أَمَرَ اللهُ أَنْ تُطَلَّقَ عَلَيهاَ النِّسَآءُ"}$$

"That is the period during which Allah has ordered the women to be divorced."[2]

So the period in which Allah has ordered women to be divorced is for her to be divorced while she is pure and not having had sexual intercourse with her husband. If he divorces her while she is menstruating, he did not divorce her according to the command of Allah. Therefore, the act is rejected. The divorce that occurred to the woman in this question, in our opinion, is a divorce that did not exist. The woman is still under the marriage contract of her husband. It is regardless of whether he knew that he divorced her while she was pure or not pure. His knowledge is not taken into consideration. However, if he knew that she was menstruating, he would be sinful and the divorce would not take effect. If he was unaware of that fact, the divorce would not have taken effect but there would be no sin upon the husband.

Shaikh ibn Uthaimin

---

[1] Recorded by al-Bukhari and Muslim.—JZ
[2] This is part of the previous hadith.—JZ

15.Questions Related to the Waiting Period (Iddah) and Mourning

What Must the Mourning Widow Abide By

Question 208: What are the laws by which the widow whose husband had just died must abide by?

Response: The Hadith states what a mourning widow is prohibited from doing and what she is requested to do.

First, she must remain in her house in which she was living when her husband died. She remains therein until her *iddah* (mourning period) comes to an end. This is four months and ten days. Unless she is pregnant, wherein her mourning period ends when she gives birth. Allah says in the Quran,

﴿ وَأُوْلَٰتُ ٱلْأَحْمَالِ أَجَلُهُنَّ أَن يَضَعْنَ حَمْلَهُنَّ ﴾   [الطلاق : ٤]

"For those who are pregnant, their waiting period is until they deliver" (*al-Talaq* 4).

She does not leave the house except due to need or necessity, such as visiting the hospital due to illness, buying what she is in need of from the market, such as food or other items, if she cannot find others to do such for her. Similarly, if the house is destroyed, she leaves it for another house. Finally, if she does not find anyone who she knows close to her and she fears for her safety, she may move due to that need.

Second, she may not wear any kind of beautiful clothing, either yellow, green or other. She must wear clothing which is not beautiful or attractive, regardless of whether it be black, green or otherwise. The important aspect is that it is not beautiful or attractive. This is what the Prophet (صلى الله عليه وسلم) ordered.

Third, she must not wear jewelry, either gold, silver, diamonds, pearls or anything of that nature. This is regardless if it be bracelets, chains or rings. She may not wear anything of this nature until her mourning period is over.

Fourth, she must refrain from using perfume. She cannot perfume herself with either incense or any other kind of items that make the body smell good. The only exception to this is when she cleanses herself after her period. In that case, there is no harm if she applies some kind of incense.

Fifth, she should not apply kohl. She can neither use kohl nor anything similar to kohl which is a beautification for the face, a beautification that may be considered something that attracts people. As for the normal beautification of using water and soap, there is nothing wrong with that. But the kohl which is a beautification of the eyes and other similar items that woman put on their faces are not to be used.

These are the five items that a woman must attend to when her husband dies.

However, there are many other acts that the general masses believe or have fabricated concerning a mourning woman. For example, they say that she cannot talk to anyone, she may not talk on the phone, she can only take a shower once a week, she cannot walk barefoot in her house, she cannot go out under the light of the moon, and other superstitions that are simply false. There is no basis for any of these. She may walk barefoot or with shoes in her house. She fulfills her needs in the house, such as cooking her food and the food of her guests. She may go out in the light of the moon on her roof[1] or in her garden. She may wash herself whenever she wishes. She may speak to anyone she wishes as long as it is not suspicious speech. She may shake hands with women and men she is related to— as for those men she is not related to, she may not shake their hands. She may remove her headscarf if she is not in the presence of men she is not related to.

---

[1] Many of the houses in the Middle East have gardens and meeting places on the rooftops.—JZ

However, she should not use henna or saffron either on her clothing or in her coffee. This is because saffron is a kind of perfume and it is not allowed for her to perfume herself. She cannot be proposed to. One may indirectly make a statement of intent to her but a clear proposal is not allowed.

Shaikh ibn Baz

Ruling Concerning Wearing a Watch During the Mourning Period

Question 209: Is it allowed for a woman to wear a watch to know what time it is and not for the sake of beautification during her mourning period?

Response: Yes. That is allowed for her due to her intention. However, if she even avoids that, that would be best because it does resemble jewelry.

The Standing Committee

What is the Mourning Period of the Pregnant Widow

Question 210: The questioner states that his father's wife is pregnant. Is her mourning period due to his father's death four months and ten days or is it until she gives birth?

Response: The conclusion of the study of the Committee is that her mourning period is until she delivers.

The Standing Committee

Does the Elderly Woman Mourn and What is the Ruling Concerning That

Question 211: A man died and his wife was elderly, over seventy years old, with little ability to think and no servant. He died while she was still married to him. Does she have to go through the mourning period like others? What is the wisdom behind such an act if someone is old like her? Why then is it that the pregnant woman mourns only until she gives birth, implying that the mourning period is just to make certain that the woman is or is not pregnant? In a case like this woman, that possibility is not present.

Response: The woman mentioned in the question goes through the mourning period of four months and ten days since she falls under the generality of Allah's words,

﴿ وَٱلَّذِينَ يُتَوَفَّوْنَ مِنكُمْ وَيَذَرُونَ أَزْوَٰجًا يَتَرَبَّصْنَ بِأَنفُسِهِنَّ أَرْبَعَةَ أَشْهُرٍ وَعَشْرًا ﴾ [البقرة: ٢٣٤]

"Those of you who die and leave wives behind, they [the wives] shall wait for four months and ten days" (*al-Baqara* 234).

From the *Shariah* wisdom of the waiting period and mourning even if the woman is old and could not possibly be pregnant is: honoring the seriousness of the marriage contract, raising the status and demonstrating the honorableness of the marriage, and fulfilling the rights of the husband, and showing the effects of one's loss by not beautifying or adorning oneself. Therefore, her mourning in that case is more than her mourning in the case of the death of a father or child. The ruling concerning a pregnant woman is until she gives birth based on the generality of Allah's statement,

﴿ وَأُوْلَٰتُ ٱلْأَحْمَالِ أَجَلُهُنَّ أَن يَضَعْنَ حَمْلَهُنَّ ﴾ [الطلاق: ٤]

"For those who are pregnant, their waiting period is until they deliver" (*al-Talaq* 4).

This verse particularizes the generality of the other verse,

﴿ وَٱلَّذِينَ يُتَوَفَّوْنَ مِنكُمْ وَيَذَرُونَ أَزْوَٰجًا يَتَرَبَّصْنَ بِأَنفُسِهِنَّ أَرْبَعَةَ أَشْهُرٍ وَعَشْرًا ﴾ [البقرة: ٢٣٤]

"Those of you who die and leave wives behind, they [the wives] shall wait for four months and ten days" (*al-Baqara* 234).

A wisdom behind relating the end of the waiting period to giving birth is that the pregnancy is the right of the first husband. If she gets married after the first husband's death or other [type of separation from him] and she is pregnant, then the second husband may be mixing his sperm with another man's. This is not allowed due to the statement of the Prophet (صلى الله عليه وسلم),

$$\text{"لا يَحِلُّ لِامْرِىءٍ مُسْلِمٍ يُؤْمِنُ بِاللهِ وَالْيَوْمِ الآخِرِ أَنْ يَسْقِيَ مَاءَهُ زَرْعَ غَيْرِهِ"}$$

"It is not allowed for a Muslim man who believes in Allah and the Hereafter to water what another has sown with his water [that is, to have intercourse with a woman impregnated by another man]."

This was recorded by Imam Ahmad, Abu Dawud and ibn Hibban on the authority of Ruwaifi ibn Thabit al-Ansari.[1]

It is obligatory upon a Muslim to apply the laws of the *Shariah* regardless of whether he knows the wisdom behind them or not. He must have belief that Allah regulates what is best and proper in His Law and His Decrees. However, if Allah blesses one with the knowledge of the wisdom, then that is light upon light and goodness in addition to goodness.

The Standing Committee

Do The Elderly or Underaged Women Have Mourning Waiting Periods

Question 212: If the husband of an elderly woman who has no desire for men or a young girl who has not yet reached the age of puberty passes away, do they have to observe the mourning-waiting period?

---

[1] According to Abdul Qadir al-Arnaut, this hadith is *hasan*. See his footnotes to Al-Mubarak ibn al-Atheer, *Jami al-Usul fi Ahadith al-Rasool* (Maktaba al-Halwani, 1972), vol. 8, p. 121.—JZ

Response: Yes, the elderly woman who has no desire for men must observe the mourning-waiting period as does the young girl who has not yet reached the age of puberty or even has approached that age. She must observe the mourning period if her husband dies until she gives birth if she be pregnant. Otherwise, it is a period of four months and ten days based on the generality of the verse,

﴿ وَٱلَّذِينَ يُتَوَفَّوْنَ مِنكُمْ وَيَذَرُونَ أَزْوَٰجًا يَتَرَبَّصْنَ بِأَنفُسِهِنَّ أَرْبَعَةَ
أَشْهُرٍ وَعَشْرًا ﴾ [البقرة: ٢٣٤]

"Those of you who die and leave wives behind, they [the wives] shall wait for four months and ten days" (*al-Baqara* 234).

And also the verse,

﴿ وَأُوْلَٰتُ ٱلْأَحْمَالِ أَجَلُهُنَّ أَن يَضَعْنَ حَمْلَهُنَّ ﴾ [الطلاق: ٤]

"For those who are pregnant, their waiting period is until they deliver" (*al-Talaq* 4).

The Standing Committee

Ruling Concerning the Mourning Widow Moving from Her Husband's House to Her Family's House

Question 213: A woman married a man and then he passed away and they did not have any children. She has no relatives in the area where her husband lived. Is it allowed for her to move from the land of her husband to the land of her guardian to pass the mourning period there?

Response: It is allowed for that woman to move to the house of her guardian or any other place in which she feels that she will be safe in order to fulfill the rest of her mourning period for her husband. This is if she fears for herself or for her honor and she finds no one to protect her. However, if she has no fear but she just wants to be closer to her family, then it is not allowed for her to move. Instead, she must remain in her place until the time expires. Then she can travel with a male relative wherever she desires.

The Standing Committee

May a Student Whose Husband Dies Continue Her Studies During Her Mourning Period

Question 214: A woman's husband died and now she must observe the mourning-waiting period while she is a student. May she continue her studies or not?

Response: It is obligatory upon the widow to observe the waiting and mourning period in the house she was living in when her husband died. This is for a period of four months and ten days. She may not stay anywhere else but there. She must avoid anything that beautifies her and makes her attractive, including perfume, kohl, attractive clothing and so forth. It is allowed for her to go out during the day if there is a need to do so. Therefore, the student in question may go out to attend her classes due to the need for such. However, she must do so while avoiding everything that a mourning woman must avoid and which may attract men and attract them to propose to her.

The Standing Committee

If a Woman's Husband Dies After the Marriage Contract but Before Consummation, She Must Still Observe the Waiting-Mourning Period

Question 215: A man married a woman and died before consummation, does she still have to observe the waiting-mourning period?

Response: The woman whose husband dies after the marriage contract yet before consummation must still observe the waiting-mourning period because simply by the conclusion of the contract she becomes his wife and falls under the command of the verse,

﴿ وَٱلَّذِينَ يُتَوَفَّوْنَ مِنكُمْ وَيَذَرُونَ أَزْوَٰجًا يَتَرَبَّصْنَ بِأَنفُسِهِنَّ أَرْبَعَةَ أَشْهُرٍ وَعَشْرًا ﴾ [البقرة: ٢٣٤]

"Those of you who die and leave wives behind, they [the wives] shall wait for four months and ten days" (al-Baqara 234).

She also falls under the hadith that al-Bukhari and Muslim recorded in which the Messenger of Allah (صلى الله عليه وسلم) said,

"لَا تُحِدَّ امْرَأَةٌ عَلَى مَيِّتٍ فَوْقَ ثَلَاثٍ إِلَّا عَلَى زَوْجٍ أَرْبَعَةَ أَشْهُرٍ وَعَشْرًا"

"It is not allowed for a woman to mourn for a dead person for more than three days—except if it is for her husband, in which case it is for four months and ten days."

Ahmad and the compilers of the *Sunan* recorded that the Messenger of Allah (صلى الله عليه وسلم) decreed concerning Buru bint Washiq, a woman whose husband had died before consummation, that she must observe the waiting period and that she was entitled to inheritance from him.

The Standing Committee

Ruling Concerning a Woman Answering the Phone During Her Mourning-Waiting Period

Question 216: Ibtisaam bint Nasir asks if it is allowed for a widow during her mourning-waiting period to answer the phone, given that she could not know if the person on the line is a man or a woman. And what is obligatory upon a woman during her mourning-waiting period?

Response: The woman in her mourning period must avoid beautification in the form of beautiful clothing, jewelry, make-up, kohl and so forth. She must not leave her house except due to necessity. She must not use perfume or incense. And she must not go in front of men she is not related to. It is allowed for her to walk throughout her house and the adjoining parts of her house. She may go up to the roof and so forth. If she needs to talk on the phone or something similar, there is no harm. If she realizes that the person calling is just one of those men who is trying to find out more about particular women, then she should get off the line as quickly as possible. It is allowed for her to speak from behind a curtain with her male relatives who are not *mahram* or over the phone in the same way that it is allowed for her when she is not in her mourning period.

Shaikh ibn Jibreen

There is No Basis for the Widow to Wear Black

Question 217: Is it allowed to wear black as a sign of grief for the deceased, especially if it is the woman's husband?

Response: Wearing black at the time of affliction is a display which is wrong and has no basis. During times of affliction, one must say what is sanctioned by the *Shariah*, "We belong to Allah and to Allah we return. O Allah, reward me during my affliction and give me a replacement better than this." If he says that with faith and expecting reward, Allah will reward him for that and replace her with someone better. However, wearing a specific clothing, such as black clothing and so forth, is a baseless act. It is, therefore, wrong and blameworthy.

Shaikh ibn Uthaimin

Ruling Concerning Delaying the Mourning-Waiting Period for no Legal Reason

Question 218: I was married for forty years and have five children. My husband passed away on 5-12-1985 but I did not observe my mourning period due to some work I had to perform related to my husband and my children. After four months, I began my mourning, that is on 9-12-1985. However, after just one

month, something happened to me that forced me to go out of my
house. Does that one month count as part of my waiting-mourning
time? Is my observing of the waiting-mourning period four
months after his death valid or not? You must understand that I
was forced to go out to fulfill some work since I do not have
anyone to take care of my household work.

Response: That action on your part is a forbidden act. It
is obligatory upon the woman to begin her waiting and mourning
period at the time that she hears about the death of her husband. It
is not allowed to delay it based on Allah's statement,

$$﴿ وَٱلَّذِينَ يُتَوَفَّوْنَ مِنكُمْ وَيَذَرُونَ أَزْوَٰجًا يَتَرَبَّصْنَ بِأَنفُسِهِنَّ أَرْبَعَةَ$$
$$أَشْهُرٍ وَعَشْرًا ﴾ \quad [البقرة: ٢٣٤]$$

"Those of you who die and leave wives behind, they [the wives]
shall wait for four months and ten days" (*al-Baqara* 234).

Delaying it for four months and then beginning your waiting
period is a sin and disobedience of Allah. You only performed ten
days of your mourning. What you did beyond that is not
considered part of the mourning period. Hence, you must repent to
Allah and increase your good deeds so that Allah may forgive you.
Once the time for the waiting-mourning period has passed, it is not
an act that may be made up later.

Shaikh ibn Uthaimin

16. Questions Related to Oaths and Vows

Ruling Concerning Saying "By Allah (*wallahi*)" Often and the Expiation for a Broken Oath

Question 219: Many times when I speak, I say "By Allah," is this considered an oath? How do I expiate it if I have violated it?

Response: If a responsible Muslim male adult or female adult often repeats the words "By Allah" for doing or avoiding something, while saying so intentionally and purposefully, like saying, "By Allah, I will visit so and so," then when he breaks that oath, by not doing what he swore he would do, or not avoiding what he swore he would avoid, then he must make the expiation for a broken vow. This expiation is to feed or clothe ten poor people or to free a slave. One must give a half of a *sa* of the staple food of a country, such as dates, rice or otherwise. Half a *sa* is about one and a half kilograms. As for clothing, it refers to what is sufficient for prayer, such as a shirt, waistcloth and overgarment. If a person is not able to do any of these three, then he must fast three days. This is based on the verse,

﴿ لَا يُؤَاخِذُكُمُ ٱللَّهُ بِٱللَّغۡوِ فِىٓ أَيۡمَٰنِكُمۡ وَلَٰكِن يُؤَاخِذُكُم بِمَا عَقَّدتُّمُ ٱلۡأَيۡمَٰنَ فَكَفَّٰرَتُهُۥٓ إِطۡعَامُ عَشَرَةِ مَسَٰكِينَ مِنۡ أَوۡسَطِ مَا تُطۡعِمُونَ أَهۡلِيكُمۡ أَوۡ كِسۡوَتُهُمۡ أَوۡ تَحۡرِيرُ رَقَبَةٖۖ فَمَن لَّمۡ يَجِدۡ فَصِيَامُ ثَلَٰثَةِ أَيَّامٖۚ ذَٰلِكَ كَفَّٰرَةُ أَيۡمَٰنِكُمۡ إِذَا حَلَفۡتُمۡۚ وَٱحۡفَظُوٓاْ أَيۡمَٰنَكُمۡ ﴾
[المائدة: ٨٩]

"Allah will not punish you for what is unintentional in your oaths, but He will punish you for your deliberate oaths; for its expiation, feed ten poor persons, on a scale of the average of that which you feed your own families, or clothe them, or manumit a slave. But whosoever cannot afford (that), then he should fast three days. That is the expiation for the oaths which you have sworn. And protect your oaths [i.e., do not swear much]" (al-Maida 89).

However, if the swearing flows on the tongue without any intent or resolve, it is considered meaningless speech. There is no expiation in that case. This is based on the beginning of the above verse that states,

﴿ لَا يُؤَاخِذُكُمُ ٱللَّهُ بِٱللَّغۡوِ فِيٓ أَيۡمَـٰنِكُمۡ ﴾   [المائدة : ٨٩]

"Allah will not punish you for what is unintentional in your oaths." (al-Maidah 89)

One expiation is sufficient for numerous oaths if they were in reference to one act, as was mentioned above. However, if they were in respect to different acts, then for each, one must make a separate expiation. For example, if a person said, "By Allah, I will visit so and so," "By Allah, I will not talk to so and so," and "By Allah, I will beat so and so." If he breaks one of them, he must do an expiation. If he broke all of them, he must make an expiation for each one separately.

Shaikh ibn Baz

I Swear Over my Children but They do Not Respond

Question 220: I have many children and I sometimes swear to them not to do a certain act but they do not listen or respond. Do I have to make an expiation in that case?

Response: If you swear with respect to your children or anyone else with a serious and intentional oath that they should do something or not do something and they violate that oath, then you must make the expiation. This is based on Allah's statement,

﴿ لَا يُؤَاخِذُكُمُ اللَّهُ بِاللَّغْوِ فِي أَيْمَٰنِكُمْ وَلَٰكِن يُؤَاخِذُكُم بِمَا عَقَّدتُّمُ
الْأَيْمَٰنَّ فَكَفَّٰرَتُهُ إِطْعَامُ عَشَرَةِ مَسَٰكِينَ مِنْ أَوْسَطِ مَا تُطْعِمُونَ
أَهْلِيكُمْ أَوْ كِسْوَتُهُمْ أَوْ تَحْرِيرُ رَقَبَةٍ فَمَن لَّمْ يَجِدْ فَصِيَامُ ثَلَٰثَةِ
أَيَّامٍ ذَٰلِكَ كَفَّٰرَةُ أَيْمَٰنِكُمْ إِذَا حَلَفْتُمْ وَاحْفَظُوا أَيْمَٰنَكُمْ ﴾

"Allah will not punish you for what is unintentional in your
oaths, but He will punish you for your deliberate oaths; for its
expiation, feed ten poor persons, on a scale of the average of
that which you feed your own families, or clothe them, or
manumit a slave. But whosoever cannot afford (that), then he
should fast three days. That is the expiation for the oaths
when you have sworn. And protect your oaths [i.e., do not
swear much]" (al-Maida 89).

However, if one swore to do or to avoid something and
then found the opposite of what he swore to do to be better, there
is no harm in breaking that oath and performing the expiation. This
is mentioned in the hadith of the Prophet (صلى الله عليه وسلم),

"إِذَا حَلَفْتَ عَلَى يَمِينٍ فَرَأَيْتَ غَيْرَهَا خَيْراً مِّنْهَا فَكَفِّرْ عَنْ يَمِينِكَ
وَأْتِ الَّذِي هُوَ خَيْرٌ"

"If you make an oath and then find that it is better to do
otherwise, then expiate your oath and do the thing that is best."

Recorded by al-Bukhari and Muslim.

Shaikh ibn Baz

She Made a Vow to Fast but She Does Not Have the Ability to Do So

Question 221: A woman vowed that if she gave birth to a
healthy baby and it lived for at least one year, she would then fast
for a year. Such did occur and the baby lived for more than a year.
But she is not able to perform the fast.

Response: There is no doubt that to make a vow of obedience is an act of worship. Allah has praised those who fulfill such vows. Allah says,

﴿ يُوفُونَ بِٱلنَّذْرِ وَيَخَافُونَ يَوْمًا كَانَ شَرُّهُ مُسْتَطِيرًا ﴾   [الإنسان : ٧]

"They are those who fulfill their vows and they fear a Day whose evil will be wide-spreading" (*al-Insan* 7).

It is confirmed that the Prophet (صلى الله عليه وسلم) said,

"مَنْ نَذَرَ أَنْ يُطِيعَ اللهَ فَلْيُطِعْهُ وَمَنْ نَذَرَ أَنْ يَعْصِيَ اللهَ فَلاَ يَعْصِهِ"

"Whoever makes a vow to obey Allah should obey Him. Whoever makes a vow to disobey Allah must not disobey Him."[1]

A man made a vow to sacrifice a camel at a certain location. He came to the Prophet (صلى الله عليه وسلم) and the Prophet (صلى الله عليه وسلم) asked him, "Was there an idol from the time of Ignorance that was worshipped there?" He said, "No," He then said, "Was there a celebration from their celebrations there?" He said, "No." So the Prophet (صلى الله عليه وسلم) then said,

"أَوْفِ بِنَذْرِكَ فَإِنَّهُ لاَ وَفَآءَ لِنَذْرٍ فِي مَعْصِيَةِ اللهِ وَلاَ فِيمَا لاَ يَمْلِكُ ابْنُ آدَمَ"

"Fulfill your oath. There is no fulfilling of oaths that are disobedience to Allah or concerning something that a human does not possess."[2]

The one who is asking the question mentioned that she vowed to fast a whole year. Fasting a whole year is a continuous type of fasting that is considered a type of permanent fasting and

---

[1] Recorded by al-Bukhari.—JZ
[2] Recorded by Abu Dawud. According to al-Albani, it is *sahih*. Al-Albani, *Sahih al-Jami*, vol. 1, p. 499.—JZ

permanent or continuous fasting is disliked. It is confirmed in the *Sahih* that the Prophet (صلى الله عليه وسلم) said,

$$ \text{"مَنْ صَامَ الدَّهْرَ فَلاَ صَامَ وَلاَ أَفْطَرَ"} $$

"Whoever performs a perpetual fast neither fasted nor broke his fast."

There is no doubt that a disliked form of worship is a type of disobedience to Allah. Therefore, one does not fulfill an oath to perform such an act. Shaikh al-Islam ibn Taimiya said, "If a person vows to perform an act of worship that is disliked, like praying the entire night or fasting the entire day, it is not obligatory to fulfill such an oath."

Therefore, the questioner must make an expiation for the oath by feeding ten poor people with a half a *sa* of dates or other common staple foods of the land. If she is not able to, then she should fast three consecutive days.[1]

The Standing Committee

Ruling Concerning Delaying the Expiation for a Broken Oath

Question 222: What is the ruling concerning delaying the expiation for a broken oath after the condition that was stated was fulfilled. For example, if a person said, "I vow to Allah to fast five days if I recover from my illness," and then he recovers but delays his fasting of those days. Also understand that he did not specify any time period. Does he have to fast those five days

---

[1] For some reason they did not mention the other options of clothing ten poor people or freeing a slave. Perhaps, they did not consider these viable options if the person is not able to feed ten poor people. Allah knows best.—JZ

consecutively? Does he have to make an expiation due to his delay even though his intention was not to deny what he had vowed?

Response: It is obligatory to fulfill one's oath of an act of worship, such as fasting, charity, *itikaf*, Hajj and reciting the Quran. If the oath is conditional, such as upon becoming healthy or returning from a journey, he should fulfill the vow as soon as possible. If he delays it and then does it, there is no sin upon him for delaying it. If he dies and he had yet to fulfill the vow, his heirs after him should fulfill it. However, one should fulfill such vows as quickly as possible so that the Muslim fulfills these obligations upon him.

Shaikh ibn Jibreen

I Made an Oath to Slaughter a Camel and Not to Eat from It but I Ate From it

Question 223: A woman and her children became ill and one of her children died. She was in the hospital between being ill and frightened, since she did not know if her children in her house were alive or dead. In that situation, she said, "O my Lord, if I find my children in my house alive, I will then slaughter a camel and not eat any of its meat. I will also fast for your sake for one month." She did actually fast for one month. She also slaughtered a camel but it happened that she ate part of that meat. The question is whether the camel she sacrificed and from whose meat she ate is sufficient or does she have to sacrifice another in its place?

Response: Since she made a vow to slaughter that camel as charity for the sake of Allah and since such is obligatory then upon her, since it was an oath of obedience to Allah, she must slaughter that camel and give all of it for the sake of Allah. Since you mentioned that she slaughtered it and ate part of its meat, it is not necessary for her to slaughter another animal. It will be sufficient for her to buy an amount of meat that she ate and give it in charity to the poor. Then she would have fulfilled her oath, Allah willing.

Shaikh ibn Jibreen

Making a Vow is Disliked and Fulfilling it is Obligatory

Question 224: What is the Islamic Law's ruling concerning making vows? Is there any punishment for not fulfilling a vow?

Response: The Islamic Law's ruling concerning making vows is that it is disliked. It is confirmed that the Prophet (صلى الله عليه وسلم) disapproved of making vows. He stated,

"إِنَّهُ لاَ يَأْتِي بِخَيْرٍ وَإِنَّمَا يُسْتَخْرَجُ بِهِ مِنَ الْبَخِيلِ"

"It does not bring about any good but it just takes by it something from the stingy."[1]

That is, some people, when they get sick, lose money in business or are afflicted, make an oath to give in charity, sacrifice an animal or give away some wealth if their situation is removed. They believe that Allah will not cure them or give them profits unless they make such an oath. The Prophet (صلى الله عليه وسلم) has stated that Allah's decree is not changed by any such thing but the stingy person will not spend anything unless he makes such a vow. It is obligatory to fulfill an oath if it is an oath to perform an act of worship, such as prayer, fasting, charity or *itikaf*. It is not allowed

---

[1] With this wording, it was recorded by Muslim. In other narrations by al-Bukhari and others, it states that it does not repel anything.—JZ

to be fulfilled if it were to do a sinful act, such as kill someone, fornicate, drink alcohol, wrongfully take someone's wealth and so forth. The person must then make an expiation for his oath which is to feed ten poor people and so forth. However, he has the choice between fulfilling the oath or making an expiation if his oath was to do something which is simply permissible, such as eat something, drink something, wear something, travel somewhere, say something and so forth. If his oath were something to be done for sake of Allah by giving to the poor and oppressed, such as food, slaughtering a sheep and so forth, he must give to the poor and oppressed. If it were a specific good act of his body or wealth, such as jihad, Hajj or *Umra*, then he must fulfill that oath. If he specifically stated where it should go to, such as to mosques, books, charitable organizations, then it is not allowed for him to give it to anyone else.

Shaikh ibn Jibreen

Ruling Concerning Changing to Whom What is Vowed is to Be Given

Question 225: Is it allowed for a person to change to whom what he has vowed is going to go to after he finds that there are more deserving recipients and after he had specifically stated what and to whom he was going to give?

Response: Before I respond to that question, I would like to make some introductory statements. A person should not make a vow, for vows are either disliked or forbidden, as the Prophet has forbidden them. It is narrated that he said,

"إِنَّهُ لاَ يَأْتِي بِخَيْرٍ وَإِنَّمَا يُسْتَخْرَجُ بِهِ مِنَ الْبَخِيلِ"

"It does not bring about any good but it just takes by it something from the stingy."[1]

The good that the one who makes a vow expects is not the result of the vow. Many people, when they become ill, make a vow that if Allah cures them they will do such and such. When others lose something they vow that if Allah returns it to them they will do such and such. If they become cured or find what they had lost, this does not mean that it was the vow that brought about that result. In fact, that is from Allah and Allah is more generous and noble than to lay down the condition that the person has stated. Instead, you should ask Allah directly to cure your illness or to bring back to you what you lost. But vowing has no effect. In fact, many people who make such vows, when what they desired comes about, become lazy when it comes to fulfilling their vows and might even abandon it completely. This is very dangerous. Listen to what Allah has said,

$$﴿ ۞ وَمِنْهُم مَّنْ عَٰهَدَ ٱللَّهَ لَئِنْ ءَاتَىٰنَا مِن فَضْلِهِۦ لَنَصَّدَّقَنَّ وَلَنَكُونَنَّ مِنَ ٱلصَّٰلِحِينَ ۞ فَلَمَّآ ءَاتَىٰهُم مِّن فَضْلِهِۦ بَخِلُوا۟ بِهِۦ وَتَوَلَّوا۟ وَّهُم مُّعْرِضُونَ ۞ فَأَعْقَبَهُمْ نِفَاقًا فِى قُلُوبِهِمْ إِلَىٰ يَوْمِ يَلْقَوْنَهُۥ بِمَآ أَخْلَفُوا۟ ٱللَّهَ مَا وَعَدُوهُ وَبِمَا كَانُوا۟ يَكْذِبُونَ ﴾$$
[التوبة: ٧٥-٧٧]

"And of them are some who made a covenant with Allah (saying,) 'If He bestowed on us of His Bounty, we will certainly give charity and will certainly be among those who are righteous.' Then when He gave them of His Bounty, they became niggardly and turned away averse. So He punished them by putting hypocrisy into their hearts till the Day whereon they shall meet Him, because they broke that [covenant with Allah] that they had promised Him and because they used to tell lies" (al-Tauba 75-77).

---

[1] With this wording, it was recorded by Muslim. In other narrations by al-Bukhari and others, it states that it does not repel anything.—JZ

Based on that, a believer should not make vows. As for the response to the question, we say that if the person made a vow for something in some place and then he found that another place is better, closer to Allah and more beneficial to Allah's servants, then there is no harm in him changing the direction of his vow in order to get the anticipated better or more virtuous results. The evidence for that is in the Hadith where a man came to the Prophet (صلى الله عليه وسلم) and said, "O Messenger of Allah (صلى الله عليه وسلم), I made a vow to Allah that if Allah conquers Makkah for you I would pray in Jerusalem." The Prophet (صلى الله عليه وسلم) told him, "Pray here [instead]." The man repeated his statement and the Prophet (صلى الله عليه وسلم) again told him, "Pray here." This happened a third time so the Prophet (صلى الله عليه وسلم) said, "Follow your own way then."[1] This indicates that if a person finds a better or more virtuous situation for his oath, he may change it to the better situation. That is permissible.

Shaikh ibn Uthaimin

---

[1] Recorded by Ahmad, al-Darimi and Abu Dawud. Al-Albani graded it *sahih*. Al-Albani, *Sahih Sunan Abu Dawud*, vol. 2, p. 635.—JZ

17. Questions Related to Expiation for a Broken Oath

The Amount of Food for Expiating an Oath

Question 226: We know that the expiation for a broken oath is feeding ten poor people. The question is: What is the amount of food to feed a poor person? What type of food should be used?

Response: The expiation for breaking an oath is feeding ten poor people, clothing them or freeing a slave. If one does not have the ability to do any of those, he fasts three consecutive days. The food is supposed to be a normal meal that the expiator feeds his own family. For example, the poor could eat with him lunch or dinner until they are full. Or he may give them enough food to satisfy them for a night. This is usually measured as one half a *sa'* of rice and so forth. As for clothing, it is what is sufficient for them to pray in.

Shaikh ibn Jibreen

Questions and Explanations Concerning Expiation for Breaking an Oath and Giving False Witness

Question 227: If I do not find ten poor people in the land I am living, is it allowed for me to give one person what is sufficient to feed ten people who are deserving?

What should I give as an expiation? May I give it in rice since that is the normal food of our land? If money is more beneficial to the poor, can I give in charity the price of the food instead of food itself? How many dollars then would I give to each person?

If a mother often invokes oaths upon her children in order to get them to perform their duties and most of the time they do not do so, does this imply that she is breaking her oath and must make an expiation for that or is such an oath considered meaningless speech only?

There was a problem between one of my schoolmates and one of my teachers. The student spoke to the teacher in a loud voice without first getting her permission. The teacher sought my witness against my classmate and I went to witness for her. I however said that she had sought her permission although I knew full well that she did not. This was because I was in front of the principal and I feared for my classmate. I have often felt remorse for that act. I wanted to ask the teacher's forgiveness but I have since then left Saudi Arabia. What should I do?

Response: You should seek out the poor people in your land. If you do not find any, then you can seek them out in a nearby land. If you do not find but one poor person, it is permissible to feed him for ten days.

Yes, it is allowed to give the expiation to the charitable organizations that collect charity and donations in order for them to distribute them to those who are in need or the oppressed or those deserving and in need.

It is allowed to gather the poor people and feed them lunch or dinner until they are full. If you prefer to give it to them, you may give them the amount of food that suffices for you and your family. You give food that is usually eaten in your land, such as rice or meat. You should give them what they need for one night. As for giving the price of the food instead of food itself, this is not acceptable, even if it is easier and more beneficial for them. Usually, they will not spend it on food that has been specifically stated by Allah in the Quran.

In our opinion, the swearing that is made often by mothers and others is considered a kind of meaningless speech because they were not said with purpose. Allah has said,

﴿ لَا يُؤَاخِذُكُمُ ٱللَّهُ بِٱللَّغۡوِ فِيٓ أَيۡمَٰنِكُمۡ وَلَٰكِن يُؤَاخِذُكُم بِمَا عَقَّدتُّمُ ٱلۡأَيۡمَٰنَ ﴾

[المائدة: ٨٩]

"Allah will not punish you for what is unintentional in your oaths, but He will punish you for your deliberate oaths" (al-Maida 89).
That is, a person will only be held accountable for those oaths that he said intentionally and with full purpose. As for those oaths that are said often, they are usually for the purpose of exhorting and threatening and one need not make an expiation for them.

You made an error by testifying to the opposite of what occurred. The expiation for that is repentance, seeking forgiveness and apologizing to the principal and teacher. You should make prayers for the teacher and ask Allah to forgive her if you are not able to reach her and seek her forgiveness.

Shaikh ibn Jibreen

Say "Allah Willing" After Making an Oath

Question 228: What is the meaning of the Hadith narrated by ibn Umar in which the Prophet (صلى الله عليه وسلم) said, "Whoever swears to an oath and then says 'Allah willing' does not violate that oath"?

Response: The meaning, of that Hadith is that if a person swears to do something and then says "Allah willing," if he does not fulfill that oath, there is no expiation upon him. For example, if he said, "By Allah, Allah willing, I will do such and such," and he does not do it. Or he says, "By Allah, Allah willing, I will not do such and such," and he does it. In those cases, there is no expiation because he said, "Allah willing." Therefore, based on that, anyone who makes an oath should also say with it, "Allah willing." In that way, if he is not able to fulfill his oath, there is no expiation to be done. There is also another benefit to saying "Allah willing" when making a vow: it will make the vow easier upon the person. This is because he has entrusted the matter to Allah and Allah has stated in the Quran,

﴿ وَمَن يَتَوَكَّلْ عَلَى ٱللَّهِ فَهُوَ حَسْبُهُۥٓ إِنَّ ٱللَّهَ بَٰلِغُ أَمْرِهِۦ قَدْ جَعَلَ ٱللَّهُ لِكُلِّ شَىْءٍ قَدْرًا ﴾ [الطلاق: ٣]

"Whoever puts his trust in Allah, then He will suffice Him. Verily, Allah will accomplish His purpose. Indeed, Allah has set a measure for all things" (*al-Talaq* 3).

Shaikh ibn Uthaimin

The Expiation for a Broken Vow

Question 229: What is the expiation for a broken vow?

Response: Allah has made the expiation for a broken vow very clear in the Quran in *surah al-Maidah*,

﴿ لَا يُؤَاخِذُكُمُ ٱللَّهُ بِٱللَّغۡوِ فِيٓ أَيۡمَٰنِكُمۡ وَلَٰكِن يُؤَاخِذُكُم بِمَا عَقَّدتُّمُ ٱلۡأَيۡمَٰنَۖ فَكَفَّٰرَتُهُۥٓ إِطۡعَامُ عَشَرَةِ مَسَٰكِينَ مِنۡ أَوۡسَطِ مَا تُطۡعِمُونَ أَهۡلِيكُمۡ أَوۡ كِسۡوَتُهُمۡ أَوۡ تَحۡرِيرُ رَقَبَةٖۖ فَمَن لَّمۡ يَجِدۡ فَصِيَامُ ثَلَٰثَةِ أَيَّامٖ ﴾ [المائدة: ٨٩]

"Allah will not punish you for what is unintentional in your oaths, but He will punish you for your deliberate oaths; for its expiation, feed ten poor persons, on a scale of the average of that which you feed your own families, or clothe them, or manumit a slave. But whosoever cannot afford (that), then he should fast three days." (*al-Maida* 89).

Unintentional oaths are those that just flow off the tongue while speaking, such as, "No, by Allah," "Yes, by Allah," and so forth. They are said without purpose or intent. There is no expiation for such words. Expiation is only when the heart had resolved on something. The expiator has a choice to free a slave, feed ten poor people a normal meal that he and his family eat in one night. He may give them lunch or dinner or give them a sufficient amount of food. He may also clothe them an amount of clothing that suffices for prayer. If he is not able to do those, then he fasts three consecutive days.

Shaikh ibn Jibreen

18. Questions Related to Injurious Crimes

There is No Expiation Upon Her

Question 230: A woman was breastfeeding her child in the bed. She then left that child to look after other children. She stayed with the other children until they slept. She also was exhausted and slept with them. When she woke, she found that the first baby cried a great deal and was being affected by the crying. He was taken to the hospital and stayed there a number of days. He then died because of that. The question is: Does that mother have to make an expiation? If so, what is it?

Response: If the events were as described in the question, there is no expiation upon the mother of the child. This is because she did not do anything that caused the child's death.

Shaikh ibn Baz

She Was Unaware of Her Young Child and This Caused the Child to "Kill Herself"

Question 231: A woman had a two year old daughter. She sat with her at a gathering which had containers of coffee and tea. The child began to play and the mother was looking in a different direction from the child in order to wash the cups. Then, all of a sudden, the little girl got to the coffee thermos, held it and spilled the cover over herself. The coffee was very hot. When it spilled over the little girl, some of the coffee got to her internal organs. After twenty four hours, the small girl died. The woman asks: Is there any expiation upon her? What is the expiation?

Response: The questioner knows best the complete circumstances and events leading up to this incident. If she feels with preponderance of thought that she was negligent in leaving the baby until what happened, the mother is then the cause of that act and she must make the expiation. The expiation is to free a slave. If she is not able to, she must fast for two months consecutively.

The Standing Committee

19. Questions Related to *Hijab*, Dress and Adornment

Ruling Concerning a Woman Uncovering Her Face in Front of Her Husband's Relatives and a Boy Sleeping with His Mother or Sister

Question 232: Is it legally permissible for a woman to uncover in front of her husband's brothers and cousins? Is it allowed for a boy to sleep in the same bed with his mother or sister after he has reached the age of puberty?

Response: First, the brothers and cousins of the husband are not *mahram* for his wife simply because they are his brothers or cousins. Therefore, it is not allowed for his wife to uncover in front of them what she cannot uncover in front of non-*mahram* men. This is true even if they are very pious and trustworthy. Allah has delineated whom a woman may expose her beauty to in the verse,

وَلَا يُبْدِينَ زِينَتَهُنَّ إِلَّا مَا ظَهَرَ مِنْهَا وَلْيَضْرِبْنَ بِخُمُرِهِنَّ عَلَىٰ جُيُوبِهِنَّ وَلَا يُبْدِينَ زِينَتَهُنَّ إِلَّا لِبُعُولَتِهِنَّ أَوْ ءَابَآئِهِنَّ أَوْ ءَابَآءِ بُعُولَتِهِنَّ أَوْ أَبْنَآئِهِنَّ أَوْ أَبْنَآءِ بُعُولَتِهِنَّ أَوْ إِخْوَٰنِهِنَّ أَوْ بَنِىٓ إِخْوَٰنِهِنَّ أَوْ بَنِىٓ أَخَوَٰتِهِنَّ أَوْ نِسَآئِهِنَّ أَوْ مَا مَلَكَتْ أَيْمَٰنُهُنَّ أَوِ ٱلتَّٰبِعِينَ غَيْرِ أُوْلِى ٱلْإِرْبَةِ مِنَ ٱلرِّجَالِ أَوِ ٱلطِّفْلِ ٱلَّذِينَ لَمْ يَظْهَرُوا۟ عَلَىٰ عَوْرَٰتِ ٱلنِّسَآءِ ﴿ [النور: ٣١]

"[Tell the believing women] not to reveal their adornments except to their husbands, their fathers, their husband's fathers, their sons, their husband's sons, their brothers or their brother's sons, or their sister's sons, or their (Muslim) women or the (female) slaves, or old male servants who lack vigor, or small children who have no sense of the shame of sex" (*al-Nur* 31).

Therefore, neither the brothers of the husband nor the children of the brothers of the husband nor the husband's cousins are from that group, even though they are related to him. Allah makes no distinction in this matter between pious people and others. This is safer for the honor of people. It also blocks the road to sin and evil. It is confirmed in authentic Hadith that the Prophet (صلى الله عليه وسلم) was asked about the male in-laws[1] and he said,

" الْحَمْــــــوُ الْمَـــــوتُ "

"The in-laws are death."[2]

The in-laws are the brother of the husband and so forth. They are not *mahram* for the wife. A Muslim must protect his religion and safeguard his honor.

Second, it is not allowed for male children, if they have reached the age of puberty or are ten years old or more, to sleep with their mothers or sisters in the same bedding or mattress. This safeguards chastity and keeps the person away from temptation. It also closes the door to evil. The Prophet (صلى الله عليه وسلم) ordered that the children be separated in their bedding when they reach the age of ten. He said,

"مُرُوا أَوْلَادَكُم بِالصَّلَاةِ لِسَبْعٍ وَاضْرِبُوهُمْ عَلَيْهَا لِعَشْرٍ وَفَرِّقُوا بَيْنَهُمْ فِي الْمَضَاجِعِ"

---

[1] Other than the husband's father or sons.—JZ
[2] Recorded by al-Bukhari and Muslim. It implies that such close relations can easily lead to adultery which has the death penalty.—JZ

"Order your children to pray when they are seven years old. And spank them [to exhort them] to do it by the age of ten and separate them in their bedding."[1]

Those who are not approaching the age of puberty still must ask permission to enter upon their parents at three times during the day. These are the times in which one is more likely to be taking off his clothing and exposing the parts that are usually covered. This has been stressed by them being called times of privacy. Allah says in the Quran,

﴿ يَـٰٓأَيُّهَا ٱلَّذِينَ ءَامَنُوا۟ لِيَسْتَـْٔذِنكُمُ ٱلَّذِينَ مَلَكَتْ أَيْمَـٰنُكُمْ وَٱلَّذِينَ لَمْ يَبْلُغُوا۟ ٱلْحُلُمَ مِنكُمْ ثَلَـٰثَ مَرَّٰتٍ مِّن قَبْلِ صَلَوٰةِ ٱلْفَجْرِ وَحِينَ تَضَعُونَ ثِيَابَكُم مِّنَ ٱلظَّهِيرَةِ وَمِنۢ بَعْدِ صَلَوٰةِ ٱلْعِشَآءِ ثَلَـٰثُ عَوْرَٰتٍ لَّكُمْ لَيْسَ عَلَيْكُمْ وَلَا عَلَيْهِمْ جُنَاحٌۢ بَعْدَهُنَّ طَوَّٰفُونَ عَلَيْكُم بَعْضُكُمْ عَلَىٰ بَعْضٍ كَذَٰلِكَ يُبَيِّنُ ٱللَّهُ لَكُمُ ٱلْءَايَـٰتِ وَٱللَّهُ عَلِيمٌ حَكِيمٌ ﴾

"O you who believe! Let your slaves and those among you who have not come to the age of puberty ask permission [before they come to your presence] on three occasions: before morning prayer, and while you put off your clothes for the noonday [rest] and after the *Isha* [Night] Prayer. [These] three times are times of privacy for you. Other than those times there is no sin for you or for them to move about, attending to each other. Thus Allah makes clear His signs to you. And Allah is All-Knowing, All-Wise" (*al-Nur* 58).

However, those who are past the age of puberty must seek permission to enter at all times of the day. Allah says,

﴿ وَإِذَا بَلَغَ ٱلْأَطْفَـٰلُ مِنكُمُ ٱلْحُلُمَ فَلْيَسْتَـْٔذِنُوا۟ كَمَا ٱسْتَـْٔذَنَ ٱلَّذِينَ مِن قَبْلِهِمْ كَذَٰلِكَ يُبَيِّنُ ٱللَّهُ لَكُمْ ءَايَـٰتِهِۦ وَٱللَّهُ عَلِيمٌ حَكِيمٌ ﴾

[النور: ٥٩]

---

[1] Recorded by Abu Dawud and Ahmad. Al-Albani has graded it *hasan*. Al-Albani, *Sahih al-Jami*, vol. 2, p. 1021.

"And when the children among you reach the age of puberty, then let them (also) ask for permission, as those senior to them (in age ask permission). Thus Allah makes clear His signs for you. And Allah is All-Knowing, All-Wise" (al-Nur 59).

All of this is to avoid any kinds of problems and temptations and to safeguard honors. It also brings an end to the means that lead to evil.

As for the child who is less than ten years old, it is permissible for him to sleep with his mother and sister in their bedding if there is some need to look after him and if there is no fear of temptation. They may also all sleep in the same area, in their own bedding, if they are of the age of puberty if there is no fear of temptation.

The Standing Committee

It is Not Allowed for a Woman to Shake the Hand of a Non-*Mahram* Man

Question 233: Some tribes have customs that go against the pure *Shariah*. For example, in some places it is customary for the guest to shake the hands of the female host. If he does not do so, it will lead to lots of problems and people will understand it in different ways. What is the best practice to follow given those circumstances?

Response: Shaking the hands of a woman for whom one is not *mahram* is not allowed. This is based on what is confirmed from the Prophet (صلى الله عليه وسلم) who said, when the women were giving the pledge of allegiance to him,

$$\text{"إِنِّي لاَ أُصَافِحُ النِّسَاءَ"}$$

"I do not shake the hands of women."[1]

---

[1] Recorded by Malik, Ahmad, al-Nasai, al-Tirmidhi and ibn Majah. Al-Albani has graded it *sahih*. Al-Albani, *Sahih al-Jami*, vol. 1, p. 494.

It is also confirmed that Aisha said, "By Allah, the hand of the Messenger of Allah (صلى الله عليه وسلم) never touched another woman [other than his wives]. He used to take their pledges verbally only."[1] Allah has said,

$$\text{﴿ لَّقَدْ كَانَ لَكُمْ فِى رَسُولِ ٱللَّهِ أُسْوَةٌ حَسَنَةٌ لِّمَن كَانَ يَرْجُوا۟ ٱللَّهَ وَٱلْيَوْمَ ٱلْأَخِرَ وَذَكَرَ ٱللَّهَ كَثِيرًا ﴾ [الأحزاب : ٢١]}$$

"Indeed in the Messenger of Allah you have a good example to follow for him who hopes in [the meeting with] Allah and the Last Day and remembers Allah much" (al-Ahzab 21).

Furthermore, shaking hands by women with men that are not *mahram* is one of the means that leads to temptation for both of them and it is obligatory to avoid it.

There is no harm in saying greetings without shaking hands. Any speech of a questionable nature or soft speech must be avoided. This is based on Allah's statement,

$$\text{﴿ يَٰنِسَآءَ ٱلنَّبِىِّ لَسْتُنَّ كَأَحَدٍ مِّنَ ٱلنِّسَآءِ إِنِ ٱتَّقَيْتُنَّ فَلَا تَخْضَعْنَ بِٱلْقَوْلِ فَيَطْمَعَ ٱلَّذِى فِى قَلْبِهِ مَرَضٌ وَقُلْنَ قَوْلًا مَّعْرُوفًا ﴾}$$

"O wives of the Prophet! You are not like any other women. If you keep your duty [to Allah], then be not soft in speech, lest he in whose heart is a disease should be moved with desire, but speak in an honorable manner" (al-Ahzab 32).

During the time of the Prophet (صلى الله عليه وسلم), the women would greet him and ask him questions that were concerning them. This is also how the women used to ask the Companions of the Prophet (صلى الله عليه وسلم) questions concerning matters of concern to them.

There is no harm in women shaking hands with *mahram* men, such as their fathers, paternal uncles, maternal uncles and so forth.

                                                    Shaikh ibn Baz

---

[1] Recorded by al-Bukhari and Muslim.—JZ

Ruling Concerning a Woman Kissing the Head of a Man

Question 234: We have a custom wherein women greet men by kissing them on their heads. It is in the following way: When the men come, they greet the women and the women respond by kissing them on their heads with the condition that upon their heads their is a headcovering or headdress without him kissing them or any soft speech. Dear Shaikh, please inform me of the ruling concerning that type of greeting. Note that there is no kissing on the cheek or anything of that nature in this greeting.

Response: That is allowed for a woman if done with one of her *mahram*, such as her father, brother and so forth. It is also permissible for those to shake each others' hands. However, if the man is not *mahram* for her, then it is not allowed for her to shake his hand or kiss him on the top of his head, regardless if he is wearing a headdress or not. This is in order to avoid any kind of temptation.

The Standing Committee

Ruling Concerning a Woman Sitting with Her In-Laws

Question 235: Is it allowed for a woman to sit with her husbands relatives while she is wearing the proper *hijab*?

Response: It is allowed for a woman to sit with her brother-in-law, her cousins and so forth if she is attired in the proper *hijab*, meaning her face, hair and all of her body is covered. This is because she is to be covered and she is a source of temptation. However, that sitting must be without any questionable or suspicious aspects and without her being in private with anyone of them. As for the sitting in which there is privacy or which may lead her to be accused of doing some evil, such gatherings are not allowed. Similarly, her sitting with them to listen to singing, music and so forth is also not allowed.

Shaikh ibn Baz

Ruling Concerning Ridiculing a Woman who Wears the Proper *Hijab* and Covers Her Face

Question 236: What is the ruling concerning one who ridicules those who wear the proper *hijab* and cover their faces and hands?

Response: Whoever ridicules a Muslim woman or man for sticking to and applying the teachings of Islam is a disbeliever. This is regardless of whether it is concerning woman's *hijab* or any other matter of the *Shariah*. This is based on the following narration from ibn Umar: At a gathering during the Battle of Tabuk, one man said, "I have not seen anyone like our Quranic readers who is more desirous of food, more lying in speech and more cowardly when meeting the enemy." A man said, "You have lied and you are a liar. I shall definitely tell the Messenger of Allah (صلى الله عليه وسلم) about that." That news was conveyed to the Messenger of Allah and the Quran was revealed. Abdullah ibn Umar added, "I saw the man holding on to the bag of the camel of the Messenger of Allah and the dust was striking him while he was saying, 'O Messenger of Allah, we were just joking and playing.' The Messenger of Allah (صلى الله عليه وسلم) was simply saying [the verse of the Quran],

﴿ أَبِٱللَّهِ وَءَايَٰتِهِۦ وَرَسُولِهِۦ كُنتُمۡ تَسۡتَهۡزِءُونَ ۝ لَا تَعۡتَذِرُوا۟ قَدۡ كَفَرۡتُم بَعۡدَ إِيمَٰنِكُمۡ إِن نَّعۡفُ عَن طَآئِفَةٍ مِّنكُمۡ نُعَذِّبۡ طَآئِفَةَۢ بِأَنَّهُمۡ كَانُوا۟ مُجۡرِمِينَ ﴾ [التوبة: ٦٥-٦٦]

"Was it Allah, and His Signs and His Messenger you were mocking? Make no excuse, you have disbelieved after you had believed. If We pardon some of you, We will punish others among you because they were sinners" (al-Tauba 65-66).[1]

So ridiculing believers has been equated with ridiculing Allah, His Signs and His Messenger.

The Standing Committee

Ruling Concerning Uncovering One's Face in Front of the Servant or Chauffeur

Question 237: What is the ruling concerning dealing with servants and family chauffeurs? Are they considered non-*mahram*? My mother wants me to uncover my face in front of the servant and just put a scarf over my head. Is this allowed in our pure religion that orders us not to disobey the commands of Allah?

Response: The chauffeur and servants are like any other men and one must wear *hijab* in front of them if they are not *mahram*. It is also not permissible to travel [alone] with them or to be in private with them. This is because the Prophet (صلى الله عليه وسلم) said,

"لاَ يَخْلُوَنَّ رَجُلٌ بِامْرَأَةٍ فَإِنَّ الشَّيْطَانَ ثَالِثُهُمَا"

"A man is never alone with a woman except that Satan is the third."[2]

---

[1] This narration may be found in al-Tabari and numerous other books of *tafseer*. There are some problems with every chain by which this and similar reports have been narrated. Muhammad Ibrahim and Abdul Munim Ibrahim did not make any clear conclusion regarding this report. However, based on supporting evidence, Alawi al-Saqaaf and Muqbil al-Wadi concluded that it is authentic. Allah knows best. See Abdul Munim Ibrahim and Muhammad Ibrahim, *Fath Dhi al-Jalaal fi Takhreej Ahadeeth al-Dhilaal* (Makkah: Maktaba Nazaar Mustafa al-Baz, 1995), vol. 2, pp. 817-818; Alawi al-Saqaaf, *Takhreej Ahadeeth wa Athaar Kitaab fi Dhilaal al-Quraan li-Sayyid Qutb* (Riyadh: Dar al-Hijra, 1991), p. 177; Muqbil bin Hadi al-Wadii, *al-Sahih al-Musnad min Asbaab al-Nuzool* (al-Maktab al-Salafi, 1401 A.H.), p. 71.—JZ

[2] Recorded by Ahmad and al-Tirmidhi. Al-Albani says it is *sahih*. Al-Albani, *Sahih al-Jami*, vol. 1, p. 234.—JZ

This is also the case due to the generality of the evidence concerning the obligation of *hijab* and the prohibition of exposing one's beauty and body to anyone other than *mahram* men. It is not allowed to obey one's mother or anyone else in something that is disobedience to Allah.

Shaikh ibn Baz

Ruling Concerning Uncovering One's Face While Abroad

Question 238: When we travel outside of Saudi Arabia is it allowed for me to uncover my face and take off the *hijab* because I am away from my land and no one there will know me? My mother becomes impossible and is encouraging my father to force me to uncover my face because they consider me to be always looked by them (people) when I cover my face.

Response: It is not allowed for you or any other woman like you to uncover her face in the lands of the disbelievers, in the same way that it is not allowed for you to do so in the land of the Muslims. It is obligatory to wear *hijab* in front of non-related men regardless if they be Muslims or non-believers. In fact, it is more important to cover in front of the disbelievers because they have no faith that will keep them from doing what Allah has forbidden. It is also not allowed for you or anyone similar to you to obey your parents or others in doing something that Allah and His Messenger have forbidden. In *Surah al-Ahzab*, Allah has stated,

﴿ وَإِذَا سَأَلْتُمُوهُنَّ مَتَٰعًا فَسْـَٔلُوهُنَّ مِن وَرَآءِ حِجَابٍ ذَٰلِكُمْ
أَطْهَرُ لِقُلُوبِكُمْ وَقُلُوبِهِنَّ ﴾ [الأحزاب:٥٣]

"And when you ask them, ask them from behind a screen, that is purer for your hearts and for their hearts"(*al-Ahzab* 53).

Allah shows in this noble verse that women must wear *hijab* in front of non-*mahram* men as that is purer for all of their hearts. In *surah al-Nur*, Allah states,

﴿ وَقُل لِّلْمُؤْمِنَـٰتِ يَغْضُضْنَ مِنْ أَبْصَـٰرِهِنَّ وَيَحْفَظْنَ فُرُوجَهُنَّ وَلَا يُبْدِينَ زِينَتَهُنَّ إِلَّا لِبُعُولَتِهِنَّ أَوْ ءَابَآئِهِنَّ أَوْ ءَابَآءِ بُعُولَتِهِنَّ ﴾ [النور: ٣١]

"Tell the believing women to lower their gaze and protect their private parts and not to show off their adornments except that which is apparent and to draw their veils over necks and bosoms and not to reveal their adornments except to their husbands, their fathers, their husband's fathers, their sons, their husband's sons, their brothers or their brother's sons, or their sister's sons, or their (Muslim) women or the (female) slaves, or old male servants who lack vigor, or small children who have no sense of the shame of sex" (*al-Nur* 31).

Obviously, the face is one of the greater sources of beauty a woman has.

Shaikh ibn Baz

The *Hijab* of a Young Girl

Question 239: What is the ruling concerning the young girls who have not reached the age of puberty? Is it allowed for them to go out without covering themselves? Can they pray without wearing a headcovering?

Response: It is a must that their guardians bring them up and teach them the manners of Islam. They should tell them not to go outside unless their bodies are covered. This is in order to avoid any temptation and to get them used to the virtuous manners so that they will not be a source of spreading evil. They should be ordered to pray with headcoverings. If they pray without it, their prayers are sound. This is because the Prophet (صلى الله عليه وسلم) said,

" لاَ يَقْبَلُ اللهَ صَلاَةَ حَآئِضٍ إلاَّ بِخِمارٍ "

"Allah does not accept the prayer of a female who has reached the age of puberty except if she is wearing a headcovering (*khimaar*)."

This was recorded by al-Tirmidhi, Ahmad, Abu Dawud and ibn Majah.[1]

The Standing Committee

Hijab of an Elderly Woman

Question 240: Is it allowed for a woman advanced in age, say 70 or 90 years old, to uncover her face in front of relatives who are not *mahram*?

Response: Allah says,

﴿ وَٱلْقَوَاعِدُ مِنَ ٱلنِّسَاءِ ٱلَّتِي لَا يَرْجُونَ نِكَاحًا فَلَيْسَ عَلَيْهِنَّ جُنَاحٌ أَن يَضَعْنَ ثِيَابَهُنَّ غَيْرَ مُتَبَرِّجَاتٍ بِزِينَةٍ وَأَن يَسْتَعْفِفْنَ خَيْرٌ لَّهُنَّ وَٱللَّهُ سَمِيعٌ عَلِيمٌ ﴾ [النور : ٦٠]

"And as for women past child-bearing who do not expect marriage, it is no sin upon them if they discard their (outer) clothing in such a way as not to show their adornment. But to refrain is better for them. And Allah is All-Hearer, All-Knower" (*al-Nur* 60).

So there is no harm if the menopausal women who are not seeking marriage and are not displaying their adornments uncover their

---

[1] According to al-Albani, this hadith is *sahih*. Al-Albani, *Sahih al-Jami*, vol. 2, p. 1280.—JZ

faces in front of non-related men. However, for them to remain covered is still better for Allah has said in the verse,

"But to refrain is better for them."

This is because some of them, when they are seen, may be a source of temptation due to their beautiful faces even though they are elderly and not displaying their adornments. However, if she is going to be having adornments [such as make-up and jewelry], she may not take off her outer covering. Having adornments includes beautifying the face with kohl and so forth.

Shaikh ibn Baz

The *Hijab* of a Female Servant

Question 241: Is it necessary for a female servant who works in the house to wear *hijab* in front of her employer?

Response: Yes, she must wear *hijab* in front of him and she may not display her adornments in front of him. Also, it is forbidden for them to be in private due to the generality of the evidences. This is because if she does not wear *hijab* or she displays her adornments, she will be a source of temptation for him. Similarly, being in private is an opportunity for Satan to make them alluring and tempting.

Shaikh ibn Baz

The Female Servant Must Wear *Hijab*

Question 242: We have a Muslim female servant who performs all of her religious obligations except she does not cover her hair. Is it obligatory upon me to instruct her in this matter?

Response: It is obligatory upon you to order her to cover her hair, face and the remainder of her body in order to be away from temptation and the spreading of evil.

The Standing Committee

A Muslim Woman Does Not Wear *Hijab* in Front of Non-Muslim Women

Question 243: We have non-Muslim female servants in our house. Is it obligatory upon us to wear *hijab* in front of them? Is it allowed for me to give them my clothes to wash and then I pray in them? Is it allowed for me to explain the falsehood of their religion to them and to explain the distinguishing features of our pure religion?

Response: First, it is not obligatory to wear *hijab* in front of them. They are like any other women according to the strongest of the two opinions among the scholars. There is no harm in them washing your clothing or utensils. However, it is obligatory to put an end to their contract because they have not embraced Islam. This is because in the Arabian Peninsula it is not allowed to have anyone except Muslims. Only Muslims may be hired in this Peninsula, regardless if it be workers, servants or whatever, regardless if they be men or women. This is because the Prophet (صلى الله عليه وسلم) ordered that the polytheists be expelled from this Peninsula and that there not be left two religions herein. This is because it was the cradle of Islam and the place of the rise of the Message. It is not allowed except for the religion of truth, the religion of Islam, to be left in this Peninsula. May Allah grant Muslims the following of truth and steadfastness in it. May Allah also guide the others to enter into Islam and leave what goes against it.

Second, it is sanctioned for you to call them to Islam and to explain to them its excellence. You may also show them what is wrong with their religion and how it opposes the truth. Also explain to them that the Law of Islam abrogates all previous laws. Tell them that Islam is the religion of truth that Allah sent all of His messengers with and by which were revealed the Books. Allah has said,

﴿ إِنَّ ٱلدِّينَ عِندَ ٱللَّهِ ٱلْإِسْلَـٰمُ ﴾   [آل عمران:١٩]

"Truly, the Religion in the sight of Allah is Islam" (al-Imran 19).

Allah also says,

﴿ وَمَن يَبْتَغِ غَيْرَ ٱلْإِسْلَـٰمِ دِينًا فَلَن يُقْبَلَ مِنْهُ وَهُوَ فِى ٱلْءَاخِرَةِ مِنَ ٱلْخَـٰسِرِينَ ﴾   [آل عمران:٨٥]

"And whoever seeks a religion other than Islam, it will never be accepted of him and in the Hereafter he will be one of the losers" (âli-Imran 85).

However, you have no right to speak about that except on the basis of knowledge and understanding. Speaking about Allah's religion without knowledge is a great evil. Allah has stated,

﴿ قُلْ إِنَّمَا حَرَّمَ رَبِّىَ ٱلْفَوَٰحِشَ مَا ظَهَرَ مِنْهَا وَمَا بَطَنَ وَٱلْإِثْمَ وَٱلْبَغْىَ بِغَيْرِ ٱلْحَقِّ وَأَن تُشْرِكُوا۟ بِٱللَّهِ مَا لَمْ يُنَزِّلْ بِهِۦ سُلْطَـٰنًا وَأَن تَقُولُوا۟ عَلَى ٱللَّهِ مَا لَا تَعْلَمُونَ ﴾   [الأعراف:٣٣]

"Say: The things that my Lord has forbidden are illicit acts, whether committed openly or secretly, sins [of all kinds], unrighteous oppression, joining partners [in worship] with Allah for which He has given no authority, and saying things about Allah of which you have no knowledge" (al-Araf 33).

Allah has put the gravity of speaking about Him without knowledge above all of the acts mentioned in the verse. This indicates how greatly forbidden it is and what a great sin it is.

Allah also says,

﴿ قُلْ هَـٰذِهِۦ سَبِيلِىٓ أَدْعُوٓا۟ إِلَى ٱللَّهِ عَلَىٰ بَصِيرَةٍ أَنَا۠ وَمَنِ ٱتَّبَعَنِى وَسُبْحَـٰنَ ٱللَّهِ وَمَآ أَنَا۠ مِنَ ٱلْمُشْرِكِينَ ﴾   [يوسف:١٠٨]

"Say: This is my way, I invite unto Allah with sure knowledge, I and whosoever follows me [must also invite

with sure knowledge]. Glorified be Allah. And I am not one
of the idolaters" (*Yusuf* 108).

In *Surah al-Baqara*, Allah states that speaking about Allah without
knowledge is one of the actions that is ordered by Satan:

﴿ يَٰٓأَيُّهَا ٱلنَّاسُ كُلُواْ مِمَّا فِى ٱلْأَرْضِ حَلَٰلًا طَيِّبًا وَلَا تَتَّبِعُواْ
خُطُوَٰتِ ٱلشَّيْطَٰنِ إِنَّهُ لَكُمْ عَدُوٌّ مُّبِينٌ ○ يَأْمُرُكُم بِٱلسُّوٓءِ
وَٱلْفَحْشَآءِ وَأَن تَقُولُواْ عَلَى ٱللَّهِ مَا لَا تَعْلَمُونَ ﴾

"O mankind! Eat of that which is lawful and good on the
Earth, and follow not the footsteps of Satan. Verily, he is to
you an open enemy. (Satan) commands you only what is evil
and sinful, and that you should say against Allah what you
know not" (*al-Baqara* 168-169).

I ask Allah for me and you support, guidance and goodness.

Shaikh ibn Baz

Ruling Concerning Wearing *Hijab* in the Presence of the Son-in-Law

Question 244: Some women wear *hijab* in front of their
son-in-laws and they refuse to greet them by shaking their hands.
Is this allowed for them or not?

Response: The son-in-law is a *mahram* for the woman due
to marriage. It is allowed for him to see of her what he can see of
his mother, sister, daughter and other *mahram* women. Covering
her face, hair, forearms and so forth from her son-in-law is a type
of extremism in the religion. Refusing to shake his hand when
meeting him is also a kind of extremism. That may lead to hard
feelings and cutting off of relations between them. Therefore, she
should not be extreme in this matter, unless she has some suspicion
about him or she does not like the way he looks at her. In that
case, what she is doing is acceptable.

The Standing Committee

Ruling Concerning a Woman Riding with a non-*Mahram* Chauffeur

Question 245: What is the ruling concerning a woman riding into town alone with a chauffeur who is not *mahram* to her? What is the ruling concerning a group of women riding in a car with a driver who is not *mahram* for them?

Response: It is not allowed for a woman to ride alone with a driver and nobody else present, as this is considered the same as being in privacy. It is confirmed that the Messenger of Allah (صلى الله عليه وسلم) said,

$$ \text{" لا يَخْلُو رَجُلٌ بِآمْرَأَةٍ إِلا وَمَعَهَا ذُو مَحْرَمٍ "} $$

"A man cannot be alone with a woman unless with her is one of her male relatives (*mahram*)."[1]

The Prophet (صلى الله عليه وسلم) also said,

$$ \text{"لاَ يَخْلُوَنَّ رَجُلٌ بِامْرَأَةٍ فَإِنَّ الشَّيْطَانَ ثَالِثُهُماَ"} $$

"A man is never alone with a woman except that Satan is the third."[2]

However, if another man or more is with them or one or more other women is with them, then there is no harm in that as long as there is no room for any suspicious activity. It is no longer considered privacy when there is a third or more present. This is for cases other than traveling. As for traveling, a woman may not travel except with a *mahram*. The Prophet (صلى الله عليه وسلم) has said,

$$ \text{"لاَ تُسَافِر آمْرَأَةٌ إِلاَّ مَعَ ذِي مَحْرم"} $$

"A woman does not travel except with a *mahram*."

---

[1] Recorded by Muslim.—JZ
[2] Recorded by Ahmad and al-Tirmidhi. Al-Albani says it is *sahih*. Al-Albani, *Sahih al-Jami*, vol. 1, p. 234.—JZ

This was recorded by al-Bukhari and Muslim. It makes no difference whether that traveling is by land, air or sea.

Shaikh ibn Baz

A Woman Does not Act as a *Mahram* for Another Woman

Question 246: Can a woman be considered a *mahram* for a woman she is not related to for purposes of traveling or sitting with others?

Response: A woman cannot be a *mahram* for another. The one who is considered *mahram* is a man that a woman cannot marry due to blood relations, such as her father and her brother, or a man related to her due to marriage, such as her husband, her father-in-law and her step-son, or a man related due to breastfeeding, such as her father from breastfeeding and so forth.

It is not allowed for a man to be in private with a woman he is not related to nor can he travel with her. The Prophet (صلى الله عليه وسلم) said,

$$\text{"لاَ تُسَافِرِ امْرَأَةٌ إِلا مَعَ ذِي مَحْرم"}$$

"A woman does not travel except with a *mahram*."

This was recorded by al-Bukhari and Muslim. The Prophet (صلى الله عليه وسلم) also said,

$$\text{"لاَ يَخْلُوَنَّ رَجُلٌ بِامْرَأَةٍ فَإِنَّ الشَّيْطَانَ ثالِثُهُماَ"}$$

"A man is never alone with a woman except that Satan is the third."

This was recorded by Imam Ahmad and others from the hadith of Umar with a *sahih* chain.

Shaikh ibn Baz

Being Held Accountable for What One Wears

Question 247: Is it correct that a person will be held accountable on the Day of Resurrection for what clothing he wore?

Response: Yes, the person will be asked about his wealth and where he acquired it from and what he spent it on. This is stated in a hadith.

Shaikh ibn Baz

Ruling Concerning Wearing Tight Clothing and White Clothing

Question 248: Is it allowed for a woman to wear tight clothing? Is it allowed for her to wear white clothing?

Response: It is not allowed for women to be in front of non-related men or in public streets or marketplaces while she is wearing tight clothing that describes her body to anyone who looks at her. This makes it like she is naked and stirring temptations. It is a cause for great evil. She also may not wear white clothing because in our country the white clothing is something specific and recognizable for men. In that case, she would be resembling men and the Prophet (صلى الله عليه وسلم) cursed those women who resembled men.

The Standing Committee

Ruling Concerning Wearing Anklets

Question 249: What is the ruling concerning wearing anklets in front of one's husband only?

Response: There is no harm in wearing such in front of one's husband, women and *mahram* men. That is because it is a type of jewelry that a woman wears on her legs.

Shaikh ibn Baz

Ruling Concerning a Woman Cutting Her Hair

Question 250: I hope you will help me concerning cutting my hair from the front of it in a certain style wherein the hair sometimes falls down over the eyebrows of a Muslim woman. Is this allowed or not? May Allah reward you.

Response: I do not know of anything [wrong] in cutting a woman's hair. It is not allowed to shave all of it off. You cannot shave off the hair of your head but you may shorten its length. I do not know of anything wrong with that. However, that should be done in a good way that is pleasing to you and your husband. You should agree upon how it is going to be done. Also, it should not be in imitation of the disbelieving women. If you leave it long, it makes it more difficult to wash it and tend to it. If it is long or thick and a women cuts it short or layers it, there is nothing wrong with that. Or she may cut part of it short to make herself more beautiful to herself and her husband. I do not know of anything wrong with that. However, one may not shave all of it off. This is not allowed except in the case of some disease or problem.

Shaikh ibn Baz

Ruling Concerning Wearing a Wig

Question 251: What is the ruling concerning a woman wearing a wig in order to beautify herself for her husband?

Response: Each spouse must beautify himself or herself for the other, in a way that is pleasing to the other and strengthens the feelings between the two. However, this must be done in a way that is within the limits of the *Shariah* and is not forbidden. The wearing of a wig is something that began among non-Muslim women and became a popular way for them to beautify themselves. If a Muslim woman wears one and beautifies herself with it, even if just for her husband, she is imitating the disbelieving women and the Prophet has forbidden that. He said,

"مَنْ تَشَبَّهَ بِقَوْمٍ فَهُوَ مِنْهُمْ"

"Whoever imitates a people is one of them."[1]

Furthermore, it takes on the same ruling as "artificially adding hair to one's hair". The Prophet (صلى الله عليه وسلم) has forbidden that act and cursed the one who did such.[2]

The Standing Committee

Ruling Concerning Shortening Eyebrows, Letting Fingernails Grow Long and Using Nail Polish

Question 252: (1) What is the ruling concerning shortening extra eyebrow hairs?

(2) What is the ruling concerning letting fingernails grow long and putting on finger nail polish, given that I make ablution before putting them on and it stays for twenty-four hours and then I remove it?

(3) Is it allowed for a woman to wear *hijab* without covering her face when she travels abroad?

Response: (1) It is not allowed to remove or shorten eyebrow hairs. It is confirmed that the Prophet (صلى الله عليه وسلم) cursed the one who has them removed and the one who removed them. The scholars have stated that the hadith is in reference to those who remove eyebrow hairs.

(2) Letting the fingernails grow is something that goes against the sunnah of the Prophet (صلى الله عليه وسلم). He said,

---

[1] Recorded by Abu Dawud. Al-Albani has graded it *sahih*. Al-Albani, *Sahih al-Jami*, vol. 2, p. 1058.—JZ
[2] Such hadith have been recorded by al-Bukhari and Muslim.—JZ

"الفِطْرَةُ خَمْسٌ: الخِتَانُ، والاسْتِحْدَادُ، وقَصُّ الشَّارِبِ، ونَتْفُ
الإبطِ، وقَلْمُ الأظْفَارِ"

"From the acts of nature are five: circumcision, removing pubic hairs, trimming the mustache, cutting the nails and plucking the hair from under the armpits."[1]

It is not allowed to leave them for more than forty nights. This is based on the Hadith of Anas who said, "The Messenger of Allah set a time limit for us for trimming the mustache, trimming nails, removing armpit hairs and removing pubic hairs. They cannot be left for more than forty nights."[2] Letting them grow long resembles animals and some of the disbelievers.

As for nail polish, it is better to avoid it. One must remove it when making ablution since it prevents water from reaching the nails.

(3) It is obligatory for women to wear *hijab* in front of non-*mahram* men both inside and outside of the country. Allah has said,

﴿ وَإِذَا سَأَلْتُمُوهُنَّ مَتَٰعًا فَسْـَٔلُوهُنَّ مِن وَرَآءِ حِجَابٍ ذَٰلِكُمْ
أَطْهَرُ لِقُلُوبِكُمْ وَقُلُوبِهِنَّ ﴾ [الأحزاب: ٥٣]

"And when you ask them, ask them from behind a screen, that is purer for your hearts and for their hearts"(*al-Ahzab* 53).

This verse refers to the face and the rest of the body. In fact, the face is the distinguishing part of the woman and it is her most alluring aspect. Allah also says,

﴿ يَٰٓأَيُّهَا ٱلنَّبِيُّ قُل لِّأَزْوَٰجِكَ وَبَنَاتِكَ وَنِسَآءِ ٱلْمُؤْمِنِينَ يُدْنِينَ عَلَيْهِنَّ
مِن جَلَٰبِيبِهِنَّ ذَٰلِكَ أَدْنَىٰٓ أَن يُعْرَفْنَ فَلَا يُؤْذَيْنَ وَكَانَ ٱللَّهُ غَفُورًا
رَّحِيمًا ﴾ [الأحزاب: ٥٩]

"O Prophet! Tell your wives and your daughters and the women of the believers to draw their cloaks (veils) all over

---

[1] Recorded by al-Bukhari and Muslim.—JZ
[2] Recorded by Muslim.—JZ

their bodies. That will be better, that they should be known (as free respectable women) so as not to be annoyed. And Allah is Ever Oft-Forgiving, Most Merciful" (al-Ahzab 59).

Another verse states,

$$ \text{﴿ وَلَا يُبْدِينَ زِينَتَهُنَّ إِلَّا لِبُعُولَتِهِنَّ أَوْ ءَابَآئِهِنَّ أَوْ ءَابَآءِ} $$

[النور: ٣١]   ﴾ بُعُولَتِهِنَّ ﴿

"[Tell the believing women] not to reveal their adornments except to their husbands, their fathers, their husband's fathers," (al-Nur 31).

This verse indicates that hijab is obligatory upon a woman both inside and outside of the country, in front of the Muslims and the non-Muslims. It is not allowed for any woman who believes in Allah and the Hereafter to be lax in this matter as such is an act of disobedience to Allah and His Messengers. Furthermore, it leads to temptation regardless if it be in or outside the country.

Shaikh ibn Baz

Ruling Concerning Circular Shaped Gold Jewelry

Question 253: What is the ruling concerning circular shaped gold jewelry?[1]

Response: It is permissible for women to wear either circular shaped or non-circular shaped gold jewelry. This is based on the general meaning of the verse,

$$ \text{﴿ أَوَمَن يُنَشَّؤُا۟ فِى ٱلْحِلْيَةِ وَهُوَ فِى ٱلْخِصَامِ غَيْرُ مُبِينٍ ﴾} $$

"[Do they then like for Allah] a creature who is brought up in adornments [wearing silk and gold ornaments, i.e., women] and in dispute cannot make herself clear?" (al-Zukhruf 18).

---

[1] This question may sound strange at first glance. However, the obvious reason behind it is that some scholars are of the opinion that such jewelry is not allowed for women although women may wear gold jewelry of other shapes.—JZ

Allah has mentioned that wearing jewelry is a characteristic of women. This is general and covers gold as well as other jewelry. Furthermore, Ahmad, Abu Dawud and al-Nasai record with a good chain from the Leader of the Faithful Ali ibn Abu Talib that the Prophet (صلى الله عليه وسلم) took silk in his right hand and gold in his left and then said,

$$ \text{"إِنَّ هذَيْنَ حَرَامٌ على ذُكُورِ أُمَّتِي"} $$

"These two are forbidden for the males of my Nation."

In the narration by ibn Majah, it ends,

$$ \text{"حِلٌّ لإِنَاثِهِم"} $$

"And permissible for its women."

Also, Ahmad, al-Nasai, al-Tirmidhi— who said it is *sahih*— Abu Dawud, al-Hakim— who also called it *sahih*— al-Tabarani and ibn Hazm— who again said it is *sahih*— all record from Abu Musa al-Ashari that the Prophet (صلى الله عليه وسلم) said,

$$ \text{"أُحِلَّ الذَّهَبُ والْحَرِيرُ لِلإِنَاثِ مِنْ أُمَّتِي وحُرِّمَ عَلَى ذُكُورِهَا"} $$

"Gold and silk have been made permissible for the females of my Nation and forbidden for its males."

Shaikh ibn Baz

Ruling Concerning High-Heeled Shoes

Question 254: What is the Islamic ruling concerning wearing high-heeled shoes?

Response: The least that can be said is that it is disliked. First, it is a kind of deception because it makes the woman look taller than she is. Second, it is dangerous for the woman because it is easy to fall in them. Third, it has negative health consequences as the doctors have concluded.

Shaikh ibn Baz

Ruling Concerning Women Using Incense[1] when They are Going to the Mosque

Question 255: During Ramadhan, some women use incense in the mosque. We advised them to stop but to no avail. We want from you, dear Shaikh, to make this issue clear to them and to us.

Response: It is not allowed for women to use incense when they go out to the mosque or inside the mosque. This is because they become a temptation, then, when they return to their homes. It has been authentically reported from the Prophet (صلى الله عليه وسلم) that he prohibited women from using any kind of perfume when leaving their house to go to the mosque. He said,

"أَيُّمَا آمَرَأَةٍ أَصَابَتْ بَخُوراً فَلاَ تَشْهَدْ مَعَنَا العِشَـــاءَ"

"Any woman who has incense over her should not attend the *Isha* Prayer with us."[2]

The same applies to them using such fragrances in the mosque because then they go outside to the market while being scented. The same is the ruling for their using it when they go some place other than the mosque.

Shaikh ibn Baz

---

[1] In many parts of the Middle East, the burning incense is passed around among the people and its scent gets clearly and noticeably attached to the clothing, skin, beard and so forth. This is the kind of incense use that is being described here. If the incense is used in a room and there is no lingering smell upon the clothing or person of a woman, then there is no harm in her using it.—JZ

[2] Recorded by Muslim.—JZ

Verily, Allah is Beautiful and He Loves Beauty

Question 256: My dear friend is a very good person, applying her religion and loving to do what is good. However, she has one thing about her: She always loves to be distinguished from her friends. For example, in her dress, she likes to be different from the others, while being properly covered, of course. She does not want anyone to be like her. It is so bad that if she finds out that one of her friends has bought the same outfit she has, she will never wear it again. The same is true for how she dresses her children and with respect to their furniture. She cannot stand to see anyone else having the same thing she has. However, at the same time, she is not envious against anyone nor does she wish that others would not have such bounties, even if it is more beautiful than what she possesses. The only thing she cares about is to be different from the others. Is this envy or arrogance, as we dislike this characteristic of her very much?

Response: I do not know what is in the heart of that lady that makes her behave in that way. If it is envy, it is forbidden. But envy implies wishing that others would lose the bounty they possess and even working to destroy it. She does not do that. If it is arrogance and having an aversion for others sharing with her, then it is also forbidden. But the arrogance that is blameworthy is to reject the truth and look down upon people, that is, belittle them. It does not include liking good clothes for oneself. Verily, Allah is beautiful and He loves beauty. Perhaps she simply likes to be different from others and have notoriety in her appearance. So one must look to see what is the cause for that. This might just be part of her character that sets in the hearts of some people without there being a forbidden cause behind it. Allah knows best.

Shaikh ibn Jibreen

Uncovering the Face While Abroad and Trimming Eyebrows

Question 257: Is a woman sinful if she travels abroad with her husband while wearing *hijab* but uncovering her face?

Is it allowed for a woman to remove part of her eyebrows as a beautification for her husband?

Response: It is not allowed for a woman to uncover her face in front of non-related men, either inside Saudi Arabia or outside of it. If a woman has the ability to wear *hijab* and cover herself completely, it is then permissible for her to travel abroad with her husband, remaining away from what is forbidden.

It is not allowed to remove some of the eyebrow hairs, nor shave them off, nor trim them, nor pluck them, even if the husband is pleased with that. It is not a beautifying act. Instead, it is changing the creation of Allah and Allah is the best of creators. The threat of punishment concerning that has been narrated from the Prophet (صلى الله عليه وسلم) as well as a curse for that act. This implies that it is forbidden.

Shaikh ibn Jibreen

No Harm in the Presence of a Blind Man

Question 258: Is it allowed for a woman to uncover her face in the presence of a blind man? If she cannot uncover her face, what is the legal reason preventing her to do so?

Response: The correct opinion is that there is no harm in a woman uncovering her face in the presence of a blind man. A woman is ordered to cover herself in front of those who can see her in order for no temptation to arise. A blind man cannot see what is in front of him and he cannot look at what will excite him in a woman, nor is he conscious of it. There is the hadith that is recorded by al-Tirmidhi, who called it *sahih*, concerning the story of ibn Umm Maktum, where the Prophet (صلى الله عليه وسلم) [told Umm Salama and Maimuna] to wear *hijab* in front of him. [When they asked about it,] he said,

" أَفَعَمْيَـاوَانِ أَنْتُمَـا أَلَسْتُمَـا تُبْصِـرَانِهِ "

"Are you two blind? Do you not see him?"

However, this hadith is considered weak by some scholars. Even assuming it is authentic, it is concerned with the woman looking at the man. Women are also ordered to lower their gaze and it is not allowed for a woman to look at a man if her desires may be stirred, regardless of whether he be blind or seeing. In fact, she should not, in that case, even look at pictures in the newspapers or in the movies if such may occur.

Shaikh ibn Jibreen

A Muslim Woman May Uncover Her Hair in Front of Non-Muslim Women

Question 259: Is it allowed for a Muslim woman to uncover her hair in front of non-Muslim women, especially if she describes the Muslim women to her male non-Muslim relatives?

Response: This question revolves around a difference of opinion concerning the interpretation of the verse:

﴿ وَقُل لِّلْمُؤْمِنَـٰتِ يَغْضُضْنَ مِنْ أَبْصَـٰرِهِنَّ وَيَحْفَظْنَ فُرُوجَهُنَّ وَلَا يُبْدِينَ زِينَتَهُنَّ إِلَّا مَا ظَهَرَ مِنْهَا وَلْيَضْرِبْنَ بِخُمُرِهِنَّ عَلَىٰ جُيُوبِهِنَّ وَلَا يُبْدِينَ زِينَتَهُنَّ إِلَّا لِبُعُولَتِهِنَّ أَوْ ءَابَآئِهِنَّ أَوْ ءَابَآءِ بُعُولَتِهِنَّ أَوْ أَبْنَآئِهِنَّ أَوْ أَبْنَآءِ بُعُولَتِهِنَّ أَوْ إِخْوَٰنِهِنَّ أَوْ بَنِىٓ إِخْوَٰنِهِنَّ أَوْ بَنِىٓ أَخَوَٰتِهِنَّ أَوْ نِسَآئِهِنَّ أَوْ مَا مَلَكَتْ أَيْمَـٰنُهُنَّ أَوِ ٱلتَّـٰبِعِينَ غَيْرِ أُوْلِى ٱلْإِرْبَةِ مِنَ ٱلرِّجَالِ أَوِ ٱلطِّفْلِ ٱلَّذِينَ لَمْ يَظْهَرُوا۟ عَلَىٰ عَوْرَٰتِ ٱلنِّسَآءِ ... ﴾ [النور: ٣١]

"Tell the believing women to lower their gaze and protect their private parts and not to show off their adornments except that which is apparent and to draw their veils over necks and bosoms and not to reveal their adornments except to their husbands, their fathers, their husband's fathers, their sons, their husband's sons, their brothers or their brother's sons, or their sister's sons, or their women or the (female) slaves, or old male servants who lack vigor, or small children who have no sense of the shame of sex" (*al-Nur* 31).

There is a difference of opinion concerning the referent of the pronoun in the phrase, "their women." Some say that it refers to the class of women as a whole. Some say that it refers to the described women only, that is, the believing women. According to the first opinion, a woman may uncover her face and hands in front of a non-Muslim woman. According to the second opinion, a Muslim woman may not do so. I am more inclined to the first opinion and believe it is more likely to be correct. That is because when a woman is in the presence of a another woman, it makes no difference if that woman is a Muslim or not, as long as there is no kind of temptation involved. However, if one fears something of that nature, such as the woman describing the Muslim women to her male relatives, then one must avoid such a cause and then the woman should not uncover her face or any part of her body in front of such a woman. This is true regardless of whether that troublesome woman is a Muslim or a non-Muslim.

Shaikh ibn Uthaimin

Ruling Concerning Wearing a Face Veil

Question 260: What is the ruling concerning women wearing clothing that has written on it verses of the Quran or statements like, "There is no God except Allah, Muhammad is the Messenger of Allah"? What is the Islamic ruling concerning wearing a *burqa'*?

Response: There is nothing wrong with wearing such clothing. However, one must make sure that there is no sense of disrespect or disdain shown to what is written. For example, she should not sleep in it or sit upon the part in which any of the names of Allah is written. She also should not wear it into the bathroom. If she is in need of that clothing for such purposes, she should first wipe away the respected names on it and then she may use it.

A *burqa'* is a type of face veil that opens for the eyes to look out from. This is allowed and there is nothing wrong with it except when one is in the state of *ihram* [for the Hajj or Umra]. The Prophet (صلى الله عليه وسلم) said,

$$\text{"} \, وَلاَ تَنْتَقِــــبُ الْمَــــرْأَةُ \text{"}$$

"Women are not to wear the face veil (*niqaab*)."[1]

This refers to the one performing the pilgrimage. She is not to wear a face veil (*niqaab*) which is the same as a *burqa'*. This indicates that such is permissible for the woman who is not making the Hajj. However, it is not allowed to widen the open space for the eyes, such that the nose and eyebrows become visible, for example. In this way, she becomes a temptation for those who see her. In addition, one must wear above the *burqa'*, a light headcovering that does not prevent one from seeing and which will cover the rest of the face that is left uncovered by the face veil.

Shaikh ibn Jibreen

The Wife of the Maternal Uncle is not *Mahram*

Question 261: Some of the older women believe that it is allowed for young men to sit with the wives of their maternal uncles and treat them like their own aunts. They say, "You accept

---

[1] Recorded by al-Bukhari and Muslim.—JZ

your uncles but do not accept your aunts!" I have tried to convince them that they are wrong and that the verse is clear about who and who is not *mahram*. I could not convince them. Could you say something to them?

Response: There is no doubt that the wife of the maternal uncle is not *mahram* for the nephew. It is permissible for the nephew to marry her if they should be separated. Therefore, it is not allowed for her to appear in front of him with her face uncovered. It is also not allowed for the two of them to be in private or for him to look at what she must cover, such as her face and her beauty. He is not mentioned among the *mahram* in the verse of the Quran,

﴿ وَلَا يُبْدِينَ زِينَتَهُنَّ إِلَّا لِبُعُولَتِهِنَّ ﴾   [النور: ٣١]

"[Tell the believing women] not to reveal their adornments except to their husbands, their fathers, their husband's fathers," (*al-Nur* 31).

She is not mentioned along with those that he cannot marry in this verse,

﴿ حُرِّمَتْ عَلَيْكُمْ أُمَّهَاتُكُمْ ﴾   [النساء: ٢٣]

"Forbidden to you (for marriage) are: your mothers..." (*al-Nisa* 23).

Therefore, the belief that they are *mahram* has no basis to it and one must avoid it.

Shaikh ibn Jibreen

Uncovering One's Face in Front of non-*Mahram* Men

Question 262: One of my friends said, "My husband permits me to uncover my face in front of his male relative that visits him. And he allows his wife to sit with my husband." Is this allowable?

Response: It is not allowed for you to obey your husband in uncovering your face in the presence of his relatives, even if they are his full brothers. They are not *mahram*. Uncovering the face is one of the causes of temptation. It is also not allowed for the wife of his relative to obey him in uncovering her face in front of your husband for the same reasons.

Shaikh ibn Jibreen

Ruling Concerning Wearing Light Colored Clothing, such as White or Yellow and Ruling Concerning Wearing Short Dresses

Question 263: What is the ruling concerning wearing light colored clothing, such as yellow, white or red, but which covers the body? What is the ruling concerning wearing short clothing that expose the legs?

Response: It is allowed for a woman to wear whatever clothing is normal for the women to wear, as long as it is not something to be specifically recognized as that for men. In that case, a woman should not wear it as the Prophet (صلى الله عليه وسلم) cursed the women who imitate men and vice-versa.

A woman must wear clothing that covers her entire body if she is in the presence of men she is not related to. She may not uncover anything of her body to them, not her face, hands or feet except in cases of need, such as handing or taking something and so forth. She also cannot wear tight clothing that shows her body shape or the size of parts of her body, such as her breasts, shoulders, chest, buttocks and so forth. One must also bring up one's children accustomed to wearing long, flowing garments. If a child grows up accustomed to something, it is very difficult to get them away from it when they get older. If the dress is short, it may show the attractiveness of her body and shows to men what will be a temptation or cause of temptation for them. There is no harm if a woman, in her house and in the presence of her relatives, wears a short dress due to some need, even if it shows her shins or upper arm, as women usually wear when they have to work.

Shaikh ibn Jibreen

Fear and Obey Allah as Much as You are Able

Question 264: I am a young girl in a very perplexing situation. I live with my family that has some very strange, distorted ideas. I used to wear *hijab*. I found great opposition and ridicule from my family. It reached the point that they physically beat me and prevented me from leaving my house. They forced me to take off the *hijab* and simply wear a long cloak but with my face uncovered. What should I do? Should I leave the house although untrustworthy people are many?

Response: This question involves two basic issues.

The family that did such an evil to this young lady have to be one of two cases: either they are ignorant of the truth or they are arrogantly refusing to follow the truth. This is very vicious and unruly behavior. They have no right to behave this way. *Hijab* is not something improper or ill-mannered. Humans are free within the limits of the *Shariah*.

If they did not know that *hijab* is obligatory upon the woman, they must be taught that. They must be taught that it is obligatory according to the Quran and sunnah. However, if they were knowledgeable but simply arrogantly refused to submit, then the crime is even greater. As a poet once said, "If you were unaware, it is a great misfortune. But if you were aware, then the misfortune is even greater."

The second issue is with respect to this young lady. We say to her that it is obligatory upon her to obey and fear Allah as much as she is able to. If she is able to wear *hijab* without her family noticing that, she should do so. However, if they beat her or force her to take it off, there is no sin upon her. Allah has said,

﴿ مَن كَفَرَ بِٱللَّهِ مِنۢ بَعْدِ إِيمَـٰنِهِۦٓ إِلَّا مَنْ أُكْرِهَ وَقَلْبُهُۥ مُطْمَئِنٌّۢ بِٱلْإِيمَـٰنِ وَلَـٰكِن مَّن شَرَحَ بِٱلْكُفْرِ صَدْرًا فَعَلَيْهِمْ غَضَبٌ مِّنَ ٱللَّهِ وَلَهُمْ عَذَابٌ عَظِيمٌ ﴾ [النحل: ١٠٦]

"Whoever disbelieved in Allah after his belief, except him who is forced thereto and whose heart is at rest with Faith— but such as open their breasts to disbelief, on them is Wrath from Allah and theirs will be a great torment" (*al-Nahl* 106). Another verse states,

﴿ وَلَيْسَ عَلَيْكُمْ جُنَاحٌ فِيمَآ أَخْطَأْتُم بِهِۦ وَلَـٰكِن مَّا تَعَمَّدَتْ قُلُوبُكُمْ وَكَانَ ٱللَّهُ غَفُورًا رَّحِيمًا ﴾ [الأحزاب: ٥]

"There is no sin for you if you make a mistake therein, except in regard to what your hearts deliberately intended. And Allah is Ever Oft-Forgiving, Most Merciful" (*al-Ahzab* 5).

But fear and obey Allah to the best of your ability. If your family does not understand the wisdom behind the obligation of *hijab*, say to them: It is obligatory upon the believer to submit to any order from Allah and His Messenger, regardless if they do or don't understand the wisdom behind it. This is because the act of submission itself is an act of wisdom. Allah says,

﴿ وَمَا كَانَ لِمُؤْمِنٍ وَلَا مُؤْمِنَةٍ إِذَا قَضَى ٱللَّهُ وَرَسُولُهُۥٓ أَمْرًا أَن يَكُونَ لَهُمُ ٱلْخِيَرَةُ مِنْ أَمْرِهِمْ وَمَن يَعْصِ ٱللَّهَ وَرَسُولَهُۥ فَقَدْ ضَلَّ ضَلَـٰلًا مُّبِينًا ﴾ [الأحزاب: ٣٦]

"It is not for a believer, man or woman, when Allah and His Messenger have decreed a matter that they should have any option in their decision. And whosoever disobeys Allah and His Messenger, he has indeed strayed in a plain error" (*al-Ahzab* 36).

When Aisha was asked about the situation of the menstruating woman, why she makes up her fasts but not her prayers, she answered, "That happened to us during the time of the Messenger of Allah (صلى الله عليه وسلم) and we were ordered to make up our fasts and we were not ordered to make up our prayers." Hence, she equated the order as being the wisdom in itself. Even given that, the wisdom behind the *hijab* is very clear as a woman displaying her beauty is a source of temptation. When temptation occurs, sin and lewdness occur. If sin and lewdness spread, that means that destruction and ruin are on the way.

Shaikh ibn Uthaimin

Ruling Concerning Wearing Gloves

Question 265: Is wearing socks or gloves on the hands in order to cover them an innovation or is it permissible? Is it forbidden for a non-*mahram* male to see a woman's hand if there is no adornment on it? Is it permissible for one spouse to prevent the other from fulfilling his or her natural right [to sexual intercourse] for a lengthy period of time without any acceptable *Shariah* excuse?

Response: It is obligatory upon a woman to wear whatever covers her body and private parts, especially if she is going out to the market or someplace similar. Therefore, she may wear socks over her feet and gloves over her hands so that nothing that could be a temptation may be seen of her. However, exposing the hand without a glove on it is permissible if there is some need, as long as the hand is not adorned with dye, jewelry or anything of that nature. This is the case since hands almost all look alike among the people.

There is no doubt that there is a psychological need for sexual contact between the two spouses. Usually, the wants of the two differ, based on different levels of desire between the man and the woman. Usually the man's desire is stronger. Therefore, he is usually the one desiring the act more. In fact, many wives complain about their husbands and the extent to which they desire sexual contact, to the point that it harms the woman.

As for avoiding such contact for a long time, this is not allowed. The woman has a right to have her needs fulfilled. The most that a woman can be asked to be patient for is four months. Therefore, the desires and needs of both should be met. The desires, abilities and shortcomings of both parties should be taken into consideration without either party being harmed.

Shaikh ibn Jibreen

Short Dresses for Young Children

Question 266: Some women, may Allah guide them, dress their young daughters in short dresses that display the shins. When we advise those women, they answer, "We used to wear those when we were young and they did not cause us any harm when we got older." What is your opinion of that?

Response: I am of the opinion that a person should not dress his daughter in such clothing while she is young. This is because if she grows accustomed to it, she will stick with it and she will consider it a light matter. However, if you trained her properly to be bashful when she was young, she would continue in that proper manner when she gets older. I advise my Muslim sisters to leave the dress of the foreigners who are the enemies of the religion and to bring up their children wearing clothes that cover their bodies and to teach them modesty, for modesty is part of faith.

Shaikh ibn Uthaimin

Uncovering the Hand and Foot

Question 267: Is it allowed for me to uncover my hand only in front of my brother-in-law? Is the ruling different if my husband is also present?

Response: The woman should cover all of herself in front of non-*mahram* men, even if it be a husband's brother, sister's husband, cousin or others, and regardless if it be in the presence of *mahram* men or not. That is to cover her beauty and the cause of temptation, be it her face, arms, shin, chest and so forth. As for the hand or foot, apparently, it is allowed to show them for some need, such as when giving something to someone or receiving something and so forth. However, if one fears some kind of temptation, then they must remain covered. For example, that would be the case if a woman notices a non-related man gazing at a woman and not moving his eyes from her. This also means that mixing or sitting with non-*mahram* men is also forbidden if one fears any harmful consequences. Allah knows best.

Shaikh ibn Jibreen

Ruling Concerning Buying and Possessing Fashion Magazines

Question 268: What is the ruling concerning fashion magazines, like *Burda*, in order to benefit from them concerning new women's fashions and accessories. What is the ruling concerning keeping them after one has already benefited from them while they are filled with pictures of women?

Response: There is no doubt that buying magazines that just contain pictures is forbidden. This is because possessing pictures is forbidden, based on the statement of the Messenger of Allah (صلى الله عليه وسلم),

" لاَ تَدْخُـــلُ الْمَلاَئِـــكَةُ بَيْتـاً فِيْـهِ صُـــورَةٌ "

"The angels do not enter a house which contains pictures."[1]

When the Prophet (صلى الله عليه وسلم) saw a picture on a cushion with Aisha, he stood and did not enter the room. His dislike could be seen on his face. Those fashion magazines must be looked into to see what they contain as not every fashion is permissible. The fashions might be such that they show the woman's body, due to their tightness or for other reasons. The fashions could be the dresses of the disbelievers that are particular to them. Imitating the disbelievers is forbidden, since the Prophet (صلى الله عليه وسلم) said,

" مَــنْ تَشَبَّــهَ بِقَـــومٍ فَهُــوَ مِنْهُـــمْ "

"Whoever imitates a people is one of them."[2]

I advise my Muslim brothers in general and my Muslim sisters in particular to avoid those fashions as either they are imitation of non-Muslims or they display what the woman should be concealing. If women follow every new fashion, then it means, in general, that our customs that have come from our religion will be changed for customs that have been taken from non-Muslims.

Shaikh ibn Uthaimin

The Islamic *Hijab*

Question 269: What is the Islamic *hijab*?

Response: The Islamic *hijab* is for the women to cover everything that is forbidden for her to expose. That is, she covers everything that she must cover. The first of those bodily parts that she must cover is her face. It is the source of temptation and the source of people desiring her. Therefore, the woman must cover

---

[1] Recorded by al-Bukhari and Muslim.—JZ
[2] Recorded by Abu Dawud. Al-Albani has graded it *sahih*. Al-Albani, *Sahih al-Jami*, vol. 2, p. 1058.—JZ

her face in front of those men that are not *mahram*. As for those who claim that the Islamic *hijab* is to cover the head, shoulders, back, feet, shin and forearms while allowing her to uncover her face and hands, this is a very amazing claim. This is because it is well-known that the source of temptation and looking is the face. How can one say that the *Shariah* does not allow the exposure of the foot of the woman while it allows her to uncover her face? It is not possible that there could be in the Esteemed, Wise and Noble *Shariah* a contradiction. Yet everyone knows that the temptation from uncovering the face is much greater than the temptation that results from the uncovering of the feet. Everyone also knows that the most sought after aspect of the woman for men is the face. If you told a prospective groom that a woman's face is ugly but her feet are beautiful, he would not propose to such a woman. However, if you told him that her face was beautiful but her hands, palms, or shins were less than beautiful, he would still propose to her. From this one can conclude that the face is the first thing that must be covered. There are also evidences from the Book of Allah and the sunnah of our Prophet (صلى الله عليه وسلم). There are also statements from the Companions, the leading Imams and the great scholars of Islam that indicate that it is obligatory for the woman to cover all of her body in the presence of non-*mahram* men. This obviously indicates that it is obligatory upon the woman to cover her face in front of such men. However, this is not the place to quote all those authorities. And Allah knows best.

Shaikh ibn Uthaimin

Ruling Concerning Wearing Ankle Bracelets

Question 270: What is the ruling concerning wearing ankle bracelets as a type of beautification?

Response: It is allowed to wear ankle bracelets for beautification. However, one is not allowed to shake them in the presence of non-*mahram* men in order to alert them to such jewelry. Allah has said,

﴿ وَلَا يَضْرِبْنَ بِأَرْجُلِهِنَّ لِيُعْلَمَ مَا يُخْفِينَ مِن زِينَتِهِنَّ ﴾[النور : ٣١]

"And let them [women] not stamp their feet so as to reveal what they hide of their adornment" (*al-Nur* 31).

Shaikh ibn Jibreen

Removing the Headcovering

Question 271: I have a skin disease on my head. The doctor told me to remove the headcovering that I wear on my head and that is truly harming me at the present time. Do I have the right to do that? What shall I do?

Response: Yes, you have the right to remove the headcovering from your head if you are not in the presence of non-*mahram* men, such as when you are with your husband, *mahram* men or women only with no men present. However, when you go to the marketplace or in the presence of non-*mahram* men, it is obligatory upon you to cover your head and your face as well as the rest of your body.[1]

Shaikh ibn Uthaimin

First, Make Your Wife Stick to the Verse

Question 272: I am married to a woman who wears, praise be to Allah, *hijab*. However, as is the custom in my country, she does not wear *hijab* in front of her sister's husband and her sister does not wear *hijab* in my presence. This is the custom. Furthermore, my wife does

---

[1] May Allah reward Shaikh ibn Uthaimin for his efforts for the sake of Allah. On this particular point, however, it seems that he has ignored the law of necessity. If the action is truly harming the woman, then it is difficult to side along with ibn Uthaimin's response to this question. Perhaps, it would have been best to reply that this sister should look for other ways by which she may cover herself and, at the same time, not cause herself any physical harm. Allah knows best.—JZ

not wear *hijab* in the presence of my brother or her cousins. Does this go against the *Shariah* and religion? What can I do while it has become the custom in my country not to wear *hijab* in the presence of those people that I mentioned. If I tell my wife to wear *hijab* in front of those people, she will accuse me of not trusting her and being suspicious about her and so forth.

Response: All of those groups of men that you mentioned in the question are not *mahram* for her. It is not allowed for her to uncover her face and beauty in front of them. Allah has only allowed her to uncover in front of the *mahram* men mentioned in the verse in *surah al-Nur*,

$$\text{﴿ وَلَا يُبْدِينَ زِينَتَهُنَّ إِلَّا لِبُعُولَتِهِنَّ أَوۡ ءَابَآئِهِنَّ ﴾}$$

"[Tell the believing women] not to reveal their adornments except to their husbands, their fathers ," (*al-Nur* 31).

First, you should convince your wife that it is forbidden to uncover her face in front of non-*mahram* men. Make her abide by that even if it goes against the customs of your people and even if she makes accusations against you. You should also make this point clear to your close relatives that you mentioned, that is, the brethren of the husband, the husband of the sister, the cousins and so forth. All of them are non-*mahram* and they all may marry her if she gets divorced.

Shaikh ibn Jibreen

May I Request My Husband to get Independent Living Quarters?

Question 273: My husband's brother wanted to get married and live with us in our house. I do not uncover my face in front of him nor do I sit with him nor have I ever seen him. He then did get married. Due to the difficult circumstances that this leads to, would my requesting from my husband independent living quarters be considered a type of causing separation between two brothers? Would that be forbidden or not? You should also know that my husband also feels that such would be best but it is my husband's mother, who lives with us, who wants them all to be together.

Response: In that situation, if the women are completely wearing *hijab* and there is no cases of privacy [with the other's husband], then staying together would be best in order to please the mother of the two husbands. However, if that is not the case, then it would be best to live separately. [Living separately would be better] if, for example, one of the woman is lax and uncovers herself in front of her brother-in-law or she stays alone with him in the house. [Similarly, separation would be best] if one of the husbands is not to be trusted with respect to the wife of his brother. That is, he follows her and tries to get an opportunity to see her, enters upon her without asking permission first, tries to see what is under her clothing and so forth. In that case, it would be best to seek independent living quarters in order to escape from the tightness and possible problems.

Shaikh ibn Jibreen

It is Forbidden for a Woman to Sit with Her Brother-in-Law

Question 274: My mother-in-law wants me to sit with her son— my brother-in-law— while wearing an outer cloak and face covering, in front of the television while they drink tea. I refused and she criticized me. Am I right in what I did or not?

Response: It is right for you to refuse to sit with them in such a situation. That would be a cause for temptation. Your brother-in-law, who is still single, is not *mahram* for you. His listening to your voice and seeing your character and behavior is a source of temptation. The same is true for your looking at him.

Shaikh ibn Jibreen

Uncovering One's Face in Front of the Husband's "Foster Father"

Question 275: What is the ruling concerning a woman uncovering her face in front of her husband's "foster father" [that is, the husband of the woman who breastfed her husband]?

Response: It is not allowed for a woman to uncover her face in the presence of her husband's "foster father" according to the strongest opinion and the chosen opinion of Shaikh al-Islam ibn Taimiya. The Messenger of Allah (صلى الله عليه وسلم) has said,

" يَحــرُمُ مِنَ الرَّضَاعَــةِ مَا يَحــرُمُ مِــنَ النَّسَـــبِ "

"Foster relationships forbid what blood relationships forbid."[1]

The father-in-law is not disallowed for marriage with his daughter-in-law due to blood relationship but due to marriage relationship only. Allah has said in the Quran,

﴿ وَحَلَـٰٓئِلُ أَبْنَآئِكُمُ ٱلَّذِينَ مِنْ أَصْلَـٰبِكُمْ ﴾

"[Forbidden to you in marriage are...] the wives of your sons who (spring) from your loins" (al-Nisa 23).

The "foster son" is not from the loins of the father. Therefore, if a woman is married to a man who has a "foster father," she must wear *hijab* in front of him and not uncover her face in front of him. If it were the case that she became separated from that man's "foster son", it still would not be permissible for him to marry her as a precautionary measure, since that is the opinion of the majority of the scholars.

Shaikh ibn Jibreen

---

[1] Recorded by al-Bukhari and Muslim with a slightly different wording.— JZ

Ruling Concerning Wearing Nose rings

Question 276: What is the ruling concerning wearing nose rings for beautification?

Response: It is permissible for a woman to beautify herself according to what is customary, even if that means she has to pierce part of her body, such as is the case with earrings. Perhaps, nose rings are permissible since it is allowed to pierce a camel's nose and put a ridle through it and that is not considered mutilation.

Shaikh ibn Jibreen

Ruling Concerning Uncovering the Face

Question 277: Is it allowed for a woman to uncover her face in front of non-*mahram* men?

Response: A woman is not to uncover her face in front of non-*mahram* men. In fact, that is forbidden. Her *hijab* is not complete without her covering her face. That is her most attractive aspect. The evidence is in Allah's statement,

﴿ وَلْيَضْرِبْنَ بِخُمُرِهِنَّ عَلَىٰ جُيُوبِهِنَّ ﴾   [النور: ٣١]

"[Tell the believing women] to draw their veils over their necks and bosoms" (*al-Nur* 31).

Allah has ordered them to lower their headcovering from their heads over the opening in the front of chest. If it comes down from the head, it covers both the face and the neck and front chest area. Allah also says,

﴿ وَلَا يُبْدِينَ زِينَتَهُنَّ إِلَّا لِبُعُولَتِهِنَّ ﴾   [النور: ٣١]

"[Tell the believing women] not to reveal their adornments except to their husbands, their fathers..." (*al-Nur* 31).

Therefore, it is forbidden for her to expose her adornments save in front of her husband and other *mahram* men.

Shaikh ibn Jibreen

Ruling Concerning Wearing Wigs

Question 278: Is it allowed for a woman to use a wig to beautify herself for her husband? Is this considered part of the prohibition of adding hair to one's hair?

Response: Wigs are forbidden and are considered a type of adding hair to one's hair. Although it is not exactly that, it makes the woman's hair look longer than it is and becomes similar to adding hair. The Prophet (صلى الله عليه وسلم) cursed the one who does the adding of hair as well as the one who requested it. However, if the woman does not have any hair upon her head, for example, if she is bald, then she may use a wig to cover up that blemish as it is considered permissible to remove blemishes. For example, the Prophet (صلى الله عليه وسلم) allowed the man who had his nose cut off during a battle to wear a fake nose of gold. The matter is more flexible than that. It might also include the question of having plastic surgery to fix a small nose and so forth. However, beautification is not the same as removing a blemish. If the matter is that of removing a blemish, there is no harm in it, such as when the nose is crooked and needs to be straightened or the removal of a beauty mark. There is no harm in such acts. But if it is not to remove a blemish, such as tattooing or removing eyebrow hairs, then it is forbidden. Using a wig, even with the permission and approval of the husband, is forbidden for there is no permission or approval in matters that Allah has forbidden.

Shaikh ibn Uthaimin

The Great Uncles are *Mahram*

Question 279: Is it allowed for a woman to uncover her face in the presence of her maternal and paternal great uncles? That is, are they considered *mahram* to her?

Response: Yes, if the woman's mother or father has maternal or paternal uncles they are considered *mahram* for that woman. This is because the paternal uncle of your father is your uncle and the maternal uncle of your father is your uncle. Similarly, the paternal uncle of your mother and maternal uncle of your mother are related to you and are considered your paternal and maternal uncles.

Shaikh ibn Uthaimin

The Muslim Women of that Land Must Not Obey Its Rulers

Question 280: A law was passed by the rulers of a Muslim land forcing the young women and all women to remove their *hijab*s, in particular their face coverings. Is it permissible for me to execute that order? You should also realize that the one who refuses to obey that command will be punished by, for example, removal from work or school or imprisonment.

Response: This trial that has befallen your land is from those events by which the servants are tested and tried. Allah has said in the Quran,

﴿ أَحَسِبَ ٱلنَّاسُ أَن يُتْرَكُوٓا۟ أَن يَقُولُوٓا۟ ءَامَنَّا وَهُمْ لَا يُفْتَنُونَ ۝ وَلَقَدْ فَتَنَّا ٱلَّذِينَ مِن قَبْلِهِمْ فَلَيَعْلَمَنَّ ٱللَّهُ ٱلَّذِينَ صَدَقُوا۟ وَلَيَعْلَمَنَّ ٱلْكَٰذِبِينَ ﴾ [العنكبوت: ٢-٣]

"Do people think that they will be left alone because they say, 'We believe,' and will not be tested. And We indeed tested those who were before them. And Allah will certainly make [it] known [the truth of] those who are true, and will certainly make [it] known [the falsehood of] those who are liars" (al-Ankabut 2-3).

In my opinion, it is obligatory upon the Muslim sisters of that land to refuse to obey the rulers in that evil order. This is because there is no obedience to evil, rejected orders. Allah says,

﴿ يَٰٓأَيُّهَا ٱلَّذِينَ ءَامَنُوٓا۟ أَطِيعُوا۟ ٱللَّهَ وَأَطِيعُوا۟ ٱلرَّسُولَ وَأُو۟لِى ٱلْأَمْرِ مِنكُمْ ﴾ [النساء: ٥٩]

"O you who believe! Obey Allah and obey the Messenger and those of you who are in authority" (*al-Nisa* 59).
If one ponders over this verse, one notes that Allah has stated,

﴿ أَطِيعُوا۟ ٱللَّهَ وَأَطِيعُوا۟ ٱلرَّسُولَ وَأُو۟لِى ٱلْأَمْرِ مِنكُمْ ﴾   [النساء : ٥٩]

"Obey Allah and obey the Messenger and those of you who are in authority" (*al-Nisa* 59).
That is, the word "obey" is not repeated directly before "those of you who are in authority". This indicates that obedience to those in authority is conditional upon obedience to Allah and obedience to His Messenger. If their orders are in contradiction to obedience to Allah and His Messenger, then they are not listened to or obeyed in that matter that they have ordered.

" ولا طَاعَةَ لِمَخْلُوقٍ فِي مَعْصِيَةِ الْخَالِقِ "

"There is no obedience to the created if it involves disobedience to the Creator."[1]

The hurt that these women face in this matter is part of what one must be patient with. They must seek Allah's help in being patient. We ask Allah to guide their leaders to the truth.

I do not think that such a compulsion can exist unless the woman leaves her house. In her house, it is not possible that they could force such a thing upon her. Hence, the sisters should try to stay in their houses until the matter is rectified. If her studies involve a disobedience to Allah, then her studies are not permissible. Instead, she should study what she needs for her religion and worldly needs and, usually, this can be done in her household. In sum, it is never allowed to obey the rulers in a command that is an evil and wrong in itself.

Shaikh ibn Uthaimin

---

[1] With this wording, this is a hadith recorded by Ahmad. However, Muslim has something very close to it.—JZ

20. Questions Related to Being Dutiful to One's Parents

That Prayer is Not Accepted

Question 281: I fast voluntary fasts so that Allah may wipe away my mistakes and errors that I have committed without any knowledge on my part. I stick to my religion, and all praises are due to Allah. However, my mother asks Allah not to accept my fasts. This is not due to any reason. My fasting does not affect my housework and she is not in need of me. I am very confused and dumbfounded that Allah may not accept my deeds and my fasting because the supplications of the parents is accepted by Allah. What is your opinion?

Response: We thank you for your concern for the acts of worship and voluntary deeds. Continue to perform those acts according to your ability. Excuse your mother. For the deeds you are doing are good deeds and the rights of your mother are more so met by you doing so. Fasting does not interfere with you being obedient to her, serving her and fulfilling her rights. In fact, she must encourage you to do such and she should take you as an example as she is in more need of voluntary prayers, fasting and acts of worship to raise her level and remove her sins. As for her supplication against you, it is not acceptable, Allah willing, especially since the deed you are doing is a good one and she only desires by that mercy and pity.

Shaikh ibn Jibreen

My Mother Loves Me Dearly and Treats Me Like a Child

Question 282: My mother loves me very dearly and has a great deal of sympathy for me, perhaps that is due to my weakness and illness. However, her love for me goes well beyond acceptable limits. I am now twenty-one years old yet my mother still treats me like I am a girl of ten. If she is able to, she feeds me by her hand. I, all praises due to Allah, am very soft in speech with her and obey her.

Response: Usually the parent loves his or her children and feels compassion for them. This effect may be much more in both or one of the parents due to no reason or because the child is so dutiful and obedient to them or due to some illness or weakness that makes them even more merciful to their weak child. The effect of this compassion may even harm the child, as in the question. The child should excuse herself to the mother or father due to the harm they cause. She should make it clear that there is no need for such protection and care. Furthermore, the parents must be equitable toward all their children with respect to love, compassion and caring. In fact, some of the early Muslims used to be equal with respect to kissing their children in a valiant attempt to fulfill the command of justice mentioned by the Prophet (صلى الله عليه وسلم),

" اتَّقُـــوا اللهَ وَاعْـدِلُـــوا بَيْنَ أُولادِكُـــمْ "

"Fear Allah and be just among your children."[1]

Shaikh ibn Jibreen

---

[1] Recorded by al-Bukhari and Muslim.—JZ

My Mother Died While She Was Angry with Me

Question 283: My mother died about six years ago during Ramadhan. When I was young, I was always arguing with her and talking back to her. When she died, she was angry with me. I became older and more mature and now I am remorseful about what happened between me and her. I cannot do anything now except ask for forgiveness and repent to Allah and pray for mercy for her and forgiveness. Is this sufficient to have Allah forgive my sin and have mercy on me for that deed on the Day that we meet?

Second, we do not fast on her behalf.[1] Are we being sinful? Is it allowed for us to fast on her behalf afterwards even though we were not aware of that matter except recently?

Response: Perhaps during the lifetime of your mother you were very young and, at the same time, ignorant and childish. You are excused for what you did during that time. Furthermore, since you are full of remorse after you have become more mature and you have repented to Allah and sought His forgiveness for that sin, Allah willing, that has erased what has occurred. Repentance wipes away what preceded it. Also, the acts of praying for her, asking for mercy and forgiveness for her, charity on her behalf and so forth all are means by which Allah wipes away sins. As for the fasting that she did not do and her breaking of her fast during the days of her illness, she is excused due to her illness that she was suffering and she did not have the ability to make up those days later.

Shaikh ibn Jibreen

---

[1] It seems that there is something missing in the text of this question. Apparently, the mother became ill and was not able to fast and her children did not make up those days on her behalf. Allah knows best.—JZ

21. Questions Related to Supplications (Du'a)

I Fear Eclipses

Question 284: My problem is that I have a fear of looking at the sky, especially during the night or when the sky is overcast. I fear the eclipses, regardless if they be lunar or solar. I want you to write a supplication for me that could remove that fear from me, by the will of Allah. Or guide me to a matter that will help me remove myself from this situation.

Response: I do not know of any reason for such a fear. The sky, earth, sun and moon are all created by Allah. Allah has erected them for His slaves. He has ordered humans to look at them and to take lessons and reminders from them. You, my sister for the sake of Allah, should increase your remembrance of Allah under all circumstances, through His names and attributes, reading the Quran, pondering over its verses and what wonderful and amazing aspects the creation of Allah contains. You should turn to Allah with the supplications that have come from the Prophet (صلى الله عليه وسلم) in the hope that such a fear will be removed from you. In its place, Allah willing, you will be given safety and tranquillity.

Shaikh ibn Jibreen

I Supplicated but Was Not Responded To

Question 285: For over ten years I prayed to Allah now and then to provide me with a pious husband and pious children... However, none of that has occurred and this is what Allah has willed and there is no one to repel His Decree. My question is this: I stopped making that *du'a* recently, not out of despair of being answered by Allah but because I began to think that that matter was not what was best for me, given that Allah did not respond to my prayer. I decided to stop making that *du'a* because Allah is more knowledgeable of what would benefit me, regardless of my great desire and hope to have my prayer answered. What is obligatory upon me in this position? Shall I continue making that supplication or should I be satisfied that such a matter is not what is best for me and simply stop making that prayer?

Response: It is mentioned in the Hadith that the servant's prayer is responded to as long as he is not hasty. Hastiness has been explained as the response being slow in coming so the person gives up and stops making the *dua*. He then says, "I prayed and prayed but I was not responded to." Allah may delay the response to a prayer for some reasons, general or specific. In a Hadith, it is stated that the supplicant receives one of three things from Allah: Either Allah responds to the *dua* and gives the person what he asks, or Allah puts something in store for him for the Hereafter or Allah keeps some harm from coming to him by His Decree. Therefore, sister, do not be hasty but continue in making that supplication, even if for a number of years. Also, you should not refuse a qualified man if he asks for your hand, even if he is elderly or is already married. Perhaps Allah may give you through him a great deal of good.

Shaikh ibn Jibreen

Supplication Against One's Children

Question 286: Many fathers and mothers make supplications against their children when they make mistakes and err. I would like you to give some words of advise to them concerning that matter.

Response: I advise parents to be forgiving and controlling of themselves when their children, while young, have shortcomings. They should be patient with respect to the words and harm they may receive from their children. Children are not completely mature so it is always the case that they make mistakes in their speech and actions. The father can be compassionate and forgiving and can teach his child with compassion and gentleness and advise him to the point that the child accepts that from him and is changed by it. However, some parents fall into a greater mistake and that is supplicating against their children by asking for death, illness, misery and so forth to come to them. They continue making such supplications and make them often. However, after their anger is over, they realize their mistake and recognize that they don't want their supplications to be answered nor do they want any of that to happen to their children, due to their compassion and mercy for them. What led them to make such *dua* was their extreme anger. Allah forgives such *dua*, as Allah has stated,

وَلَوْ يُعَجِّلُ ٱللَّهُ لِلنَّاسِ ٱلشَّرَّ ٱسْتِعْجَالَهُم بِٱلْخَيْرِ لَقُضِيَ إِلَيْهِمْ أَجَلُهُمْ ﴾ [يونس: ١١]

"Were Allah to hasten for mankind the evil [they have earned] as they would hasten on the good, their respite would already be settled" (*Yunus* 11).

Parents must have patience and calmness. They must raise the child in the best way. The child may be beaten in a way that will keep him from what is wrong as a child is often more affected by a spanking than by teaching and moral training. Obviously, making *dua* against the child does not benefit the child. One does not know what to say about it. Perhaps, what is stated against the child may be recorded and the parent will not benefit at all from it. Allah knows best.

Shaikh ibn Jibreen

22. Questions of a Miscellaneous Nature

Meaning of the Women Having a Shortcoming in Reasoning and Religion

Question 287: We always hear the Hadith, "Women have a shortcoming in understanding and religion." Some of the men state it to insult women. We would like you to explain to us the meaning of that Hadith.

Response: The Prophet's words and their explanation is as follows:

"مَا رَأَيْتُ مِنْ نَاقِصَاتِ عَقْلٍ ودِينٍ أَغْلَبَ لِلُبِّ الرَّجُلِ الحَازِمِ مِنْ إِحْدَاكُنَّ، فِقِيلَ يَارَسُولَ اللهِ ما نُقْصَانُ عَقْلِها؟ قَالَ أَلَيْسَتْ شَهَادَةُ الْمَرْأَتِينِ بِشَهَادَةِ رَجُلٍ؟ قِيلَ يَارَسُولَ اللهِ! مَا نُقْصَانُ دِينِهَا ؟ قَالَ: أَلَيْسَتْ إِذَا حَاضَتْ لَمْ تُصَلِّ وَلَمْ تَصُمْ؟ "

"I have seen none having more of a shortcoming in reasoning and religion yet, at the same time, robbing the wisdom of the wisest men than you." They said, "O Messenger of Allah (صلى الله عليه وسلم), what is the shortcoming in our reasoning?" He said, "Is it not the case that the testimony of two women is equivalent to that of one man?" They said, "O Messenger of Allah (peace be upon him), what is the shortcoming in our religion?" He said, "Is it not the case that when you have your menses you neither pray or fast?"[1]

---

[1] Recorded by al-Bukhari and Muslim.—JZ

The Prophet (صلى الله عليه وسلم) explained that their shortcoming in reasoning is found in the fact that their memory is weak and that their witness is in need of another woman to corroborate it. Therefore, it is related to nonproficiency in witnessing due to woman's forgetfulness or she may add something in her witnessing. As for the shortcoming in her religion, it is because when they are menstruating or having post-partum bleeding, they neither pray nor fast, and they do not make up their prayers, and this is their shortcoming in the religion. However, they are not to be blamed for that shortcoming. This has been imposed by the Law of Allah. He is the one who laid down such legislation in kindness and ease upon her. This is because if she were to fast while menstruating or post-partum bleeding, this would harm her. It is from the mercy of Allah that she is sanctioned not to fast. As for the prayer, during menses, she is in a situation that keeps her from being purified. It is again from Allah's mercy that He has commanded that they do not pray while they are menstruating as well as during post-partum bleeding. He has also ordered that they do not make up their prayers. This is because if they were ordered to make up their prayers, it would be a hardship upon them. Prayer is repeated five times in a day and night. Menses may last for a number of days, up to seven or eight or more. Post-partum bleeding lasts for forty days. It is from the mercy of Allah and His goodness to them that they are not obliged to perform or make up the prayers of such conditions. However, this does not mean that they have a shortcoming in understanding in everything or that they have a shortcoming in religion in every matter. The Prophet (صلى الله عليه وسلم) made it clear that their shortcoming in understanding is with respect to their nonproficiency and in religion with respect to their not praying or fasting during menstruation or post-partum bleeding. This also does not mean that she is less than men in every matter or that men are superior to her in every aspect. Yes, as a class, men are superior to women in general. This is true for a number of reasons, as Allah has stated,

﴿ الرِّجَالُ قَوَّمُونَ عَلَى النِّسَاءِ بِمَا فَضَّلَ اللَّهُ بَعْضَهُمْ عَلَى بَعْضٍ وَبِمَا أَنفَقُوا مِنْ أَمْوَلِهِمْ ﴾ [النساء : ٣٤]

"Men are the protectors and maintainers of women, because Allah has made the one of them to excel the other, and because they spend [to support them] from their means" (*al-Nisa* 34).

However, she may excel him in many matters. How many women are greater than many men with respect to their intelligence, religion and proficiency. It has been narrated from the Prophet (صلى الله عليه وسلم) that women as a species or class are less than men in understanding and religion from the point of view of the matters that the Prophet (صلى الله عليه وسلم) himself explained.

A woman may perform many good deeds and exceed many men in her good deeds, her fear of Allah and her place in the Hereafter. She may concentrate on some matters and her proficiency may be much greater than many men in many issues that concern her and in which she exerted her memory and proficiency. She may be a reference, for example, in Islamic history and many other matters. This is something very clear to anyone who pondered the state of the women during the time of the Prophet (صلى الله عليه وسلم) and afterwards. From this, one knows that her shortcoming does not mean that she cannot be relied upon for narrations. Similarly, if her witness is supported by another woman, it is accepted. There is nothing that prevents her fear of Allah from making her one of the best of the servants of Allah and one of the best women-servants of Allah. This is if she is steadfast in her religion and she is not obliged to fast or pray while menstruating or having post-partum bleeding. If she does not have to pray or make up her prayers that does not necessitate that she has a shortcoming in every matter related to fear and obedience of Allah or her fulfilling of her duties upon her. With respect to her proficiency, she has a specific shortcoming, as the Prophet (صلى الله عليه وسلم) explained, and that does not mean that it can be generalized. A believer may not accuse her of having a shortcoming in everything or a weakness in her faith in every matter. It is a particular shortcoming in her religion and a particular shortcoming in her reasoning that is related to the proficiency of the witness and so forth. One must be fair to her and understand the words of the Prophet (صلى الله عليه وسلم) in the best and most appropriate manner. And Allah knows best.

Shaikh ibn Baz

There is no Harm in Joking as long as it is Truthful

Question 288: What is the ruling concerning joking? Is it considered useless and vain speech? Note that it does not contain any ridiculing of the religion.

Response: There is no harm in joking by words and anecdotes, if they are truthful and real, especially if it is not done often. The Prophet (صلى الله عليه وسلم) used to jest but he would only speak the truth. If it is with lying, then it is not allowed. The Prophet (صلى الله عليه وسلم) said,

"وَيْلٌ لِّلَّذِيْ يُحَدِّثُ فَيَكْذِبُ لِيُضْحِكَ بِهِ القَومَ ، وَيْلٌ لَّهُ ، ثُمَّ وَيْلٌ لَّه"

"Woe to the one who speaks and tells a lie in order to make the people laugh at it. Woe to him. Then again, woe to him."
This was recorded by Abu Dawud, al-Tirmidhi and al-Nasai with a good chain.

Shaikh ibn Baz

The Hadith of the Seven is Not in Reference to Men Only

Question 289: Is the hadith that talks about the seven whom Allah will shade on the Day in which there is no shade except Allah's specific just for men or is it for anyone, such as women, who perform those acts and, therefore, they will receive that reward mentioned in the hadith?

Response: The merits mentioned in the hadith are not specifically for men. In fact, they are general for both men and women. If a young woman grows up in the worship of Allah, she is included among them. Similarly, two women who love each other for the sake of Allah alone are also included. Again, any woman who is invited to illegal sexual intercourse by a man of nobility and beauty and she refuses his advances, saying, "I fear Allah," will be one of those in the shade of Allah. Any woman who gives in charity from her legal earnings to the extent that her left hand does not know what her right hand has given will be included among them. If a woman remembers Allah when she is alone by herself, she will be included among them like any man. However, the righteous leader is something specific for men. Similarly, performing the prayers in congregation in the mosque is something specific for men. The prayer of the woman in her house is more virtuous as has been stated in the authentic Hadith of the Prophet (صلى الله عليه وسلم).

Shaikh ibn Baz

Ruling Concerning Women Driving Automobiles

All praises are due to Allah. May the peace and blessings of Allah be upon the Messenger of Allah, his family, his Companions and all who follow his guidance. To proceed:

There have been numerous questions concerning the ruling of women driving automobiles. The response is the following:

There is no doubt that such is not allowed. Women driving leads to many evils and negative consequences. Included among these is her mixing with men without her being on her guard. It also leads to the evil sins due to which such an action is forbidden. The Pure Law forbids those acts that lead to forbidden acts and considers those means to be forbidden also. Allah has ordered the wives of the Prophet (صلى الله عليه وسلم) and the women of the believers to remain in their houses, to wear *hijab* and not to display their adornments to non-*mahram* males as that leads to promiscuity that overruns a society. Allah has stated,

﴿ وَقَرْنَ فِي بُيُوتِكُنَّ وَلَا تَبَرَّجْنَ تَبَرُّجَ ٱلْجَٰهِلِيَّةِ ٱلْأُولَىٰ وَأَقِمْنَ ٱلصَّلَوٰةَ وَءَاتِينَ ٱلزَّكَوٰةَ وَأَطِعْنَ ٱللَّهَ وَرَسُولَهُۥ ﴾

"Stay in your houses and do not display yourselves like that of the times of ignorance and offer prayer perfectly and give Zakat and obey Allah and His Messenger" (*al-Ahzab* 33).

Allah also says,

﴿ يَٰٓأَيُّهَا ٱلنَّبِيُّ قُل لِّأَزْوَٰجِكَ وَبَنَاتِكَ وَنِسَآءِ ٱلْمُؤْمِنِينَ يُدْنِينَ عَلَيْهِنَّ مِن جَلَٰبِيبِهِنَّ ذَٰلِكَ أَدْنَىٰٓ أَن يُعْرَفْنَ فَلَا يُؤْذَيْنَ ﴾ [الأحزاب: ٥٩]

"O Prophet! Tell your wives and your daughters and the women of the believers to draw their cloaks (veils) all over their bodies. That will be better, that they should be known (as free respectable women) so as not to be annoyed. (*al-Ahzab* 59)

Yet another verse states,

﴿ وَقُل لِّلْمُؤْمِنَٰتِ يَغْضُضْنَ مِنْ أَبْصَٰرِهِنَّ وَيَحْفَظْنَ فُرُوجَهُنَّ وَلَا يُبْدِينَ زِينَتَهُنَّ إِلَّا مَا ظَهَرَ مِنْهَا وَلْيَضْرِبْنَ بِخُمُرِهِنَّ عَلَىٰ جُيُوبِهِنَّ وَلَا يُبْدِينَ زِينَتَهُنَّ إِلَّا لِبُعُولَتِهِنَّ أَوْ ءَابَآئِهِنَّ أَوْ ءَابَآءِ بُعُولَتِهِنَّ أَوْ أَبْنَآئِهِنَّ أَوْ أَبْنَآءِ بُعُولَتِهِنَّ أَوْ إِخْوَٰنِهِنَّ أَوْ بَنِىٓ إِخْوَٰنِهِنَّ أَوْ بَنِىٓ أَخَوَٰتِهِنَّ أَوْ نِسَآئِهِنَّ أَوْ مَا مَلَكَتْ أَيْمَٰنُهُنَّ أَوِ ٱلتَّٰبِعِينَ غَيْرِ أُولِي ٱلْإِرْبَةِ مِنَ ٱلرِّجَالِ أَوِ ٱلطِّفْلِ ٱلَّذِينَ لَمْ يَظْهَرُوا۟ عَلَىٰ عَوْرَٰتِ ٱلنِّسَآءِ وَلَا يَضْرِبْنَ بِأَرْجُلِهِنَّ لِيُعْلَمَ مَا يُخْفِينَ مِن زِينَتِهِنَّ وَتُوبُوٓا۟ إِلَى ٱللَّهِ جَمِيعًا أَيُّهَ ٱلْمُؤْمِنُونَ لَعَلَّكُمْ تُفْلِحُونَ ﴾ [النور: ٣١]

"Tell the believing women to lower their gaze and protect their private parts and not to show off their adornments except only that which is apparent and to draw their veils over necks and bosoms and not to reveal their adornments except to their husbands, their fathers, their husband's fathers, their sons, their husband's sons, their brothers or their brother's sons, or their sister's sons, or their women or the (female) slaves, or old male servants who lack vigor, or small children who have no sense of the shame of sex. And let them not stamp their feet so as to reveal what they hide of their adornment. And beg Allah to forgive you all, O believers, that you may be successful" (al-Nur 31).

The Prophet (صلى الله عليه وسلم) himself said,

"مَا خَلاَ رَجُلٌ بِامْرَأَةٍ إِلا كَانَ الشَّيْطَانُ ثَالِثَهُمَا"

"A man is never alone with a woman except that Satan is the third."[1]

The Purifying Law forbids all of the causes that lead to depravity. Such depravity leads to the innocent and pure women being accused of indecencies. Allah has laid down one of the harshest punishments for such an act in order to protect society from the spreading of the causes of depravity. Women driving cars, however, is one of the causes that lead to that. This is something obvious. But some people are ignorant of the laws of the *Shariah* and the evil ends that being lax lead to. When such evils are also accompanied by what has inflicted many of diseased hearts of love for promiscuity and the enjoyment of looking at women, it leads to people jumping into this discussion without knowledge and without any consideration of the evils that are behind it. Allah has clearly stated.

---

[1] Recorded by 'Ahmad and al-Tirmidhi. Al-Albani says it is *sahih*. Al-Albani, *Sahih al-Jami*, vol. 1, p. 234.—JZ

﴿ قُلْ إِنَّمَا حَرَّمَ رَبِّيَ ٱلْفَوَٰحِشَ مَا ظَهَرَ مِنْهَا وَمَا بَطَنَ وَٱلْإِثْمَ وَٱلْبَغْيَ بِغَيْرِ ٱلْحَقِّ وَأَن تُشْرِكُوا۟ بِٱللَّهِ مَا لَمْ يُنَزِّلْ بِهِۦ سُلْطَٰنًا وَأَن تَقُولُوا۟ عَلَى ٱللَّهِ مَا لَا تَعْلَمُونَ ﴾

[الأعراف: ٣٣]

"Say: The things that my Lord has forbidden are illicit acts, whether committed openly or secretly, sins [of all kinds], unrighteous oppression, joining partners [in worship] with Allah for which He has given no authority, and saying things about Allah of which you have no knowledge" (al-Araf 33).

Another verse in the Quran states,

﴿ وَلَا تَتَّبِعُوا۟ خُطُوَٰتِ ٱلشَّيْطَٰنِ إِنَّهُ لَكُمْ عَدُوٌّ مُّبِينٌ ٠ إِنَّمَا يَأْمُرُكُم بِٱلسُّوٓءِ وَٱلْفَحْشَآءِ وَأَن تَقُولُوا۟ عَلَى ٱللَّهِ مَا لَا تَعْلَمُونَ ﴾

[البقرة: ١٦٨-١٦٩]

"Follow not the footsteps of Satan. Verily, he is to you an open enemy. [Satan] commands you only what is evil and sinful, and that you should say against Allah what you know not" (al-Baqara 168-169).

The Prophet (صلى الله عليه وسلم) said,

" مَا تَرَكْتُ بَعْدِي فِتْنَةً أَضَرَّ عَلَى الرِّجَالِ مِنَ النِّسَاءِ "

"I have not left behind me any temptation more harmful for men than women."[1]

Hudhaifah ibn al-Yamaan said, "The people used to ask the Messenger of Allah (صلى الله عليه وسلم) about good but I used to ask him about evil out of fear that it may reach me. I said, 'O Messenger of Allah, we used to be living in the Times of Ignorance and Evil. Then Allah brought this good [to us]. Will there be after it evil again?' He said, 'Yes.' I said, 'After that evil, will there be good again?' He said, 'Yes, but it will be tainted.' I said, 'How will it be tainted?' He said, 'There will be a people

---

[1] Recorded by al-Bukhari and Muslim.—JZ

who would guide without guidance, you will approve of some of their deeds and disapprove of some others.' I said, 'Will there be evil after that good?' He said, 'Yes, there will be callers from the gates of the Hell-Fire. Whoever responds to them shall be flung into it.' I said, 'O Messenger of Allah, describe them to us.' He said, 'They will be from our own people and speak our language.' I said, 'What do you order me to do if I should come across that time?' He said, 'Stick to the community of the Muslims and their leader.' I said, 'Suppose they do not have a leader or a community?' He said, 'Then separate yourself from all of those factions, even if you have to eat the roots of trees until death comes to you while you are in that state.'" Recorded by al-Bukhari and Muslim.

I call upon every Muslim to fear Allah in his speech and action and to be wary of the trials and temptations. Also, be wary of those who call to such things. Everyone must remain far away from that which brings about Allah's anger or leads to it. Each must take every precaution from those callers that the Prophet (صلى الله عليه وسلم) has spoken about in this noble Hadith. May Allah protect us from the evil of temptation and trials and its people. May Allah protect for this Nation its religion and repel the evil of those callers to falsehood. May Allah bless and guide all the Muslims to what pleases Him and what is best for them and their success in both this life and the Hereafter. He is the One who is in Control of that and Able to do that.

And may the peace and blessings of Allah be upon our Prophet Muhammad, his family and his Companions.

Shaikh ibn Baz

Women Working Alongside Men

Question 290: What is Islam's view of women working alongside men?

Response: It is known that when women go to work in the workplaces of men this leads to mixing with men and being in private with them. This is a very dangerous matter that has dangerous consequences and negative results. It is in clear opposition to the texts of the *Shariah* that order the women to remain in their houses and to fulfill the type of work that is particular for her and upon which Allah has fashioned her nature, which is far from the place where she will mix with men.

The clear, authentic evidences that indicate that it is forbidden for men and non-related women to be in private together and for men to look at women are numerous. There are also much evidence that what leads up to those forbidden ends are also forbidden. The evidences are many, clear and decisive that the mixing between the sexes is forbidden as it leads to negative and blameworthy results. Among those evidences are the following:

﴿ وَقَرْنَ فِى بُيُوتِكُنَّ وَلَا تَبَرَّجْنَ تَبَرُّجَ ٱلْجَـٰهِلِيَّةِ ٱلْأُولَىٰ وَأَقِمْنَ ٱلصَّلَوٰةَ وَءَاتِينَ ٱلزَّكَوٰةَ وَأَطِعْنَ ٱللَّهَ وَرَسُولَهُۥٓ إِنَّمَا يُرِيدُ ٱللَّهُ لِيُذْهِبَ عَنكُمُ ٱلرِّجْسَ أَهْلَ ٱلْبَيْتِ وَيُطَهِّرَكُمْ تَطْهِيرًا ﴾

"Stay in your houses and do not display yourselves like that of the times of ignorance and offer prayer perfectly and give Zakat and obey Allah and His Messenger. Allah only wishes to remove evil deeds and sins from you, O members of the family [of the Prophet] and to purify you with a thorough purification." (*al-Ahzab* 33).

﴿ يَـٰٓأَيُّهَا ٱلنَّبِىُّ قُل لِّأَزْوَٰجِكَ وَبَنَاتِكَ وَنِسَاءِ ٱلْمُؤْمِنِينَ يُدْنِينَ عَلَيْهِنَّ مِن جَلَـٰبِيبِهِنَّ ذَٰلِكَ أَدْنَىٰٓ أَن يُعْرَفْنَ فَلَا يُؤْذَيْنَ وَكَانَ ٱللَّهُ غَفُورًا رَّحِيمًا ﴾ [الأحزاب: ٥٩]

"O Prophet! Tell your wives and your daughters and the women of the believers to draw their cloaks (veils) all over their bodies. That will be better, that they should be known (as free respectable women) so as not to be annoyed. And Allah is Ever Oft-Forgiving, Most Merciful" (*al-Ahzab* 59).

﴿ قُل لِّلْمُؤْمِنِينَ يَغُضُّوا مِنْ أَبْصَـٰرِهِمْ وَيَحْفَظُوا فُرُوجَهُمْ ذَٰلِكَ أَزْكَىٰ لَهُمْ إِنَّ اللَّهَ خَبِيرٌ بِمَا يَصْنَعُونَ ۝ وَقُل لِّلْمُؤْمِنَـٰتِ يَغْضُضْنَ مِنْ أَبْصَـٰرِهِنَّ وَيَحْفَظْنَ فُرُوجَهُنَّ وَلَا يُبْدِينَ زِينَتَهُنَّ إِلَّا مَا ظَهَرَ مِنْهَا وَلْيَضْرِبْنَ بِخُمُرِهِنَّ عَلَىٰ جُيُوبِهِنَّ وَلَا يُبْدِينَ زِينَتَهُنَّ إِلَّا لِبُعُولَتِهِنَّ أَوْ ءَابَآئِهِنَّ أَوْ ءَابَآءِ بُعُولَتِهِنَّ ﴾

"Tell the believing women to lower their gaze and protect their private parts and not to show off their adornments except only that which is apparent and to draw their veils over necks and bosoms and not to reveal their adornments except to their husbands, their fathers, their husband's fathers, their sons, their husband's sons, their brothers or their brother's sons, or their sister's sons, or their women or the (female) slaves, or old male servants who lack vigor, or small children who have no sense of the shame of sex. And let them not stamp their feet so as to reveal what they hide of their adornment. And beg Allah to forgive you all, O believers, that you may be successful" (al-Nur 31).

﴿ وَإِذَا سَأَلْتُمُوهُنَّ مَتَـٰعًا فَسْـَٔلُوهُنَّ مِن وَرَآءِ حِجَابٍ ذَٰلِكُمْ أَطْهَرُ لِقُلُوبِكُمْ وَقُلُوبِهِنَّ ﴾ [الأحزاب: ٥٣]

"And when you ask them, ask them from behind a screen, that is purer for your hearts and for their hearts"(al-Ahzab 53).

The Prophet (صلى الله عليه وسلم) himself said,

"إِيَّاكُمْ وَالدُّخُولَ عَلَى النِّسَاءِ – يَعْنِي الأَجْنَبِيَّاتِ – قِيلَ يَارَسُولَ اللهِ أَفَرَأَيْتَ الحَمْوَ؟ قَالَ: الحَمْوُ المَوْتُ"

"Beware of entering upon women. the women who are non-mahram." They said, "O Messenger of Allah, what do you say about the in-laws?" He said, "The in-laws are death." [1]

---

[1] Recorded by al-Bukhari and Muslim. It implies that such close relations can easily lead to adultery which has the death penalty.—JZ

The Messenger of Allah (صلى الله عليه وسلم) categorically prohibited privacy between a man and a non-related woman. He said,

"إِنَّ ثَالِثَهُما الشَّيْطَانُ"

"Satan is the third."[1]

He also prohibited traveling except in the presence of *mahram* males in order to close the door to the roads that lead to evil and sins and to protect the two parties from the plotting of Satan. That is why it is confirmed from him that he said,

"اتَّقُوا الدُّنْيا واتَّقُوا النِّسَاءَ فإنَّ أَوَّلَ فِتْنَةِ بَنِي إِسْرَائِيلَ كَانَتْ فِي النِّسَاءِ"

"Be wary and cautious of this world and be wary and cautious of women. Verily, the first trial that afflicted the Tribes of Israel was with respect to women."[2]

Another hadith states,

"مَاتَرَكْتُ بَعْدِي فِي أُمَّتِي فِتْنَةً أَضَرَّ عَلَى الرِّجَالِ مِنَ النِّسَاءِ"

"I have not left behind me any temptation more harmful for men than women."[3]

These clear verses and Ahadith indicate that it is obligatory to avoid the mixing of the sexes that leads to evil and lewdness and the destruction of societies. When we look at the plight of women in some of the Muslim countries we see that she has become a disrespected working servant because of her leaving her house and taking roles that are not her responsibility. The wise people in those lands and in the lands of the West are calling for the return of the woman to her natural roles that Allah has

---

[1] Recorded by Ahmad and al-Tirmidhi. Al-Albani says it is *sahih*. Al-Albani, *Sahih al-Jami*, vol. 1, p. 234.—JZ
[2] Recorded by Muslim.—JZ
[3] Recorded by al-Bukhari and Muslim.—JZ

prepared her for and for which her body and mind are more attuned to. But this call is coming too late.

There are enough jobs for women in their houses, in teaching positions and other places related to women that make it unnecessary for her to take on jobs in the workplace of men. We ask Allah to protect our land and the lands of all Muslims from the plots and machinations of their enemies. May Allah guide those in charge and the rest of the media to lead people to what is best for them in both this life and the Hereafter. May Allah guide them to executing the commands of their Lord and Creator who is most knowledgeable of what is in their best interests. May Allah bless and guide the leaders of the lands of the Muslims to what is best for the Muslims and the country with respect to their livelihood here and their resurrection. May Allah save us and them and all the Muslims from the misguidance of temptation and the causes of destruction. He is the One with the Power and Ability to do that.

Shaikh ibn Baz

Ruling Concerning a Woman Remaining with Her Alcoholic Husband

Question 291: I have three sons and a daughter. My husband, may Allah protect us, is an alcoholic. He has been imprisoned in the past. He is addicted to alcohol and has injured me and my children. I have been divorced from him and I am currently with my family. He does not spend anything on us and I do not have any desire to return to him. However, he has threatened to take my children and that would be something that I could not bear. After all, I am, first and foremost, a mother. Please help me.

Response: This is something that definitely needs to be taken up in the courts of law. One should not remain with an alcoholic as he harms his wife and his children. One should remain away from him unless Allah guides him and he returns to what is correct. If the judge separates the two, usually, the children are given over to the mother as she is most qualified for them while he is not qualified. As long as he has the problem of being an alcoholic, he is not suited to bring up his children as he will destroy and ruin them. Therefore, she has more right to her children than him, even if they be boys. This is what is usually done by the judges and this is what is obligatory. The children must be with her because she is better than him and he is an evil-doer. If she refuses to go back to him, she has done well, as such a living condition is harmful and dangerous for her. If he also does not pray, then it is obligatory not to return to him for the one who abandons the prayer is a disbeliever— and protection is sought from Allah. The Prophet (صلى الله عليه وسلم) said,

"العَهْدُ الَّذِي بَيْنَنَا وَبَيْنَهُمُ الصَّلَاةُ فَمَنْ تَرَكَهَا فَقَدْ كَفَرَ"

"The covenant between us and them is the prayer. Whoever abandons it has committed disbelief."[1]

It is not obligatory to remain with the one who does not pray.[2]

﴿ لَا هُنَّ حِلٌّ لَّهُمْ وَلَا هُمْ يَحِلُّونَ لَهُنَّ ﴾ [الممتحنة : ١٠]

"They are not lawful [wives] for the disbelievers nor are the disbelievers lawful [husbands] for them" (al-Mumtahina 10).

[That is,] until Allah guides them and they repent. The woman should go to her family or stay with her children and not let her husband come to them until he repents to Allah and returns to what is right.

---

[1] Recorded by Ahmad, al-Nasai, al-Tirmidhi and ibn Majah. Al-Albani calls it *sahih*. Al-Albani, *Sahih al-Jami*, vol. 2, p. 760.—JZ
[2] This sentence, as is clear from the remainder of the response, must not be misunderstood. It does not mean that one may stay with one who does not pray if one wishes to do so. It is not an option to remain with a husband who has been deemed a disbeliever.—JZ

If he prays but drinks alcohol, then that is a great sin and a great crime. However, he is not a disbeliever but an evildoer. The woman has the right to prevent him from her and to leave him. She is excused for that act. If she remains patient and has the ability to be patient, there is no harm in that option either.

Shaikh ibn Baz

Ruling Concerning Producing Deviant Magazines, Working for Them, Distributing Them and Buying Them

Question 292: What is the ruling concerning producing magazines that display women uncovered and in seductive manners? What about magazines that are concerned only with news about actors and actresses? What is the ruling concerning those who work for such magazines, who distribute them and who buy them?

Response: It is not allowed to produce or support magazines that are comprised of distributing pictures of women or encouraging people to fornication, lewdness, homosexuality, drinking alcohol or any other type of wrong act. It is not allowed to work for such magazines, either by writing for it or distributing it. This would be a type of helping one another in sin and transgression as well as spreading evil on earth and calling others to ruin society and spread depravity. Allah has stated in his Clear Book,

$$ \text{﴿ وَتَعَاوَنُوا۟ عَلَى ٱلْبِرِّ وَٱلتَّقْوَىٰ وَلَا تَعَاوَنُوا۟ عَلَى ٱلْإِثْمِ وَٱلْعُدْوَٰنِ ﴾} $$
[المائدة: ٢]

"Help you one another in righteousness and piety, but do not help one another in sin and transgression. And fear Allah, verily, Allah is severe in punishment" (al-Maidah 2).

The Prophet (صلى الله عليه وسلم) also said,

"مَنْ دَعَا إِلَى هُدَىً كَانَ لَهُ مِنَ الأَجْرِ مِثْلُ أُجُورِ مَنْ تَبِعَهُ لاَ يَنْقُصُ ذَلِكَ مِنْ أُجُورِهِمْ شَيْئاً، وَمَنْ دَعَا إِلَى ضَلاَلَةٍ كَانَ عَلَيْهِ مِنَ الإِثْمِ مِثْلُ آثَامِ مَنْ تَبِعَهُ لاَ يَنْقُصُ ذَلِكَ مِنْ آثَامِهِمْ شَيْئاً"

"Whoever calls to guidance shall receive the same reward as the one who follows that guidance, without the reward of either of them being lessened. And whoever calls to misguidance shall bear that sin as well as the sin of the one who follows his call without the burden of either of them being lessened."

This was recorded by Muslim in his *Sahih*.

The Prophet (صلى الله عليه وسلم) stated in another hadith,

"صِنْفَانِ مِنْ أَهْلِ النَّارِ لَمْ أَرَهُمَا بَعْدُ، رِجَالٌ بِأَيْدِيهِمْ سِيَاطٌ كَأَذْنَابِ الْبَقَرِ يَضْرِبُونَ بِهَا النَّاسَ، وَنِسَاءٌ كَاسِيَاتٌ عَارِيَاتٌ مَائِلاَتٌ مُمِيلاَتٌ رُؤُوسُهُنَّ كَأَسْنِمَةِ الْبُخْتِ الْمَائِلَةِ لاَ يَدْخُلْنَ الْجَنَّةَ وَلاَ يَجِدْنَ رِيحَهَا وَإِنَّ رِيحَهَا لَيُوجَدُ مِن مَسِيرَةِ كَذَا وَكَذَا"

"There are two groups of people from the inhabitants of Hell that I have not yet seen: Men having flogs like oxen tails with them and they would be beating people and women who would be dressed but naked, their heads would be like the humps of the *bukht*[1] camel inclined to one side. They will not enter Paradise and they would not smell its odor although its odor can be smelled from such and such a distance."

This was also recorded by Muslim in his *Sahih*.

The verses and Ahadith with this meaning are many. We ask Allah to bless and guide Muslims to what is best for them and their salvation. We ask him to guide those in charge of the media in all of its forms to what is best for society. We also ask Allah to protect them from the evils of their own souls and from the plots of Satan. He is Generous, Noble.

Shaikh ibn Baz

---

[1] This is a certain type of camel.

Ruling Concerning Reading Such Deviant Magazines

Question 293: What is the ruling concerning the women who look at such [deviant] magazines?

Response: It is forbidden for every adult and sane person, man or woman, to read the books of innovation and misguidance as well as the magazines that spread deviations, have false propaganda and claims, call others to deviance and depraved characters. The only exception is if the person is reading them to refute what it contains of godlessness and deviance. We advise their husbands and fathers to guide them and to repel what they are doing and to warn the people from their evil.

The Standing Committee

The Quran is the Replacement

Question 294: What is your advice, dear Shaikh, for those people who go a month or many months without reading the Quran and who have no excuse whatsoever for that behavior? However, you will find some of them following closely and reading the magazines that have no benefit to them?

Response: It is recommended for every believing man and woman to recite often the Book of Allah with thought and understanding. This may be done from a copy of the Quran or from one's memory.

Allah has said,

﴿ كِتَٰبٌ أَنزَلْنَٰهُ إِلَيْكَ مُبَٰرَكٌ لِّيَدَّبَّرُوٓاْ ءَايَٰتِهِۦ وَلِيَتَذَكَّرَ أُوْلُواْ ٱلْأَلْبَٰبِ ﴾
[ص: ٢٩]

"[This is] a Book which We have sent down to you, full of blessings that they may ponder over its Verses, and that men of understanding may remember" (Sad 29).

﴾ إِنَّ ٱلَّذِينَ يَتْلُونَ كِتَٰبَ ٱللَّهِ وَأَقَامُوا ٱلصَّلَوٰةَ وَأَنفَقُوا مِمَّا
رَزَقْنَٰهُمْ سِرًّا وَعَلَانِيَةً يَرْجُونَ تِجَٰرَةً لَّن تَبُورَ
○ لِيُوَفِّيَهُمْ أُجُورَهُمْ وَيَزِيدَهُم مِّن فَضْلِهِۦٓ إِنَّهُۥ غَفُورٌ
شَكُورٌ ﴿ [فاطر : ٢٩-٣٠]

"Verily, those who recite the Book of Allah, and offer prayer
perfectly, and spend [in charity] out of what We have
provided for them, secretly and openly, hope for a [sure]
trade-gain that will never perish.   That He may pay them
their wages in full, and give them [even] more, out of His
Grace.   Verily!   He is Oft-Forgiving, Most Ready to
Appreciate [good deeds]" (*Fatir* 29-30).

The aforementioned reciting of the Quran includes both its
recitation and its following. The recitation is with both reflection and
understanding. Sincerity to Allah is a means of following and executing
the Quran. It contains a great reward. The Prophet (صلى الله عليه وسلم) said,

"اقْرَؤُوا الْقُرْآنَ فَإِنَّهُ يَأْتِي شَفِيعاً لِأَصْحَابِهِ يَوْمَ القِيَامَةِ"

"Recite the Quran for it shall come on the Day of
Resurrection as an intercessor for its companion."
Recorded by Muslim in his *Sahih*. The Prophet (صلى الله عليه وسلم) also said,

"خَيْرُكُمْ مَـنْ تَعَلَّـمَ القُـرْآنَ وعَلَّمَـهُ"

"The best of you is he who learns the Quran and teaches it."

This was recorded by al-Bukhari in his *Sahih*. Another hadith states,

" مَنْ قَرَأَ حَرْفاً مِنَ القُرْآنِ فَلَهُ حَسَنَةٌ وَالْحَسَنَةُ بِعَشْرِ أَمْثَالِهـا لا
أَقُولُ [ألم] حَرْفٌ. ولكِنْ أَلِفٌ حَرْفٌ، وَلامٌ حَرْفٌ، وَمِيمٌ حَرْفٌ"

"Whoever reads one word (*harf*)[1] of the Quran shall receive
a good deed and ten good deeds similar to it. I do not say

---

[1] Many people seem to misunderstand this hadith. The word *harf* in the
language of the Prophet (peace be upon him)— as opposed to the
language of the Arabs of today— meant a complete word. However, in

that *Alif Lam Mim* is a word but *Alif* is a word, *Lam* is a word and *Mim* is a word."[1]

The Prophet (صلى الله عليه وسلم) told Abdullah ibn Amr ibn al-As, "Read the Quran once a month." He said, "I am able to do more than that." He told him, "Then read it once in seven days." The Companions of the Prophet (صلى الله عليه وسلم) used to recite the entire Quran once every seven days.

I advise all the readers of the Quran to increase their readings with reflection and understanding as well as sincerity to Allah, with the goal of benefiting from and learning the Quran. They should read the entire Quran once a month. If they are able to do so without difficulty, they should do it in less than that time. That is a very great good deed. One may even finish the entire reading in less than seven days. However, it is best not to recite the entire Quran in less than three days. This is the least amount of time that the Prophet (صلى الله عليه وسلم) mentioned to Abdullah ibn Amr ibn al-As.[2] This is because if it is read in less than three days, the person becomes hasty and lacks thought and concentration. It is not allowed to read it from a *mushaf* [physical copy of the Quran] unless one is in the state of purity. However, one may still read it from his memory even though he is not in a state of ablution. As for the sexually defiled, he should neither read it from a copy of the Quran nor from his memory until he makes *ghusl*. This is based on what Imam Ahmad and the compilers of the *Sunan* recorded with a good chain from Ali who said that nothing kept the Prophet (صلى الله عليه وسلم) from the Quran except being in a state of sexual defilement.

Shaikh ibn Baz

---

this hadith, he is showing that the reward for reciting the Quran is not simply for each word but it is, in fact, for each individual letter.—JZ

[1] Recorded by al-Tirmidhi and al-Hakim. Al-Albani says it is *sahih*. Al-Albani, *Sahih al-Jami*, vol. 2, p. 1103.—JZ

[2] Recorded by al-Bukhari.—JZ

Ruling Concerning Listening to Radio Programs that Contain Music

Question 295: What is the ruling concerning listening to radio programs that contain music, such as news programs?

Response: There is no harm in listening to them and benefiting from them as long as one turns down the volume from the time the music commences until it is finished. This is because it is from the aspects of useless speech that Allah has commanded Muslims to avoid and remain away from its evil.

Shaikh ibn Baz

Ruling Concerning Singing and Watching Programs

Question 296: What is the ruling concerning listening to singing and music? What about watching television programs in which women appear displaying their adornments?

Response: The ruling concerning that is that it is forbidden. It keeps the person from the way of Allah, it sickens the heart and may lead the person to be involved in other lewd and sexual acts that Allah has forbidden. Allah has stated in the Quran,

﴿ وَمِنَ ٱلنَّاسِ مَن يَشۡتَرِي لَهۡوَ ٱلۡحَدِيثِ لِيُضِلَّ عَن سَبِيلِ ٱللَّهِ بِغَيۡرِ عِلۡمٍ وَيَتَّخِذَهَا هُزُوًا أُوْلَٰٓئِكَ لَهُمۡ عَذَابٌ مُّهِينٌ ٥ وَإِذَا تُتۡلَىٰ عَلَيۡهِ ءَايَٰتُنَا وَلَّىٰ مُسۡتَكۡبِرًا كَأَن لَّمۡ يَسۡمَعۡهَا كَأَنَّ فِىٓ أُذُنَيۡهِ وَقۡرًا فَبَشِّرۡهُ بِعَذَابٍ أَلِيمٍ ﴾ [لقمان: ٦-٧]

"And of mankind is he who purchases idle talk [music, singing] to mislead (men) from the Path of Allah without knowledge, and takes it [the Path of Allah] by way of mockery. For such there will be a humiliating torment. And when Our Verses are recited to such a one, he turns away in pride, as if he heard them not, as if there were deafness in his ear. So announce to him a painful torment" (*Luqman* 6-7).

In these two noble verses is evidence that listening to musical instruments and singing is a cause for straying and misguiding as well as taking the Verses of Allah as a mockery and arrogantly refusing to listen to the Verses of Allah.

Shaikh ibn Baz

They Say that I Am a Troublemaker

Question 297: I am a young woman who lives in the dormitory with the other female students. Allah has guided me to the truth and I am sticking to my religion, and all praises are due to Allah. However, what I see around me from my fellow students disturbs me very much. I see them committing sins and evil, like listening to music, backbiting, tale spreading. I have advised them often but some of them ridicule me and some insult me. They say that I am just causing trouble. Dear Shaikh, I hope you will help me. What shall I do? May Allah reward you.

Response: It is obligatory upon you to repel evil to the best of your ability, with good words, kindness and a good approach. You should use the verses of the Quran and narrate hadith according to your level of knowledge. You should not join them in listening to songs or other forbidden words or actions. Separate yourself from them as much as possible until they engage in some other activity. This is what Allah has stated,

$$ \text{﴿ وَإِذَا رَأَيْتَ ٱلَّذِينَ يَخُوضُونَ فِىٓ ءَايَٰتِنَا فَأَعْرِضْ عَنْهُمْ حَتَّىٰ يَخُوضُوا۟ فِى حَدِيثٍ غَيْرِهِۦ ﴾ } $$

[الأنعام: ٦٨]

"When you see those engage in a false conversation about Our Verses by mocking at them, stay away from them till they turn to another topic" (al-Anam 68).

When you have rebuked them with your speech according to the best of your ability and remain away from what they have done, then their deeds will not harm you in the least nor will their disapproval of you. Allah has stated,

﴿ يَـٰٓأَيُّهَا ٱلَّذِينَ ءَامَنُوا۟ عَلَيْكُمْ أَنفُسَكُمْ لَا يَضُرُّكُم مَّن ضَلَّ إِذَا ٱهْتَدَيْتُمْ إِلَى ٱللَّهِ مَرْجِعُكُمْ جَمِيعًا فَيُنَبِّئُكُم بِمَا كُنتُمْ تَعْمَلُونَ ﴾

[المائدة: ١٠٥]

"O you who believe! Take care of your ownselves. If you follow the right guidance no hurt can come to you from those who are in error. The return of you all is to Allah, then He will inform you about (all) that which you used to do" (al-Maidah 105).

Allah has made it clear that a believer is not harmed by those who stray as long as he sticks to the truth and remains steadfast upon guidance. This is done by eradicating evil and remaining firm upon the truth along with calling others to that path in a good way. Allah will then make for the person an escape and refuge. Allah willing, Allah will benefit them by your guidance if you are patient and hope for reward from Allah. Have the glad tidings of a great deal of good and a praiseworthy end as long as you stick to the truth and reject what opposes it. As Allah has said,

﴿ وَٱلْعَـٰقِبَةُ لِلْمُتَّقِينَ ﴾ [القصص: ٨٣]

"And the good end is for the God-fearing" (al-Qasas 83).

Allah also says,

﴿ وَٱلَّذِينَ جَـٰهَدُوا۟ فِينَا لَنَهْدِيَنَّهُمْ سُبُلَنَا وَإِنَّ ٱللَّهَ لَمَعَ ٱلْمُحْسِنِينَ ﴾ [العنكبوت: ٦٩]

"And for those who strive hard in Our Cause, We will surely guide them to Our Paths. And verily, Allah is with the good doers" (al-Ankabut 69).

May Allah grace you with what is pleasing to Him and grant you patience and steadfastness. May Allah bless your sisters, families and companions with that which is beloved and pleasing to Him. He hears and is Close. He is the Guide to the Straight Path.

Shaikh ibn Baz

Being Too Shy to Rebuke Those who Backbite and Spread Tales

Question 298: I am a young woman who hates backbiting and tale spreading. Sometimes I am amidst a group of people who talk about others and they begin to backbite and spread tales. In my soul, I hate and despise what they are doing but I am much too shy. So I do not have the ability to make them stop. Furthermore, I have no place to go to get away from them. Allah knows that I wish they would start talking about something else. Am I sinful because of my sitting with them? What is obligatory upon me to do? May Allah grant you what is best for Islam and Muslims.

Response: You are sinful in that case unless you repel the evil. If they accept that from you, all praises are due to Allah. If they do not respond to you, then you must leave them and not sit with them. This is because Allah has stated,

﴿ وَإِذَا رَأَيْتَ ٱلَّذِينَ يَخُوضُونَ فِىٓ ءَايَٰتِنَا فَأَعْرِضْ عَنْهُمْ حَتَّىٰ يَخُوضُواْ فِى حَدِيثٍ غَيْرِهِۦ ﴾ [الأنعام: ٦٨]

"When you see those engage in a false conversation about Our Verses by mocking at them, stay away from them till they turn to another topic" (*al-Anam* 68).

Furthermore, the Prophet (صلى الله عليه وسلم) said,

"مَنْ رَأَى مِنْكُمْ مُنْكَراً فَلْيُغَيِّرْهُ بِيَدِهِ فَإِنْ لَم يَسْتَطِعْ فَبِلِسَانِهِ فَإِنْ لَّمْ يَسْتَطِعْ فَبِقَلْبِه وَذَلِكَ أَضْعَفُ الإِيمَانِ"

"When one of you sees an evil he must change it by his hand. If he is not able to do so, he must change it by his tongue. If he is not able to do so, then by his heart and that is the weakest of faith."

Recorded by Muslim in his *Sahih*. Verses and Ahadith of that meaning are numerous.

Shaikh ibn Baz

You Must Order what is Good Even if the One You Ordered Becomes Upset

Question 299: If we try to keep people away from spreading tales and backbiting among people, the one who orders good and stops evil is usually abused. The people get angry with him. Are we committing sins because of their anger? Even if it is with respect to one of our parents, shall we stop them or let them be and not consider that matter important?

Response: One of the most important obligations is that of ordering good and preventing evil. Allah says,

﴿ وَٱلْمُؤْمِنُونَ وَٱلْمُؤْمِنَتُ بَعْضُهُمْ أَوْلِيَآءُ بَعْضٍ يَأْمُرُونَ بِٱلْمَعْرُوفِ وَيَنْهَوْنَ عَنِ ٱلْمُنكَرِ ﴾ [التوبة: ٧١]

"The believers, men and women, are helpers and supporters of one another; they enjoin the good and forbid evil" (*al-Tauba* 71).

In this verse, Allah has made it clear that one of the obligatory attributes of believing men and women is ordering good and eradicating evil. Allah also says,

﴿ كُنتُمْ خَيْرَ أُمَّةٍ أُخْرِجَتْ لِلنَّاسِ تَأْمُرُونَ بِٱلْمَعْرُوفِ وَتَنْهَوْنَ عَنِ ٱلْمُنكَرِ وَتُؤْمِنُونَ بِٱللَّهِ ﴾ [آل عمران: ١١٠]

"You are the best of peoples ever raised for mankind, you enjoin what is good and you forbid evil and believe in Allah" (*ali-Imran* 110).

The Prophet (صلى الله عليه وسلم) said,

"مَنْ رَأَى مِنْكُمْ مُنْكَراً فَلْيُغَيِّرْهُ بِيَدِهِ فَإِنْ لَمْ يَسْتَطِعْ فَبِلِسَانِهِ فَإِنْ لَّمْ يَسْتَطِعْ فَبِقَلْبِهِ وَذَلِكَ أَضْعَفُ الإِيمَانِ"

"When one of you sees an evil he must change it by his hand. If he is not able to do so, he must change it by his tongue. If he is not able to do so, then by his heart and that is the weakest of faith."

This was recorded by Muslim in his *Sahih*. The verses and Ahadith concerning the obligation of ordering good and eradicating evil as well as blaming those who do not do such are many. Therefore, it is obligatory upon you and upon every believing man and woman to order good and eradicate evil, even if those who you are rebuking should get upset with you and even if they abuse you. You must have patience. You should follow the example of the messengers (peace be upon all of them) and follow them in the good they performed. While addressing the Prophet (صلى الله عليه وسلم), Allah has stated,

$$ ﴿ فَٱصۡبِرۡ كَمَا صَبَرَ أُوْلُواْ ٱلۡعَزۡمِ مِنَ ٱلرُّسُلِ ﴾ \quad [الأحقاف : ٣٥] $$

"Therefore, be patient (O Muhammad) as were the Messengers of strong will" (*al-Ahqaf* 35).

Another verse states,

$$ ﴿ وَٱصۡبِرُوٓاْ إِنَّ ٱللَّهَ مَعَ ٱلصَّٰبِرِينَ ﴾ \quad [الأنفال : ٤٦] $$

"Be patient. Surely, Allah is with those who are patient" (*al-Anfal* 46).

In another place, Allah quotes the wise man Luqman as saying,

$$ ﴿ يَٰبُنَيَّ أَقِمِ ٱلصَّلَوٰةَ وَأۡمُرۡ بِٱلۡمَعۡرُوفِ وَٱنۡهَ عَنِ ٱلۡمُنكَرِ وَٱصۡبِرۡ عَلَىٰ مَآ أَصَابَكَ إِنَّ ذَٰلِكَ مِنۡ عَزۡمِ ٱلۡأُمُورِ ﴾ \quad [لقمان : ١٧] $$

"O my son! Establish the prayer and enjoin the good and forbid evil, and bear with patience whatever befalls you. Verily, that is of the firmness of the affairs" (*Luqman* 17).

There is no doubt that the reformation of society and its being built on solid ground comes about by it being, first, for the sake of Allah and then by the ordering of good and eradicating of evil. Evil in society tears it apart and presents itself for a general punishment. One of the greatest causes for such a general punishment is the lack of ordering what is good and preventing evil. It has been authentically narrated from the Prophet (صلى الله عليه وسلم) that he said,

"إِنَّ النَّاسَ إِذَا رَأَوُا الْمُنْكَرَ فَلَمْ يُغَيِّرُوهُ أَوْشَكَ أَنَّ يَعُمَّهُمُ اللهُ بِعِقَابِهِ"

"If the people see an evil and they do not change it, soon Allah will inflict them all with His punishment."[1]

Allah has warned His servants from following the way of the disbelievers of the Tribes of Israel. He says,

﴿ لُعِنَ ٱلَّذِينَ كَفَرُوا مِنۢ بَنِىٓ إِسۡرَٰٓءِيلَ عَلَىٰ لِسَانِ دَاوُدَ وَعِيسَى ٱبۡنِ مَرۡيَمَۚ ذَٰلِكَ بِمَا عَصَوا وَّكَانُوا يَعۡتَدُونَ ٠ كَانُوا لَا يَتَنَاهَوۡنَ عَن مُّنكَرٍ فَعَلُوهُۚ لَبِئۡسَ مَا كَانُوا يَفۡعَلُونَ ﴾ [المائدة : ٧٨-٧٩]

"Those among the Tribes of Israel who disbelieved were cursed by the tongue of David and Jesus, son of Mary. That was because they disobeyed [Allah and the messengers] and were transgressing beyond bounds. They used not to forbid one another from the evil which they committed. Vile indeed was what they used to do" (al-Maidah 78-79).

We ask Allah to bless all Muslims with rulers and ruled who establish and fulfill this obligation in the best possible way. We also ask Him to make their affairs good and to protect them from all of the causes of His wrath and punishment. He is Hearing, Responding.

Shaikh ibn Baz

Ruling Concerning Women Removing Hairs

Question 300: What is the ruling concerning the following:
(a) Removing pubic and underarm hairs?
(b) Removing leg and arm hairs for a woman?

---

[1] Recorded by Ahmad with a slight change in the word order. Al-Albani has graded it *sahih*. Al-Albani, *Sahih al-Jami*, vol. 1, p. 398.—JZ

(c) Removing eyebrow hairs at the request of the husband?

Response: (a) Removing pubic and underarm hairs is *sunnah*. It is best to pluck the armpit hairs and shave the pubic hairs. There is no harm if they are removed by different means.

(b) There is no harm in the woman removing her leg and arm hairs. I do not know of any harm in that.

(c) Removing eyebrow hairs at the request of the husband is not allowed. The Messenger of Allah (صلى الله عليه وسلم) cursed the one who does the removing and the one who has it done. This is in reference to the one who has eyebrow hairs removed.

Shaikh ibn Baz

Ruling Concerning Giving Preference to One Child Over the Others with Respect to Wealth and Other Matters

Question 301: Is it allowed for me to give to one of my children and not to the other because the other one is wealthy?

Response: It is not allowed for you to single out any of your children, male or female, over the others. It is obligatory upon you to be just between them, taking into consideration their inheritance or leaving them all of it. The Prophet (صلى الله عليه وسلم) said,

"اتَّقُـوا اللهَ وَاعْـدِلُـوا بَينَ أَوْلادِكُـمْ"

"Fear Allah and be just among your children."

This was recorded by al-Bukhari and Muslim. However, if they accept that one of them gets preferential treatment, this is permissible as long as those who approve of it are adult and competent. That would be the case, for example, if one of his children is in need and not able to earn for himself, due to illness or other preventive reason, and he does not have a son or child to maintain him or a stipend from the government to support him. In that case, it is obligatory upon you to spend on his behalf according to his needs until Allah makes him self-sufficient.

Shaikh ibn Baz

Ruling Concerning Exchanging Old Gold for New

Question 302: A woman goes to the market with her old gold and says to the goldsmith or jeweler, "Estimate for me its price." He does so and then she says, "Give me, for that price, new gold." Is there any contradiction between this act and what the *Shariah* states?

Response: Such a transaction is not allowed because it is selling gold for gold without making sure it is for an equivalent amount. It has been authentically narrated from the Messenger of Allah (صلى الله عليه وسلم) who said,

$$ \text{"الذَّهَبُ بِالذَّهَبِ مِثْلاً بِمِثْلٍ سَوَآءً بِسَوَآءٍ وَزْناً بِوَزْنٍ يَداً بِيَدٍ فَمَـنْ زَادَ أَوِ اسْتَزَادَ فَقَدْ أَرْبَى"} $$

"Gold for gold must be like for like, the same amount for the same amount, weight for weight and in a hand to hand transaction. Whoever adds more or requests more has taken interest."

Recorded by Muslim in his *Sahih* with more than one wording. It is not allowed to sell gold for an additional amount of gold. This contradicts the equivalency principle that makes the transaction valid. The *Shariah*'s way to handle such a transaction is to sell the gold that she has first for a specific price that she receives from the goldsmith. Then she can buy whatever she needs from him or from someone else in another independent transaction. Therein there will be no interest. One of the allowed transactions of this nature is for her to buy a gold item for currency note or silver currency, hand to hand, or for other wealth, such as coffee, cardamom, rice, sugar, clothes or so forth, even if payments are made over time. This is because there is no interest between the gold item and these commodities.

Shaikh ibn Baz

Ruling Concerning Left-overs in the Garbage and Using Newspapers[1] as Tablecloths

Question 303: (1) Is it allowed to use newspapers like tablecloths to eat on? If that is not allowed, what should one do with them after reading them?

(2) Concerning left-overs, some people put them in cartons and then put them in the streets so the animals can eat them. However, the street cleaners then come along and put them with the rest of the garbage. The question is: Is it allowed to put food with the rest of the garbage?

Response: (1) It is not allowed to use newspapers as tablecloths to eat upon nor should one use them as a kind of wrapping paper. Nor should one put them in despicable places if they contain verses of the Quran or mention of Allah. What must be done in those cases is either preserve them in a proper place, burn them or bury them in clean soil.

(2) One must give the leftovers to poor people to eat them, if one can find them. If one finds no poor people to eat them, then one should place them in a place far from the garbage so that the animals can eat from it. If that is not possible, then one should put them in cartons, bags or containers and the city officials should take on the responsibility to collect them and put them in a clean place where

---

[1] The newspapers in many Arab Muslim countries have a religion section in them. Hence, they contain verses of the Quran in Arabic. If a person eats on the floor, as is also customary, and uses them as tablecloths, it could seem that he is disgracing the Quranic verses in the newspaper. This is what leads to this particular question.—JZ

the animals can eat them or people can come and take it for their animals. This is to keep the food from being mistreated or wasted.

Shaikh ibn Baz

Sins and Effacing of Blessings

Question 304: I read that one of the results of sins is punishment from Allah and effacing of blessings. I cried out of fear of that. Please guide me, may Allah reward you.

Response: Every Muslim man and woman must be aware of sins and repent for what sins he did previously. He must also have good expectations of Allah and hope for His forgiveness as well as fearing His anger and punishment. In Allah's Noble Book, He says about His righteous servants,

$$ ﴿ إِنَّهُمْ كَانُوا يُسَٰرِعُونَ فِي ٱلْخَيْرَٰتِ وَيَدْعُونَنَا رَغَبًا $$
$$ وَرَهَبًا ۖ وَكَانُوا لَنَا خَٰشِعِينَ ﴾ [الأنبياء: ٩٠] $$

"Verily, they used to hasten on to do good deeds, and they used to call on Us with hope and fear, and used to humble themselves before Us" (al-Anbiya 90).

Another verse states,

$$ ﴿ أُوْلَٰٓئِكَ ٱلَّذِينَ يَدْعُونَ يَبْتَغُونَ إِلَىٰ رَبِّهِمُ ٱلْوَسِيلَةَ أَيُّهُمْ أَقْرَبُ $$
$$ وَيَرْجُونَ رَحْمَتَهُۥ وَيَخَافُونَ عَذَابَهُۥٓ ۚ إِنَّ عَذَابَ رَبِّكَ كَانَ مَحْذُورًا ﴾ $$
$$ [الإسراء: ٥٧] $$

"Those whom they [the disbelievers] call upon [like Jesus and others] desire (for themselves) means of access to their Lord, as to which of them should be the nearest and they hope for His Mercy and fear His torment. Verily, the torment of your Lord is something to be afraid of" (al-Isra 57).

Again,

$$ ﴿ وَٱلْمُؤْمِنُونَ وَٱلْمُؤْمِنَٰتُ بَعْضُهُمْ أَوْلِيَآءُ بَعْضٍ ۚ يَأْمُرُونَ بِٱلْمَعْرُوفِ $$
$$ وَيَنْهَوْنَ عَنِ ٱلْمُنكَرِ وَيُقِيمُونَ ٱلصَّلَوٰةَ وَيُؤْتُونَ ٱلزَّكَوٰةَ $$
$$ وَيُطِيعُونَ ٱللَّهَ وَرَسُولَهُۥٓ ۚ أُوْلَٰٓئِكَ سَيَرْحَمُهُمُ ٱللَّهُ ۗ إِنَّ ٱللَّهَ عَزِيزٌ $$
$$ حَكِيمٌ ﴾ [التوبة: ٧١] $$

"The believers, men and women, are helpers and supporters of one another; they enjoin the good and forbid evil. They offer their prayers perfectly and give the zakat and obey Allah and His Messenger. Allah will have His mercy on them. Surely, Allah is All-Mighty, All-Wise" (al-Tauba 71).

At the same time, believers must follow the causes that Allah has allowed them. They must combine together the aspects of fear and hope. In their actions, they must apply the outward causes and put their trust in Allah, trusting in Him to bring about the desired result free from any blemish. Verily, He is the Generous, the Noble.Allah has said,

$$ ﴿ وَمَن يَتَّقِ ٱللَّهَ يَجْعَل لَّهُ مَخْرَجًا ٠ وَيَرْزُقْهُ مِنْ حَيْثُ لَا يَحْتَسِبُ ﴾ $$

[الطلاق: ٢-٣]

"Whoever fears Allah and keeps his duty to Him, He will make a way for him to get out [from every difficulty]. And He will provide him from (sources) he never could imagine." (al-Talaq 2-3).

And Allah also says,

$$ ﴿ وَمَن يَتَّقِ ٱللَّهَ يَجْعَل لَّهُ مِنْ أَمْرِهِ يُسْرًا ﴾ $$ [الطلاق: ٤]

"Whosoever fears Allah and keeps his duty to Him, He shall make his matter easy for him" (al-Talaq 4).

And again Allah says,

$$ ﴿ وَتُوبُوٓا۟ إِلَى ٱللَّهِ جَمِيعًا أَيُّهَ ٱلْمُؤْمِنُونَ لَعَلَّكُمْ تُفْلِحُونَ ﴾ $$

[النور: ٣١]

"And beg Allah to forgive you all, O believers, so that you may be successful" (al-Nur 31).

It is a must upon you, O sister for the sake of Allah, to repent to Allah for the sins you committed in the past and to become steadfast in His obedience. At the same time, you should have good thoughts and expectations of Allah. Be aware of all of the causes of His anger. Accept the glad tidings of plentiful good and a praiseworthy end.

Shaikh ibn Baz

Pictures of any Living Creature are Forbidden except Due to Necessity

Question 305: It has reached us from some people that pictures are forbidden and that the angels do not enter a house in which there are pictures. Is this true? Is what is meant by such pictures those that take on the shape of humans or animals, that is, three dimensional statues or such? Or does it also include two dimensional pictures that are kept for the sake of memory or that is found on money? If the prohibition applies to all of them, what is the solution to rid one's house of all such pictures?

Response: Yes, pictures of any living creature, human or animal, are forbidden, regardless of whether they be three dimensional statues or two dimensional drawings or colors on paper or drawn on cloth and so forth. The angels do not enter houses in which there are pictures as the generality of the authentic Hadith indicates. The exception to that is what is needed due to necessity, such as pictures of criminals and the like to identify them, pictures on passports and for identification purposes. We hope that such pictures do not keep the angels from entering the houses due to the necessity of keeping and preserving them. The same is true for those pictures that are degraded, such as those on pillows and cushions. From the Hadith related to this topic is one where the Prophet (صلى الله عليه وسلم) said,

"إِنَّ أَصْحَابَ هَـذِهِ الصُّـوَرِ يُعَذَّبُـون يَـومَ الْقِيَامَـةِ وَيُقَـالُ لَهُـمْ
أَحْيُوا مَا خَلَقْتُمْ"

"The artists who made these pictures will be punished on
the Day of Resurrection. They will be told, 'Give life to
what you have created.'"

This was recorded by al-Bukhari. It is also narrated on the
authority of Abu Juhaifah that the Prophet (صلى الله عليه وسلم) cursed
the one who takes interest, pays interest and makes pictures.[1]

The Standing Committee

Collecting Pictures for Memory's Sake

Question 306: Is it allowed to collect pictures for the sake
of memories?

Response: It is not allowed for any Muslim, male or
female, to collect pictures of living creatures, human or otherwise,
for memory's sake. In fact, one must destroy them for it is
confirmed that the Prophet said to Ali,

"لا تَدَعْ صُورَةً إِلا طَمَسْتَهَا وَلا قَبْراً مُشْرِفاً إِلاَّ سَوَّيْتَه"

"Do not leave an image but efface it and do not leave a
grave elevated but level it."[2]

It is also confirmed from him (صلى الله عليه وسلم) that he forbade
pictures in the House. When he (صلى الله عليه وسلم) entered the Kaaba
after the Conquest of Makkah, he saw pictures on its curtain and
he requested water and a cloth and he wiped them away. There is
nothing wrong with pictures of inanimate objects, such as
mountains, shrubbery and so forth.

Shaikh ibn Baz

---

[1] Recorded by al-Bukhari.—JZ
[2] Recorded by Muslim.—JZ

The Voice of a Woman

Question 307: Some say that the voice of the woman is *aurah* [something which must be concealed and not displayed publicly]. Is this correct?

Response: Women are a place for fulfillment of desire for men. They are inclined to them by natural impulses that make them desire and appreciate them. If a woman is flirtatious in her speech, it increases the temptation and desire. For that reason, Allah has ordered the believers, that when they ask anything of women, that they ask from behind a curtain. Allah states,

﴿ وَإِذَا سَأَلْتُمُوهُنَّ مَتَٰعًا فَسْـَٔلُوهُنَّ مِن وَرَآءِ حِجَابٍ ذَٰلِكُمْ
أَطْهَرُ لِقُلُوبِكُمْ وَقُلُوبِهِنَّ ﴾   [الأحزاب: ٥٣]

"And when you ask them, ask them from behind a screen, that is purer for your hearts and for their hearts"(al-Ahzab 53).

He has also prohibited women, when they speak with men, to be flirtatious or soft in their speech in order that those in whose hearts is a disease may not desire them. Allah has stated,

﴿ فَلَا تَخْضَعْنَ بِالْقَوْلِ فَيَطْمَعَ ٱلَّذِى فِى قَلْبِهِۦ مَرَضٌ ﴾

"Be not soft in speech, lest those in whose heart is a disease should be moved with desire" (al-Ahzab 32).

If that was the situation at a time when the believers were strong in their faith, what must be the situation in a time like now when faith has been weakened and very few stick to the religion? You must mix with non-*mahram* men as little as possible and speak to them but little. You must do so only if there is truly a need to do so and, when doing so, you must not use flirtatious and soft speech, as is stated in the above verse.

Based on that, one can see that the voice, free of soft or flirtatious speech, is not *aurah* in itself. The women used to speak to the Prophet (صلى الله عليه وسلم) and ask him questions about their religion. Similarly, they used to speak to the male Companions when they needed to do so and no one objected to that.

The Standing Committee

Ruling Concerning a Woman Leaving Her House without Her Husband's Permission

Question 308: What is the ruling concerning a woman going out to the marketplace without her husband's permission?

Response: If a woman wants to leave her husband's house, she may inform him of where she wants to go and he may permit her to go there as long as it is not someplace where harm is expected, as he is most knowledgeable of what is in her best interest. This is based on the generality of Allah's statement,

$$ ﴿ وَلَهُنَّ مِثْلُ ٱلَّذِى عَلَيْهِنَّ بِٱلْمَعْرُوفِ وَلِلرِّجَالِ عَلَيْهِنَّ دَرَجَةٌ ﴾ $$

"And they (women) have rights similar to [those] over them according to what is reasonable, but men have a degree [of responsibility] over them" (*al-Baqara* 228).

And Allah's statement,

$$ ﴿ ٱلرِّجَالُ قَوَّٰمُونَ عَلَى ٱلنِّسَآءِ بِمَا فَضَّلَ ٱللَّهُ بَعْضَهُمْ عَلَىٰ بَعْضٍ ﴾ [النساء: ٣٤] $$

"Men are the protectors and maintainers of women, because Allah has made the one of them to excel the other" (*al-Nisa* 34).

The Standing Committee

A Forbidden Gift

Question 309: I used to live in a society in which men and women intermix. One man gave me a present as a sign of his devilish desire. It was an expensive necklace. All praises be to Allah, I have left that society and I now know the way of truth. I feel remorse for what I did. Do I have a right to that gift and is it allowed for me to adorn myself with it or should I give it in charity or what should I do? I am not able to return it to its giver due to my dislike for that society.

Response: Thank Allah for your safety and what He saved you from. As for that gift, do not return it to its giver but give it away in charity.

The Standing Committee

The Voice of the Woman is *Aurah*

Question 310: What is the ruling concerning a man listening to the voice of a woman over the radio or other form of media?

Response: The voice of the woman is *aurah* according to the correct opinion.[1] It is for this reason that she does not say *subhanallah* aloud in the prayer when the Imam makes a mistake, but she simply claps. She is also not allowed to make the general call to prayer in which she would raise her voice. Also, during the pilgrimage, she raises her voice during the *talbiyah* [the words one recites during the pilgrimage rites] only so loud that her companions can hear her. However, some scholars say that it is permissible for her to converse with men according to what is needed, such as responding to a question. However, this is conditional upon it being free of any questionable or suspicious aspects and being free from anything that may arouse one's desires. Allah says,

$$\text{﴿ فَلَا تَخْضَعْنَ بِٱلْقَوْلِ فَيَطْمَعَ ٱلَّذِى فِى قَلْبِهِ مَرَضٌ ﴾}$$

[الأحزاب: ٣٢]

---

[1] In an earlier response, the Standing Committee has convincingly argued that the voice of the woman by itself is not *aurah*. The examples that ibn Jibrin presents in this response are related to the prayer, wherein men should be concentrating on the prayer, or the call to prayer, where the voice is made beautiful, and so forth. However, all of these respected scholars agree that the conversation between women and non-related men must be kept to a minimum and only according to need.—JZ

"Be not soft in speech, lest those in whose heart is a disease
should be moved with desire" (*al-Ahzab* 32).

The disease in the heart is the desire for fornication. This may be
planted in the heart when the woman is soft in speech or when she
is flirtatious, like that speech between a husband and wife. Based
on that, a woman should only speak on the telephone [with a man]
according to what is needed, regardless of whether she was the one
doing the calling or if she answered the call. In that case, she is
forced to do so.

Shaikh ibn Jibreen

Ruling Concerning a Woman Riding with a Non-Related Male Chauffeur

Question 311: What is the ruling regarding a woman
riding with a non-related male driver or chauffeur?

Response: It is not allowed for a man to be alone with a woman
in a car unless he be a *mahram* for her. The Prophet (صلى الله عليه وسلم) said,

" لا يَخْلُوَنَّ رَجُلٌ بامْرَأَةٍ إلا مَعَ ذِي مَحْرَم"

"A man cannot be alone with a woman unless in the
presence of a *mahram* of hers."

However, if there are two or more women, then there is no harm
because in that case it is not privacy. That is conditional upon it
being a state which is considered "safe" and it is not a situation of
them traveling together.

Shaikh ibn Uthaimin

Keeping a Dog in the House

Question 312: We have a female dog in our house that we
imported. We did not know the ruling concerning owning dogs and we
were not in need of the dog. After we knew the ruling, we threw the dog
out but he would not leave because he grew up in the house. We did not
want to have him killed. What is the solution?

Response: There is no doubt that it is forbidden to keep a dog except for those cases that the *Shariah* has specifically permitted. Whoever has a dog— unless it be a hunting, livestock or farm dog— will lose a *qirat's* [a very large portion] worth of his reward for every day. If he loses a *qirat's* worth of reward, it means that he is committing a sin because one does not lose reward except by committing sin. Hence, both of these aspects show that it is forbidden, due to the result of that. In this case, I advise all of those who are deceived into following what the disbelievers do concerning having dogs as pets, that such dogs are evil and a great impurity. They are one of the most impure of animals. The impurity of the dog is not cleansed except by washing a container [in which it licked] seven times, one of them being with soil. Even the pig, that Allah has declared in the Quran to be unlawful and impure, has not reached that extent. Therefore, dogs are impure and dirty. However, with deep apologies, we find some people deceived by the ways of the disbelievers who like impure things and, therefore, they also keep dogs as pets without any need or necessity. They keep the dogs, bring them and clean them, although they can never become cleansed even if one uses an entire sea. This is because their impurity is a physical impurity. Furthermore, they waste a lot of money on such dogs and this is wasted money. The Prophet (صلى الله عليه وسلم) has forbidden the wasting of money. I advise those who have been deceived to repent to Allah and to get the dogs out of their houses. As for those who need the dogs for hunting, farming or livestock, there is no harm in that because the Prophet (صلى الله عليه وسلم) has permitted that.

The question still remains to be responded to. I say to you that if you let the dog leave your house and throw him out, then you will not be responsible for him. Do not leave him in your house. Perhaps if you leave the door open for him to leave, he may go out and eat from what Allah has provided them, as the other dogs do.

Shaikh ibn Uthaimin

Shaking Hands with a non-*Mahram*

Question 313: In our village, we have many evil customs. For example, if a guest comes to the house, everyone, men and women, shake his hands. If I refuse to do that, they will say that I am strange or deviant. What is the ruling concerning that?

Response: A Muslim must obey Allah by applying His commands and remaining away from what He has forbidden. Following such commands is not being strange or deviant. In fact, the one who is strange or deviant is the one who does not follow what Allah has ordered. That custom that the questioner mentioned is an evil custom. The shaking of a woman's hand by a non-*mahram* man, regardless if it be directly touching the hand or if the hand is covered, is forbidden as it leads those who touched to temptation. There are Hadith about this that warn those who do such an act. Although these Ahadith are not strong in their chains, their meanings are corroborated. And Allah knows best.

I say to the questioner not to submit to the blame of his family. In fact, it is obligatory upon him to advise them to stop that evil custom and to behave in a way that is pleasing to Allah and His Messenger.

Shaikh ibn Uthaimin

Lying is Forbidden— Jokingly or Seriously

Question 314: When some people speak with their friends they say some things which are not true in order to make the people laugh. Is this not allowed in Islam?

Response: Yes, that is not allowed in Islam. All lying is forbidden and it is a must to remain away from it. The Prophet (صلى الله عليه وسلم) said,

"عليكُمْ بِالصِّدْقِ فإنَّ الصِّدْقَ يَهْدِي إلى البِّرِّ وإنَّ البِّرَّ يَهـدِي إلى الَجَنةِ وَلا يَزَالُ الرَّجُلُ يَصْدُقُ ويَتَحَرَّى الصِّدْقَ حَتَّى يُكْتَبَ عِنـدَ اللهِ صِدِّيقاً. وإيَّاكُمْ والْكَذِبَ فإنَّ الكَذِبَ يَهْدِي إلَى الفُجُورِ وإنَّ الفُجُورَ يَهْدِي إلى النَّارِ وَلاَ يَزَالُ الرَّجُلُ يكْذِبُ ويَتَحَرَّى الكَـذِبَ حَتَّى يُكْتَبَ عِنْدَ اللهِ كَذَّاباً"

"You should be truthful for truthfulness leads to piety and piety leads to Paradise. A person continues being truthful and seeks truthfulness until he is recorded with Allah among the truthful. Stay away from lying for lying leads to wickedness and wickedness leads to the Hell-fire. A person continues lying and seeking falsehood until he is recorded with Allah as a liar."[1]

It is also narrated that the Prophet (صلى الله عليه وسلم) said,

"وَيْلٌ لَّمَنْ كَذَبَ لِيُضْحِكَ بِهِ الْقَوْمَ. وَيْلٌ لهُ ثُمَّ وَيْلٌ لَّهُ"

"Woe to the one who speaks and tells a lie in order to make the people laugh at it. Woe to him. Then again, woe to him."[2]

Therefore, one must be aware of any type of lying, regardless if it is to make people laugh, joking or serious. If a person trains himself to be honest and tries his best to be honest, he will become an honest and sincere person both on the outside and the inside. That is why the Messenger of Allah (صلى الله عليه وسلم) said,

"وَلا يَزَالُ الرَّجُلُ يَصْدُقُ ويَتَحَرَّى الصِّدْقَ حَتَّى يُكْتَبَ عِنـدَ اللهِ صِدِّيقاً."

---

[1] Recorded by Muslim.—JZ

[2] As mentioned earlier by Shaikh ibn Baz, this was recorded by Abu Dawud, al-Tirmidhi and al-Nasai with a good chain.—JZ

"A person continues being truthful and seeks truthfulness until he is recorded with Allah among the truthful."

None of us are unaware of the results of truthfulness and the results of lying.

Shaikh ibn Uthaimin

Interpretation of Seeing the Deceased in a Dream

Question 315: What is the interpretation of seeing a deceased every time in dreams?

Response: If one sees a deceased in a good state in a dream, this lends hope that he is in a good state. If one sees him in another type of state, this could simply be devils taking on the form of people. Devils take on the shapes of people in a disliked situation in order to grieve the living. This is because devils are very avaricious to do anything that brings grief, worry and sadness to the believers. Allah has said,

$$\text{﴿ إِنَّمَا ٱلنَّجْوَىٰ مِنَ ٱلشَّيْطَٰنِ لِيَحْزُنَ ٱلَّذِينَ ءَامَنُوا وَلَيْسَ بِضَآرِّهِمْ}$$
$$\text{شَيْئًا إِلَّا بِإِذْنِ ٱللَّهِ ﴾ [المجادلة : ١٠]}$$

"Secret counsels are only from Satan, in order that he may cause grief to the believers. But he cannot harm them in the least, except as Allah permits" (*al-Mujadalah* 10).

So if a person sees something evil for a deceased in a dream, he must seek refuge in Allah from the evil of Satan and the evil of what he saw. He should not communicate that dream to anyone concerning that deceased. In that way, the deceased will not harm whatsoever. In fact, any time a person sees something disturbing in a dream, he should then seek refuge in Allah from the evil of Satan and the evil of what he saw. Then he should spit three times on his left side. He should then change his side upon which he was sleeping to the other side. If he makes ablution and prays, that is better and superior. He should not communicate that dream to anyone and, in that case, he will not be harmed by it at all.

Shaikh ibn Uthaimin

Buying Magazines

Question 316: I am very much bent on reading beneficial magazines. I benefit from them in my life. However, the problem of the pictures in those magazines disturbs me. Is there any harm on my part if I buy them? What shall I do with them as I keep them with me, for I am in need of them, or should I simply burn them?

Response: You may read beneficial magazines or newspapers that contain aspects related to religion, literature, manners or so forth. As for the pictures, you may blot them out with ink or remove them or disfigure them when you are storing the magazines in a storage or box. When you are finished with them, have them burned.

Shaikh ibn Jibreen

Plastic Surgery or Other Operations to Fix a Disfigurement or Deformation is Permissible

Question 317: What is the ruling concerning operations done for beautification? What is the ruling concerning learning how to be a beautician?

Response: Beautification is of two types. One is beautification to remove a blemish or disfigurement that is the result of an accident or something else. There is nothing wrong with that. The Prophet (صلى الله عليه وسلم) allowed a man who had his nose broken in a battle to wear a nose made of gold.

The second type of beautification is superfluous and is not done to remove a blemish or disfigurement. It is done only to increase one's beauty. This is forbidden and not permissible. This is based on the Messenger of Allah (صلى الله عليه وسلم) cursing the one who had her eyebrow hairs removed, the one who does the act of removing eyebrows, the one who adds hair to hers and the one who does the adding, the one who gets tattooed and the tattooer. This is because this is simply to add to one's beauty and is not in order to remove a blemish or disfigurement. As for one who is studying and in his coursework he takes courses on plastic surgery and the like, there is no harm in taking those courses and learning such but one may not use them in forbidden ways. I advise the one who wants such a surgery to remain away from it as it is forbidden. Perhaps if this advise came from a doctor himself it would have more of an effect on the people.

Shaikh ibn Uthaimin

Ruling Concerning a Wife Taking from Her Husband's Wealth and then Making an Oath that She Did not Take Anything

Question 318: What is the ruling concerning a wife who took money from her husband on a number of occasions, without his knowledge, to spend it on her children, and she swore that she did not take anything from him? What is the ruling concerning such an act?

Response: It is not allowed for a woman to take wealth from her husband without his permission. Allah has forbidden anyone from taking anybody else's wealth. The Prophet (صلى الله عليه وسلم) announced that during his Farewell Pilgrimage, when he said,

"إنَّ دِمَاءَكُم وأَمْوَالَكُمْ وَأَعَرَاضَكُمْ عَلَيكُمْ حَـرَامٌ كحُرْمـةِ يَومِكُمْ هذَا فِي شَهْرِكُمْ هذَا فِي بَلَدِكُمْ هذَا أَلا هَل بَلَّغْتُ"

"Verily, your blood, wealth and honor are inviolable like the inviolability of this day of yours in this month of yours in this land of yours. Have I not conveyed the message?"[1]

However, if her husband is miserly and does not give her and her children what is sufficient for them of maintenance, according to what is customary, then she has the right to take that amount of maintenance from his wealth for her and her children. She may not take more than that. She may not take something more than what is needed for herself and her children. This is based on the Hadith of Hind bint Utbah who came to the Prophet (صلى الله عليه وسلم) and described her husband as a stingy man who does not give her what is needed for her and her children. The Prophet then said to her,

$$\text{"خُذِي مِنْ مَّالِهِ مَا يَكْفِيكِ وَيَكْفِي بَنِيكِ"}$$

"Take from his wealth what is sufficient for you and your children."

In another narration, it states,

$$\text{"مَايَكْفِيكِ ويكفِي وَلَـــدَكِ بِالمَعْـــرُوفِ"}$$

"What suffices for you and for your child according to what is reasonable and customary."[2]

In the question, the woman states that she swore to her husband that she had not taken anything. Her swearing is forbidden unless there is some explanation behind it. For example, she could have meant by what she said, "By Allah, I did not take anything which was forbidden for me to take," or, "By Allah, I did

---

[1] This was recorded by al-Bukhari.—JZ

[2] This translator is not familiar with the first version stated above. However, the second version has been recorded by Muslim and many others.—JZ

not take anything in addition to the maintenance that is obligatory
upon you," or some other kind of interpretation that is consistent
with that she rightfully deserved. Such an interpretation or way of
speaking is permissible for the one who is being wronged.
However, if a person is wronging another, or is neither wronging
another nor being wronged, then such reinterpretation or way of
speaking is not permissible. A woman whose husband is being so
miserly that he is not spending upon her or her children is a
woman who is being wronged.

Shaikh ibn Uthaimin

Remove the Uncommon Hairs from Your Face

Question 319: Is it allowed for a woman to remove or lighten
the hairs of her eyebrows if they appear in a disfigured manner?

Response: This question has two aspects to it. The first is
if that is done by plucking out those hairs. That is forbidden.
Indeed, it is a great sin. It is an act whose performer the Prophet
(صلى الله عليه وسلم) cursed. Second is to have the hair trimmed or
clipped.   On this point there is a difference of opinion among the
scholars. Is this also a kind of removing the eyebrows or not? It is
best to avoid that act and for the woman not to do it. As for the
hair that is uncommon or unusual for women to have, such as what
grows on part of the face wherein women usually do not have hair
growth, such as a woman having a mustache or cheek hair growth,
there is no harm in removing that kind of hair. This is because it
goes against what is normal and is a kind of disfigurement for the
woman.   As for eyebrows, it is normal for them to be either very
thin or very thick and wide. Both of these are normal.   If
something is normal, it should not be opposed because the people
will not view it as a blemish. In fact, they may consider its non-
existence or its existence as a thing of beauty. Therefore, it is not
a type of blemish that calls for removal.

Shaikh ibn Uthaimin

Women Wearing Their Hair in a Fashion Wherein it is Gathered On Top of the Head

Question 320: What is the ruling concerning a woman putting a hair in a fashion where all of it is gathered on the top of the head?[1]

Response: If the hair is gathered on top of the head then, according to the scholars, such a fashion is prohibited as the Prophet (صلى الله عليه وسلم) warned about it in his statement,

$$"صِنْفَـــانِ مِـنْ أَهْـلِ النَّـارِ لَمْ أَرَهُمَـا بَعْـدُ"$$

"There are two groups of people from the inhabitants of Hell that I have not yet seen..."

He mentioned the women who would be dressed but naked, their heads would be like the humps of the *bukht*[2] camel inclined to one side.[3] So it is prohibited if it is all gathered on top of the head. However, if it falls upon the neck, for example, there is no harm in it— unless, of course, the woman goes out to the marketplace like that.   Then that would be a type of displaying her adornments as [her amount of hair and hair style] could be clearly noted even when covered by her outer garment. Hence, that would be a type of public display of her beauty and a source of temptation. Thus, it would not be allowed.

Shaikh ibn Uthaimin

It is Not Allowed for a Woman to Kiss a non-*Mahram* Man

Question 321: A woman kisses her sister's husband when she greets him after he has come from a journey. He does not shake her hand. Is that allowed or not? Note that one of the

---

[1] Like the beehive style that was popular in the United States during the 1950s and 1960s.—JZ

[2] This is a certain type of camel.

[3] This was recorded by Muslim in his *Sahih.*—JZ

husbands is her cousin but the second is not, it is simply her sister's husband.

Response: It is not allowed for a woman to kiss any non-*mahram* man, such as the husband of her sister or her cousin. In the same way, it is not allowed for her to display her beauty and adornments in front of any non-*mahram* man. It is allowed for her to greet them without shaking hands, while she is properly covered and while not being in private with him. The one who sees that act must forbid it and explain that it is a custom of the Days of Ignorance that Islam has brought an end to.

Shaikh ibn Jibreen

Women Shall Also Have Spouses in Paradise

Question 322: We know that when the men go to Paradise they shall have wives from the *hoor al-'ein*. However, when women go to Paradise shall they have spouses or not?

Response: When talking about the bounties of Paradise, Allah states,

$$ ﴿وَلَكُمْ فِيهَا مَا تَشْتَهِىٓ أَنفُسُكُمْ وَلَكُمْ فِيهَا مَا تَدَّعُونَ ﴾ $$

$$ ﴿ نُزُلًا مِّنْ غَفُورٍ رَّحِيمٍ ﴾ [فصلت: ٣١-٣٢] $$

"Therein you shall have all that your inner-selves desire, and therein you shall have (all) for which you ask. An entertainment from (Allah), the Oft-Forgiving, Most Merciful." (*Fussilat* 31,32).

Allah also states,

$$ ﴿وَفِيهَا مَا تَشْتَهِيهِ ٱلْأَنفُسُ وَتَلَذُّ ٱلْأَعْيُنُ وَأَنتُمْ فِيهَا ﴾ $$

$$ ﴿ خَٰلِدُونَ ﴾ [الزخرف: ٧١] $$

"[There will be] therein all that the one's inner-selves could desire, all that the eyes could delight in, and you will abide therein forever" (*al-Zukhruf* 71).

It is given that having a spouse is one of the most sought after desires of the soul. The inhabitants of Paradise will have that desire met, regardless if they be men or women. A woman will be married by Allah in Paradise to the one that she was married to in this life. Allah states,

$$ ﴿ رَبَّنَا وَأَدْخِلْهُمْ جَنَّتِ عَدْنٍ ٱلَّتِي وَعَدتَّهُمْ وَمَن صَلَحَ مِنْ ءَابَآئِهِمْ وَأَزْوَٰجِهِمْ وَذُرِّيَّٰتِهِمْ ﴾ [غافر: ٨] $$

"Our Lord! And make them enter the Everlasting Gardens which you have promised them, and to the righteous among their fathers, their wives, and their offspring" (*Ghafir* 8).

If a woman had two husbands in this world, she will choose between them in Paradise. If a woman was not married in this life, Allah will marry her to one who is pleasing to her in Paradise. The bounties of Paradise are not simply for the men. They are for men and women. Among those bounties is having a spouse. One might then say, "Allah has mentioned the *hour al-ain* as spouses for men and He did not mention any such spouses for women." The reply is: He mentions the wives for the husbands because it is the husband who usually seeks such and he is the one who desires it.

Shaikh ibn Uthaimin

That Deed is not Allowed

Question 323: Is it allowed for a woman to trim her eyebrows if they are long and wide, similar to that of men, in order to beautify herself for her husband?

Response: That is not allowed no matter what the case may be. The Prophet (صلى الله عليه وسلم) has cursed the one who does it and the one who has it done. A curse implies prohibition of the act whose doer has been cursed. There is no doubt that beauty lies in the way that Allah has made the creation. Eyebrows are created on the human body as part of the beauty of the face. They are also beneficial, protecting the eyes from what falls from above. Removing them or trimming them is a type of changing the creation of Allah and is not allowed.

Shaikh ibn Jibreen

The Worse People are the Two-Faced

Question 324: I witness some people who are two-faced in their speech with respect to me and others. Should I be silent about that or inform them of it?

Response: It is not allowed to be two-faced. The Prophet (صلى الله عليه وسلم) said,

"تَجِدُونَ شَرَّ النَّاس ذَا الوَجهَينِ الَّذِي يَأْتِي هؤُلاءِ بِوَجْهٍ وهؤُلاءِ بِوَجْهٍ"

"You will find the worse people to be the two-faced ones who come to this one with one face and to the other with another face."[1]

The meaning of that is that he greatly praises a person to his face for some worldly benefit and then in his absence he berates him in front of the people. This is usually done by people who have no dignity or class. It is obligatory upon one who knows about such behavior to advise such people and to warn them about that behavior, which is one of the characteristics of the hypocrites. Furthermore, people will definitely find out that such a person has this terrible characteristic sooner or later. They will then despise him, be wary of him and remain away from him. Therefore, he will not meet his goal. If he does not change after being advised, then you must warn the others about him and what he is doing, even behind his back. This is based on the hadith that states,

---

[1] Recorded by al-Bukhari and Muslim.—JZ

"آذْكُرُوا الفَـاسِقَ بِمَـا فِيـهِ كَـي يَحـذَرَهُ النَّـاسُ"

"Mention the characteristics of the evildoer so that the people may be warned about him."[1]

Shaikh ibn Jibreen

Ruling Concerning Giving Preference to Some Children Over Others

Question 325: Is it allowed for a woman to give preference to one child over another with respect to greeting and welcoming them, while in their treatment of her they are the same? What about for the grandchildren while they are also the same with respect to how they treat and greet her?

Response: The father[2] must be just and equitable among his children. He cannot give preference to one over the other with respect to what he gives them, grants them or presents to them. This is based on the hadith,

"اتقُّـوا اللهَ وَاعْـدِلُـوا بَيـنَ أوْلادِكُـمْ"

"Fear Allah and be just among your children."[3]

---

[1] This is part of a hadith recorded by Abu Yala, al-Tirmidhi al-Hakeem, al-Uqaili, ibn Adi, al-Tabarani, al-Baihaqi and others. It is from Jarood ibn Yazid on the authority of Bahz. Jarood has been deemed a liar and forger of hadith by some. After recording the hadith, al-Uqaili said, "It has no source in the hadith of Bahz whatsoever, nor in the hadith of anyone else and there is no corroboration for it." Al-Daraqutni stated that Jarood fabricated it. Al-Tabarani also records it with another chain that contains liars. It is very strange that the Shaikh would mention a hadith of this caliber in his response to the question— especially without pointing out the great weakness of this hadith. See Abu Jafar al-Uqaili, *Kitab al-Dhuafa al-Kabeer* (Makkah: Dar al-Baaz, 1984), vol. 1, p. 202; al-Sakhawi, p. 562.—JZ

[2] The question explicitly mentions "woman" while the answer explicitly mentions "the father". However, the ruling for both parents is one and the same.—JZ

[3] Recorded by al-Bukhari and Muslim.—JZ

The Prophet (صلى الله عليه وسلم) also said,

"أَتُحِبُّ أَنْ يَكُونُوا لَكَ فِي البِرِّ سَوَاءً فَسَوَّ بَيْنَهُمْ"

"Don't you like for them to be the same with respect to their being dutiful to you? So treat them all the same."[1]

Some of the great scholars used to prefer to be equitable among their children even with respect to kissing them, smiling and welcoming them based on the clear order to be just among the children. However, one may be pardoned concerning that matter sometimes. A father may prefer one child due to his being younger or ill and so forth, out of compassion for him. Otherwise, the basic rule is that one must be just with respect to all dealings with one's children.

Shaikh ibn Jibreen

---

[1] Until now, this translator could not find a hadith with such a wording, even in the relevant section of *Kanz al-Ummal*. Perhaps the closest narrations are: "Fear Allah and be equitable among your children in the same way that you love for them to be dutiful towards you,"; "Fear Allah and be just between them as you have a right upon them to be dutiful to you." In *Kanz al-Ummal*, it states that both of these have been narrated from al-Numan ibn Basheer by al-Tabarani. However, this translator could not locate it there and they were not mentioned by al-Haithami in *Majma al-Zawaid*. Another interesting aspect is al-Albani's declaring this narration weak in *Dhaeef al-Jami al-Sagheer* and then adding the footnote, "Until now I have not come across its chain. I do not think it is authentic. In the *Sahih*s of al-Bukhari and Muslim there is the hadith without the additional words, 'in the same way that you love them...'" Previous to al-Albani, al-Syuti gave it the notation of being weak and al-Manawi did not comment upon that. See Ala al-Din al-Hindi, *Kanz al-Ummaal fi Sunan al-Aqwal wa al-Afaal* (Beirut: Muassassat al-Risalah, 1989), vol. 16, pp. 444-445; Muhammad Nasir al-Din al-Albani, *Dhaeef al-Jami al-Sagheer* (Beirut: al-Maktab al-Islami, 1988), p. 19; Abdul Rauf al-Manawi, *Faidh al-Qadeer Sharh al-Jami al-Sagheer* (Beirut: Dar al-Marifah, 1972), vol. 1, p. 127.—JZ

Applying Henna During the Menses is Permissible

Question 326: What is the ruling concerning applying henna [as a beautification for the hands] during the menses? Is it considered impure as long as the color of the henna remains on the hands?

Response: It is allowed for a woman to apply henna to her hands while she is menstruating for the body of a menstruating woman is pure. That is why it is permissible to shake her hand. It is confirmed that the Prophet (صلى الله عليه وسلم) drank from the same cup as Aisha while she was menstruating, and put his mouth where her mouth was.[1] [In another hadith,] he told her,

" إنَّ حَيْضَتَـكِ لَيْسَـتْ فِـي يَـدِكِ ؟ "

"Your menses are not in your hands."

Henna is pure and it is applied to a pure place. Hence, there is nothing forbidden concerning it.

Shaikh ibn Jibreen

The Inheritance of a Divorced Woman

Question 327: Does a divorced woman inherit whose husband died unexpectedly after he had divorced her and she was in her "waiting period" (*iddah*)? What about if he dies after the end of the "waiting period"?

Response: If the husband of a divorced woman who is in her "waiting period" dies, then either the divorce was a revocable divorce or an irrevocable divorce.

If the divorce was revocable, then she is legally considered his wife and she now changes from the waiting period of divorce to the waiting period of being a widow. A revocable divorce is where a woman was divorced, after consummation, without her giving up any money for the purpose of divorce. The divorce must

---

[1] Recorded by Muslim.—JZ

have been either the first or the second pronouncement of divorce. In that case, if her husband dies, she inherits from him. This is based on the Quranic verse,

﴿ وَٱلْمُطَلَّقَٰتُ يَتَرَبَّصْنَ بِأَنفُسِهِنَّ ثَلَٰثَةَ قُرُوٓءٍ وَلَا يَحِلُّ لَهُنَّ أَن يَكْتُمْنَ مَا خَلَقَ ٱللَّهُ فِىٓ أَرْحَامِهِنَّ إِن كُنَّ يُؤْمِنَّ بِٱللَّهِ وَٱلْيَوْمِ ٱلْءَاخِرِ وَبُعُولَتُهُنَّ أَحَقُّ بِرَدِّهِنَّ فِى ذَٰلِكَ إِنْ أَرَادُوٓا إِصْلَٰحًا وَلَهُنَّ مِثْلُ ٱلَّذِى عَلَيْهِنَّ بِٱلْمَعْرُوفِ . . ﴾ [البقرة: ٢٢٨]

"And divorced women shall wait [as regards their marriage] for three menstrual periods, and it is not lawful for them to conceal what Allah has created in their wombs, if they believe in Allah and the Last Day. And their husbands have the better right to take them back in that period, if they wish for reconciliation. And they [women] have rights similar [to those of their husbands] according to what is reasonable..." (al-Baqara 228).

Allah also says,

﴿ يَٰٓأَيُّهَا ٱلنَّبِىُّ إِذَا طَلَّقْتُمُ ٱلنِّسَآءَ فَطَلِّقُوهُنَّ لِعِدَّتِهِنَّ وَأَحْصُوا ٱلْعِدَّةَ وَٱتَّقُوا ٱللَّهَ رَبَّكُمْ لَا تُخْرِجُوهُنَّ مِنۢ بُيُوتِهِنَّ وَلَا يَخْرُجْنَ إِلَّآ أَن يَأْتِينَ بِفَٰحِشَةٍ مُّبَيِّنَةٍ وَتِلْكَ حُدُودُ ٱللَّهِ وَمَن يَتَعَدَّ حُدُودَ ٱللَّهِ فَقَدْ ظَلَمَ نَفْسَهُ لَا تَدْرِى لَعَلَّ ٱللَّهَ يُحْدِثُ بَعْدَ ذَٰلِكَ أَمْرًا ﴾ [الطلاق: ١]

"O Prophet! When you divorce women, divorce them at their prescribed periods and count [accurately] their periods. And fear Allah your Lord, and turn them not out of their [husbands'] homes, nor shall they themselves leave, except in case they are guilty of some open illegal sexual act. And those are the set limits of Allah. Whosoever transgresses the set limits of Allah, then indeed he has wronged himself. You know not, it may be that Allah will afterward bring some new thing to pass" (al-Talaq 1).

Allah has ordered the divorced woman to remain in the house of her husband during the waiting period. The words, "You know not, it may be that Allah will afterward bring some new thing to pass," is in reference to the husband returning to the marital state with his wife.

But if the divorce during which the husband dies unexpectedly is an irrevocable divorce, such as if it were the third divorce, or if she paid something to get him to divorce her or if it were a waiting period due to nullification of the marriage contract, and it is not a waiting period of divorce, in these cases, she does .not inherit nor does her waiting period change from that of divorce to that of being a widow.

There is one case wherein she still inherits although she has been divorced irrevocably. This is, for example, if in his final illness he divorces her, it seems, just to keep her from inheriting from him. In that case, she still inherits from him even if her waiting period has ended. This is so as long as she has not rewed. If she has rewed, she does not inherit.

Shaikh ibn Uthaimin

Ruling Concerning Selling Gold that Contains an Etching or Picture

Question 328: What is the ruling concerning selling gold that contains an etching or a picture, such as a drawing of a butterfly or the head of a snake and so forth?

Response: Gold or silver jewelry that is made into a picture of a live animal is forbidden. It is forbidden to sell it or buy it. It is also forbidden to wear it. And it is forbidden to take it. This is because it is obligatory upon the Muslim to efface the picture and to remove it. It is recorded in *Sahih Muslim* on the authority of Abu al-Hayaj that Ali ibn Abu Talib said, "Shall I not send you for the same purpose that the Prophet (صلى الله عليه وسلم) sent me. This is to not leave any picture but to erase it and to not leave any raised grave but to level it." It is also confirmed that the Prophet (صلى الله عليه وسلم) said,

"أَنَّ الْمَلاَئِكَــــةَ لاَ تَدْخُــــلُ بَيتــاً فِيهِ صُـــــورَةٌ"

"The angels do not enter a house in which there are pictures."

(Recorded by al-Bukhari and Muslim from the Hadith of ibn Abbas.) Therefore, a Muslim must refrain from using, buying or selling such jewelry.

Shaikh ibn Uthaimin

Removing Extra Teeth

Question 329: What is the ruling concerning removing extra teeth?

Response: There is no harm in removing extra teeth because it is a visible deformation and it disturbs the one who has it. Similarly, it is allowed to straighten them by braces and so forth. However, it is not allowed to add spaces between them or file them down. These have been prohibited.

Shaikh ibn Jibreen

Ruling Concerning Beating Students [as a Matter of Discipline]

Question 330: What is the ruling concerning beating students that need some instruction in their manners or learning?

Response: It is best for teachers to be gentle and soft with younger and older students. However, if the situation calls for them to be punished or beaten, without causing injury to them, then it is permissible. It is the custom of the foolish and ignorant not to have proper behavior and respect. Therefore, sometimes it is needed to treat them with harshness and force. The effect of this, in their cases, is greater than kindness and gentleness.

Shaikh ibn Jibreen

Is it or Is it Not *Sunnah* to Bury One's Nails and Hairs After Cutting Them?

Question 331: I have seen some people, especially women, burying their hair and nails after they have cut them on the basis that leaving them in the open is a sin. To what extent is this correct?

Response: The scholars state that it is best and preferred to bury such hairs and nails. Such has been reported from some of the Companions. However, it is not true to say that leaving them in the open or throwing them in a specific place is considered a sin.

Shaikh ibn Uthaimin

Selling Gold

Question 332: Many goldsmiths buy used (and broken) gold jewelry and then go to a gold trader and exchange that gold for new gold jewelry. The weights are exactly the same. The person receives wages for making the new gold. What is the ruling concerning this?

Response: It is confirmed that the Prophet (صلى الله عليه وسلم) said,

"الذَّهَبُ بِالذَّهَبِ وَالفِضَّةِ بِالفِضَّةِ وَالبُرُّ بِالبُرِّ وَالتَّمْرُ بِالتَّمْرِ وَالشَّعِيرُ
بِالشَّعِيرِ وَالمِلْحُ بِالمِلْحِ مِثْلاً بِمِثْلٍ سَوَاءً بِسَوَاءٍ يَداً بِيَدٍ"

"Gold for gold, silver for silver, wheat for wheat, dates for dates, barley for barley and salt for salt: All must be the same quantity for the same quantity, the same amount for the same amount, in a hand to hand transaction"[1]

It is also confirmed that he said,

" مَنْ زَادَ أَوِ اسْتَزَادَ فَقَدْ أَرْبَى"

---

[1] Recorded by Muslim.—JZ

"Whoever increases any one or requests an increase has participated in interest."[1]

It is also confirmed that he came across good quality dates and when he asked about them, he was told that they exchanged twice or three times the amount of poorer quality dates for better quality dates. He forbade that practice also.

Shaikh ibn Uthaimin

Take the Best Approach!

Question 333: Is it allowed to inform about a relative or close friend who continues to do forbidden acts, such as drinking alcohol, even after we have advised him a number of times? Or would this be considered exposing him and making his case known, although a person who is being quiet about the truth is considered a silent devil?

Response: It is obligatory upon a Muslim to advise his brother when he sees him doing something forbidden. And he must warn him about continuing to disobey Allah. He should also explain to him the punishment for sins and the evil results they have on the heart, soul, body, individual and society. Perhaps by advising him often, one will stop him and guide him to what is right. However, if such advising does not seem to benefit him, then one may follow the best or closest means to make him stop the act of disobedience that he is performing. This could be done by informing people of authority or another person whom he respects more than the first brother who tried to advise him. The important thing is to follow the best path that will bring about the desired result, even if it means going to the legal authorities who will then stop him.

Shaikh ibn Uthaimin

---

[1] Also recorded by Muslim.—JZ

The One Who Reads the Quran Without Knowing Its Meaning will be Rewarded

Question 334: I continually read the Quran but I do not understand its meaning. Will I be rewarded by Allah for that?

Response: The Noble Quran is full of blessings. Allah has said,

﴿ كِتَـٰبٌ أَنزَلۡنَـٰهُ إِلَيۡكَ مُبَـٰرَكٌ لِّيَدَّبَّرُوٓاْ ءَايَـٰتِهِۦ وَلِيَتَذَكَّرَ أُوْلُواْ ٱلۡأَلۡبَـٰبِ ﴾

[ص:٢٩]

"[This is] a Book which We have sent down to you, full of blessings that they may ponder over its Verses, and that men of understanding may remember" (*Sad* 29).

A person is rewarded for reciting the Quran regardless of whether he comprehends it or not. But a believer must not recite the Quran without understanding it while he is responsible to apply it. If a person wants to learn medicine, for example, and he studies the books of medicine, he will not benefit from them until he understands their meanings and explanations. In fact, he will be very desirous to take advantage of every opportunity to understand their meanings in order to apply them. If that is the case with books like medicine, what must be the case with respect to reading the Book of Allah without thought and understanding of its meaning while it is a cure for what is in the hearts and an admonition for mankind? This is why the Companions would not go beyond ten verses until they understood the meanings of those verses with respect to what they contain of knowledge and how to apply them. A person is rewarded and recompensed for reciting the Quran whether he understands it or not. However, he must be most anxious and use every opportunity to understand its meaning and to take that meaning from the trustworthy scholars, like [studying] the Quranic commentaries by ibn Jarir al-Tabari, ibn Katheer and others.

Shaikh ibn Uthaimin

It is not Allowed to Throw Away Anything Containing Verses of Allah

Question 335: We use newspapers and magazines which contain the name of Allah and then we throw them into the trash. [Is this proper?]

Response: It is not allowed to throw anything containing the verses of Allah or Ahadith of the Messenger of Allah (صلى الله عليه وسلم) into a despised and filthy place. This is because it is the great word of Allah and it must be respected. That is why one does not read them while he is sexually defiled and one does not touch the *mushaf* except while in a state of ablution, according to the opinion of many scholars— in fact, the majority of scholars. Instead, one must burn them completely or use a paper shredder by which nothing is left of them.

Shaikh ibn Uthaimin

An Invalid Bequeath

Question 336: My father wrote that his son is to be the owner of a farm after his death. He has four daughters other than that son. Is that permissible? If that farm is divided over the son and four girls, how is that division to be?

Response: Allah has made it clear how the estate of the deceased is distributed:

﴿ يُوصِيكُمُ ٱللَّهُ فِىٓ أَوْلَٰدِكُمْ لِلذَّكَرِ مِثْلُ حَظِّ ٱلْأُنثَيَيْنِ ﴾
[النساء: ١١]

"Allah commands you as regards your children's [inheritance]; to the male, a portion equal to that of two females" (*al-Nisa* 11).

The Prophet (صلى الله عليه وسلم) also said,

"إِنَّ اللهَ أَعْطَى كُلَّ ذِي حَقٍّ حَقَّهُ فَلاَ وَصِيَّةَ لِوَارِثٍ"

"Allah has allotted his share to everyone who has a right.
Therefore, there is no bequeathing on behalf of an heir"[1]

Based on that, the bequest of that father for that child is an invalid
bequest and it is not allowed to be executed — unless all the other
heirs are pleased with it and they agree that there is no harm in it. If
they do not agree to it, that farm must be returned to his estate and
divided according to the portions Allah has designated in the Quran. It
will be divided among all of the heirs. If he does not have an heir
besides that one child and those daughters, then the male receives
twice the share of one female. The value of that farm is then
distributed. Similarly, any shares that the deceased left behind will be
one share for each daughter and two shares for the son.

Shaikh ibn Uthaimin

Ruling Concerning Women Attending Educational Meetings

Question 337: Is it allowed for Muslim women to attend
educational meetings and fiqh study sessions in the mosques?

Response: Yes. It is allowed for her to attend educational
meetings, regardless if they are related to practical matters or to
matters of faith and monotheism. This is given the condition that
she is not perfumed or displaying her beauty. She must also be
distant from the men and not mixing with them. This is based on
the Messenger of Allah's (صلى الله عليه وسلم) statement,

$$\text{"خَيْرُ صُفُوفِ النِّسَاءِ آخِرُهَا. وَشَرُّهَا أَوَّلُهَا"}$$

"The best rows for the women are the last ones and the
worst are the front ones."[2]

---

[1] Recorded by al-Tirmidhi. Al-Albani has graded it *sahih*. Al-Albani,
Sahih al-Jami, vol. 1, p. 354.—JZ
[2] Recorded by Muslim.—JZ

This is because the front rows are those closest to the men and, therefore, the back rows are better than the front rows.

Shaikh ibn Uthaimin

Newspapers After they are Read

Question 338: What shall we do with newspapers after we read them?

Response: There is no doubt that newspapers contain the names of Allah as well as some verses and Ahadith. For that reason, it is not allowed to disrespect them. Unfortunately, some people use them as tablecloths to eat upon and this is ignorance on their part. As for what a person may possess of newspapers, if he is able to have them burned, that is best. Otherwise, he should put them in a container or bag and wrap them up so that they will remain separate from the rest of the household trash.

Shaikh ibn Uthaimin

Ruling Concerning Suicide

Question 339: What is the ruling concerning suicide?

Response: Suicide is for a person to intentionally kill himself regardless of the reason. It is a forbidden act and is one of the great sins. It falls under the general meaning of the verse,

﴿ وَمَن يَقْتُلْ مُؤْمِنًا مُّتَعَمِّدًا فَجَزَآؤُهُۥ جَهَنَّمُ خَٰلِدًا فِيهَا وَغَضِبَ ٱللَّهُ عَلَيْهِ وَلَعَنَهُۥ وَأَعَدَّ لَهُۥ عَذَابًا عَظِيمًا ﴾

[النساء: ٩٣]

"Whoever kills a believer intentionally, his recompense is Hell to abide therein, and the Wrath and the Curse of Allah are upon him, and a great punishment is prepared for him" (al-Nisa 93).

It is also confirmed in the Hadith from the Prophet (صلى الله عليه وسلم) that if anyone kills himself with something, he will be punished with that thing in the hell-fire forever. In general, the one who commits suicide does so due to difficulties he is facing in life, regardless if those are the acts of Allah [such as, what the West calls "natural disasters"] or the acts of creation. He is not able to bear what has happened to him. He is, in reality, like one who jumps from the frying pan into the fire. He has, perhaps, moved from one bad situation to a worse one. If he were to be patient, Allah would help him bear his troubles. As it is said, it is impossible for one state to continue forever.

Shaikh ibn Uthaimin

Permissible Work for a Woman

Question 340: What are the permissible types of work for a Muslim woman to work in without being in contradiction with the teachings of her religion?

Response: The places of work for women are those places that are specific for women. For example, she may work in woman's education, either in administration or otherwise. She can also work in her house by being a tailor for women and so forth. It is not allowed for her to work in areas which are exclusive for men because in that case she must mix with men and this is a great source of trial and temptation that one must beware of. One must realize that the Prophet (صلى الله عليه وسلم) said,

"مَا تَرَكْتُ بَعْدِي فِتْنَةً أَضَرَّ عَلَى الرِّجَالِ مِنَ النِّسَاءِ وإِنَّ فِتْنَةَ بَنِي إِسْرَآئِيلَ كَانَتْ فِي النِّسَاءِ"

"I have not left behind me any temptation more harmful for men than women."[1]

"Verily, the [first] trial that afflicted the Tribes of Israel was with respect to women."[2]

---

[1] Recorded by al-Bukhari and Muslim.—JZ
[2] Recorded by Muslim. The Arabic text of this work presents these two hadith as one hadith. In reality, they are two hadith.—JZ

A man must keep his family and wife from falling into such temptations and their causes under all circumstances.

Shaikh ibn Uthaimin

Sexual Intercourse with a Pregnant Woman

Question 341: Is it allowed for a man to have intercourse with his wife while she is pregnant? Is there any text of the Quran or sunnah that indicates that this is either permissible or forbidden?

Response: It is allowed for a man to have intercourse with his wife while she is pregnant, for Allah has said,

﴿ نِسَآؤُكُمْ حَرْثٌ لَّكُمْ فَأْتُوا حَرْثَكُمْ أَنَّى شِئْتُمْ ﴾ [البقرة: ٢٢٣]

"Your wives are a tilth for you, so go to your tilth when or how you will..." (*al-Baqara* 223).

Allah also says,

﴿ وَٱلَّذِينَ هُمْ لِفُرُوجِهِمْ حَٰفِظُونَ ٠ إِلَّا عَلَىٰ أَزْوَٰجِهِمْ أَوْ مَا مَلَكَتْ أَيْمَٰنُهُمْ ﴾ [المؤمنون: ٥-٦]

"Those who guard their private parts except from their wives or their slaves..." (*al-Muminoon* 5-6).

The words "except for their wives" is stated in an unrestricted sense. Therefore, the basic ruling is that it is allowed for a man to enjoy the pleasure of his wife under all circumstances except those in which the Quran and sunnah have clearly stated that he must refrain from such acts. Therefore, it is not necessary to prove that he may have intercourse with his pregnant wife because the basic ruling is one of permissibility. It is not allowed for a man to have intercourse with his menstruating wife, in the sense of sexual intercourse through the woman's private part, but he may enjoy her pleasure in any other way. It is also not permissible for him to have anal intercourse with her as it is a place of filth and harm. Similarly, he cannot have intercourse with her while she has post-partum bleeding until she becomes pure from such post-partum or menstrual bleeding. But he may have intercourse with her if she becomes clean of post-partum bleeding, even if it is before the expiration of the forty day period.

Shaikh ibn Uthaimin

I Advise My Mother who Has Some Deviations and She Gets Angry at Me

Question 342: I see my mother following a path that is not correct. Every time I advise her she gets upset with me and she will pass many days without even talking to me. How can I advise her without earning her anger and the anger of Allah upon me? Or should I just leave her without advising her to earn her good pleasure and then the pleasure of Allah?

Response: You should repeat your advising of your mother and explain to her what kind of sins she is committing and their punishment. If she is not affected by them, inform her husband or her father or her guardian to advise her. If she is committing a major sin, then there is no sin upon you because of her boycotting you and it will not harm you if she supplicates against you or if she says to you that you are disobedient and cutting off the ties of kinship. You are not doing that except for the sake of the honor of Allah and to forbid evil. If it is a small sin, then you should not cause the cutting of relations with her.

Shaikh ibn Jibreen

Birth Control is Not Allowed Except in Cases of Necessity

Question 343: I am a woman who is 37 years old. I am diabetic. During my last pregnancy, I suffered a lot from my diabetes and had to take insulin shots. The birth was through Cesarean section. Due to that reason, I had my tubes surgically tied. Is that permissible or forbidden? Please help me. [Know that] I have eight boys and girls. May Allah bless you.

Response: It is not allowed to use a remedy that either causes permanent or temporary birth control except in the case of necessity, such as if respected doctors decide that pregnancy will increase a woman's illness or they have a probable fear that she may die due to pregnancy. This must be done with the approval and agreement of the husband to permanently or temporarily cut off the means to pregnancy. If the cause no longer exists, then the woman returns to her original state. Among the conditions that are considered necessities is where the woman has an illness or her body is weak such that she will then not be able to carry the baby, or bring it up or care for it and so forth.

Shaikh ibn Jibreen

Light Sporting Between Spouses

Question 344: Can we understand from the Messenger of Allah (صلى الله عليه وسلم) racing with his wife Aisha that women can participate in athletics? We would like you to clarify this issue.

Response: That race was in a particular circumstance. It is apparent that it was at night and the people had retired to their quarters. The race took place in the mosque, close to it or at the end of the city. Perhaps the purpose behind it was to complete the good relations between them and increase the love and affection between the spouses. Based on that, one may use that as evidence for similar acts. Therefore, it is allowed for a man to do something similar with his wife on the condition that they are concealed and not a source of distraction or temptation. As for her practicing publicly in athletics, be it sports, racing, wrestling or so forth, one cannot derive that from that story of the Prophet (صلى الله عليه وسلم). That story is limited to actions between spouses and in the manner we have described. And Allah knows best.

Shaikh ibn Jibreen

The Wealth and Dower of a Wife

Question 345: Is it allowed for a husband to take his wife's wealth and to include it with his if such was done with her permission or must he first get the permission of their children?

Response: There is no doubt that a woman has the most right to her dowry and her wealth that she got through her work, as a gift, inheritance and so forth. It is her wealth and her possession. She may dispose of it herself and no one else may do so. But if she allows her husband to take all of it or part of it, this is permissible and it becomes permissible for him. As Allah says in the Quran,

$$\text{﴿ وَءَاتُوا ٱلنِّسَآءَ صَدُقَـٰتِهِنَّ نِحْلَةً ۚ فَإِن طِبْنَ لَكُمْ عَن شَىْءٍ مِّنْهُ نَفْسًا فَكُلُوهُ}$$

$$\text{هَنِيٓئًا مَّرِيٓئًا ﴾}   \qquad [النساء : ٤]$$

"And give to the women their dower with a good heart, but if they, of their own good pleasure, remit any part of it to you, take it, and enjoy it without fear of any harm [as Allah has made it lawful]" (*al-Nisa* 4).

This is conditional upon her giving it of her free will and pleasure. There is no need for the approval of her children or anyone else as long as she is competent and mature. However, it is not allowed for the wife to then use that for her benefit, continuing to praise what she did and continuing to remind her husband of the favor she did for him. In the same way, it is not allowed for the husband to mistreat her if she refused to give him her wealth. He cannot make things difficult for her or harm her if she does not give it to him as it is her personal property and she has the most right to it. And Allah knows best.

Shaikh ibn Jibreen

Looking at Pictures of Women in Magazines or in Films

Question 346: Is it allowed to view pictures of nude women in magazines or to see them in movies?

Response: It is not allowed to look at pictures of non-related[1] women who are not wearing *hijab*. It is not allowed to buy such films or magazines which contain such pictures. In fact, they must be burnt so that the evil is not spread and lewdness does not occur due to the existence of its causes.

Shaikh ibn Jibreen

Ruling Concerning Listening to Music and Watching Depraved TV Shows

Question 347: What is the ruling concerning listening to music and singing? What is the ruling concerning watching TV shows in which women are shown displaying their beauty and adornments [that is, without proper *hijab*]?

Response: Listening to music and singing is forbidden. There is no doubt about its prohibition. Some of the Companions and Followers stated that singing develops hypocrisy in the heart and listening to singing is a kind of idle amusement and indulging in it. Allah has said,

﴿ وَمِنَ ٱلنَّاسِ مَن يَشْتَرِى لَهْوَ ٱلْحَدِيثِ لِيُضِلَّ عَن سَبِيلِ ٱللَّهِ بِغَيْرِ

عِلْمٍ وَيَتَّخِذَهَا هُزُوًا أُوْلَٰئِكَ لَهُمْ عَذَابٌ مُّهِينٌ ﴾   [لقمان : ٦]

"And of mankind is he who purchases idle talk [music, singing] to mislead (men) from the Path of Allah without knowledge, and takes it [the Path of Allah] by way of

---

[1] It seems that the Shaikh has understood the question to mean "women who are not wearing *hijab*". This is one possible understanding. Allah knows best.—JZ

mockery. For such there will be a humiliating torment."
(*Luqman* 6).

In explaining this verse, the Companion ibn Masud said, "By Allah, this refers to singing." The explanation of a Companion is authoritative. It comes third in the sources of Quranic commentary. Quranic commentary has three levels to it: explaining the Quran by other verses of the Quran, explaining the Quran by the sunnah of the Prophet (صلى الله عليه وسلم) and explaining the Quran by the statements of the Companions. In fact, some scholars even state that the statements of the Companions in Quranic exegesis are considered to have come from the Prophet (صلى الله عليه وسلم) himself. However, the correct opinion is that they do not have such a ruling. This is the closer opinion to what is right. In addition, the Prophet (صلى الله عليه وسلم) warned about such listening to music and singing when he said,

"لَيَكُونَنَّ أَقْوَامٌ مِنْ أُمَّتِي يَسْتَحِلُّونَ الْحِرَ وَالْحَرِيرَ وَالْخَمْرَ وَالْمَعَازِفَ"

"There will be a people from my Nation who will try to make fornication, silk, alcohol and musical instruments permissible."[1]

That is, they will consider permissible fornication and alcohol. They will also make silk permissible although for men it is not allowed. And musical instruments are the tools of idle amusement. This was recorded by al-Bukhari from the hadith of Abu Malik al-Ashari or Abu Amr al-Ashari. Based on that, I advise all of my Muslim brethren to be on one's guard concerning listening to singing and music. I also advise them not to be deceived by the statements of those people of knowledge who say

---

[1] Recorded by al-Bukhari.—JZ

that musical instruments are permissible. The evidence showing their prohibition is clear and straightforward.

As for watching shows which contain women, this is forbidden since it leads to temptation and attachment to such women. Most of the shows are harmful, even if they do not show women. Their purpose, in general, is to harm society's culture and behavior. I ask Allah to protect the Muslims from this harm and to guide the Muslim leaders to what is best for the Muslims.

Shaikh ibn Uthaimin

It is Not Allowed to Shake Hands with a Woman Even if She is Wearing Gloves

Question 348: Is it allowed to pray while facing a scenic landscape? Is there a sin upon a woman if she shakes hands with a man while she is wearing gloves?

Response: It is not allowed for a woman to shake hands with a man who is not *mahram* to her, even if she is wearing gloves or if her hand is under a garment or such. All of this is handshaking even if there is some barrier between the two hands. As for the aforementioned prayer, it is not allowed if the landscape is an illustration and something that takes the person's attention while he is praying. If it is something one is accustomed to, there is no harm in it.

Shaikh ibn Jibreen

Mixing Between Men and Women in Hospitals

Question 349: I work in a hospital and the nature of my work requires constant mixing and communication between women and non-related men. What is the ruling concerning that? What is the ruling concerning a woman shaking hands with non-related men, especially during Ramadhan?

Response: Mixing between men and women is not allowed. It is very dangerous, especially if the woman is displaying her beauty and is not covered. You must avoid such mixing. You should seek a job that is free of such mixing. There are many types of jobs available, and all praises are due to Allah. It is forbidden for a man to shake hands with a non-related woman who is not *mahram* as it is also a source of temptation and may arouse desires. The Prophet (صلى الله عليه وسلم) never touched the hand of a non-related woman and he used to take their oath of allegiance verbally.

Shaikh ibn Jibreen

Ruling Concerning Cutting a Woman's Hair... Wearing High Heeled Shoes... Using Items for Beautification

Question 350: What is the ruling concerning a young lady cutting her hair to shoulder length as an act of beautification, regardless if she is married or not? What is the ruling concerning wearing high heeled shoes, whether they have tall or short heels? What is the ruling concerning the different beautification items to beautify oneself for one's husband?

Response: It is forbidden for a woman to cut her hair in a fashion that resembles that of a man's haircut. This is one of the major sins. The Prophet (صلى الله عليه وسلم) cursed those women who imitate and resemble men. However, if it is done in a way that is not resembling that of men, then there is a difference of opinion among the scholars. Some say that it is permissible and there is no harm in it. Others say that it is forbidden. Yet others say that it is disliked. The most well-known opinion in the school of Ahmad ibn Hanbal is that it is disliked. In reality, as I stated in an earlier response, it is not necessary for us to receive every type of custom that comes from others. Not too long ago, we would see women boasting about how much hair was on their head and how long it was. How come now they are taking on this new approach that has come from outside of our lands? I do not reject every thing that is new. However, I do reject everything that leads our culture to become a culture that is following the ways of the non-Muslims.

As for high-heeled shoes, they are not allowed since they are besides the norm and they lead the woman to expose her beauty and make people look at her. Allah has said,

$$ ﴿ وَلَا تَبَرَّجْنَ تَبَرُّجَ ٱلْجَٰهِلِيَّةِ ٱلْأُولَىٰ ﴾ \quad [الأحزاب : ٣٣] $$

"Do not display yourselves like that of the times of ignorance" (al-Ahzab 33).

Everything that leads to the woman displaying herself and showing her beauty and in such a beauteous way distinguishing herself from the other women is forbidden and not allowed.

As for using items of beautification, such as make-up for the face, I do not see any harm in it, especially for those who are married. However, the beautification that some women do, of removing or thinning some of their eyebrows, is not allowed for the Prophet (صلى الله عليه وسلم) cursed the woman who performs that and the one who has it done. Also, a woman filing down her teeth for the sake of beauty is also forbidden and accursed.

Shaikh ibn Uthaimin

Such Papers Should be Burnt and Buried

Question 351: What is the ruling concerning using newspapers as tablecloths to eat on?

Response: Those newspapers and papers usually contain the names of Allah or some verses of the Quran or some noble hadith. Therefore, it is not allowed to degrade them, sit upon them, use them as table cloths and so forth. Instead, one should burn them after he is finished using them.

Shaikh ibn Jibreen

It is not Allowed for Her to Take From His Pocket

Question 352: I am a woman who is married. I have a house and a husband and children, all praises be to Allah. I pray, fast and perform all of the duties Allah has obliged upon me. However, I need clarification concerning a matter. That is, I store away some of the money set aside for house expenditures without my husband's knowledge. I also take some money from his pockets, also without his knowledge. I, praise be to Allah, do not spend it in ways that are displeasing to Allah. Instead, I save it since I do not know what might happen and I fear for myself and my children. Am I committing a sin in this case, I do fear Allah and I do fear His punishment?

Response: In my view, it is not allowed for you to take money from his pocket without his knowledge in order to save, as long as he is not being miserly and he is maintaining you in a comparable fashion. It is not allowed for you to ask for money for expenditures that have already been covered. It is the husband who should save for different circumstances. He is the one who invests or saves his money. Therefore, you must return the money you saved to him or you must inform him of what you have done and try to get his approval for it is his wealth that you have taken from him without his knowledge.

Shaikh ibn Jibreen

It is Not Allowed to Let Fingernails Grow Long

Question 353: Is letting the fingernails grow long for the sake of beauty forbidden?

Response: It is not allowed to allow the fingernails to grow long. In fact, it has been commanded to cut them every week or, at the most, every forty days.

Shaikh ibn Jibreen

Performing Voluntary Fasts is Not Proper Before Making Up What Was Missed

Question 354: If a woman has to make up some days from Ramadhan, is it allowed for her to perform voluntary fasts, like fasting the Day of Ashura, while she has yet made up those days from Ramadhan?

Response: One must make up the missed days of Ramadhan quickly. It is not proper to perform voluntary fasts before those days are made up. If a person fasts the Day of Ashura or a similar day with the intention of performing a voluntary fast, then she still has to make up her obligatory days that she missed. If, however, she fasts it with the intention that it is one of the days that she must make up, this is then proper and she will be rewarded for that, Allah willing.

Shaikh ibn Jibreen

It is not Allowed for a Husband to Spend the Wife's Wealth

Question 355: Does the husband have the right to object to the fact that I have given my inheritance to my mother? Does he have the right to spend the wealth and salary of the wife?

Response: A wife's wealth is her possession and she has the right to spend it, give it as a gift, give it in charity, pay off loans, give up her right to some money, such as when someone owes her money or her inheritance, to whomsoever she wishes, a relative or non-relative. The husband has no right to object to that as long as she is adult and mature. Her husband has no right to spend her wealth unless she approves of that. If she has a job and receives a salary and the job makes her not fulfill some of his rights, then he could keep her from that job unless she agrees to the condition that they share the salary in return for his allowing her to work and her not fulfilling some of his rights and also in return for him taking her back and forth to work.

Shaikh ibn Jibreen

Shall I Serve My Father-in-Law?

Question 356: I am a woman who serves my father-in-law. He has no one except my husband. Do I have the right to wash him and see him?

Response: As for your serving your father-in-law, this is a deed that deserves to be thanked as it is part of your goodness to that elderly man and to your husband also. You may wash him except for his private parts (back and front). As for his private parts, if he can wash them himself, he should do so and it would not be allowed for you to wash them. However, if he cannot do so, there is no harm upon you doing it for him with the condition that you wear gloves on your hands, so you do not directly touch his private parts. At the same time you must lower your gaze and not look at his private parts. It is not allowed for you to look at anyone's private parts except for that of your husband.

Shaikh ibn Uthaimin

Cheating on Scientific/Secular Exams

Question 357: What is the ruling concerning cheating in English classes or science classes, like math classes, and so forth?

Response: Cheating is not allowed in any class whatsoever. The purpose of the examinations is to determine the level and the grades of the students in that class. Cheating also is laziness and deception. It allows a weaker student to excel beyond those who actually work.

The Messenger of Allah (peace be upon him) said,

" مَنْ غَشَّنَـا فَلَيْـــسَ مِنَّـا "

"Whoever deceives us is not one of us."[1]

Deception here is general for any kind whatsoever. Allah knows best.

Shaikh ibn Jibreen

Cutting One's Hair

Question 358: What is the ruling concerning a woman cutting her hair?

Response: Among the Hanbalis, it is disliked for a woman to cut her hair. But if the haircut is like that of men, it becomes forbidden. This is based on the Prophet's saying,

" لَعَنَ اللهُ الْمُتَشَبِّهَـــاتِ مِنَ النِّسَــآءِ بالرِّجَـــالِ "

"Allah has cursed those women who imitate and be like men."[2]

Similarly, if she cuts her hair in such a way as to resemble the disbelievers, it is also forbidden. It is not allowed to imitate the disbelieving, Godless women. The Messenger of Allah (صلى الله عليه وسلم) said,

" مَنْ تَشَبَّـــهَ بِقَـــومٍ فَهُـــوَ مِنْهُـــمْ "

"Whoever resembles or imitates a people is one of them."[3]

---

[1] Recorded by Muslim.—JZ
[2] Recorded by Ahmad. In the version by al-Bukhari and others, it is the Prophet (peace be upon him) who cursed such women.—JZ
[3] Recorded by Abu Dawud. Al-Albani has graded it *sahih*. Al-Albani, *Sahih al-Jami*, vol. 2, p. 1058.—JZ

If it is neither an imitation of men or of the disbelievers, then it is disliked among the Hanbali scholars.

Shaikh ibn Uthaimin

Does the Harshness of Illness Remove Sins?

Question 359: Does the harshness of the pangs of death remove sins? Similarly, does illness also remove sins?

Response: Yes, everything that afflicts a person of illness, difficulty, grief or sadness, even a thorn that pricks him, acts as an expiation for sins. Furthermore, if he is patient and hoping for rewards from Allah, then in addition to it being an expiation, he is also rewarded for that patience with which he faced that affliction. There is no difference on this point between that which afflicts a person at death or beforehand. Afflictions are an expiation of sins for the believer. This is indicated in Allah's words,

$$﴿ وَمَآ أَصَـٰبَكُم مِّن مُّصِيبَةٍ فَبِمَا كَسَبَتْ أَيْدِيكُمْ وَيَعْفُواْ عَن كَثِيرٍ ﴾ [الشورى: ٣٠]$$

"And whatever of misfortune befalls you, it is because of what your hands have earned. And He pardons much" (*al-Shura* 30).

If it is due to what our hands have earned, this indicates that it is an expiation for what we have done and earned. Similarly, the Prophet (صلى الله عليه وسلم) stated that a believer is never afflicted by any grief, sadness or injury, even a prick of a thorn, except that Allah expiates sins from him due to it.

Shaikh ibn Uthaimin

It is Permissible to Use Eggs, Honey and Milk to Cure

Question 360: Some of my friends use eggs, honey and milk to remove freckles and spots that appear on the face. Is that allowed?

Response: It is well-known that those are types of food that Allah has created to feed the body. If a person needs to use them for another purpose, that is not improper, such as a cure, then there is no harm. This is based on Allah's statement,

﴿ هُوَ ٱلَّذِى خَلَقَ لَكُم مَّا فِى ٱلْأَرْضِ جَمِيعًا ﴾ [البقرة: ٢٩]

"He it is Who created for you all that is on earth" (*al-Baqara* 29).

His saying, "for you," means that, in general, it may be used in any beneficial way as long as there is nothing to indicate its prohibition. As for using it for beautification, there are other sources that are preferred to be used. However, there is nothing wrong with beautification. In fact, Allah is beautiful and He loves beauty. However, to exaggerate in this matter until it becomes the number one concern, and one neglects many other things and forgets many of the beneficial aspects of his religion and worldly life, is not allowed. It is a type of extravagance and Allah does not love extravagance.

Shaikh ibn Uthaimin

Ruling Concerning Applauding and Whistling

Question 361: What is the ruling concerning applauding (clapping) and whistling that many people do at parties?

Response: The ruling concerning that is that it is something that has been taken, apparently, from the non-Muslims. Therefore, Muslims should not do it. If a person is very pleased by something, he should extol Allah's greatness [say *Allahu akbar*] or glorify Allah [say *Subhanallah*]. Furthermore, this should not be done as a group chant, like some people do today. A person says such things between himself and his soul. There is no basis whatsoever for everyone saying *Allahu akbar* together in an audible voice when something occurs which pleases them.

Shaikh ibn Uthaimin

It is Not Allowed to Cheat on Exams

Question 362: I gave my classmate the answers to some questions during the exams after she has exhorted me to give her the answer in any way possible. What is the view of the religion on such a practice?

Response: It is not allowed to cheat during exams or to help someone cheat on something, regardless if it be by whispering or any other form of trickery and deception. It is something that harms everyone for the cheater then receives positions that he is not qualified for or deserving of. This is harmful and deceiving. And Allah knows best.

Shaikh ibn Jibreen

Ridiculing Teachers and Giving Them Nicknames

Question 363: Some of the female students ridicule their teachers and give them foul and evil nicknames or they laugh about them. They say that they do not mean those things and that they are only joking.

Response: A Muslim must guard his tongue from anything that hurts another Muslim or degrades him. A hadith states,

"لا تُـؤْذُوا الْمُسْلِمِـينَ وَلاَ تَتَّبِعُـوا عَـورَاتِهِــمْ"

"Do not harm Muslims nor search for their private matters"[1]

Allah says,

﴿وَيْلٌ لِّكُلِّ هُمَزَةٍ لُّمَزَةٍ﴾ [الهمزة: ١]

"Woe to every slanderer and backbiter" (*al-Humazah* 1).

And,

---

[1] Recorded by al-Tirmidhi. Al-Albani called it *hasan sahih*. Muhammad Nasir al-Din al-Albani, *Sahih Sunan al-Tirmidhi*, vol. 2, p. 200.—JZ

﴿ هَمَّازٍ مَّشَّاءِ بِنَمِيمٍ ﴾   [القلم : ١١]

"A slanderer going about with calumnies" (al-Qalam 11).

And, finally,

﴿ وَلَا تَنَابَزُوا بِالْأَلْقَابِ ﴾   [الحجرات : ١١]

"Nor insult one another by nicknames" (al-Hujurat 11).

To belittle or harm a Muslim is forbidden.

Shaikh ibn Jibreen

It is not Allowed for a Teacher to Cheat a Student

Question 364: Some teachers do not give students their full rights and fail them simply because of the teacher's emotions and feelings. What is the opinion of the *Shariah* concerning that?

Response: It is forbidden for a teacher to wrong a student and to keep him from getting what he deserves, whether it be a particular grade or advancement to the next level. When he does not give him what he deserves, he is hurting the student's interest. Instead, he must be just and fair and give everyone what they deserve.

Shaikh ibn Jibreen

She Did Well and She Did Wrong

Question 365: A woman collected her husband's money that was in addition to what was needed for household items and stored them until they became thousands of dollars, without telling her husband about it. She did that so she could repay a debt that he had from her brother. Then, all of a sudden, she told him about it and he was pleased with what she had done. Then, afterwards, he became disturbed about it and began to doubt her and not trust her anymore, even though she is a very religious believer and her intention was good. However, he has some evil friends that are pushing him to think such thoughts. She wants to know if she was sinful or not in what she did.

Response: That woman did well in some aspects and wrong in other aspects. She was doing well in trying to relieve her husband of the debt as he was in debt to another and she wanted to free him from that. Her intention could have also been to help her brother by giving him his right as her husband was delaying in returning what was rightfully his although he had the ability to do so. She wanted her brother to receive his right that he was in need of. But the method she took was one of deception. However, she was wrong in doing it in a deceiving fashion that was like stealing and hiding some of the money that she had taken to meet the household needs. In that case, she was lying. I advise the husband to forgive her and have good thoughts about her. And he should return to trusting her and believing in her.

Shaikh ibn Jibreen

Perhaps You Dislike Something Whereas Allah Has Put a Great Deal of Good Therein

Question 366: I have been at my place of work for about five years now and I am not happy with my situation. I would like to change my job because I am not able to fulfill it properly. Before I thought of moving to another place, I prayed *Salat al-Istikhaara* hoping that my steps would be on a firm foundation. My heart was resolved to leave that job and I stated to do so. However, every hope I had to leave was soon exhausted and everything returned to how it used to be. Since that time I have been trying to leave this job but without any benefit.

Is *Salat al-Istikhaara* in those circumstances permissible or not? If it is legally sanctioned, what is the Divine wisdom behind me staying in my work for five years while I hate it and have not had an opportunity to change it?

Response: Do not dislike your staying in that job, even for a long period of time. Perhaps, it is better for you than other jobs. You should fulfill your job to the best of your ability and if you have any shortcomings, they are to be pardoned. There is nothing wrong with you also trying to find another job. However, do not despair of Allah's mercy and do not think that the response is slow in coming. Perhaps it is best for you. *Salat al-Istikhaara* is a sunnah and virtuous act. Perhaps Allah knows that you staying in that job is better for you although you personally dislike it.

﴿ وَعَسَىٰٓ أَن تَكۡرَهُواْ شَيۡـًٔا وَهُوَ خَيۡرٌ لَّكُمۡ وَعَسَىٰٓ أَن تُحِبُّواْ شَيۡـًٔا وَهُوَ شَرٌّ لَّكُمۡ وَٱللَّهُ يَعۡلَمُ وَأَنتُمۡ لَا تَعۡلَمُونَ ﴾ [البقرة ٢١٦]

"And it may be that you dislike a thing which is good for you and that you like a thing which is bad for you Allah Knows but you do not Knows. (al-Baqarah 216)[1]

Shaikh ibn Jibreen

---

[1] Verse added by publisher

Glossary

Asr, Salat al- (صلاة العصر): This is the obligatory afternoon prayer.

aurah (عورة): This is a reference to the portions of a person's body that are to be covered and covered properly. Under different circumstances, a person's *aurah* will be different. For example, for women, their *aurah* in the prayer when no men are around is different from their *aurah* when they go out in public which is yet different from their *aurah* when they perform the pilgrimage.

Dhuhr, Salat al- (صلاة الظهر): This is the obligatory midday prayer.

Eid al-Adha (عيد الأضحى) and *Eid al-Fitr* (عيد الفطر): These are the two Islamic festivals. One occurs at the end of the pilgrimage while the second occurs at the end of the fasting of the month of Ramadhan.

Fajr, Salat al- (صلاة الفجر): This is the obligatory dawn prayer.

fiqh (فقه): Islamic jurisprudence.

ghusl (غسل): This is the complete ritual washing of the body. It is required, for example, after sexual intercourse or after a woman has completed her menses.

Hajj (حج): This is the Major Pilgrimage. It is obligatory upon every Muslim to perform this once in his life if he has the means to do it. It is made up of specific rites and is performed at a specific time of the year.

Hasan (حسن): This is an acceptable hadith although it does not reach the level of authenticity of a *sahih* hadith. It is still considered an authority in Islamic Law.

hijab (حجاب): Herein it is a reference to the proper dress of a Muslim woman which cover her completely.

iddah (عدة): This is the woman's waiting period. It could be the result of divorce or the result of becoming a widow. In both cases, there are special rulings that she must abide by.

Ifadha, Tawaf al- (طواف الإفاضة): This is the circumambulation of the Kaaba which is performed on the Tenth of Dhul-Hijjah. It is one of the pillars or essential acts of the Hajj.

ihram (إحرام): Herein it is a reference to the inviolable state of the Pilgrimage. In this state, one is not allowed to perform certain acts that on another occasions he may be able to do.

Isha, Salat al- (صلاة العشاء): This is the obligatory night prayer.

Istihaadha (إستحاضة): This is a prolonged or continuous flow of blood from the vagina or a flow of blood of outside of the monthly menses.

jilbab (جلباب): This is the outer cloak that woman are commanded to wear in *Surah al-Ahzab*. It covers the woman's entire body from her head to her feet.

Maghrib, Salat al- (صلاة المغرب): The is the obligatory prayer said immediately after sunset.

mahram (محرم): In general, it is used herein as a reference to a woman's husband and all the men that are within the prohibited degrees of marriage, such as her father, brothers, father-in-law and so forth. It is allowed for a woman to be alone with such men, travel with them and so on. It can also be used in reference to a man's wife and all the women relatives within the prohibited degrees, such as his mothers, sisters and so forth. He is allowed to be alone with such women, travel with them and so forth.

mustahaadha (مستحاضة): This is in reference to the physical condition of a woman characterized by the condition of *istihaadha*.

qiraan (قِرَان): This is where a person performs Hajj and Umrah at one time, with one intention, and entering the state of *ihram* only once.

rakah or *rakat* (رَكعة): This is a "unit" of the prayer. For example, the *Fajr* or Morning Prayer consists of two *rakat*s.

sa' (صاع): This is a measure of food. It is approximately equivalent to three kilograms of specific types of foods. In reality, it is four times what a person can hold when he cups both of his hands together.

sahih (صحيح): This is an authentic hadith, a hadith of the highest level of authenticity. It is an authority in Islamic law.

Salat al-Istikhaarah (صلاة الإستخارة): When a person has a choice between doing a particular act, he asks Allah to guide him to that act if it is better for him and to take him away from that act if it is not good for him, and to bring him what is good for him. This is done by performing two *rakat*s of voluntary prayer and then making a special supplication afterwards.

Shariah (شريعة): This is the Islamic Law; in particular, what is stated in the texts of the Quran and sunnah.

tahajjud (تهجد): These are the voluntary late-night prayers. They are said between the performance of the Night (*Isha*) Prayer and the Dawn (*Fajr*) Prayer.

tamattu' (تَمتّع): This is where a person performs the Umrah during one of the months of Hajj. Then he leaves the inviolable state and re-enters it to begin his Hajj.

tayammum (تيمم): This is the ritual cleansing with soil in the absence of water.